High-Quality Psychosocial Interventions Research

High-Quality Psychosocial Interventions Research

From Conception to Piloting to Population Based Trials

Second Edition

Patricia A. Areán
and
Michael D. Pullmann

OXFORD
UNIVERSITY PRESS

OXFORD
UNIVERSITY PRESS

Oxford University Press is a department of the University of Oxford. It furthers the University's objective of excellence in research, scholarship, and education by publishing worldwide. Oxford is a registered trade mark of Oxford University Press in the UK and in certain other countries.

Published in the United States of America by Oxford University Press
198 Madison Avenue, New York, NY 10016, United States of America.

First Edition published in 2013
Second Edition published in 2026

Library of Congress Cataloging-in-Publication Data
Names: Areán, Patricia A. author | Pullmann, Michael D. author
Title: High-quality psychosocial research : from conception to piloting to population based trials / Patricia A. Areán and Michael D. Pullmann.
Other titles: High-quality psychotherapy research
Description: Second edition. | New York, NY, United States of America : Oxford University Press, 2026. | Includes bibliographical references and index.
Identifiers: LCCN 2025044139 (print) | LCCN 2025044140 (ebook) | ISBN 9780197681923 hardback | ISBN 9780197681947 epub | ISBN 9780197681954
Subjects: LCSH: Psychotherapy—Research | Evidence-based psychotherapy
Classification: LCC RC337 .A74 2026 (print) | LCC RC337 (ebook)
LC record available at https://lccn.loc.gov/2025044139
LC ebook record available at https://lccn.loc.gov/2025044140

DOI: 10.1093/oso/9780197681923.001.0001

Printed by Marquis Book Printing, Canada

The manufacturer's authorized representative in the EU for product safety is Oxford University Press España S.A. of Parque Empresarial San Fernando de Henares, Avenida de Castilla, 2 – 28830 Madrid (www.oup.es/en or product.safety@oup.com). OUP España S.A. also acts as importer into Spain of products made by the manufacturer.

MIX
Paper | Supporting responsible forestry
FSC® C103567
FSC www.fsc.org

Contents

Foreword by Dr. Areán

The first edition of this book was written over 10 years ago, with my colleague, Dr. Helen Kraemer, one of the most influential and inspirational biostatisticians with whom I ever had the pleasure to meet. The inspiration from the first edition came from the fact that while there were many methods books focused on randomized clinical trials, there were few focused on clinical trials involving psychosocial interventions. And of those that existed at the time, most were mired in the eternal debate over which was better, internal or external validity (with few recognizing that the importance depended on the question being answered), and none were focused on the practicalities of this research, of how to plan and run a study. Dr. Kraemer and I set out to create a how-to manual that anyone could use, and to our delight, this has been a moderately popular book.

Much has changed in the world, and in the field of science since Dr. Kraemer and I penned the first edition of this book, including my having met and worked closely with a brilliant methodologist, Dr. Michael Pullmann, co-author of this second edition. Dr. Pullmann and I have had the distinct fortune of working together on all trial types, from small-scale exploratory studies to identify treatment targets to larger-scale pragmatic trials involving digital mental health tools. The world of psychosocial interventions research is indeed a very different one since I was a junior researcher, and since I wrote the first edition with Dr. Kraemer. The changes to this book in its second edition are inspired and guided by the events over the last decade and more and are meant to better prepare researchers interested in developing and testing psychosocial interventions for the next century.

The first major change in the field is the increased emphasis on mechanistic trials. Around the time the first edition was published, the National Institute of Mental Health in the United States began to strongly encourage the use of the *experimental therapeutics approach*, which it then made required for all clinical trials in 2016. This approach was really nothing new, it merely stated that all clinical science must be theory-driven, and as part of hypothesis testing, one must also study whether the proposed theory-based mechanism is demonstrated. In other words, rather than just studying if an intervention works, we must also study how it works. I say this is nothing new, because all along, most scientists who studied psychosocial interventions were also testing the "how" of the intervention; the difference however was that the "how" questions were often relegated to exploratory hypotheses, largely because of the complexity in answering "how" questions. Although many people were concerned (and still are concerned) that the "how" will be seen as more important than the "does it work" question, most have come to realize that the "how" question is important, particularly in the development of novel treatments, and in understanding the voltage-drop between efficacy (which usually have large effect sizes) and effectiveness (where the effect sizes tend to drop considerably). For this reason, this book now discusses how to identify targets (Chapter 2) and test mechanisms (Chapters 6 and 8).

A second major change in the field is the introduction of a new trial type, the Hybrid-Effectiveness Trial. Hybrid trials were introduced as a potential solution to shortening the "science to service" gap in the United States, which can be as long as 30 years. By combining questions about implementation strategies with questions about intervention effectiveness, scientists can simultaneously address questions about an intervention's population impact while addressing challenges to their implementation, potentially speeding up the time between development and deployment. We have included a new chapter dedicated entirely to effectiveness and hybrid-effectiveness trials (Chapter 9).

The third, major, change to the field was the COVID-19 epidemic and the ability to not only conduct research remotely but also to deliver psychosocial interventions using personal technology. Technology has opened many opportunities to conduct clinical research at a scale never heard of before, but at the same time, it has ushered in new, unexpected challenges to clinical research. There is little guidance in the field regarding best practices for this type of research. For this reason, we added a new chapter on remote clinical trials (Chapter 10).

It is important to note here that because of technology and the need to innovate research methods, there have been many other changes to the field that we briefly discuss in Chapter 11. These include the Just-In-Time Adaptive Interventions, which are mini-interventions triggered by a sensor or some other event; Sequential Multiple Assignment Randomized Trials (SMART), which allow for testing sequential interventions and treatment algorithms; Stepped-Wedge Designs, which are useful for system-level interventions; and the Multiphase Optimization Strategy (MOST), which is a process for optimizing treatments. We also do not provide details about pure implementation studies, system-level trials, or policy trials. While all of these trial types and designs are valuable to know about, and we do discuss them briefly, the how-to's of these trials and designs are beyond the scope of this book.

I end by thanking all the past, present, and future consumers of this book. Good luck in making the world a better place through clinical research!

Acknowledgments

We thank Kevin King for providing the raincloud chart in Chapter 2, and Pedja Klasnja for consultation on Micro-Randomized Trials in Chapter 11. We also would like to thank Brittany Mosser for her contributions to Chapters 5 and 10. We thank all the students and junior investigators we have worked with over the years and served as the inspiration for the first edition and this new edition of the book. Your wonderful questions, brilliant ideas, and unstoppable energy are an inspiration. Keep thinking outside of the box and challenging senior investigators.

About this Book

This book, *How to Conduct High-Quality Psychosocial Interventions Research*, is the second edition of the book *How to Conduct High-Quality Psychotherapy Research*, written by Drs. Patricia Areán and Helena Kraemer in 2013. It has been nearly 10 years since the first edition. Much has changed during that time, including the use of digital technology to deliver psychotherapies, the importance of Social Determinants of Health in understanding response to treatments, and even advances in the design of clinical trials, particularly effectiveness research. We felt it was important to provide an update to the original book to reflect these changes, as well as correct some errors we found recently in the first edition.

Why change the title? When the first book was written, much of the technical assistance that Areán and Kraemer provided, which served as an inspiration to write the book, was focused squarely on psychotherapies. However, over the decade, we found that the technical assistance provided in this book was applicable to any psychosocial or behavioral intervention. So as not to limit the audience that could potentially benefit from the knowledge compiled here, Drs. Areán and Pullmann decided to change the title. We hope this does not confuse any of our original readers.

What is the goal of the book? This book is meant to serve as a straightforward primer on the clinical trial research pipeline as it applies to psychosocial interventions. It is meant to serve alongside other works that delve into the theory of research methods and the conduct of data analysis, to be the "how-to" book for running a clinical trial, and the guide for planning a course of investigation into a psychosocial intervention. To that end, we try to provide a step-by-step process for investigators to follow, discussing the daily running of these studies and common concerns, such as how to write a treatment manual, manage your study team, recruit participants, and finance and cost your trial. We provide in this book the street smarts of clinical trials for psychosocial interventions; things we know are not often taught in a classroom and are often learned through apprenticeships and trial and error.

Who is the intended audience? We intend this book to be of use to anyone who conducts clinical trials of psychosocial interventions research, junior or senior investigators. Junior and first-time clinical trialists will likely read the whole book, and as a result, this book would be useful in classrooms or other training venues regarding psychosocial interventions research. We anticipate that selected chapters would be of interest to senior investigators, for instance, investigators who have spent their careers in treatment development and efficacy testing would benefit from the chapters on hybrid effectiveness trials. Investigators who have never conducted research using remote trial technologies (apps, wearable sensors) would likely benefit from Chapter 10, on how to conduct remote clinical trials. We have something for everyone in this book.

Ethics, Equity, and Budgets. In writing this book, we grappled with whether ethics, equity, and budgets should be their own chapters or integrated into chapters as needed. Our concern in separating these topics into their own chapters is that it is easy for readers to skip over these important topics when they are not integrated. It is also complicated to dedicate a chapter to, say, ethics, when ethical considerations in trials vary by trial type and stage of science. For this reason, each chapter has sections on ethics, equity, and budgets as they are relevant to the topic.

A note on language in this book. Language reflects the social power dynamics within a culture. Language and terms change as quickly as the social and political movements and evolving belief systems that drive them, and the same underlying concepts may be referred to by varying terms depending on the discipline. We have attempted to use the most modern and respectful language and terms for the wide range of clinical trialists that will read this book. However, we recognize that this language may quickly become out of date in a changing culture. We interchangeably use "client," "patient," "consumer," or "participant" to refer to the people who receive health services and/or take part in clinical trials. We use "consumer" as an empowering term. For some readers, it may connote an industrialist or capitalist dehumanization; however, this term emerged from mental health advocacy movements as an effort to signify active participation in treatment selection, as opposed to being passively treated as patients. We also intermittently use "they," "he," and "she" to refer to people when we present hypothetical examples as gender-balanced language.

About the authors. Drs. Areán and Pullmann began this work when collaborating on several studies at the University of Washington. Both were leaders in the NIMH-funded UW ALACRITY Center, which was focused on the implementation of evidence-based psychosocial treatments in underserved and rural communities, as well as the Mental Health America/Talkspace (MHATS) digital laboratory, focused on optimal engagement with therapy apps for depression and anxiety. Dr. Areán is an internationally known expert in research focused on increasing access to and quality of psychotherapy for underserved, rural, inner-city, and geriatric communities. She is also an international expert in digital technologies for mental health care. Dr. Pullmann is an internationally known expert in implementation science and the implementation of evidence-based psychosocial interventions, research methods, and data science.

We both have moved from being academic researchers to working in research funding agencies in the United States. Dr. Areán is a former, retired director for the Division of Services and Interventions Research at the National Institute of Mental Health and Dr. Pullmann is the Implementation Science Senior Program Officer at the Patient Centered Outcomes Research Institute (PCORI). We note here that, as authors of this book, readers should not interpret any of our writing as representing the position of our respective agencies. This book represents our experience as researchers, not as funders.

A final note of thanks. We want to acknowledge and thank Dr. Helena Kraemer for her contributions to the first edition, and her frank and thoughtful approach to clinical trials research. We also want to thank our mentors who showed us the ropes, people who have participated in our trials (and also showed us the ropes), our colleagues who have been inspiring partners in our research, our former students and mentees, our funders, and to our research teams, in particular Brittany Mosser, who contributed mightily to the chapters on team building and remote clinical trials, and who is one of the best project managers in the world.

Enjoy the book!

Patricia (Pat) A. Areán, Ph.D. and Michael (Mike) Pullmann, Ph.D.

1

Introduction to Psychosocial Intervention Trials

Critical Research Questions This Chapter Will Address

- How do I apply the scientific method to planning a psychosocial clinical trial?
- What is the purpose of a randomized clinical trial?
- What are the phases of clinical trials research?
- What are the elements of a high-quality psychosocial interventions study?

Psychosocial interventions research is a field of science that investigates the best methods for providing care to people with mental illness or behavioral challenges. The most common type of study conducted by psychosocial interventions researchers is what the National Institutes of Health (NIH) defines as a clinical trial (NIH, 2010), and that is the type of study on which this book will focus. A clinical trial is conducted to determine the impact an intervention has on behavior and symptoms, such as social, physical, emotional, and cognitive functioning. This chapter provides an overview of the different types of clinical trial methods used to study the impact of psychotherapy on mental health and behavioral issues, and when to use a particular trial design. Here, we set the stage for the ensuing chapters that will describe how to conduct high-quality psychosocial intervention research. In the Appendix, we will provide a list of resources and sample tools from our own studies.

How Do I Apply the Scientific Method to Planning a Psychosocial Clinical Trial?

The scientific method is the process by which people objectively test questions through experimentation. This process involves observing, forming hypotheses or questions, designing and conducting an experiment and then ma king inferences from the resulting data analysis and making them available to the public.

High-Quality Psychosocial Interventions Research. Second Edition. Patricia A. Areán and Michael D. Pullmann,
Oxford University Press.
DOI: 10.1093/oso/9780197681923.003.0001

Formulating a question and hypothesis

All good psychosocial intervention research starts with a question that can come from a variety of sources, including (and not limited to) clinical observation, a review of the literature, attendance at scientific meetings, and curious findings from a completed trial. After the investigator reviews the literature further and explores existing datasets that may have variables of interest, these questions are refined and put into the form of a hypothesis, which is a testable statement that describes or explains a phenomenon. A final hypothesis should be developed based on a combination of existing literature, theory, and exploration of datasets that can shed light on the question.

Example: While working in a county hospital, an investigator began to suspect that older adults suffering from depression benefited more from group-based psychotherapy than from individual psychotherapy because of the opportunity to socialize with others from their age group. This was an observation they had made when treating older adults with psychotherapy, listening to past group members say how much meeting others was helpful in recovery. With this hunch, they developed two hypotheses, one descriptive and one explanatory: (1) Older adults suffering from depression who receive group psychotherapy will have greater improvement in depression scores over time than comparable adults receiving individual psychotherapy, and (2) improved social connection is a mechanism of depression treatment in group therapy for older adults. To test these hypotheses, she obtained Institutional Review Board (IRB, see Chapter 2) approval to explore the clinic's health record, which included 400 older adults who participated in either therapy format. They found two interesting results:

1. There was no apparent difference between the group and individual treatment in depression outcomes.
2. Older patients who reported improved social connection after treatment seemed more likely to be treated to remission than those who did not report improved social connection.

The investigator's question changed from "group therapy is more effective than individual therapy in treating late life depression" to "interventions that provide opportunities for social connections are more effective than those that do not provide these opportunities."

Designing the experiment

The next step in the process is to design a study that will test this hypothesis. If there are questions as to the feasibility of the study design, one should consider doing a *pilot study* (see Chapter 7) to resolve these questions. Not all research designs require pilot studies, but where there are such questions, pilot studies are vital for testing the feasibility and quality of the methods used to test the hypothesis to avoid catastrophic results once the study has begun. Providing evidence for feasibility is often a precondition for funding a larger trial.

A recent example of a pilot trial we conducted was in preparation for a large-scale study of the effectiveness of video-based versus text message-based digital therapy on reducing depression. In the pilot study, we sought to answer several critical research questions to inform the larger trial: (1) treatment feasibility: would people with depression be willing to be re-randomized to a different treatment after six weeks of their assigned care, (2) research feasibility: would participants complete daily and weekly text-based research assessments for 12 weeks, and (3) incentive optimization: what was the optimal amount of monetary incentive ($75 USD versus $125 USD). Our primary outcomes of interest for these research questions were rates of measure completion and study retention (Areán et al., 2021). As you will learn in Chapter 10 these are critical problems in the digital mental health research field, where participants are recruited remotely, and before we could move on to a much larger version of the study, we needed to answer these questions. We note that while the pilot study was comparatively large (N = 250), because of the design of the study and the incentive arms, we were not able to test the clinical outcomes with certainty, though we published these data as preliminary findings, with all caveats disclosed (Areán et al., 2024; Griffith Fillipo et al., 2022).

Once the study design is completed, the hypothesis testing study can be proposed and, if funded, implemented. The methods by which hypotheses are tested are very important and include the elements detailed later in the book. Without these elements, investigators will have a difficult time interpreting their data and confirming the outcomes.

After the trial's completion, the data are analyzed and the outcomes reported, according to the proposed a priori, analytic plan. This is usually done in collaboration with an expert in biostatistics, who will have helped you select the best analytic plan prior to beginning the study and should be regularly involved in tracking study progress (see Chapter 5). There are instances where the analytic plan may change, owing to advances in the statistical field, and as long as those changes are made *before* you analyze your data, and the regulatory bodies who oversee your research give the OK, then this is fine. However, as we discuss below (see Cherry-Picking), changing your analysis plan based on which plan best supports your hypothesis is a major no-no.

Interpreting the findings

The next step after analyzing your data is dissemination: publishing, presenting, and communicating the results to other scientists and the public. When you write the results from your primary study aims, you will need to be sure you report on all the hypotheses you had planned to test whether they were supported or not. As we discuss in more detail below, it is unethical to do otherwise, and currently, with trial registration, journals will insist on it. It is true that you may have a more difficult time publishing in the top journals if you have null results (if none of your hypotheses are supported), but it is not impossible. There is a growing appreciation for the importance of discovering an intervention doesn't work that well—why would any clinician or organization invest their time and money implementing an intervention that was not effective?

The scientific method accepts that no hypothesis can ever be completely proven true; rather, hypotheses have degrees of probability that are only applicable within the specific context under which they were examined. Every study is just one piece of evidence that supports a hypothesis to a certain degree. One standard that greatly increases the probability of a hypothesis is independent replication (Jacobson, 1999). It is important that investigators without allegiance to the experimental intervention replicate any study done by investigators who have a vested interest in the intervention. Investigator bias, confirmation bias, and allegiance effects can occur when, consciously or unconsciously, researchers make design, analysis, and reporting decisions that favor an experimental intervention. Therefore, it is important for investigators to test other people's interventions for confirmatory purposes.

What Is the Purpose of Randomized Clinical Trials?

A clinical trial is conducted to determine the effect an intervention has on behavior and symptoms, such as social, physical, emotional, and cognitive functioning.

This *effect of treatment* is defined as the patient's response to treatment compared to the patient's response had that treatment not been given (a control/comparison condition). It tries to separate that part of the response due to treatment from any other changes that would have spontaneously occurred without treatment. Since a treatment cannot be both given and withheld from an individual patient, the effect of treatment is generally assessed by comparing the responses of a sample of patients given the treatment to the responses of a comparable sample of patients in the control/comparison condition. Every clinical trial has two necessary components:

- The prospective assignment of human participants to treatment and control or comparison conditions (or multiple of each).
- The measurement of a health-related outcome in each condition.
- The assessment of how the experimental intervention results in changes in the outcome (*mechanism of action*).

What Are the Phases of Clinical Trials Research?

There are several steps in the clinical trial process to test the impact of an intervention on a mental or behavioral health problem. The below figure illustrates the clinical trial phases, which include:

- *Target identification:* What is the problem we are meant to solve?
- *Proof-of-concept*: Does my intervention look like it changes the underlying cause or correlate of the problem I want to solve?
- *Confirmatory efficacy:* Does my intervention solve the problem better than no treatment or some other treatment, under ideal circumstances?
- *Effectiveness/Hybrid Effectiveness:* Does my intervention work as well in actual practice as it did in the research setting? Who does the intervention works best? Is a modified version of the intervention as effective as the original intervention?

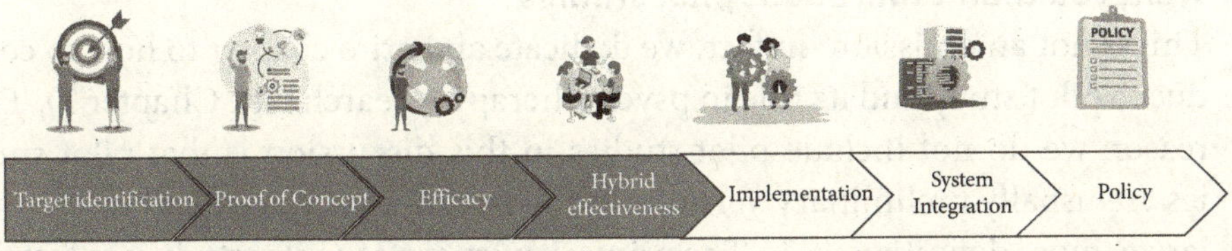

Target identification and proof-of-concept are discussed in detail in Chapters 2 and 6, Efficacy trials in Chapter 8, and Hybrid Effectiveness in Chapter 9.

The above figure includes three other phases of clinical trials: implementation, systems, and policy research. This book will not cover in detail these last three trial types; however, it is important to understand their purpose. *Implementation trials* are conducted when there are aspects of an intervention that make it challenging for clinicians, consumers, and systems of care to use. Current evidence-based psychosocial interventions are often difficult to implement because of their complexity. As a result, implementation research studies methods to improve the uptake of interventions by developing strategies that train, support, and incentivize clinicians, consumers, and administrators to adopt them. While the most important outcome should always be consumer improvement, the primary questions include clinician skill and skill drift, access to treatment, and the number of consumers treated. *System-level intervention trials* are focused on addressing the structures of an organization that impede the implementation of best practices. These are often multi-component interventions that involve the introduction of new staff into the system, redesigning clinical practice, and reorganizing an entire care pathway to improve consumer experiences with care. These studies are usually done at the system level, meaning that while it may be possible to randomize consumers to conditions, it is more typical to randomize at the organizational level. While the ultimate outcome is consumer improvement, the main outcomes tend to be focused on system-level efficiency, cost of services, and reach to populations. Finally, *policy-level intervention trials* are rather rare, and focus primarily on strategies to influence how policy makers decide to select and support interventions at a system, county, state, or federal level. The focus of the intervention is on the decision-maker, with the outcome being changes in policy to support best practices. These latter steps in the clinical trials process are clearly important, as it is this research that changes how care is provided and is responsible for getting your new intervention into practice, once you find it to be effective.

Wait, you didn't talk about pilot studies

This is not an omission; in fact, we dedicate an entire chapter to how to conduct a pilot study and its role in psychotherapy research (see Chapter 7). The reason we do not include pilot studies in this discussion is that pilot studies are usually preliminary versions of the trial design you intend to use in a larger, more definitive study. The primary purpose of a pilot study is to test the feasibility of your research design and make refinements to the design so that when you conduct your adequately powered trial, you are prepared. Because in a pilot study, you often make changes to the design as you go, including how you recruit participants, how you train providers, and even the number of measures you use, the design may undergo several protocol violations that impact the ability to make interpretations from the data collected about intervention impact. Thus, the only questions a pilot study answers are "Can I do this study as I designed it? Can I feasibly recruit the sample size I need to test my hypotheses? Are participants willing to engage in the study?" These questions provide essential information about the feasibility of supporting more definitive trials. To quote Drs. Leon, Davis and Kraemer (2011).

> *"Pilot results can inform feasibility and identify modifications needed in the design of a larger, ensuing hypothesis testing study. Investigators should be forthright in stating these objectives of a pilot study. Grant reviewers and other stakeholders should expect no more."*

One last note, which will be reiterated in Chapter 7, you should not use pilot studies to estimate effect sizes for your hypothesis testing study. Pilot studies are usually quite small, only large enough to make methodological decisions, and are usually funded as small studies. The *statistical power* to detect a true effect size is not large enough in these studies. So, what is the basis for your effect size decision? It is based on clinical meaningfulness, the degree to which a change in outcome is felt to be meaningful by the person who is suffering from the condition in question (*Pilot Studies*, n.d.).

Clinical Trial Deliverables

Clinical trials can have different types of deliverables depending on the hypotheses being investigated. Most randomized clinical trials provide the field with an effect of treatment on clinical problems relative to no treatment or other treatments. Randomized clinical trials also yield useful information about the *moderators and mediators* of treatment outcomes. Depending on the type of study and where it lies on the efficacy/effectiveness spectrum, clinical trials are designed to determine or document one or more of the following:

- Overall effect of treatment on a target mechanism
- Overall effect of treatment on a population
- Moderators of treatment
- Mediators of treatment
- Methods for implementing treatment

Estimating the Effect Size of Treatment

The primary purpose of most clinical trials is to assess the effect of treatment in the populations from which the patients are sampled. The usual and minimal assessment is whether the sample size was large enough to detect any effect of treatment at all, a statistical test usually reported in the form of a *p-value* (probability score). Usually, if the p-value is less than 5% the result is declared statistically significant.

However, more important than a *p*-value (indicating statistical significance) is an effect size (indicating clinical significance), a measure that quantitatively compares the typical response in the treatment group to that in the control/comparison group. There are many effect sizes, but the most those that are standardized and have a value of zero when no difference exists between the treatment and control/comparison group responses. The easiest effect size to understand is simply the mean difference between two group averages: how many points is the intervention group higher (or lower) than the control/comparison. As an example of a standardized effect size, Cohen's *d* is the mean of the intervention group minus the mean of the control group and divided by the standard deviation. Dividing the means by the standard deviation standardizes the mean difference between the groups into standard deviation units. It therefore provides the average standard deviation points that the intervention group is better (or worse) than the control/comparison group. Generally, larger, positive effect sizes for the intervention indicate that the intervention was more beneficial compared to the control/comparison, and smaller, negative effect sizes indicate the control/comparison was more beneficial than the treatment. Whether or not an effect size is considered of clinical significance depends on the context: the severity of the condition, the consequences of inadequate treatment, the costs and risks of the treatments, and so forth.

Interpreting effect sizes always involves clinical value judgments, and perhaps even different value judgments from clinicians, patients, policymakers, and researchers. It is up to the investigator and the field to determine what is a small, medium, or large effect size and to that end what is a meaningful effect size. The effect size chosen must be defensible to those reading the study's outcomes. While benchmarks exist, effect sizes should always be interpreted using clinical judgment, the content, and the research method, and this should be done prior to the results being known. Even Cohen, who provided conventional effect size benchmarks, strongly cautioned against their thoughtless application (Cohen, 1988, 1990).

Since there must be a theoretical rationale and empirical justification for undertaking a clinical trial, the population effect size is seldom absolutely zero—this is a strawman for statistical testing. For instance, consider a measure such as average height or mental health ratings on two very large groups; one will always have a larger average score, even if it is only by the thousandths of an inch or a single point on the thousandths decimal place. Given a large enough sample size, it is always possible to show "statistical significance" for an effect size not absolutely zero. Thus, it is a mistake to interpret a *p*-value as indicating the clinical effect of a treatment. The function of an effect size is to convey the information to those processing the results that might provide the basis to judge clinical significance.

The effect size in any clinical trial estimates the population effect size. Its accuracy (usually indicated by a confidence interval) depends on the sample size. While the p-value should be reported to document that the sample size was large enough to show some deviation from a zero result, it is more important that an effect size and its confidence intervals be reported. From the effect size, readers can assess the clinical, not merely the statistical significance of the treatment.

Moderators of Treatment: Who Does This Treatment Work For?

What has long been abundantly clear is that some people respond to certain types of psychosocial interventions and others do not (Baron & Kenny, 1986; Kraemer et al., 2002; Kraemer et al., 2006a). In other words, the impact of a psychosocial intervention may differ greatly from one person to another. A moderator is a baseline characteristic of the patient, provider, or setting that can influence the effect size of the treatment. Moderators of treatment can help to "target" the treatment to those who would be most likely to respond and support the search for other treatments for those who would not be likely to respond. When there are multiple outcomes on which patient response is measured, it should be noted that the moderators of treatment for one outcome may not be the same as the moderators of treatment for another. For example, a study of trauma-focused cognitive behavioral therapy in Zambia found that primary caretaker type moderated treatment such that those who identified mothers as their primary caretaker had greater trauma reductions, whereas those who identified fathers as their primary caretaker had better functioning (Kane et al., 2016). While identifying different moderators for different outcomes might be of scientific interest, it certainly confuses clinical decision-making—yet one more reason for a single, primary outcome measure on which the treatment decisions should be based.

In the United States, moderation research has been a major area of interest to the National Institute of Mental Health, which under its strategic plan (*The National Institute of Mental Health Strategic Plan—National Institute of Mental Health (NIMH)*, 2024) as indicated that the field would be better served by developing new interventions for those who do not respond well to existing evidence-based practices. An example of a moderation study would be evaluating the impact that mild cognitive impairments have on the relative effectiveness of a structured versus process-based psychosocial intervention. Moderation studies:

- Investigate the impact that patient, provider, or setting characteristics have on subsequent treatment outcomes.
- Can be part of efficacy or effectiveness research.
- Can be the sole purpose of the study.

Perhaps the most important moderation research in the future will seek to identify which people are most likely to benefit from psychosocial treatments versus medication, as well as determining which types of psychosocial interventions are effective for specific populations.

Mediators of Treatment: How and Why Does This Treatment Work?

The purpose of mediation studies is to uncover how or why psychosocial interventions work (Baron & Kenny, 1986; Kraemer et al., 2002). This analysis is particularly important in proof of concept, efficacy, and in some effectiveness trials, as knowing how an intervention produces its effects is as important as knowing that there is an effect. In some funding agencies, for instance, the National Institute of Mental Health, this approach is currently required under the experimental therapeutics mandate. Historically, if you do not propose a mechanistic hypothesis, your study will not be considered for funding. Mediators are patient characteristics that change as a function of a specific intervention and account for all or part of the effect of the treatment on outcomes. Mediator variables are always expected to change before the primary outcome of interest changes, since it is hypothesized that the treatment is effective on the outcome (say depression) because of its ability to change a person's pretreatment negative mindset to a more positive mindset (the mediator); changes in positive mindsets should happen before there is an impact on depression. Because identifying the kinds of changes in the person associated with better outcomes can guide the development of better treatments, mediators of treatment can be used to tailor treatments to the needs of the individual person. An example of a mediator study would be to test whether problem-solving therapy's effect on depression outcomes is due to patient improvement in problem-solving skills. As of 2025, the NIMH requires that clinical trials include mediational hypotheses, with the aim of refining existing evidence-based practices or developing more potent interventions. Mechanisms are a particular type of mediator of the greatest interest to clinical research. Mechanisms are causal in nature; that is, they specify the rationale for how and why mediation works. While mediators are identified by a statistical association of direct and indirect effects, mechanisms must have additional evidence for their causal impact (Tryon, 2018). Studying mediation can point toward possible mechanisms important for clinical research as mechanisms can be harnessed to improve interventions. Mediator studies:

- Test whether an intervention's impact on the primary outcome is because it changes a feature of the patient.
- Tests whether the mediator changes before the outcome changes.
- Can be used to develop personalized psychosocial interventions.
- Can be used to understand why an evidence-based practice is effective.

What Are the Elements of a High-Quality Psychosocial Interventions Study?

In many ways, psychosocial interventions research is like any intervention trial, but there are a few important methodological differences. A well-designed clinical trial has the following features (and will be discussed in detail in subsequent chapters):

- A clearly stated hypothesis that is of public health significance.
- A sample that is representative of the target population.
- A sample that is large enough to test the hypothesis accurately.
- A clear method for recruiting and retaining participants.
- Informed consent.
- Defined outcomes and methods for measuring them.
- Defined treatments and/or implementation strategies and methods for determining if an adequate dose was given.
- Clearly defined comparison group.
- Random assignment to a group.
- A well-trained research team that delivers the treatments and performs the measurements with fidelity to the study protocol.

- Personnel who administer the intervention are unaware of the details of the hypotheses to be tested, and if possible, the participant's treatment assignment.
- Personnel who assess outcomes are unaware of the participant group assignment and study hypothesis.
- Participants are unaware of the hypotheses and if possible, the treatment condition to which they are assigned.
- A detailed methodological design with a clear protocol that can be replicated by another investigator.
- State-of-the-art data analysis plan.
- Clear reporting of results according to the original protocol, with any additional insights clearly labeled as exploratory.

Psychosocial intervention studies can meet these requirements but some of these elements are more difficult to meet than others. Efforts to keep participants, providers, and research assistants unaware of the participant's group assignment can be very difficult. It is important in clinical research to try and maximize masking the assignment because participants, providers, and research assistants may behave differently if they believe the participant is in the comparison/control or experimental condition, which may in turn influence the research outcomes. Also, by virtue of providers being trained to provide a specific intervention and deliver it, they will always know what treatment the participant is receiving. Like providers, participants will know the treatment they are given (although they may not know if they are in the experimental intervention) and by virtue of the research interview, in our experience, participants will sometimes talk about the details of their treatment to the research assistant, even when instructed not to do so. It is of particular importance to mask the assessment of outcomes, either by using objective measures that cannot be influenced by the biases of the participants or providers, or by having outside evaluation examine the response records masked to group membership.

Ethical Considerations

In addition to the basic elements of intervention research, high-quality psychosocial intervention research must also be conducted ethically, with every consideration for participant safety thought through. First, deciding to do a clinical trial, particularly a randomized clinical trial, requires *clinical equipoise*, the assumption that one treatment is not superior for either the control or intervention group. It is not ethical to randomize people unless the researcher has a reasonable doubt as to which of the two treatments is clinically preferable; that is, both treatment and control conditions must be credible. Thus, if a researcher is sure that the treatment is better than placebo (or any other comparison condition), based on previous research, the existence of guidelines or a known standard of practice, it is not ethical for that researcher to randomize participants to a nontreatment group. Ethicists have their own arguments for this requirement, but there is also a very practical argument: It is very difficult to remain unbiased in the design, implementation, and analysis of the results of a trial when the person designing, implementing, and analyzing the results is already quite convinced of what the answer should be. Moreover, in conducting and analyzing the results of a study, it is often difficult to see ourselves as others see us. Innovation bias is a widespread, normal phenomenon caused by an intense focus on the desired immediate consequences of a new intervention, and it can create tunnel vision in researchers that impacts their decision-making. Consequently, researchers must involve external oversight bodies, such as Institutional Review Boards (IRB) and Data Safety and Monitoring Boards (DSMB). We additionally recommend that a Participant Advisory Board (PAB) be added to the mix, particularly for studies that include high-risk or hard-to-reach populations.

An Introduction to the IRB

IRBs consist of scientists and community representatives who work together to determine the safety of a proposed study before it begins and continue to monitor a trial's safety. IRB members are all trained in the ethical conduct of research and are overseen by an administrative team to facilitate the review process. Although there are firm ethical guidelines regarding the conduct of human science, IRBs will vary from institution to institution in the rigor with which those guidelines are applied and have been found to apply different decisions to the very same research protocol (Pritchard, 2011). Be prepared to encounter some interesting comments from IRBs concerning psychosocial interventions research but also keep in mind that the comments are made in the interest of the participant, not to annoy the investigator. Decisions are not immutable, in fact, if the IRB is in error or a decision is based on an uninformed impression, your job as an investigator is to educate the board about the latest information or how the IRB's decision could compromise the research.

The IRB will classify your study into one of these categories: exempt, minimal risk, moderate risk, or high risk. For the most part (although we have heard of exceptions), psychosocial interventions are considered minimal risk studies. Studies that include vulnerable populations (i.e., prisoners, children, and those who cannot consent for themselves) or problems with high potential for mortality (i.e., suicide), will often be rated as high or moderate risk. Exempt status is very rare for psychosocial interventions research. Designation of risk will determine the degree of safety monitoring expected for a study (see DSMB below).

As an example of how IRB decisions can be debated, one investigator had been told by her IRB that to enroll participants with major depression into a psychotherapy trial without also prescribing an antidepressant medication to all the participants was unnecessarily withholding treatment and was therefore unethical. The investigator responded to the recommendation by:

- Providing extensive documentation from leading professional organizations stating that psychotherapy is an effective treatment for depression.
- Showing that the populations she was studying tended to either refuse medication treatment or could not afford it (hence the purpose of the study).
- Reminding the IRB that the purpose of the study was to determine the effectiveness of the treatment for depression, and as such had incorporated several safeguards to ensure that any participant who appeared to be significantly worse as a function of participating in the trial would be provided with other treatment.

In this instance, the IRB overturned its own decision and approved the original study. Once caveat requires mention: We are not suggesting that every decision made by an IRB that changes the methods of a trial be resisted. IRBs can have important insight into the safety of research that we as investigators may overlook in our enthusiasm for the study. Always consider the decisions made by an IRB first before deciding to argue your own methodological decision. But do not shy away from defending an approach if it is imperative for the study to succeed.

Data Safety and Monitoring Boards (DSMBs)

The DSMB is an independent body of scientists and ethicists that is sometimes selected by the investigative team and sometimes selected by the funding organization. The DSMB should have statistical, clinical, methodological, and ethics and sometimes regulatory representation to ensure proper monitoring of the research study. The DSMB's role is similar to the IRB's role, but rather than approve proposed study designs on the basis of ethics, the DSMB's role is to determine if participants are being managed safely as they progress through the study. The DSMB is also responsible for ensuring that the study is being conducted as originally planned and that any deviation from the original plan is justified and will not compromise the ability of the investigative team to test hypotheses. The frequency with which the DSMB will meet is often determined by the anticipated safety issues in the study. It can meet as often as once a month for high-risk studies and no less than once a year for minimal risk studies. The investigative team provides the DSMB with information regarding adverse events, recruitment and retention of participants, and any changes the team would like to make to the study protocol, if needed. The DSMB provides a report to the funder about the study's progress and the board's impression regarding the safety of the study. If at any point the DSMB concludes that one or more of the treatment arms proves to be harmful, the DSMB can recommend early termination of the clinical trial. In some cases, the design of the clinical trial study protocol plans for interim analyses with criteria to stop a trial early, either because the results are convincing or there is a need to evaluate any potential harm participation in research may result in, such as in cases where the intervention is very new, or mortality is the outcome. In such cases, again, it is the DSMB that evaluates the evidence from the interim analysis based on these sequential *stopping rules* and decides on early termination. The determination and use of sequential stopping rules is complex and beyond the scope of this book. We recommend working closely with a biostatistician when determining these rules. Early termination of a clinical trial is never, and should never be, an easy decision. For a view of how difficult a decision can be, you might read the report of a study of the effectiveness of hormone replacement therapy on prevention of heart disease that was terminated (Wittes, 1993).

A DSMB can be helpful to investigators by asking the kinds of questions reviewers may later raise but asking them at an early point at which problems can be dealt with. It can also help in unexpected ways. For example, in a multisite Randomized Clinical Trial (RCT), one site was found not only to be much slower in recruitment than promised, but also to be deviating from the protocol. Recognizing that this would compromise both the validity and power of the entire study, the DSMB chose to intervene, warning that the site would recommend termination if the site did not recruit adequately and adhere to the protocol within the next month and thereafter, the DSMB would recommend termination of that site and return unexpended funds to the funder. Not surprisingly, the site chose to adhere to protocol. Such action would have been very difficult for the lead investigator, but coming from the DSMB the intervention was highly effective and did not compromise the working relationship between sites.

Participant Advisory Boards (PAB)

Participant advisory boards are not required entities but can be very helpful when considering the potential burden and undue influence a study design may have on participants. We argue here that while not required, they should be part of the research process, owing to decades or scientific misconduct, particularly in historically underrepresented groups. This misconduct has led to mistrust in science and scientific practice, and lower willingness to participate in research, even when the research would result in beneficial outcomes. PABs should be made up of people representative of the population of interest, or advocates of the population in cases where the participants of interest cannot participate fully (i.e., caregivers of people with dementia in a study of dementia treatment), have experience with the problem in question, and be thoughtfully involved throughout the study lifetime, from designing the research methods to interpreting and disseminating the outcomes. While the DSMB sees the study from the perspective of researchers, the PAB sees the study from the perspective of the participants. The number of members may vary depending on the purpose of the PAB, but in general, you will want one or two people representing each perspective. For example, in a study regarding the treatment of depression, alcohol misuse, and anxiety in older people seeking care in primary care medicine (Areán et al., 2008), investigators recruited two members to represent each disorder (N = 6) and a member of each racial and ethnic community we wanted to recruit (two Latine, two Black, N = 4). In this study, the PAB was involved in selecting measures and testing the burden, informing us of the best way to approach people about research. They reviewed the progress of our study, participated in helping us understand the findings, and then helped to disseminate the findings.

The PAB can also be involved in considering the ethics of the study. For example, in this same study, the PAB helped us understand why, when a participant agreed to research interviews, they would not be home for any scheduled home visits. They let us know that in their community, people were reluctant to be interviewed in their homes because they were concerned that neighbors would associate regular visits from research assistants with the depression study and thus violate confidentiality. Based on this concern, the PAB provided us with a community alternative, interviews in neighborhood churches and libraries.

Trial Registration

Another important part of ethical conduct of research is the need to register your trial, even if it is a small proof-of-concept or pilot study. Trial registration happens differently from country to country but always consists of some public and accessible way of posting your study protocol, the hypotheses you are testing and how you are measuring the variables in your study. Importantly, trial registration occurs before the trial begins recruitment; it is a means of keeping researchers accountable to the study protocols that were approved for funding and by IRBs. In the United States, federally funded studies are registered in ClinicalTrials.gov and must be registered before the study begins. It is through this system that changes to protocols are not only updated, but a record of when those changes were made is kept for public scrutiny. In other countries, trials are registered through the publication of a protocol paper, and many top journals either have a section or subjournal dedicated to these manuscripts. Protocol papers must be published within one year of the study beginning. Many investigators will do both, register in clinicaltrials.gov and publish their protocol in a scientific journal. It's not necessary but it does help with transparency (plus, it's another paper to add to your CV). The need for registration arose from—you guessed it—scientific misconduct. Historically, very little information was made available about a study prior to the publication of the outcomes, with only the funding agency having a record of the original protocol. Some scientists, driven we assume by the "publish or perish" rule and the tendency for top journals to only publish positive outcomes (meaning the main hypotheses were supported) would only report on outcomes that proved their hypotheses (cherry-picking), even though they were not the primary outcome measures. Although industry-sponsored research has been the poster child for selective reporting of clinical trial outcomes, this problem is not limited to industry-funded studies. In a meta-analysis conducted in 2014, it was found that over half of published trials failed to report on the planned primary outcomes, thus cherry-picking what was reported, and as much as 65% of trials did not report on the safety outcomes the protocol specified would be studied (Wager & Elia, 2014).

Ethics and the Research Team

The investigative team must also be prepared and trained in the ethical conduct of research, and not to complete training once, but to keep abreast of advances in scientific ethics as often as possible. In the United States, training in ethical conduct of human research is required every four years. Most universities and funding agencies require this training, which is often conducted online. To be clear, everyone on the investigative team must undergo training, as is anyone who is in contact with a research participant. This not only includes ethical conduct of science but also understanding financial conflict and how that can impact the conduct of a study and reporting of those outcomes. We will not go into detail here about the nuance of ethics, however, most chapters in this book will discuss ethics related to the chapter topic, if relevant, for instance, the chapter on creation of study materials has a discussion about the need for the IRB to review these materials.

Gender Issues, Equity and Disparities, Children and Advanced Age

In 1993, Congress passed, and then-President Clinton approved, the NIH Revitalization Act (NIH Revitalization Act of 1993 Public Law 103-43, 1994) that mandated the NIH provide support and guidelines for the inclusion and recruitment of women, minorities, and children into clinical research samples. The basis for this mandate was the result of a review of the clinical trial literature that noted most studies had been conducted on white men between the ages of 21 and 60. As such, recommendations about treatment were based on research that did not consider the potential differential response to treatment that women and minorities would have. In 2002, NIH created guidelines for investigators and reviewers of grant proposals to follow regarding this mandate (NIH, 2024). Specifically, this mandate indicates that women, historically under-represented racial and ethnic groups and children must be included in research and that exclusion of any of these groups—including children—must be justified, with the cost of recruitment not being a valid reason for exclusion. More recently, NIH has gone further to require that clinical research include in the aims the intention to assess sex as a biological variable in any data analysis.

Clearly, if one were studying depression in pregnant women, one would not include children or men; if one were studying Alzheimer's patients, one would not include children or young adults. Such exclusions are easy to justify.

More difficult is the situation in which the community one is sampling from has very low representation of, say Pacific Islanders. Should one over-sample Pacific Islanders in the community to bring representation up to national levels, thereby risking having a biased sample of the community population? Or should one take a representative sample of the community population and risk being criticized for under-representation of Pacific Islanders? If race does not moderate the effect of treatment—and you have data that demonstrates this—it doesn't matter which tactic is taken. If the effect of treatment is dependent on race, there is a real problem faced. Generally, the investigator would overrecruit—or *enrich*—Pacific Islanders in this case, consider race a possible moderator of treatment. The representation of racial and ethnic groups in the population samples (*sampling weights*) is used to estimate and test the parameters in the population sampled.

Another complication in including people from different ethnic or racial groups is that eventually, you will be in a position to analyze the data to determine if racial or ethnic variables influenced outcomes. Most people, when conducting clinical trials, usually do not have sufficient sample sizes of each group to compare outcomes by group or even detect whether one race is a moderator, and if membership in another race is not a moderator. Sadly, limited sample sizes result in the tendency to lump people into White/Not White categories which treats the sample as if people from nonwhite racial groups are all the same (which they are not).

A Word on Advanced Age

The global population is aging rapidly, and many countries are faced with how to best manage mental and behavioral health problems in these age groups (World Population Aging 2019: Highlights, 2019). Older adults are not just old adults, there is considerable evidence that the older brain functions differently from young or middle-aged brains, and that late age is a moderator of treatment outcome and acceptability, particularly in psychosocial interventions (Murman, 2015). Untreated or poorly treated behavioral health problems confer considerable societal and economic costs, and if these issues are treated appropriately, problems such as morbidity and mortality in this group dissipate (Gallo et al., 2016). While this can be a challenging group to recruit into research, particularly into psychosocial research, once recruited they are known to be less likely to drop from a study. Because countries and funding organizations continue to ignore this demographic grouping as a necessary group to ensure it is represented in research, we encourage readers of this book to consider including older samples in your future research to correct this unfortunate and continued disparity.

Chapter Summary

The field of psychosocial interventions research is most concerned with the best way to treat behavioral health conditions using techniques based on psychosocial theories. The best studies begin with developing a question of high public health significance, turning that question into a hypothesis that is supported by current thinking in the field as well as preliminary data, piloting the project to work out the methodological bugs in the study protocol and obtain pilot data, then testing the intervention's efficacy and effectiveness, what variables moderate outcomes and the processes by which the intervention produces its effect (mediation), and finally testing the best methods for implementing the intervention into real world settings.

The study design is important for adequately testing questions of interest, and several important elements need to be in place for readers to trust the study's outcomes. These include a specific, replicable protocol, reliable and valid measures, a well-trained and unbiased research team, a representative sample large enough to test the hypotheses, and the use of state-of-the-art data-analytic methods.

The investigative team must work with an IRB and DSMB and should work with a PAB. The sample must be representative of the population of interest and ensure that there is appropriate and adequate inclusion of women, historically under-represented racial and ethnic groups, and children.

2

Selecting and Supporting Your Hypotheses

Critical Research Questions This Chapter Will Address

What do innovation, public health significance, and impact mean in psychosocial interventions research?

- What does a clear and concise hypothesis look like?
- What are the best analytic methods for data exploration?
- What are the ethical issues in exploratory research?
- How much does it cost to do exploratory work?
- What are some common ethical mistakes made during analysis?
- How do you ensure your hypotheses consider equity and diversity?

One of the most important aspects of a psychosocial intervention trial is the question you are attempting to answer. High-quality psychosocial intervention research tests well-defined, innovative, significant, and incremental sets of questions likely to impact the scientific and clinical field. Study aims, the accompanying hypotheses, and the theory that support your aims should be clearly stated and written and supported by preliminary data. The research process is lengthy, incremental, and iterative. New researchers often too quickly identify research questions, resulting in aims that are overly ambitious and not grounded in the specific gaps in the field. Especially for junior researchers, it can be best to identify a highly feasible research question while you learn the ropes about the complexities that even a "simple" research study may bring. The purpose of this chapter is to help you identify compelling psychosocial intervention research questions, determine their innovation, impact, and significance, and better understand how to use existing data and theory to support and refine the study question. Part of this discussion will include how to apply the experimental therapeutics and mechanistic approach to clinical trial research, which includes identifying mechanisms that drive the outcomes in your intervention. We will also discuss here, under the discussion of theory, how the Research Domain

High-Quality Psychosocial Interventions Research. Second Edition. Patricia A. Areán and Michael D. Pullmann, Oxford University Press.
DOI: 10.1093/oso/9780197681923.003.0002

Criteria (*Research Domain Criteria (RDoC)—National Institute of Mental Health (NIMH),* 2025) applies to psychosocial interventions research.

Sources for Generating Psychosocial Interventions Research Questions

Most psychosocial interventions researchers generate research questions from a variety of sources. These sources include clinical observation, literature review, participating in research and clinical conferences, collecting preliminary data, and exploring existing data. We advise that investigators not rely solely on one source of information to generate questions. For instance, an idea generated from clinical observation should be investigated using existing theory, data exploration, and observations others have made and documented in the field. Theory and current thinking in the field should support questions arising from data exploration. In short, not every novel observation is worth a research project; there must be a strong justification to spend the effort, time, and resources to design, fund, and conduct a research study. As we discuss in this chapter, other factors must be considered before planning a research study, such as public health significance, innovation, and potential impact.

Reviewing the Literature

One important way to generate hypotheses is to read the literature and attend conferences about recent developments in your field. Sometimes good sources of hypotheses are systematic reviews, discussions about next directions for an area of research, and clinical journals that report on interesting case findings. Another strategy that can be helpful in generating hypotheses is to read papers from outside your area of research, expertise, or discipline. For instance, geriatrics experts can sometimes find interesting perspectives from pediatrics literature, and psychotherapy researchers can sometimes find interesting avenues of intervention by reading psychopharmacology literature. Case in point: one of the book authors had read about correlations of poor antidepressant response in older adult populations, where a consistent correlate was executive dysfunction. In reading the clinical description of executive dysfunction, she found a potential avenue for an intervention she is an expert in, namely Problem-Solving Therapy. Her research question from this review of the literature, coupled with her expertise was: Can Problem

Solving Therapy, an intervention that theoretically addresses behaviors associated with executive dysfunction, serve as a better treatment than antidepressants in this population of older adults?

Clinical observation

Isaac Asimov is quoted as saying, "The most exciting phrase to hear in science, the one that heralds new discoveries, is not 'Eureka!' (I found it!), but 'That's funny....'" Direct observation of presentation of symptoms, clinical characteristics that appear to influence treatment outcomes, and overall response to treatment are frequently the source of the most interesting, innovative, and exciting psychotherapy questions. Observation can be as simple as noting a clinical pattern while treating patients, noting in a chart review a pattern of response among a particular group of people to a specific treatment, or even just a single unusual case.

To illustrate the use of observation to generate questions, we turn to Dr. B, who noticed that they and other therapists in their clinic were struggling to provide a structured, problem-focused therapy for depression to patients who were particularly anxious and reported past abuse experiences. Dr. B and their colleagues speculated that patients with past abuse might have trouble focusing on specific problems because of poor affect regulation. These and other data led to an initial question: Do early childhood trauma and current affect regulation deficits differentially impact the effectiveness of structured, problem-focused therapy?

Collecting preliminary data

It is often helpful to collect preliminary data to investigate hypotheses generated from observation. Investigators will sometimes ask patients to participate in research to clarify the question they are interested in exploring. Using Dr. B's example above, one question that came to mind was whether childhood abuse and affect regulation were problematic only in structured psychotherapies, or if this poor response was common across all psychotherapies. To gain insight into this question, Dr. B obtained IRB approval to survey clinicians in their practice about clinical presentations of depression they felt were most difficult to treat and listed several potential problems including affect regulation and childhood abuse. Dr. B found that therapists who provided other forms of psychotherapy also found these patients to have a poorer response to depression treatment. Based on this data, Dr. B modified the research question to determine the impact of childhood abuse and poor affect regulation on all psychotherapies.

Using existing data to generate hypotheses (one type of secondary data analysis)

A *hypothesis-testing* study has very few primary research hypotheses, each with a theoretical rationale and empirical justification, and is specifically designed to test those hypotheses with a specific, predetermined analytic plan. An *exploratory study* is conducted with the general goal of trying to understand a certain phenomenon, and each analysis tends to stimulate further analyses. This is not to say that unintended observations made during exploration should be ignored; sometimes the best discoveries in science come from trying to explore one question and finding another, better question to explore.

The exploration of existing datasets is always helpful in supporting, refuting, or refining new hypotheses. Having results of such exploration is crucial to providing empirical support to justify the hypothesis in any proposal for funding a hypothesis-testing study. It is important to note here that exploratory research offers insights into an issue and adds to comprehension; it is not likely to provide the definitive answer to any question.

There are two major reasons why secondary data analysis is only useful for hypothesis generation. First, any hypothesis generated from exploration cannot be validly tested on the same data. This is called *post hoc* testing and is a source of many erroneous conclusions in research. Legitimate hypothesis testing requires that the hypothesis tested be stated a priori, that is, generated before the data is collected and used to test the hypothesis. This would, of course, be a full statement of the hypothesis, including stipulation of the outcome measure, of any covariates to be included, whether interactions of covariates with treatment choice would or would not be included, and so forth. Second, such exploration is meant to, and likely will, suggest the appropriate sample, the appropriate design and measure, and the appropriate analyses for the study necessary to provide a definitive answer regarding the hypothesis posed. While it can occasionally happen, the exploratory dataset is unlikely to be optimally designed to address a research question that was not a priori. Consequently, any hypothesis that arises from data exploration must be formally tested with a study designed specifically to address that research hypothesis before being accepted as a research conclusion. Exploratory studies should have actual research questions in mind; random exploration without a clear idea of what one is looking for is a waste of time and effort.

If you generate an idea that seems innovative and exciting from exploratory analyses, be ruthless: consider alternative explanations for that idea in the same dataset, particularly those less innovative and exciting. Let's say you are interested in whether or not group psychotherapy for depression is more effective than individual psychotherapy for depression in older people accessing services in community mental health, the hypothesis being that late-life depression may be a function of social isolation, and the group experience would enhance the effects of therapy (true example, by the way). The clinic you work in offers individual and group psychotherapy and collects clinical outcomes regularly. You conduct an analysis of the data from encounters covering four years (N = 500), and you find that individual psychotherapy results in greater treatment outcomes than group psychotherapy. You may be inclined to think that this would be initial, compelling evidence to support a hypothesis that individual psychotherapy is more effective than group psychotherapy, and this may be particularly exciting, given the effort involved in scheduling and leading group psychotherapy. You might even be able to argue that this finding is accurate, given the large sample size. However, being a critical thinker, you acknowledge that the sample was not randomized, and while you found no group difference in depression or functional outcomes prior to initiating treatment, there may be other differences that may be driving the outcome. Because you can find no theory to support why such a difference would exist (indeed all the literature up to that point suggests the opposite), you speak to the clinicians in your clinic about alternative explanations for your findings and you discover a major difference between individual therapy and group therapy. In group therapy, the clinicians followed a structured manual, and while they did make minor adaptations to the content for understandability, by and large the group stuck to just the psychotherapy content. In individual psychotherapy, the clinicians provided psychotherapy and case management services, such as linkages to housing and food assistance, helping schedule medical appointments and other advocacy work. The clinicians further pointed out that since the older adults in the clinic were often struggling with problems associated with social determinants of health, the addition of case management services made it easier to address psychological issues, since patients receiving case management tended to be less distracted in session by problems related to basic human needs. While the original idea of comparing group to individual psychotherapy could not be supported by the exploratory aims, this exploration did lead to and provisionally support another interesting hypothesis, "does the addition of case management to psychotherapy improve depression outcomes more than either intervention alone," a study which was eventually funded (Areán et al., 2005). Interestingly, in the larger, randomized study comparing psychotherapy with case management to the two interventions alone found a different outcome, that of the three conditions, psychotherapy alone performed the worst, with the combined condition and the case management condition being the two superior interventions, the only significant difference being between the combined condition and the psychotherapy condition.

As can be seen in this example, investigators should draw conclusions from findings in exploratory studies with extreme caution. Unfortunately, exploratory studies (referred to with derogatory terms such as "fishing expeditions" or "torturing the data until they confess") have a bad reputation, largely because in the past, investigators have ignored this caveat. To be sure your exploratory work is well guided, follow these rules:

- Approach your exploration with a particular goal in mind. In the example above, the investigator had a specific purpose in looking at the clinic data, whether there were differences in outcomes between people who received group psychotherapy and those who received individual psychotherapy.
- Consider alternative explanations for any new idea generated but cross-reference your findings with existing theory, literature, and expert opinion. As was done above, the investigator further explored the reasons for their findings through literature review and discussions with clinicians offering these services.
- Interpret your data with caution. Although the investigator was initially excited by this contradictory finding, they also knew that the sample was not randomized, and the results could be trusted only so far.
- If you wish to publish the results of these analyses, emphasize that the study is "preliminary" or "exploratory." Indeed, since the last version of this book, many journals request authors qualify the study type in its title, for instance, "The Effectiveness of Individual Psychotherapy and Group Psychotherapy in a Clinic Sample of Older, Low-Income Elderly: Results from an Exploratory Chart Review." In your discussion, remind readers that the result is a hypothesis to be tested in future studies, not a conclusion that might be used to inform practice.

Where to Find Data to Explore

Since the last version of this book, there have been tremendous strides in making datasets collected with public funds readily available to anyone (within reason) who wishes to use the data for exploratory purposes. In Chapter 4, we will discuss the different ways to make your data available, data sharing methods, and examples of how to manage data sharing efforts. Technically, you can use any source to explore data, though the quality of the data is an important selection issue. If the sample is haphazardly assembled, or the data are carelessly and incompletely collected, it is not worth the time and effort necessary to explore it. Sample size is less of an issue here, as even single case histories can be included, for any hypothesis generated in one source should be checked in multiple sources. Data can come from chart reviews, open-access datasets, other research studies, electronic claims data from health companies, and now from digital datasets from mobile health applications (apps). Places to find open-access data include the National Library of Medicine website in the United States, the NIH Data Repository, the WHO's Global Health Observatory, the Global Health Data Exchange, and Sage Bionetworks' Synapse Database. Datasets are available from epidemiological studies, the Centers for Disease Control and Prevention, the Agency for Healthcare Quality and Research, the Substance Abuse and Mental Health Data Archive, and even Subreddits have open-sourced data to mine.

The prime sources of data for exploration are our own data generated in previous hypothesis-testing studies, now to be explored to guide your own future research efforts, and data from well-done hypothesis-testing studies that might be shared by your colleagues. In 2003, the NIH in the United States mandated that investigators should make data available to others for exploration, data merging, and confirmation purposes. Datasets created from US federal dollars are to be made publicly available under the Freedom of Information Act (*Freedom of Information Act, 2025*). There are some guidelines as to how the data should be shared, but also some grey areas, such as whether raw or preprocessed data should be shared and depending on the type of data shared (for instance, social media data), the decision to share raw or preprocessed data will depend on whether it is possible to identify specific participants based on the data they do share. Most top-tier journals now expect to have a data sharing statement in any document, and some even ask the data to be published in a peer-reviewed journal (this is more common in studies of digital interventions). Be prepared to have at least a statement available and a means for sharing your data.

Foundations that fund mental health research have varying policies related to data sharing. A quick review of data-sharing policies revealed that the Robert Wood Johnson Foundation will make some large datasets available, while the MacArthur Foundation encourages its investigators to share their data without providing resources to access the information. Insurance and pharmaceutical companies often have strict rules regarding data sharing, but some health plans in the United States participate in the NIH Collaboratory, where de-identified data are shared and merged into a large repository specifically to encourage health science. In most circumstances, for outside investigators to access these companies' data, they must establish a relationship with another investigator inside the organization.

Data Analytic Methods for Exploration

Any data analytic method can be used for exploratory data analysis. However, analyzing data in multiple ways until a significant finding is obtained is inappropriate. Significance values are not legitimate unless adjusted for the familywise error that occurs when conducting multiple tests, and any findings that are reported need to be specified as exploratory with a full description of the number and type of analyses that were conducted. Occasionally, studies conducting many tests using large datasets will produce clickbait-style attention. In 2019, newspapers and websites reported that a study conducted by Skittles candy found people whose favorite flavor was red were more likely to identify as hopeless romantics, lovers of purple were more likely to be introverts, and lovers of yellow were more likely to leave on their read receipts for texts. These kinds of absurd results are a predictable consequence of collecting hundreds of variables from thousands of people, analyzing all possible combinations, and reporting on the few significant findings, most of which are false positives. For this reason, any hypothesis that emerges from exploratory analyses needs to be aligned with existing theory and results from other studies before it can be taken too seriously.

There is a fundamental difference in the use of statistical analyses in exploratory (hypothesis-generating) studies and in hypothesis-testing ones. In hypothesis-testing studies, sampling, measurement, design, and analytic decisions should be driven by the a priori hypothesis, or the hypothesis made before the results are known. Hypothesis testing is inherently a deductive process, where existing theories or ideas about the world are tested. Hypothesis generation is an inductive process, in which ideas about the world are created based on observed data. This process can be driven by descriptive statistics, depicting data through figures and tables, exploring associations among variables, and other methods with fewer mathematical assumptions than hypothesis testing. There are many approaches to exploratory data analysis (Tukey, 1977), and here we will describe a few. Let's return to Dr. B. If you recall, Dr. B noticed that patients with anxiety and past abuse did not benefit from structured, problem-focused therapy for depression. Once they observed the pattern in their own clinical work, and that pattern was supported in their clinician survey, what happened next? Was this pattern some sort of "clinician's illusion," or did it really objectively exist? Dr. B could explore an existing dataset to find out which patterns would emerge—specifically, would past abuse and affective dysregulation affect response to psychotherapy overall, and would past abuse and affective dysregulation have a particularly negative impact on structured, problem-focused therapy? Dr. B conducted a search for large-scale clinical trials comparing psychotherapy types, including a structured problem-focused therapy for treating depression, in the NIH REPORTER, the online search engine, and found a study that fit their needs. They then contacted the authors of the study and were given permission to use their dataset for their purposes.

The crucial data here for each patient are (1) their treatment group (problem-focused therapy versus some other approach); (2) whether or not there was past abuse; (3) a measure of affective dysregulation at baseline; and (4) a measure of treatment response such as a pre-post change score on depression. (A note that while change scores are sometimes criticized when used in statistically modeled data as compared to other approaches, despite the criticisms they can still be useful for exploration and modeling.) The first step is to familiarize yourself with the data by examining the relevant distributions. Finding out what the sample sizes of subjects in each treatment group are, how much missing data there is, and computing what percentage of subjects in each treatment group reported past abuse are easy tasks. If your variable is categorical, compute frequencies and proportions so you know how many participants are in each category. Using bar charts can help you visually display your data and may give you a better understanding of the categorical proportions.

Where exploratory analyses really get exciting is when you begin to analyze two or more variables in conjunction to explore for unexpected patterns and associations in your data. Dr. B may be interested in first examining whether the proportion of patients in the problem-focused therapy group who had a treatment response above a clinical cutoff was higher than the proportion in the therapy-as-usual group. For this analysis, one would use crosstabulations, which are the stratified frequencies for two categorical variables. When running crosstabulations, you obtain the proportions or percentages between groups, in addition to frequencies, to better identify patterns that could be obscured due to different sample sizes. For instance, you could compute the percentage of patients in each treatment group that had a positive treatment response. Alternatively, you could compute the percentage of patients who had a positive treatment response that were in the problem-focused group versus the other group. This example illustrates a common problem we see when people compute crosstabulations. Sometimes it is difficult to know which variable to base the percentage on. While you can always compute both, this can become confusing. You may find it easier to formulate an exploratory research question and then, using that question, conceptualize one of your variables as a pseudo-dependent variable and one as a pseudo-independent variable. Then, use the independent variable as the denominator, or the basis for the percentage computation. In our example, Dr. B would compute the percentages of patients who improved within each treatment group. We find it easiest to usually place our "independent variable" in the column of a crosstabulation, and then request percentages by column.

In crosstabulations of variables that have more than two categories, it can be difficult to identify which categories have possible patterns. Therefore, we like to compute expected values and standardized residuals for each cell. The expected value is what the count in the cell would be if the data were evenly distributed across the two variables. The standardized residual is a statistic demonstrating how extremely different the observed value is from the expected value, with a zero indicating no difference. The more extreme this statistic, the more likely there is an odd pattern in the data associated with that combination of variables. Standardized residuals above or below 1.96/-1.96 could be considered "statistically significant," though we are usually not highly concerned with that when exploring data.

Examining continuous variables such as the baseline measure of dysregulation and continuous scores on treatment response can be a bit trickier than categorical variables. They are often summarized using four commonly used "moments"—mean (mathematical average), variance, skewness, and kurtosis. You'll also want to examine two other measures of central tendency: the median (middle value) and the mode (most common value), and you'll want to examine the range (lowest and highest value). These statistics will help you understand the distribution of your data. Graphically depicting your data can provide a visual analysis of these moments and further help you to understand how your data is distributed across the population. Histograms are a type of bar chart used for continuous data. Histograms show frequencies of binned scores to better display the frequency of ratings, and binned scores are ranges within the continuous variable. In the hypothetical example in Figure 2.1, most participants had an Affective Disregulation score ranging from 0 to 38 and the distribution is fairly normal, with one outlier scoring around 78. That outlier should be examined for a possible out-of-range value or data error. Boxplots or box-and-whisker plots display the median (middle value), 25th and 75th percentiles (i.e., upper and lower quartiles), low and high expected values (1.5 times smaller or larger than the upper and lower quartiles), and

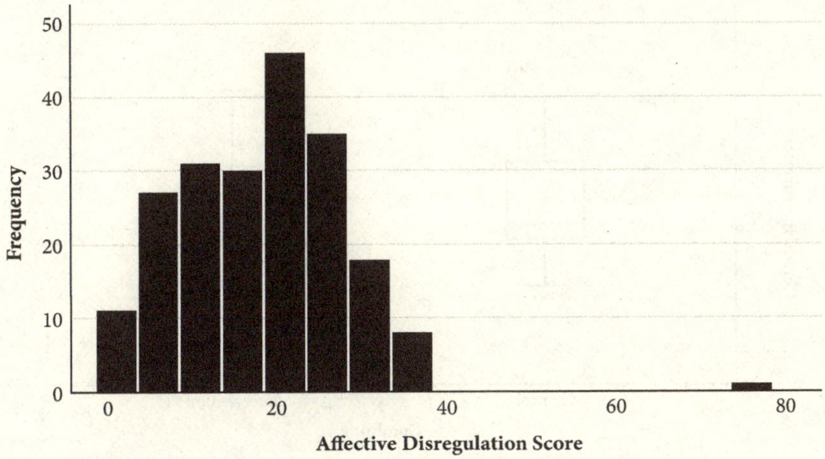

Figure 2.1 Histogram

outlier cases that are smaller or larger than these expected values. Figure 2.2 displays hypothetical boxplots for an intervention and control condition on the clinical change score. The median (heavy line in the middle of the chart) is very similar between the groups, but the intervention group appears to have greater variance, with 25th and 75th percentiles ranging from 3 to 69, whereas the control group percentiles range from about 23 to 65. There is an outlier in the control group, case 3 which scored an 80, that should be examined. Raincloud or half-violin charts, so named because they sometimes look like the curves of a half of a violin, combine boxplots with histograms to display the specific frequency of datapoints across the distribution. (Violin charts also exist, which provide a mirror image of the vertical plane, but these provide redundant information, so the raincloud is more efficient.) Figure 2.3 shows a hypothetical raincloud chart of the exact same data as Figure 2.2. In this figure, the dots are each individual person's score (jittered so they are offset horizontally, so the reader can better see the frequency of identical scores). The shaded area or cloud is the histogram frequency. We can now see that there are two potential outliers, the case identified in the control group from the boxplot plus a case in the intervention group that scored low. We can also see increased detail on the distribution of the two groups, with the intervention group having greater kurtosis (flatness) and the control group having greater positive skew. However, rainclouds do not show the median or percentiles like boxplots.

Outliers can be easily identified using these graphical approaches and are always worth examining as they may be errors that need to be addressed. A common mistake is forgetting to specify a value (such as 999) as missing or

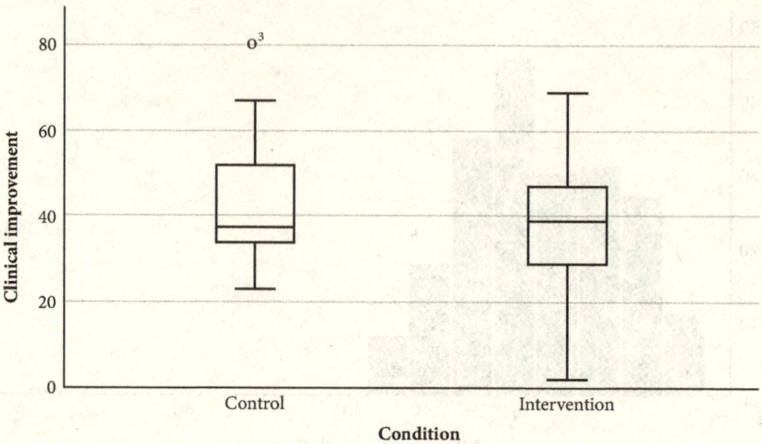

Figure 2.2 Boxplot

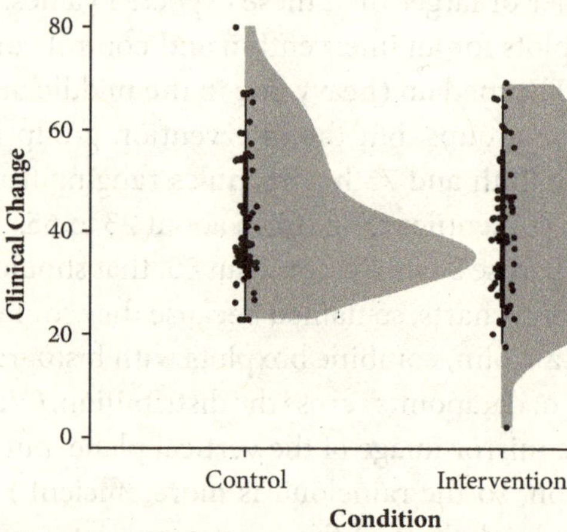

Figure 2.3 Raincloud or half-violin chart

not applicable. These could also be caused by mistakes in data entry (missing a decimal point) or calculation. Thus, every individual outlier is examined to determine whether it is in error or is a "real" outlier, and errors are corrected before any further analysis. Each "real" outlier should be considered as a case history, for outliers often provide unique insights into their origin. However, real outliers can skew the data and have overly large impacts on analyses. Consider Windsorizing your data in these situations; that is, identify a natural cut-off above which only one or a few extreme scores are located, or examine all scores above a high percentile, such as the 95th, and recode these to the next highest value.

So, Dr. B might compute these data and visualizations for the scaled measures of affective dysregulation and for treatment response in each treatment group. If participants were randomized to a treatment condition, the box-and-whisker plots for baseline scores on affective dysregulation should be approximately the same for all treatment groups. If not, that raises a question about randomization that should be examined further before proceeding; however, randomization does not guarantee baseline equivalence. If randomization is done correctly any differences between the group are, by definition, random, even if statistically significant.

The box-and-whisker or violin plots for the treatment outcome for each treatment group are of particular interest. While standard methods for testing group differences focus on comparing treatment group means, these visualizations provide additional context. For instance, while the means may be similar, there may be differences in the proportion of patients that are outliers, or differences between groups in the range of treatment responses such that one treatment is associated with both higher and lower change scores. If, in fact, there are strong predictors or moderators of treatment (e.g., if a history of abuse and affective dysregulation is associated with the response to some treatments and not others), this is often suggested by differences in within-group variance, depicted as the sizes of the boxes and whiskers and the frequency of outliers.

To explore whether the history of abuse might be moderated with treatment response, you might then divide each treatment group into those with and without a history of abuse and get separate box-and-whisker, histogram, or violin plots for these. If abuse is indeed a predictive factor for response, one should see two different plots, each with a much smaller range (smaller boxes and shorter whiskers). If not, the shape and size will change very little from that of the total treatment group. Now one might see more clearly which treatments, if any, are influenced by a history of abuse. If the situation differs for different treatment groups, that suggests a history of abuse as a moderator of treatment outcome.

Dr. B may also be interested in how baseline affective dysregulation is associated with treatment outcome. To do this, they could dichotomize these scores and proceed as described above. But it is usually best to leave continuous variables uncategorized because you sacrifice valuable information when doing this. The exception to this rule is when disseminating results, it can often be easier for people to understand relationships among variables

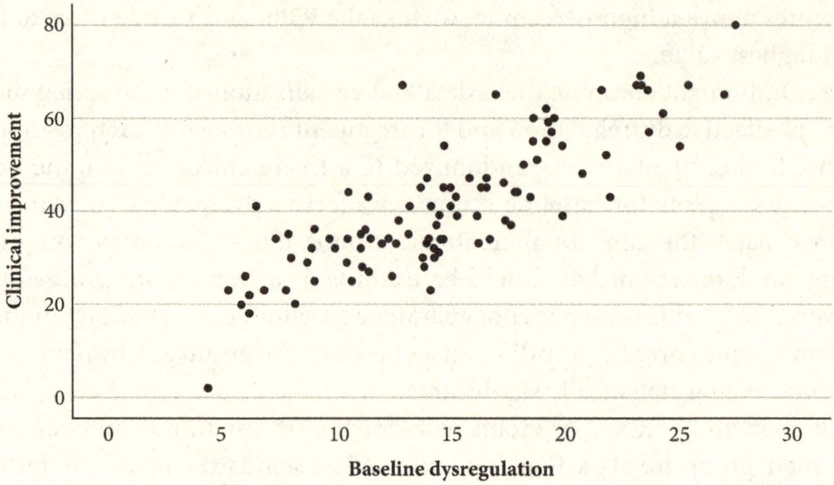

Figure 2.4 Scatterplot of baseline dysregulation by clinical improvement

when findings are categorized. Therefore, instead of categorization during this exploration of the data, you might compute a scatterplot that displays baseline affective dysregulation scores on the x-axis (the horizontal line) and treatment response on the y-axis (the vertical line) and each patient's scores as one point on the graph. Figure 2.4 displays a hypothetical scatterplot that indicates a positive correlation between baseline affective dysregulation and treatment change. The higher one's baseline dysregulation scores, the more likely they were to show improvement.

If the variables are unrelated, the scatterplot points would appear nebulous and cloud-like, or maybe in a horizontal or vertical line. If they are related, you may see a detectable pattern. Points clustered around a non-horizontal or vertical line would indicate linear relationships. Standard statistical methods (linear regression, product-moment correlation) are based on assuming such a pattern. However, you may also see other patterns nondetectable in standard statistical analyses. For example, an inverse U-shaped curve would indicate that for both high and low values of affective dysregulation, treatment response is poor, and that the best response is seen for those in the middle of the affective dysregulation scale. Or perhaps there is only an association between affective dysregulation and treatment outcome in certain areas. This is what is assumed to be true when one dichotomizes a scale at the optimal point. However, when researchers choose to dichotomize at an arbitrary point, that point is not likely to be optimal and findings will be obscured.

To examine Dr. B's primary question, whether those with abuse are less responsive to problem-focused therapy, you may also label your scatterplot points using different colors or shapes to highlight those with or without abuse. Any differences between the groups in the linear quality or clustering of the points may indicate a moderating relationship of abuse on the association between treatment. If those with a combination of a history of abuse and high affective dysregulation are least likely to respond to treatment, that pattern should be visible in the graphic as a clustering of points.

These two methods illustrate the basic principles of exploratory data analysis: first, visualize your data whenever possible. Second, make as few statistical assumptions as possible—don't assume normal distributions, equal variance, linear associations, etc., unless the data indicates that these assumptions are valid. Third, don't throw away useful information in the data by categorizing continuous variables prematurely. Fourth, let the data guide you, don't simply examine the data for confirmation, but also actively examine the data to try to disprove your suspicions and let the data lead to new hypotheses. Finally, use data exploration to indicate the most appropriate methods to test your hypotheses by examining the underlying assumptions of some statistical analyses, such as linearity.

Are Pilot Studies Exploratory Studies?

The reader may have noticed that we did not include the use of pilot studies for determining if a research question is worth pursuing. Technically, the purpose of a *pilot study* is to determine the *feasibility* of research methods proposed for a future larger scale, hypothesis-testing, clinical trial. In contrast, an exploratory study is a study done to identify and support proposed hypotheses, to provide a theoretical and empirical justification for a specific set of hypotheses and to guide the design of the study to test those hypotheses.

The term "pilot study" (discussed in detail in Chapter 7) has come to be used very generally to include any study not well designed to test a hypothesis, covering both what we call pilot studies and exploratory studies, as well as poorly designed and executed hypothesis-testing studies. In the past (and all too often, currently), grant reviewers inappropriately expected data from pilot studies to determine if the hypotheses were worthy of study. They made that determination based on effect sizes and significance testing on samples that were too small to provide sufficient statistical power. Owing to efficiency and the need to tweak study design to enhance recruitment and retention and select the least burdensome assessment, nearly all pilot studies are underpowered as they have too few participants (often in the range of 30–70), too much variability, and too small effect sizes. We discuss power in more detail in Chapter 4. Thus, the expectation that a pilot study can provide signals of efficacy or test hypotheses is flawed (Kraemer et al., 2006b). This myth has been repeatedly debunked, and sadly keeps reappearing in proposal reviews, and we strongly caution against using data from pilot studies in this manner. Despite this, federal funding mechanisms for pilot trials such as the R34 Clinical Trial still reads that it "...provides resources for evaluating the feasibility, tolerability, acceptability and safety, and *preliminary effectiveness* of approaches to improve mental health/functional outcomes..." (*PAR-21-131: Pilot Effectiveness Trials for Treatment, Preventive and Services Interventions (R34 Clinical Trial Required)*, 2025). The prudent grant applicant should carefully walk the line between examining preliminary effectiveness versus basing the rationale for a larger trial on these analyses.

You may read in other texts and hear from other investigators who still report pilot study effect sizes in grant applications, because of the strong tradition of doing so and the expectation that reviewers want to see this data to justify funding a larger grant proposal. We further argue that it is not currently necessary to provide that information. Many reviewers have come around to the idea that pilot studies have a specific purpose and the value of a study should be based on the study's public health significance, innovation, and impact (discussed in the next section). While the determination of target sample sizes for proposals of large trials is often made based on pilot effect sizes, these estimates are best made based on the smallest effect size of clinical interest. Finally, reviewer opinion is not immutable and is constantly changing as new information becomes available.

The pearls of wisdom we offer regarding pilot studies are simple. Do not use pilot study data to demonstrate the importance of a hypothesis, or the basis of sample size determination unless no other basis such as a clinically relevant effect size is available. You should be deciding on a sample size that tests the hypothesized effect you feel is clinically important. Use theory and multiple sources of exploratory studies to provide theoretical rationale, empirical justification and public health significance for your hypotheses and to provide guidance as to how best to design a study to test your hypotheses. Use pilot studies to ensure that what you are proposing to do in a hypothesis-testing study is feasible, logical, or optimal. Finally, a poorly designed hypothesis-testing study is neither a pilot study nor an exploratory study, it is merely a poorly designed study.

Judging a Question's Public Health Significance, Innovation, and Impact

Not every question generated from observation or data exploration is worth pursuing. Journal editors and research funders generally ask three questions when reviewing the importance of a research question: (1) Does the question address an important public health problem (termed *significance*); (2) Is the question new/not tested before (termed *innovation*); and (3) Will the answer to the question significantly influence how researchers think of the problem, or will the answer significantly change how the problem is managed by clinicians (termed *impact*)? A question does not need to address all three to be deemed important. For instance, a study exploring predictors of psychotherapy outcomes may be innovative and may have public health significance but may not have an immediate impact on the field. A study of clinician implementation of Cognitive Behavioral Therapy with Asian adolescents may not be innovative (if nothing new is tested about the therapy) but may have an impact on health care delivery. For a question to be considered worthwhile to pursue, it should address at least two of these three questions.

The best way to determine whether or not a question has public health significance, is innovative and impactful, is to consider at a minimum:

- Has the question been studied before (overall innovation)?
  - If Yes:
    - Is there a better way to answer the question (methodological innovation)?
    - Does the question require replication (public health significance)?
    - Are there aspects to the question that have been left unanswered (innovation)?
  - If no:
    - Does the question address an important problem or barrier to the field (public health significance)?
    - Will the answer to the question improve scientific knowledge (public health significance)?
    - Will the answer improve some technology related to psychosocial interventions (public health significance)?
    - Will the answer change clinical practice (impact)?
- Will answering the question change clinical paradigms (innovation)?
- Will answering the question result in new interventions (innovation)?

It is best to answer these questions about your proposed research in consultation with other experts in the field, by reading the literature, and in discussion with program officers at funding organizations. In the United States, each institute within the National Institutes of Health has a publicly available strategic plan that details the areas of research that are deemed to be of public health importance. This plan is updated every five years and is a great resource to review in deciding the relevance of your question to the funder. When consulting with others, it is a good idea to have a well-formulated question so that the advice you receive will be maximally helpful.

Ethical Considerations When Using Existing Data

Chart Reviews

While IRBs have always been careful to ensure investigators have a plan to safely and ethically handle data from chart abstraction or review, the advent of the Health Insurance Portability and Accountability Act of 1996 (HIPPA) drastically changed the ability of investigators to access clinical chart data. Most IRBs acknowledge that obtaining consent to review charts from everyone in a health system is not feasible, and many will want to ensure that no private information will be used in research or that patients will not be contacted because of the chart review. If in your practice you prospectively intend to use chart data for research purposes, you will often need to gain consent from patients before that information is collected.

Digital Data

Data collected from people's smart phones, wearable electronics, search engine requests, and social media use are all highly sensitive information because of a number of factors, including the potential to inadvertently identify people without their permission, the expectation people have that the information they put into these tools is private, and because of misuse on the part of companies to influence behavior. There is little guidance available to date about the best use of this data, and most concerns center around expectations of privacy and potential under-representation of populations who do not use technologies in the exploration of this data for health science purposes (Conway & O'Connor, 2016; Moreno et al., 2013; Nebeker et al., 2019). Some digital datasets are curated from people who donate their information for scientific purposes (the Health eHeart Study is one example), but donations do not solve all the ethical challenges involved in using digital datasets for exploration. The management of this data is very sensitive and requires that data be housed in such a way that prevents attempts to hack such data. In Chapter 10, we will cover this issue of secure digital dataset management.

Secondary Data Analysis

As with chart reviews, when using information from existing datasets, most IRBs will exempt investigators from the requirement of collecting consent from participants who have already consented to donate and share their data. However, investigators must prove to the IRB that the data is de-identified, meaning that no information that could identify the participant will be part of the dataset. There are different operational definitions of de-identification depending on the relevant law, but for health-related data, HIPAA specifically outlines several variables that must be omitted, such as participant name, social security numbers, email, and IP addresses. For a full list, please go to the HIPAA Journal (*De-Identification of Protected Health Information: How to Anonymize PHI, 2025*). Further, IRBs will often ask for proof that the original study was approved by another IRB. Although not technically an IRB issue, most people sharing their datasets will ask you to complete a Data Use Agreement (see Appendix), specifying that you cannot share the data with anyone else, as it is not your data, and that you promise to keep the data secure.

Budgetary Issues in Secondary Data Analysis

Preliminary data analysis has its costs. You will need the following resources in place to conduct your preliminary research.

Your Time

You will need to estimate how much of your time to set aside to do the research. For studies involving primary data collection, if you intend to train, supervise, and oversee the data collection, you can anticipate that approximately 20% of the time you spend conducting the study will go toward those efforts, primarily in supervision and team meetings, double-checking data collection, and recruitment efforts. If you plan to conduct some of the interviews yourself, you will need to add more time.

If you plan to conduct secondary data analysis, the time you will need to allocate will depend on what tasks you will take on. If you plan to work with the data yourself rather than engaging methodologists or biostatisticians, you will need to set aside approximately 20–30% of your time.

Research Assistants

Because of the potential for investigator bias, it is preferable that you, as the principal investigator, do not collect data. Research assistants who will collect data can be volunteers, graduate students, or professionals you hire to collect, code, and enter your data into a database. Whatever level they are, these assistants will need to possess specific skills. If they do not, someone will have to train the assistants in these skills. In Chapters 5 and 7, we discuss the composition of the team, what research assistant skills should be, how to train and how to supervise research assistants.

Biostatistical Help

Having biostatistical help is very useful in all stages of research. However, since it is often difficult to fund such help, it is worth considering what type of statistical help is most useful at each stage of research. We must first distinguish between a statistician, a biostatistician as a collaborator, a biostatistician as a consultant, and a statistical analyst. Both statisticians and biostatisticians typically have PhD-level training in statistics, but their discipline may be in mathematics, statistics, psychology, epidemiology, sociology, and so forth. It is the level of training and experience, not the specific degree that matters. We note here that statistical expertise is needed, even if you have someone who is an expert in Artificial Intelligence (AI) methods, such as Machine Learning or Natural Language Processing, methods that are currently very popular in exploratory or hypothesis-generating research. People with a background in Artificial Intelligence often do not have expertise in statistics. In fact, we have yet to meet an AI expert who can also conduct statistical analyses beyond descriptive analyses. Although that person may exist, it is rare, and so be prepared when partnering with an AI expert for that expert to ask whether there is a statistician on the team.

Biostatisticians are statisticians with a specific interest and experience in the application of statistics in biological and behavioral research. A *statistician*, not a biostatistician, will likely not be interested in the problems you are interested in and will not be very helpful in your research. As we point out in Chapter 5 under team building, the people on your team will only be so productive if they have an interest in the problem being solved. This goes for the people analyzing your data. The biostatistician will be more likely to read up on the latest methods for the analysis of behavioral data and clinical trials and will also be interested in applying these methods to your problem. In other words, any old statistician will *not* do, you will want to work with someone who has an interest in public health.

Cherry-Picking, *P*-Hacking, and Fishing

Several related problems in the clinical research field spring from a tendency to selectively choose analyses to run and report on. Cherry-picking outcomes is reporting outcomes that find the hoped-for difference between interventions while hiding unfavorable findings (Andrade, 2021). This is unethical behavior, but such behavior has been historically hard to detect in publications and has resulted in serious adverse consequences. Cherry-picked results are misleading as they do not portray the full balance of outcomes including unintended consequences and can mislead clinical decision-making and clinical research.

P-hacking occurs when researchers probe their original research question by analyzing their data in multiple ways until a significant finding results. Researchers may change certain aspects, such as their approach to missing data, the addition of covariates, and participant grouping or splitting. As an example of how different approaches to analyses can dramatically change findings, a recent study assigned the same dataset and research question to 29 teams and found widely different analytic approaches and effect sizes, with 69% of the teams finding a statistically significant positive effect and 31% not finding a significant relationship (Silberzahn et al., 2018). The variation in results was not explained by analysts' prior beliefs, level of expertise, or peer ratings of the quality of the analyses. Therefore, even subtle differences in analytic approaches can have dramatic impacts on findings even when researchers try to avoid bias.

Similarly, data mining and dredging are synonymous terms like p-hacking but applied to indiscriminate post-hoc analysis. An investigator analyzes the data in several ways without a hypothesis and reports only on significant findings. This is also wrong because your "important finding" may have only been identified by chance. Post hoc exploratory analyses should be labeled as such, and if multiple tests are done, you should report the results of every test.

Because of these unfortunate practices, registration of clinical trials prior to conducting the study is now required by funding agencies and most top-tier journals. Chapter 2 has a full discussion of this requirement and how one registers a trial. In short, it is always important to plan your study and your analysis and stick to that plan. If changes to the analytic plan, or exploratory unplanned analyses are made, they should be judicious, rare, and explained during dissemination.

We believe that cherry-picking and fishing arose largely because of the belief held by many investigators that the only studies that can be published are those that find statistically "significant" treatment differences and confirm hypotheses. With adequately powered and valid studies, we contend this should not be the case. This belief also confuses statistical "significance" (mathematically finding that an observed relationship is not likely to be spurious) with the significance, or importance, of a study. As long as a study is well designed and the data are properly analyzed, even studies that find no differences between interventions can yield valuable information. A recent example of such a study randomized approximately 6000 people who were identified as at high risk for suicide to one of two interventions: online mental health care based on an evidence-based treatment for suicidal ideation or to receive supported care management. Not only did the online intervention not find any significant improvement in suicidal ideation, but more people in that condition took their lives than in the control (Simon et al., 2022). Clearly, this was a very important finding to the field, even though the hypotheses were not supported.

Changing the Question and HARKing

There are research studies designed and funded to ask one research question but change the research question to another when that research question does not pan out. Other studies may "Hypothesize After the Results are Known" or HARK. This may occur after fishing or data mining, when the results of exploratory analyses are then used to construct a post-hoc hypothesis yet report it as if it were a priori. A major reason why clinical trials are required to be registered before they begin is that this is a very common practice. This is not meant to deter you from exploratory analyses, which can be extremely useful. But exploratory analyses should be reported as such and not be regarded as hypothesis testing or the basis for conclusions.

Interpreting Non-Statistically Significant Results as Proof of the Null Hypothesis

As we described earlier, there are almost always real differences between groups; non-statistically significant results are usually the outcome of inadequate power in the design. Statistical testing for clinical trial outcomes generally involves a null hypothesis (that is, a hypothesis of no difference between the groups), and null hypotheses cannot be proven, only rejected or failed to reject. Absence of proof is not proof of absence. If you are really interested in determining if interventions have equivalent outcomes (non-inferiority trials), you often need a larger sample size, on the order of 300 to 800 participants for a prespecified "clinically significant difference." This sample size will be based on the largest effect size, or real difference between groups, that is possible while still being recognized by the field as an effect that has no or negligible clinical difference. The larger the clinically significant difference, the smaller the number of participants you need to recruit.

Avoiding These Sins

There are many more of these "sins," although these tend to be the most common. It is important to be aware of the motivations that drive these practices. The most innocuous reason is simple ignorance of these practices as errors that may obscure, rather than reveal, the truth. But sometimes there may be motivations that cloud a researcher's thinking. The research endeavor can create a form of myopia, what Robert Merton termed "the imperious immediacy of interest" (Merton, 1936), when researchers are so focused on solving a social problem that they ignore conflicting data, weak methods, and unintended consequences of their work. Researchers face enormous pressure for research projects to "succeed," which is unfortunately often seen as equivalent to the discovery of statistically significant results. Years of focused effort builds momentum that is difficult to adjust in the light of disappointing findings. This may be combined with pressure from colleagues and departmental leadership and the need to build a career. An unsuccessful project may even cut off future funding for investigators and the lab staff who depend upon them. Many researchers face this dilemma and hopefully embrace the importance of quality science as the ultimate best path for their career. Sloppy methods may address a short-term problem, but it does not take long for one's reputation to be marred by inadequate attention to ethical practices.

To ensure adherence to good practices, you should familiarize yourself with analysis and publication guidelines described in this book, such as the CONSORT guidelines for clinical trials, the American Psychological Association publication manual, field-specific journal reporting requirements, and guidelines for open science including trial registration and data sharing. Additionally, consult a trained and experienced biostatistician or research methodologist in the design and analysis of your study, use peer review (not only those reviewing for funding, but also by colleagues willing to give a critical reading of your proposal or paper), and learn from mistakes in one study to avoid making the same mistake in future studies. Although PhD-level mental health professionals are trained to read, understand, and in some cases, conduct data analyses, statistics is an ever-evolving and very specialized field. Unless you are a regular consumer of statistical literature, you will eventually be using outdated analytic techniques and will be interpreting your data with old assumptions in mind.

How to Finance Exploratory Research

It is possible to find funds to support exploratory research, and since the first edition of this book, most science funders will support this research well. Depending on where you work and live, you may have access to more than just public or federal funds and foundations for your work. Universities and medical centers will often have seed grants for junior faculty and students, and in the United States, the Veterans Administration has funding available for preliminary research. In the United States, the NIH has two specific mechanisms aimed toward data exploration. The first is the R03 grant, which supports small research studies that can be carried out over two years. The second is the R21 grant, which is for more complex exploratory or developmental work and is intended for early phases of research. It is feasible to apply for larger pots of money in the United States. In our example of Dr. B, they were able to successfully apply for a multi-million dollar award from NIMH by partnering with other investigators around the country to share datasets.

Equity Considerations

Health inequities are systematic, and often systemic, differences between groups in determinants of health, healthcare access, healthcare quality, and health functioning and outcomes. These inequities are pervasive in social science research yet have received far too little attention as to root causes and context-based interventions. It is important to intentionally consider health inequities when formulating your hypotheses, doing background research, and analyzing existing data. The Cochrane and Campbell Equity Methods group advocates for a framework known as PROGRESS-Plus (*Cochrane Methods Equity, 2025*; Oliver et al., 2008), which is an acronym that summarizes several social determinants of health, including place of residence, race/ethnicity, occupation, gender and sexual orientation, religion, education, social capital, socioeconomic status, plus personal characteristics associated with discrimination (e.g., age, disability), features of relationships (e.g., parents with disabilities, exclusion from school), and time-dependent relationships (e.g., respite care or times when a person is temporarily at a disadvantage). By deeply considering these socially stratifying factors, you may uncover new ways of thinking about the causal processes underlying the health phenomena in which you are interested. Applying the PROGRESS-Plus framework to systematic reviews may help you identify important gaps in the research (if researchers have not investigated equity), contextual factors that could moderate the clinical effectiveness of interventions, and potential variables to explore in your datasets. For instance, during your literature review, you may examine whether race, ethnicity, gender, age, or any of the other PROGRESS-Plus variables were included as moderators in the published literature. Similarly, you may include these variables yourself when exploring your data, which could be by stratifying the data as described above in the section on exploring data, including these variables as control variables and interaction terms in more advanced statistical modeling.

A two-step process borrowed from Implementation Science (Gaias et al., 2022 may be useful for broadening your equity thinking when exploring the impact of interventions on health outcomes. In Step 1, identify your underlying assumptions about the intervention: how, why, and for whom it is supposed to work, and what is essential for the intervention to result in equitable outcomes. In Step 2, consider potential sources of inequities. Who was involved in the development of the intervention? Who is involved in implementing it? What resources are necessary for clients to use the intervention? Who determined the primary health outcomes of interest? Later, after your analyses are done, you may find that the intervention is associated with inequitable outcomes. A key line of research could then lead you to a third step: adapt the intervention or implementation strategy to ensure that equity is embedded in the underlying assumptions and intervention causal pathway.

A key aspect of equity examination is to try to avoid exploring only causal explanations that blame the victim. Socially determined inequities in health have often been misattributed to personal, cultural, or biological causes while neglecting the potential causes of racism, homophobia, sexism, and other forms of social control over resources. Simply identifying a phenomenon is not enough for a career-oriented program of research. We urge you to dig deeper to explore causal mechanisms to identify what works (and doesn't work) for whom, when, and under what circumstances.

Chapter Summary

Research questions can be generated by several sources of information but should never rely on just one source. It is fine to explore existing datasets, provided you have a question you wish to explore, the exploration is guided by theory, the data are interpreted cautiously, and the results are not treated as definitive. The importance of a hypothesis should be judged by its public health significance, innovation, and impact, not the effect size generated from a pilot study.

3

Selecting and Creating Materials for a Psychosocial Interventions Study

Therapy Manuals, Training Materials, and Fidelity Measures

Critical Questions This Chapter Will Address

- What is RDoC/Experimental Therapeutics
- How do I design and adapt therapy manuals?
- Do I need to develop training methods and materials?
- How do I create fidelity measures, and when do I need them?
- What is Human-Centered Design and how can that help me create usable materials?

Psychosocial interventions studies differ from other clinical trials in that they rely significantly on treatment manuals, training protocols for the study therapists, and methods for measuring how well the study therapists administered the intervention. Although all clinical trials have manualized protocols, in psychosocial intervention trials, the treatment manual, training model, and fidelity measures are the methods by which we determine and document that study participants are receiving the treatments being studied. This chapter explains how these materials are selected, created, and adapted for populations and contexts.

Creating and Adapting Treatment Manuals

What do we mean by a treatment manual? Treatment manuals are intervention guidelines that detail the specifics of the intervention, the therapeutic elements, and the structure. The manual or treatment guideline is the blueprint for how treatment is to be delivered and serves as a reference point for determining whether the treatment provider was adherent to the treatment protocol. If the treatment is proven to be successful, a manual allows other

High-Quality Psychosocial Interventions Research. Second Edition. Patricia A. Areán and Michael D. Pullmann, Oxford University Press. © Patricia A. Areán and Michael D. Pullmann (2026).
DOI: 10.1093/oso/9780197681923.003.0003

providers in the field to replicate the therapeutic methods. Manuals take many forms. Some are literally textbooks you can purchase from a publisher or bookseller, and some are merely guidelines that walk a therapist through the process of treatment delivery. There are even attempts to digitize these manuals to guide providers in the treatment methods in real time. An intervention may have more than one manual; there may be a manual for the treatment provider, a manual for the patient, and a training manual for the person who trains other providers in the treatment. In some circumstances, there may be a manual to help organizations implement the treatment.

Depending on your research question, you may or may not need to create a manual or adapt an existing manual for a given context. If your intent is to use an existing treatment that has a well-developed manual, you need not do more than seek permission from the developer to use the manual and to train yourself and the study therapists in the delivery of the treatment. It is not always possible to seek permission from the intervention developer, nor is it always necessary to do so. If one cannot seek permission from the developer, the investigator has the burden of demonstrating that they are an expert in the intervention or have employed an expert in the intervention on the study team as a consultant.

If there is no existing manual, or if you wish to modify the intervention or adapt it to the local context, there is a set of procedures that psychosocial interventionists use to create effective manuals. Human-Centered Design (HCD) is a process by which the intended users of the intervention (treatment provider and patient) are involved in the creation or adaptation of the intervention, usually by providing feedback or participating in user testing sessions to identify usability problems with the intervention. HCD methods intentionally focus on the needs of the end user, developing tools that are easy to use, learn, and operate with efficiency, and are accessible, engaging, and contextually appropriate (Lyon et al., 2020). HCD involves a hands-on and rapid iterative process, such as having the developer and representative end users interact with the manual by testing it out with simulated cases or patients, or through a process called a *cognitive walk-through*, which we describe below. The developer uses data collected from the end users to adjust the intervention to enhance its usability, acceptability, and potential for engagement. Key to this process is understanding the context in which an intended intervention will be deployed. Here, we are referring to the intervention setting (clinic, organization, community, and patient environment), the providers who will be delivering the intervention and patients using them.

Why are usability, appropriateness, engagement, and context so important when developing or adapting a treatment? Technically, you could develop a very effective intervention without consideration of these factors, but unfortunately, this tendency to believe that "if you build it, they will come" has yet to pan out for most psychosocial interventions. Indeed, most psychosocial interventions end up needing substantial modification to be usable in most contexts, and while some adaptation is necessary for implementation (Damschroder & Lowery, 2013), most interventions are not adopted in the first place, not implemented with fidelity, abandoned after implementation efforts, or require costly methods to sustain. Indeed, there is at least a decade of research focused on changing the attitudes of clinicians toward evidence-based practice (Lilienfeld et al., 2013), which often centers on low perceived clinical utility (Keepers et al., 2023). Perhaps the problem to be solved is not by directly addressing clinician attitudes, but ensuring the intervention is appropriate, usable, and fits the clinical context (Butler et al., 2015). We argue that if one considers intervention usability, appropriateness, and context, the historic challenges in evidence-based treatments becoming standard practice may be mitigated, or at least become easier to address (Lyon et al., 2019; Lyon et al., 2021b; Munson et al., 2022). The traditional linear pathway of treatment development, which has followed that of drug development via a multistage path of safety testing and highly controlled efficacy trials before real-world efficacy trials can begin, has slowed the implementation of psychosocial innovations. For psychosocial interventions, which frequently re-align existing practices into multi-component and multi-level interventions, the safety of individual components has already been established. The effectiveness of these interventions is highly dependent upon context, so testing within rigorously controlled settings may lack generalizability to real-world settings. While we agree with calls to expedite science by beginning the process with effectiveness or pragmatic trials rather than efficacy trials (Beidas et al., 2023), researchers must focus on preliminary development work to ensure the intervention is usable before the effectiveness trial begins.

Whether you are designing a new intervention or are adapting an existing intervention, we recommend you use a process we have developed in the UW ALACRITY Center, called the Discover, Design/Build, and Test framework (Lyon et al., 2019). This model is an integration of methods from HCD and Implementation Science to ensure an intervention is usable and easily deployed once data on its efficacy and effectiveness is tested. The process proceeds through the following steps:

(1) *Discover:* Identify or define the treatment and its elements; Identify the context in which it will be delivered.

(2) *Design and Build:* Design the manual or manuals for optimal implementation using iterative design.
(3) *Test:* Test the manual for finalization of feasibility.

As we describe these steps below, we will use the example of Engage, a novel psychotherapy for late-life depression (Alexopoulos & Areán, 2014) which was based on the National Institute of Mental Health's Research Domain Criteria (RDoC) experimental therapeutics approach and employed HCD methods to develop the intervention process. But before we move on, let's take a moment to talk about the National Institute of Mental Health's Research Domain Criteria Project (RDoC) and the experimental therapeutics approach.

What Is RDoC, How Does It Relate to the Experimental Therapeutics Paradigm, and Why Is It Important?

So, let's get RDoC out of the way first. RDoC was a project that began in 2012 at the National Institute of Mental Health in the United States and was meant to provide a paradigm for understanding psychopathology that would then inform novel treatment development and thus is largely focused on mental health (National Institutes of Mental Health, 2025). Those of you who study other conditions can skip to the next section on the experimental therapeutics approach. The RDoC project delineates the different units of analysis that should be studied when exploring the causes and correlates of psychopathology, in particular, genes, molecules, cells, neurocircuits, physiology, behavior, and self-report measures. These units of analysis are meant to measure different constructs, largely neurological or neuropsychological constructs, specifically positive and negative valence systems, cognitive and social processes, arousal, and sensory motor systems. These constructs are further divided into subconstructs, such as fear, reward responsiveness, attention, attachment, sleep, and agency. Although some have mistaken RDoC to be a new diagnostic system, that is not its intent at all. It is merely meant to be a way to study specific dysfunction that may cut across illnesses and lead to the identification of new treatment targets for mental health. This concept has become quite popular in basic mental health research, pathophysiology research and novel treatment development and other organizations around the world have begun to embrace this approach. For instance, the Wellcome Trust in England has its own version of RDoC (Farber et al., 2020). Why is this important for manualization and treatment development? The end goal of RDoC and efforts like it is to lead to the development of novel mental health treatments. The developers of RDoC and similar projects, however, admit that these variables are not quite ready to be targets for treatment development, although some have been used successfully for behavioral and neuropsychologically based treatments. What is really important for those of you who are developing new treatments, or modifying existing treatments is not so much a reliance on RDoC, but the importance of the Experimental Therapeutics Approach to intervention research. Let's now talk about that; we will return to RDoC momentarily.

The experimental therapeutics approach

This approach to health research has been around for centuries and has accelerated in the last century. The point of this approach is to use information from basic science to identify targets for treatments; the most successful example of this approach is the application of the genetics of cancer to developing chemotherapies and other somatic therapies to target the specific genes of different cancers. Take, for instance, breast cancer. Based on genetics research, there are now several different types of breast cancer based on the expression of different genes. After the genetic makeup of the tumor is identified from a biopsy, oncologists can create a treatment regimen consisting of chemotherapy, surgery, or radiation; the number and level of treatment intensity a patient receives will be based on the genetics of the tumor. This success has led to the development of "personalized medicine" which is meant to help clinicians identify subtypes of illnesses based on genes, biomarkers, and, as in RDoC, constructs that are associated with subtypes of illnesses, and match patients to the treatment that has the highest likelihood of curing or managing the illness (Waldman et al., 2009). In mental health, we do not have this level of understanding of our illnesses in the same way that oncology and other medical fields have. However, at least in the United States, identifying a target for your intervention is important. Although we may not have clear subtypes for, say depression, we also do not want our treatments to be "black boxes," we want to know if a treatment works and how it works. As we discussed in the last chapter and will discuss in future chapters, identification of how a treatment works can be very informative to understand under what conditions it should work well and when it may not be effective.

Back to RDoC; in using the experimental therapeutics approach, your intervention may target factors associated with a behavioral health condition. RDoC is one framework that can drive your selection of targets (we provide an example of that below). Other frameworks are just as valid, for example, Social Determinants of Health, which is not part of RDoC, would be highly important to study as drivers for psychopathology and treatment outcome. Now let's turn our attention back to the use of HCD in manual development.

Discover Phase

Identify/define the treatment and its elements: the RDoC/experimental therapeutics approach

Before you write your manual, you will need to identify the essential, active ingredients of your intervention, and their functions and causal mechanisms. These functions and causal mechanisms will articulate the rationale for why the core components are expected to have desired impacts. If you are developing a new intervention, these active ingredients may be entirely theory-based or hypothetical, and you will want to test your hypothesis about their therapeutic importance in a proof-of-concept study (see Chapter 6). If you are modifying an existing intervention, then those therapeutic elements will be prespecified by the developer and may have been verified as necessary elements in previous research. Either way, you will need to know what the necessary content is, and what content is just supportive or what content is just the structure of the therapy. The supports and structures (often termed the "adaptable periphery" in Implementation Science) can be changed to accommodate quality delivery of the therapeutic elements. The therapeutic elements (termed "core components" in Implementation Science) generally should remain in the intervention, although by identifying the functions and causal mechanisms, you may determine ways to modify, substitute, or rearrange the core components in a way that serves the same function but has other advantages.

Let's take the example of Engage to illustrate how the therapeutic elements were identified. The impetus for Engage was based on challenges Dr. Areán and colleagues had in implementing evidence-based psychotherapies for late-life depression, in particular Problem-Solving Treatment (PST), Cognitive Behavioral Therapy (CBT), and Behavioral Activation (BA), into community mental health and primary care settings serving older adults. We found that despite extensive costs on the part of health care organizations to train front-line clinicians in these treatments, trained and certified clinicians would not implement the treatment. Even those who seemed engaged with the intervention reported that over time they had made certain adjustments to it, as they felt the intervention was burdensome to deliver because of its structure, that it did not allow for time to get to know the patient, and it was occasionally not appropriate for a given patient (Crabb et al., 2012). These experiences led us to determine that we needed to create a new intervention for late-life depression, one that would be seen as less burdensome and was deemed appropriate for any older client in a variety of contexts.

In creating a new, more usable intervention, we wanted to verify the elements that would go into such a treatment, as well as develop a theory for why these treatments worked for some patients but not for others. Our first step in identifying therapeutic elements that would be part of this new intervention was to identify the therapeutic elements that were common across PST, CBT, and BA. We used a method similar to Chorpita's Distillation and Matching Model (Becker et al., 2018), whereby we looked at the evidence-based treatments for late-life depression and identified which elements were shared in common. These were: cognitive appraisal work, problem solving, goal setting, and action planning.

Our second step was to conduct a *systematic chart review* to identify relevant clinical evidence for practices used in real-world delivery. Using qualitative research methods, two advanced research assistants reviewed clinical notes from our own studies of BA, PST, and CBT, two of which were large, pragmatic trials (Areán et al., 2010; Farrand et al., 2024). The charts were coded using thematic content analysis (Nuendorf, n.d.). This process involves reviewing notes and looking for themes or content that appear in the notes commonly across therapists and patients. Codes and their definitions were developed by two independent reviewers. Then the reviewers compared, codified, and confirmed the common themes. When chart reviewers did not agree on themes, a third reviewer was available to resolve the discrepancy. The thematic analysis identified an interesting pattern in the notes. Most therapists started these treatments with simple, activity-based goals, such as cleaning up the house, meeting a friend for lunch, or going for walks. Patients who responded well to these initial interventions tended to be ready to take on more challenging goals, whereas patients who did not either meet the initial goals or did meet the goals but did not show any emotional response to the work tended to struggle in treatment and have a poor response. Many cases responded well to these treatments, but about one-third struggled with activity-based goal setting. Although some of these cases did eventually respond to treatment, usually when the therapist tried to use other approaches to encourage goal engagement, many did not. It was also noted that therapists who struggled the most with these treatments (defined as having a higher proportion of patients not completing tasks) tended to continue encouraging patients to work on easier goals (like house cleaning), despite patients raising other issues, such as interpersonal challenges. We interpreted the latter finding to mean that because the patient was not responding to activity-based goals, the therapist seemed stuck as to what to do next in treatment.

It appeared to us that when an older adult responded well to initial attempts at goal setting, the therapists were able to use these treatments effectively. However, when patients did not respond to initial, activity-based goals, we noticed five common clinical presentations emerged. Patients who did not respond to activity-based goal setting tended not to try the goal discussed in treatment. The reasons therapists listed in the notes could be defined as "low motivation," "distracted by a different problem," "too anxious to try," or "pessimistic about the utility of activity-based goals." The fifth category was like the last one mentioned, except in this case, patients did engage in the activity-based goal, but did not feel it helped and only focused on the negative aspects of the outcome, a common theme being, "I should have been doing this all along. What is wrong with me?" This led us to conclude that in addition to the common therapeutic elements we identified as necessary for late-life depression, cognitive appraisal work needed to have a specific focus on anticipatory negativity bias and post-reward appraisal of success. We also found that including strategies to manage affect would be important. The identification of these barriers was then applied to the RDoC matrix, which helped us to identify both ways to measure these constructs and potential interventions that could target these barriers.

Focus-groups

Chart reviews are very helpful in identifying initial problems for intervention focus, but they need to be triangulated with outside sources. We interviewed five clinicians who had been involved in our studies to determine if we could ground our findings within their experiences using PST, BA and CBT. This was done using *focus-group interviews*. The process involves creating an interview guide of questions to guide a group discussion, in this case, challenges in implementing PST, BA, and CBT with older adults. It is important, though, not to influence group participants' answers to these questions and to make them open-ended or phrased in such a way that a conversation can ensue (asking, "What challenges did you experience using PST?" rather than "Did you find CBT challenging?"). We therefore did not share our chart review findings until the end of the focus group, and our intent in sharing the findings was to get more information from the therapists about what we found.

The results of the focus group were largely confirmatory of our chart review findings and in general, clinicians had no objection to interventions like

PST, CBT, or BA. The problem for them was when patients had low motivation, heightened anxiety, or were easily distracted or overly pessimistic, the interventions became very challenging. They also noted that the most challenging cases had a hard time identifying goals they found useful to address. The focus group participants indicated that if an intervention had strategies they could easily use in these situations, they may be able to implement the intervention more frequently than they typically did. However, the focus group participants also became concerned with piling on too many active ingredients into a session and voiced strong objections to making these interventions even more cumbersome. They unanimously felt that they would like to exercise their clinical judgment in determining when a specific intervention would be necessary, rather than teaching a patient all the possible skills to motivate behavior change. We will discuss more on this later under an HCD approach to manual development.

Applying the experimental therapeutics approach to intervention identification, using the RDoC

Our chart review and focus group seemed to indicate that older adults who engaged with rewarding activities tended to show improvements in their mood and social function. These findings were no surprise, as much of research on depression in older adults had already identified that engagement in rewarding activities served as a protective factor against depression later in life (Fancourt & Tymoszuk, 2019), and most evidence-based psychosocial interventions for depression in older adults had goal setting, pleasant activity scheduling, and BA as a main therapeutic element, or the *outcome mediator* (see Chapters 4 and 6 for more discussion on mediators). Thus, the central active ingredient of Engage had to be engagement in rewarding activities, or *reward exposure* (Alexopoulos & Areán, 2014; see Figure 3.1).

Our chart review and focus groups also found five clinical features that influenced whether a patient would engage in activity-based goals or would benefit from engaging in these goals. These challenges are: (1) pessimism regarding the utility of activity-based goal engagement, which leads to poor

Figure 3.1 Exposure to reward as a mediator of engagement on depression

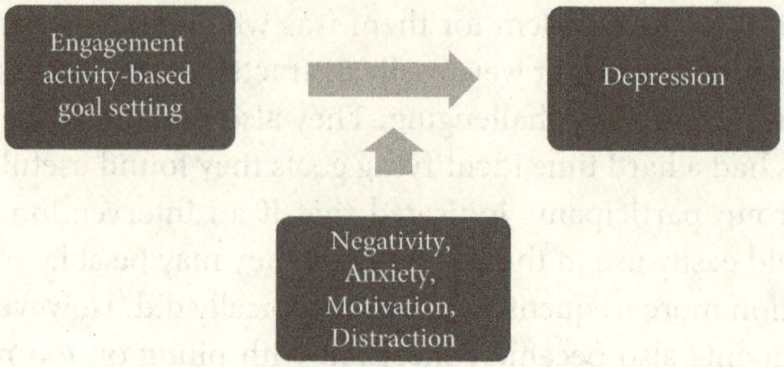

Figure 3.2 Moderators of engagement on depression

patient engagement; (2) pessimism regarding the outcome of goal engagement, which leads to a poor response to engagement; (3) feelings of anxiety about the potential outcome of goal engagement, which leads to avoidance of the goal; (4) lack of motivation to engage in the goal, leading to poor engagement; and (5) distractibility, which leads to de-prioritizing goal engagement and prioritizing emergent issues. These we identified as the *treatment moderators* (see Figure 3.2).

Identify the context in which it will be delivered

When designing your intervention and its manual, you will need to have a thorough understanding as to where the intervention will be used (clinic, school, online), the training level of the typical provider (MD, PhD, MA, lay person), and details about the typical client (language, culture, education, social determinants of health). These are some important questions to consider in designing your intervention:

1. What resources does the setting you are developing the intervention for have to support its use? For the new intervention, we already had some knowledge of the typical setting older adults seek mental health care from, either primary care medicine or senior centers. These are clearly two very different settings, but they also had considerable overlap. Neither settings are primarily a mental health setting, so the usual resources available to support mental health intervention are not present, such as easy access to private space. We had to consider that issues such as office availability and the existence of trained mental health providers would be limited in these settings. We elected to design the intervention primarily for senior centers in this context, believing that adaptation for primary care medicine would be the next step, but we would design the intervention with that setting in the back of our minds.

2. What level of training does the clinician have? In both primary care medicine and senior centers, most clinicians available to provide intervention have a Masters in Social Work (MSW). However, while some MSWs have training in mental health, many in aging services do not, and thus any intervention we develop for this setting would need to be easy enough to learn so that someone without a background in mental health could implement it.
3. How much time does the clinician typically have with the patient? This is where senior centers and primary care medicine diverge. In primary care medicine practices that have integrated behavioral health, most patients are seen monthly and usually only have 30 minutes of the provider's time. In senior centers, providers have more time to meet with patients, although this, too, depends on the number of social workers a center has available, and the other tasks that the providers have at hand. We decided that the intervention needed to be streamlined and efficient so that providers could deliver the intervention and still do any other work needed during the visit.
4. How much time does the clinician have to learn a new intervention? This is often a more challenging problem than most treatment developers realize. In fact, evidence-based treatments are challenging to learn as illustrated by the limited impact workshops and continuing education has on adoption of practices ("train and hope"; Beidas & Kendall, 2010), the need to demonstrate competencies by most treatment developers, and successful implementation programs either have ongoing consultation embedded as part of the practice (e.g., Project ECHO; Komaromy et al., 2016) or involve lengthy commitment by health plans to dedicate clinician time to education and supervision (e.g., NHS Talking Therapies for Anxiety and Depression, 2025). While we have no objection to ensuring clinician competencies are maintained, the cost of these approaches for most settings, particularly public health and community settings, is greater than they can afford, and clinicians argue that their time should be in billable hours seeing cases, not talking to academics. You may not be able to get around needing extensive training and supervision for your intervention, however, you should consider the fact that time in training will be an important implementation barrier for your treatment. For our new intervention, we purposely designed it to minimize the time needed for training and the need for ongoing supervision.
5. What resources do patients have? The life context of your selected population is a major determinant of treatment engagement. Most people

will want to improve as soon as possible, and many find the typical psychotherapy process where patients drive to the therapist's office for a once-a-week 45-minute visit to be a large time commitment. Some may prioritize their treatment visit in principle but may be forced to put other demands before treatment. Employment is a common barrier; being paid hourly or not having flexible work hours makes it difficult to attend treatment when it conflicts. It is for this reason that it is so important to talk to people from your selected population about what is reasonable for treatment, and even as important to talk to people who have tried to use the mental health system when designing your intervention. For Engage patients, the therapeutic hour was not objectionable to most older adults, but there was consensus from patients that tying the treatment to other doctors' visits would make engagement easier.

Design and Build Phase

Once you have identified the therapeutic elements and the context in which they will be delivered, the next step is to design the manual. You will create a face-valid draft manual with representatives of the intended clinician and patient user groups. The process we recommend at the UW ALACRITY Center is to engage in iterative design of the intervention manual and guidelines until you reach a satisfactory level of usability, appropriateness, and engagement. The process for developing a face-valid manual using interactive design involves writing a draft of the manual in collaboration with representative end users and field experts and iteratively testing and designing the manual with the end users and experts to improve the manual's design. Iterative design begins with a sacrificial concept that will serve as the starting point for designing the manual. When adapting an existing treatment, the current manual would serve as the sacrificial concept. Be prepared, this process will take at least three separate meetings to finalize an initial draft manual to be tested later. In each meeting, you will be engaged in activities with the "end user" (clinician or consumer) to redesign the intervention. You can hold these meetings as one-on-one meetings or as focus groups. The one-on-one meetings take more time because you will need to integrate feedback from each session to proceed to the next design and then iteration. Focus groups tend to go faster, and for each meeting, you will have a consensus on the next design. However, you may miss some nuance in a focus group that would come up in one-on-one sessions. The decision to go one way or the other is based on time, money, and convenience for the end user. When conducting the iterative design of your manual, you will be addressing these questions:

1. What will be the challenges in using the therapeutic elements, and can they be designed for ease of use?
2. How should each element be introduced? What is the best sequence and under what circumstances under which elements are introduced, withheld, or modified?
3. What tools, resources, and skills need to be in place for the typical provider and patient to use the treatment effectively?
4. How often and how long do the clinician and patient need to meet? One additional question you need to ask your intended end users is: what is a reasonable expectation for the number of visits and the length of treatment?

Question 1: What will be the challenges in using the therapeutic elements, and can they be designed for ease of use?

When developing our new intervention, we were interested in treating late-life depression, but there was another problem we wanted to address: intervention usability. To best understand what aspects of evidence-based treatments clinicians found complex to use, we interviewed five clinicians who had been certified in one of these treatments and used the intervention with older adults with depression in settings serving older adults. The settings represented were primary care medicine, community mental health, and senior housing. We used two procedures to identify the usability challenges with evidence-based practices. The first was a general focus group interview and is described above in identifying the needed therapeutic elements. We also learned from this first group's additional insights about the interventions' usability. The results reveal the following insights: (1) the structure of these therapies was cognitively onerous. To repeat the same therapeutic process with every patient was exhausting and boring, and as one clinician put it, "I'm not going to spend my day repeating myself like a robot, it's a soul draining enterprise." (2) the reliance on forms and steps made the treatment seem artificial and took away the interpersonal aspects of therapy; (3) cognitive reappraisal was seen as important, but the psychoeducational process was seen as a waste of time, as most older adults didn't quite understand it until they engaged in goal setting first; putting cognitive reappraisal before activity scheduling didn't work well.

The next set of questions focused on intervention steps and structures. This discussion started with an explanation as to why evidence-based treatments follow a stepped approach, and that the intervention developers recognized that it took incredible skill and facility with these interventions to remain on schedule. The focus group participants reported that time constraints were indeed a challenge because there was often too much material to cover in sessions, and the amount of material interfered with conducting other critical tasks clinicians felt eased the burden of psychotherapy, such as establishing a relationship with patients. While we, the interventionists, had always heard this to mean a therapeutic relationship to gain trust with the patient, this group of clinicians said it was also beneficial to the *clinician* to have a relationship with the patient; otherwise, treatment felt impersonal to them. The clear message here was, yes, we need to engage patients in the therapeutic elements of a treatment, but we also need to make the process relational and beneficial for the clinician. Whether an intervention developer agrees with this position or not, we felt that addressing this need was essential for engaging clinicians in the new intervention.

Question 2: How should each element be introduced?

This next question was addressed in our second design group. Here, we were interested in learning how the clinicians would incorporate the therapeutic elements if it were up to them to design the intervention. We showed them, based on the previous discussion, what we heard were critical therapeutic elements: time socializing with the patient, helping patients identify meaningful goals to work toward, goal setting and when faced with challenges in goal setting, strategies to address motivation, pessimism, distraction, and emotion. We then let them design the structure of the therapy in whatever way they felt was feasible without losing the therapeutic elements. They all felt that a conversation about values-based living was important before beginning any treatment. This process allowed the clinician to get to know the patient while also learning more about where to start treatment. Clinicians felt that rather than engaging in a psychoeducational lecture about the importance of values-based living, depression in late life, and reward processing, a simple pamphlet for patients would be sufficient, and during conversations with the patient, they could introduce these concepts. The next step was to talk to the patient about values-matched activities they could engage in over a week. This would lead to an action plan that included a simple prescription (e.g., "Walk two blocks three times a week."). The group determined that follow-up sessions would continue like this, with one exception, which was a check-in on whether the patient engaged in the plan and if there was any change in mood. If the plan was successful, then they would not change anything about the treatment. If it wasn't, then they would talk to the patient about what got in the way, keeping the common barriers in mind, and creating a plan for overcoming the barriers.

Question 3: What tools, resources, and skills need to be in place for the typical provider and patient to use the treatment effectively?

For this question, we referred back to the original worksheets and materials that are commonly used in PST, CBT, and BA and asked the clinicians to determine which, if any, of these materials were necessary and if the necessary ones needed to be changed. The initial reaction to materials such as homework sheets, psychoeducation, and the like was that they got in the way of treatment and were not at all helpful. However, nearly all clinicians felt that having patients list their values on paper and refer to them when selecting goals was a helpful tool. This then led to the creation of a very simple goal-setting sheet and prescription pad (see Appendix). The clinicians also agreed they needed some way to determine successful goal setting, and after discussion agreed that a simple 7-point scale to evaluate mood that week and action planning could serve to address success. Finally, the clinicians felt examples of simple strategies to address barriers would be useful as well.

Question 4: How often and how long do the clinician and patient need to meet?

For this question, we are determining the dose of treatment and often that cannot be really determined until one tests the intervention's impact on the intended clinical outcomes. However, it is a good idea to have in mind the minimum amount of exposure needed to engage in a treatment. If you are uncertain, you can use other evidence-based treatments as examples. For instance, a dose of CBT for depression is weekly sessions for 16–20 weeks. For Exposure Therapy, the frequency of treatment is 1–2 times a week for the initial phases of treatment, with 90-minute sessions. For PST, the dose is a weekly session for 6–10 weeks. When we asked clinicians what they thought the optimal dose should be, they answered "however long it takes." When we asked patients, they said, "A month." We therefore decided to make the new intervention a four-two-nine-week intervention, to allow the clinician to adjust to patient need, but also to allow the client the opportunity for brief treatment.

Getting expert feedback

It is usually a good idea to talk to experts in the field to refine your manual further. In deciding to whom to show your theory and intervention, you should consider getting feedback from experts in the disorder and population, other representative therapists who work with the population you are treating, and patient representatives who would be eligible for the treatment.

Additionally, you may consider involving the directors of programs where the patients receive care and therapists work. This last step may increase your chances of developing a manual that could be easily implemented.

In our experience reviewing grant proposals for intervention development, we have seen a variety of methods for receiving expert feedback on a manual. The most common (and cost-effective) method is to send your experts a specific set of questions you would like them to answer, have them read your manual, and then have them provide you with feedback. The advantage of this approach is that it is easy to do and relatively cost-effective. In our experience, most people are happy to provide this feedback free of charge. Offering monetary incentives is always helpful, but not always necessary.

Sometimes, collecting information in a focus group format (having experts meet and discuss your manual in a group context) generates insights into your manual that would not be generated individually. For this reason, some developers prefer to collect feedback in a group setting. Focus groups are similar to individual survey methods in that the participants are presented with the manual and a series of questions. However, discussion among the group is highly encouraged to generate more ideas about the manual. There are several ways to run these meetings, including the Delphi method and step-back consultation.

The Delphi method is a form of consensus building used traditionally for expert forecasting, such as predicting how the stock market will look based on economic challenges. The principle behind the Delphi method is that forecasts from structured groups of experts are more accurate than those from unstructured groups or from individual predictions. Applied for this purpose, the Delphi method has been proposed as a method for identifying potential problems in a new treatment and remedies for them.

The process is as follows. After a group of experts is identified, each expert is given a copy of the manual and a series of questions. The experts never meet one another, nor are they identified in any of the feedback. This anonymity is useful for minimizing the tendency for individuals to defer to those in authority and is believed to minimize the "bandwagon" effect that occurs in face-to-face meetings. Answers to these questions as well as additional impressions are compiled and filtered for irrelevant content and then fed back to the experts. Experts then comment on their own responses as well as the responses from others and can change their responses at any time. The feedback process stops when consensus has been reached, or further iterations of feedback are not likely to yield new results.

Step-back consultation was developed from business consultation methods and was used originally in situations where the individual was "too close" to a problem and needed a fresh set of eyes to develop new solutions. In our opinion, most developers can be too close to their manuals and as a result may miss important solutions or approaches. Step-back consultation works in this way. A group of experts is given the rationale for the manual and a set of questions about it at the beginning of the meeting—ideally the members have read the manual prior to the session. The group members are instructed to think about these questions and the manual, as if they were the manual developers. To facilitate this mindset, rather than use phrases like, "What Dr. T should do is..." the group uses phrases such as "What I need to do..." or "I should break the session down further." The group is instructed to brainstorm and not limit their ideas to issues (finances and so forth) that the developer did not impose already. The rationale is to develop innovative ideas that the developer may be able to use and refine to fit the manual.

Finally, the developer does not sit at the table with the group or participate in the conversation in any way. Instead, the developer sits in the corner of the room, facing away from the group, and takes notes or manages the recording of the meeting. The rationale behind removing the developer from the conversation is based on observations made in problem-solving meetings in business settings; too often, the developer will inadvertently influence the direction of the conversation, and as a result limit the number of new ideas.

Let's return to the new intervention and the process we used for obtaining feedback and how it changed the intervention. We elected to solicit individual feedback from experts because it was too logistically complicated to hold a group feedback session. Content experts were spread across the world, and thus, even a web-based meeting would not be feasible due to time zone differences. Additionally, process experts (program directors) schedules were too busy to align for a group session. We sent a copy of Engage to the experts with this description of the rationale behind the manual:

Thank you so much for taking the time to read this manual and give me feedback. As we discussed earlier, I would like to create a new behavioral treatment for late life depression that can be easily implemented in aging care settings. As you know, counselor training varies considerably in these settings, and not everyone can do CBT, IPT, or PST well; rather than develop an intensive training program that my colleagues have found to be too costly and time-consuming (also subject to poor sustainability because of high provider turnover), we would like to develop a user-friendly, yet effective, treatment. Please read this manual with that purpose in mind.

We then attached a series of questions to guide the review:

a. What is your overall impression of the manual and the treatment?
b. In your opinion, does the treatment address the important issues in late-life depression?
c. Do you think the treatment is particularly innovative? Why or why not?
d. Do you think the number of sessions is too few, too many, too demanding, or just right?
e. Is the frequency of visits too small, too many, or just right?
f. Do you think the treatment material provided in each session is reasonable?
g. Do you think the typical counselor can do this treatment? What would you add, leave out, or change?
h. Do you think the typical low-income older adults can understand and apply the treatment strategies? What would you change and how would you change it?
i. Do you think the treatment team approach makes sense? How would you change it? What concerns do you have about the team?
j. Any other suggestions?

Why Do Treatment Manuals Fail to Be Used by Clinicians?

As of this writing, very few psychosocial intervention manuals take into consideration the setting and the therapists who are most likely to use the intervention, and as a result, these interventions that have an evidence base have a difficult time finding their way into standard practice. Traditional psychosocial intervention research has occurred in academic settings, using study therapists who belong to the research team, rather than an external organization, and as a result, information about how to implement these interventions is lacking. Consideration of the system of care the treatment is meant to be used in is critical for rapid uptake in the community, even as efficacy and effectiveness are demonstrated.

Adapting an intervention

Some investigators are interested in applying an existing evidence-based psychotherapy to a population or context for which it has not yet been studied, and thus the manual needs to be adapted. The most common type of adaptation is cultural adaptation. In a previous version of this book, we made distinctions between a simple adaptation, where adaptation included cultural, language, and population adjustments that do not significantly change the therapeutic elements of the treatment, and complex adaptation, which involves changing the intervention by adding new treatment components, eliminating treatment components, and changing the delivery of the intervention to fit a new setting. However, over the last decade, a growing body of research and theory has shown that rarely do psychosocial interventions need simple adaptations; often, the adaptations for age groups, racial and ethnic groups, and novel settings and provider types tend to be complex and require far more than changing the structure or language of the intervention manual. To illustrate best practices in intervention adaptation, we will focus on how to conduct cultural adaptations, since many times, not only does the manual need to be adapted for the patient, but it will also need to be adapted for the provider delivering care and the settings in which the patient lives and the provider works.

Early models of cultural adaptation largely focused on the following cultural dimensions: (a) language, (b) persons, (c) metaphors, (d) content, (e) concepts, (f) goals, (g) methods, and (h) context (Alegria et al., 2010). While these dimensions are highly relevant and important in cultural adaptation, there is not much guidance as to how to address these dimensions when adapting a psychotherapy. Recent recommendations go a step further in describing the process for addressing these dimensions of care. The Cultural Adaptation Framework has been recommended by the American Psychological Association's Division 12 as an important and thorough model that has resulted in successful adaptations that account for the early model dimensions but it is also clear that sometimes the intervention therapeutic elements do need to change for the intervention to be acceptable (Fendt-Newlin et al., 2020). The Cultural Adaptation Framework also uses elements of HCD, although not explicitly named. For instance, there is an emphasis on iterative design and the inclusion of the provider and patient voice through the adaptation process.

Let's walk through the Cultural Adaptation Framework using the example of Dr. M's cultural adaptation of CBT for postpartum depression, specifically, in the Latino population.

Rationale

Dr. M was interested in determining whether CBT was as effective in preventing depression in young, pregnant women as it was in treating depression in the general population. Because he wanted his intervention to be broadly generalizable to racially diverse young pregnant women, he wanted to recruit young women who were Black, Hispanic, and White. Because in his setting, most of the young Hispanic women preferred to talk to their providers in Spanish, he wished to translate the CBT manual into that language.

CAF Phase 1 Activities

Step 1: *Content, Concepts, and Goals*: Before translating the CBT manual into Spanish, Dr. M's first task was to modify the manual so that it focused on the goals of prevention of depression, pregnancy, parenting examples, and other topics specific to the issues that young pregnant women encounter that could contribute to their depression. These initial examples were derived from his own clinical experience, by talking to clinicians and patients about their goals in managing stress and mood as new parents, and by interviewing a group of five experts in postpartum depression in Latinas. There is no magic number of experts you need to have comment on your manual. The best rule of thumb is to determine what expertise you would like represented in the review. Dr. M first modified the manual's content, driven largely by what patients and therapists recommended. These recommendations were driven by therapist and patient identification of the goals of the intervention; specifically, in this cultural group, the primary goal is to support someone in becoming a caring parent, with subgoals focused on managing stress, emotion, fatigue, and how to ask for help when needed. Rather than focusing on improving mood, they felt the manual should shift its focus to parenting and "self-parenting." The metaphor is: to be a good parent to your child, you need to be a good parent to yourself. All reviewers felt the concepts for preventing depression in the original manual were important but needed to be explained using the self-parenting metaphor.

Step 2: *Context and methods.* Dr. M's next step was to talk to representative patients about their living context and the feasibility of using CBT strategies considering the context. Dr. M also spoke to therapists about the context in which they work, and the feasibility of the structure of therapy, including time constraints and other issues that often arise in treatment. Patient feedback from this process (which therapists concurred was important) was that patients had very little time to engage in action plans and homework assignments that were outside the scope of parenting, caring for the home, doctors' appointments, and other demands. Patients felt that for any action plan to be taken seriously, it had to be embedded in their normal routine. Strategies such as thought record keeping and mood tracking were seen by both patient and therapist representatives as onerous and had poor cultural fit. If necessary, these elements would need to be modified for the patient context.

Therapists believed it was complicated and onerous to explain the use of these tools to new mothers. Instead, therapists recommended using novella-like storyboards to demonstrate and explain therapeutic elements and concepts and in-session practice, without requiring patients to complete forms outside of the therapeutic session.

Step 3: *Language and Metaphors.* Once Dr. M had the information needed to create the culturally adapted manual, he began the process of translating the manual and materials into Spanish. This translation consisted of both forward-back translation and consensus translation. Forward-back translation consists of taking material written in one language (e.g., English) and translating it into another (e.g., Spanish). The Spanish version is translated back by a translator different from the one in the first step, into the English language, and the two English manuals are compared. Any discrepancies in the two versions are discussed to ensure the translations accurately reflect the intent of the original text. Consensus translation takes this process a step further by showing the Spanish translation and original English version to a group of bicultural and bilingual participants and having them discuss whether the translation reflects the intent of the English version and if the new translation is understandable to all people from the culture. For example, although people from different Latin American countries can communicate easily with one another in Spanish, certain idioms are country-specific. The Latino media gets around this issue by using what is called "broadcast Spanish." Broadcast Spanish uses Spanish terms all countries are aware of (even though they may not use them in conversation) and is understood by most of the Hispanic populace. The intent of consensus translation is to get the translation to be as close as possible to the broadcast version of the language. An important aspect of translation is the use of metaphors. Metaphorical translation involves not simply translating terms from one language into another, but from one worldview to another. For instance, many Latin cultures have a strong religious worldview, and thus values, behaviors and attitudes are based on Judeo-Christian worldviews, and in some Caribbean cultures, this worldview also includes aboriginal Caribbean and African religions. These religions are often very community and family-focused, patriarchal with profound love of art, music, and food. Dr. M's manual included an infusion of religion, art, food, and respect for elders and the patriarchal structure, which was then vetted with patients for acceptability and clarity.

CAF Phase 2: Model and Validate the Intervention and Create Training

For this next phase, Dr. M circulated his culturally adapted manual to therapists, advocates, and experts in Latine culture and in post-partum depression, using the Delphi method to evaluate and improve the intervention flow and adaptations of the therapeutic elements. His decision to use the Delphi method with input from multiple roles was due to concerns that academic experts may overshadow therapist and advocate voices. See the section on Delphi method above for more details.

To develop the training program, Dr. M worked closely with clinic administrators and representative therapists to determine how much time he would realistically have to train and certify clinicians in a typical clinic. Clinics serving Latina mothers often have limited time and resources. In reviewing efficient training models, he decided to integrate a flipped classroom (Merlin-Knoblich et al., 2019) approach to training with a model similar to the ECHO model for ongoing support (Komaromy et al., 2016). He then piloted the training model in one clinic. Based on participant feedback, he made additional modifications to the at-home educational modules.

CAF Phase 3

With the culturally translated manual and training materials in hand, Dr. M. tested the intervention in a sample of five Spanish speakers, and following the steps presented earlier, the manual was further modified for the intended study.

Manualizing and existing intervention that has no manual

Many researchers and treatment providers are interested in studying the effectiveness of widely used treatments developed by community mental health clinicians that have guidelines but no detailed manuals. There is a tendency in our field to apply psychosocial interventions based solely on the hearsay results from other providers. This is not to say these interventions are not effective, and some speculate that if certain interventions are broadly adopted by large communities of providers, there may be very positive reasons for their adoption (this is sometimes deemed "practice-based evidence"). The difficulty here is that these interventions still need to be tested empirically to be sure that the observed treatment effects are due to the treatment itself and not to some other factor, such as attention. The best way to answer this question is to create a manual of the intervention and compare it to another intervention.

The process of creating a community-based manual is different than creating a new manual. The intervention is already developed, but it lacks a clear description of the key elements and the process by which it should be delivered. Creating a manual for an existing treatment consists of these steps:

1. Discussion with providers proficient in the treatment about the key strategies and elements of the treatment.
2. Observation of providers administering the intervention until no more new information is obtained.
3. Designing the manual with expert input.
4. Comparing the delivery of the treatment following the manual to the delivery of the treatment without the manual.

The first step in the process may seem straightforward. If therapists were proficient in delivering the intervention, they would likely agree on the key elements that make the intervention effective. However, our experience tells us otherwise. Although therapists may agree on general concepts concerning why an intervention works, they will occasionally disagree about how it works, or which elements are most important. As an example, early in her career, Dr. Areán was asked to help manualize a clinical case management program that had been in existence for a decade in San Francisco County. The case management program was to be part of a larger study of the treatment of dual diagnosis (substance abuse and severe mental illness). Dr. Areán elected to perform a provider focus group with the original developer present. What ensued was a clear disagreement about the importance of certain aspects of the program, even the program's mission and philosophy; in fact, a discussion between two case managers and the developer began over who was really an expert in the program! Due to this approach's limited success, the author applied the Delphi method to find the common elements that the care managers could agree were important and used that information for the next step in creating a manual. Reliance on the Delphi method helped to zero in on the critical elements of the intervention that expert providers all agreed were critical to the intervention's success, those elements that were not important and minimized the development of unnecessary conflicts.

The second step is relatively straightforward and can be done either by shadowing therapists and making observations about the treatment or by watching videotapes of therapists providing the intervention. It is especially important to conduct this observation. Therapists will sometimes forget about important aspects of the treatment when trying to describe it to you, or they may have difficulty conveying how a particular strategy is done. Dr. Areán experienced the latter when trying to create a manual for strength-based treatment in severely mentally ill populations (a strategy that emphasizes on identifying patients' strengths rather than focusing on illness). When she asked therapists to describe the principles and elements of strength-based treatments, the therapists' explanations were hard to follow, even when they were asked to provide examples. One area of confusion was how to use strengths to address areas of need (e.g., social isolation) without specifically focusing on the area of need. It was not until she shadowed four therapists that she was finally able to describe using strengths to overcome needs.

The third step involves getting feedback on the draft manual. As already discussed in the section on the development of a new manual, this step involves identifying experts in the field (including experts in the intervention) and determining whether the manual accurately reflects the treatment.

The final step is to compare the delivery of the manualized version of the intervention to the natural delivery of the intervention. Returning to the case management example, the investigative team identified two case managers who had never used this mode of case management before and trained them in the model using the manual. Two other case managers who were experts in the intervention were also identified but were not given access to the manual. Ten sessions with representative patients were videotaped and then shown to an independent set of experts. The experts were asked to rate the case managers on their effectiveness and fidelity to the intervention and were not told which case managers were trained using the manual and which were existing experts. This process helps the investigative team refine the manual and determine how closely the intervention could be duplicated for research purposes.

Structuring a treatment manual

The structure of treatment manuals has, thankfully, evolved considerably over time. Older manuals resembled textbooks for psychotherapy courses and would review in depth the theory and research support and provide endless examples to illustrate one technique. Although these manuals are very comprehensive, and terrific for providers with the time and wherewithal to read textbooks, they are hardly a useful toolkit for study or community providers if they have a quick question about a procedure or need to review how to explain a technique to a patient. In our expert opinion, manuals selected, created, and adapted for research (and for future dissemination) should possess these qualities:

- The content should focus specifically on how to implement the intervention.
- The manual should be divided into these general sections:
  - Overview and purpose.
  - Basic skills providers need to implement the treatment (e.g., Does the therapist need experience with brief treatment? Does the therapist need a specific type of basic training?).
  - The therapeutic stance (Is it collaborative, reflective, coaching, or neutral?) and session organization (How should the therapist time the session to complete all the tasks?).
  - Clear, succinct outline and description of the therapeutic strategies.
  - Common implementation challenges and methods for overcoming them.
  - Materials needed.
- The manual should have case examples to illustrate the therapy. However, in our experience, the best examples are videos rather than written.

There are several good examples of contemporary psychotherapy manuals that investigators can use as models for their own manual development. One particularly good example of how manuals should be organized is *High-Yield Cognitive-Behavioral Therapy for Brief Sessions: An Illustrated Guide* by Wright, Sudak, Turkington, and Thase (Wright, 2010). This is a very concise and clearly written guidebook that offers not only case examples but also exercises for readers to use in practicing the skills, free access to additional treatment materials, and very helpful DVD case examples.

Not all manuals need to be in paper—online manuals are becoming increasingly popular and easy to use. One example is the AIMS Center website https://aims.uw.edu/. The Problem Solving Treatment (PST) manual is online and is accompanied by a podcast of a workshop, PowerPoint slides from the workshop, and a series of video clips of different clinicians using PST with different types of patients and addressing common issues that come up in treatment of depression while using PST (e.g., suicide, past traumatic experiences, reluctance to engage in treatment).

Increasingly popular are online tools that agglomerate resources such as manuals, training materials, tools to support high-fidelity treatment delivery, videos, discussion boards, communication tools for providers and consultants/trainers, and/or patient dashboards. For instance, iBESTT (https://www.education.uw.edu/ibestt/) is a website and app for supporting youth with behavior problems in school by coaches and teachers that features instructional videos, manuals, team-based communication links, and a patient dashboard that guides coaches and teachers in high-fidelity development and delivery of Applied Behavior Analysis. Another example is PracticeWise's Managing and Adapting Practice, which provides users with research summaries on which evidence-based treatment components (such as relaxation or cognitive restructuring) work best for certain mental health problems, short manuals (1–3 pages) for each component to instruct clinicians on delivery techniques, and a dashboard to track component delivery and patient response over time.

Do I need a manual for my comparison condition?

Selecting and creating the manual for your comparison condition is also important. It is not a good methodology to invest all your efforts in developing materials for a new intervention while failing to treat the comparison condition with the same attention to detail. Comparison conditions, whether they are placebo conditions or not, also need to follow a specific protocol in efficacy and some effectiveness study, and in Hybrid studies, or pragmatic trials, you will need to define "usual care" or the comparator and document its delivery through the study. The importance of detailing or manualizing comparison conditions became particularly relevant in effectiveness research's early years. Effectiveness researchers would compare their interventions to "usual care" but then fail to define what usual care was. When usual care was deconstructed in later years, the psychotherapy field learned that often usual care was *no* care, which led therapists to question the value of effectiveness studies. Even more striking, some patients assigned to the control group may seek out the type of intervention described for the treatment group on their own, in which case the separation between treatment and control begins to disappear. This happened with the introduction of support groups for breast cancer patients. At first the control groups were indeed "medical treatment only" groups. After the literature reported on the effectiveness of such support groups, later trials found it harder and harder to find patients who were not already involved in a support group, or who would not seek out a support group if assigned to the "medical treatment only" group. Since then, services and effectiveness researchers have gone the extra mile to define what usual care is and to continue to monitor it during a randomized trial.

Therapist/provider training manual and quality measures

Once you have developed your manual, the next step is to develop how your study therapists (and future therapists, should you choose to disseminate your treatment) are to be trained in the intervention. Therapist training generally involves two steps. The first step includes didactics to provide the therapists with an overview of the intervention, the theoretical rationale, and the steps involved in delivering the intervention. Therapist supervision and technical assistance are given while delivering the treatment for the first time.

The second step involves having the therapists apply the therapy on three to five test cases. How this second step unfolds will vary from study to study. Currently, there is no one perfect method. The most common method is to use video or audio recordings of treatment sessions to observe how well the therapists apply the therapy and provide corrective feedback to the therapists until they reach a high degree of proficiency. As we will discuss in Chapter 10, for electronic text-based (or secure messaging) interventions, the quality of session content can be assessed through the review of text transcripts. The degree of proficiency must be rated using a quality assessment tool, which is an observational measure used to assess the degree to which the therapist follows the study protocol. These tools will be discussed in the next section. The advantage of this method is that study therapists learn to administer the intervention on representative patients and receive feedback from experts prior to subsequent sessions. This method is also particularly useful in trials that involve several clinical sites or sites that are distant from the investigator's institution. The challenge with this method is that the feedback must be given quickly. Recorded sessions must be reviewed prior to subsequent sessions for the feedback to be helpful. Additionally, study therapists must see their training cases close in time to one another, but with enough time between cases so that feedback from the previous case can be applied to the next case.

A third approach is to have the study therapists co-lead therapy sessions with an expert and receive real-time feedback. In this approach, the expert takes the lead in early treatment sessions but eventually becomes less involved as the study therapists become more comfortable with the intervention. The study therapists are still rated on the degree to which they can implement the intervention effectively, but only in sessions they lead on their own. The advantage of this approach is that the study therapists tend to prefer seeing the expert apply the intervention before doing it themselves. This approach also solves the problems researchers encounter with audio and video recordings (equipment failure, participant reluctance to be recorded). The main disadvantage is that this approach requires expert time, which can be costly for a study on a limited budget.

A final method for training study therapists is using simulated case actors, people who are hired to act like patients with the illness in question. This method of therapist training is becoming a popular model in medical schools in the United States, particularly in situations where therapist error can have dire consequences. Study therapists are rated using the quality measures, as in the other forms of training, but additionally receive feedback from the actors about how they felt the intervention went, whether they felt the therapists addressed their problems, and other interpersonal issues they feel would affect a patient's willingness to continue in treatment. This approach has the benefits of being able to collect audiotaped or videotaped reviews and minimizes the impact of clinical error on participants. The only disadvantage is identifying actors who can emulate the population under study.

How can I ensure my intervention will be implemented broadly if successful?

Some of the success in therapist use of the intervention will be due to your preparatory work in co-designing a new intervention or in adapting an existing one. Successful dissemination and implementation are also determined by the communities' perceived need for a new intervention, perceived fit with local context, community buy-in, quality of leadership, and multiple other factors. Those who are interested in learning more can study the Consolidated Framework for Implementation Research (https://cfirguide.org/). However, there are a few things you can do to make the process of adoption easier for organizations, and that often begins with optimizing training. In creating the training program for your intervention, try to keep in mind how easily the training method you use can be implemented in regular practice, should your intervention be found effective. Developing training tools that anyone could access, and that would be relatively inexpensive to sustain over time, will help bridge the gap between science and service. Again, keep in mind your target audience, the burden your training may impose on their time, and the potential overall cost of the training method. Consider that training alone is usually not very effective and that most implementation efforts will need to supplement with other implementation strategies such as coaching or supervision. The Expert Recommendations for Implementing Change (ERIC) study identified 73 implementation strategies for you to consider (Powell et al., 2015). There are multiple methods for selecting and tailoring the right implementation strategies for your context, such as concept mapping and intervention mapping (Powell et al., 2017). Thoughtful implementation via the planning and execution of a variety of aligned strategies will help ensure that your intervention is adopted and used well.

Treatment and quality measures

Good execution of an intervention in an efficacy or some effectiveness studies does not stop with initial use of the treatment. To sustain quality treatment delivery, you can consider sustainment strategies such as ongoing monitoring of the treatment delivery. Even excellent therapists are known to begin adapting an intervention as they become more familiar with it, and while some degree of adaptation is necessary, you will want to be sure the providers do not stray too far afield. It is important to measure how well the study clinicians adhere to the treatment at initial use and over time to ensure fidelity and minimize "drift." Treatment quality and fidelity measures are assessment tools that researchers use to determine how well study therapists adhere to the treatments and the quality of the therapeutic relationship. In efficacy studies, these tools are useful for ensuring high quality and fidelity of intervention delivery, and the results of these ratings are shared with the therapists regularly to ensure quality is maintained. The degree to which information is shared in an effectiveness study will vary depending on the study's purpose. If an effectiveness study intends to evaluate the effects of an evidence-based practice in a new population, feedback may be provided in the same way it is provided in efficacy trials. If the intent is to determine an intervention's effectiveness without frequent expert feedback, then the information from the fidelity ratings would not be shared. Quality ratings would still be collected to determine how well the therapists adhered to the intervention without feedback.

Creating a quality tool

Creating a treatment quality tool is relatively straightforward. The tool should have the following components:

- A well-defined and anchored rating method that is clearly understood by any person using the tool. This will aid in having good inter-rater reliability, which is important to ensure that fidelity raters agree on whether the therapist is delivering the treatment with fidelity.
- A detailed checklist of the therapy components that must be delivered in a given session. As an example, in one quality rating of problem-solving treatment (Mynors-Wallis et al., 2000), the problem-solving steps are detailed on the rating form, but each step is further broken down into the specific actions the therapist is expected to do. The overall rating for the "problem definition" step is a numeric quality rating (e.g., 0 = not done at all, to 5 = all aspects of the step done exceptionally well), and the rating is supported by a checklist of actions:

- The patient picked the problem to work on.
- The problem is broken down into smaller steps.
- The problem was free of untested assumptions.
- The problem is defined concretely and in actionable terms.
- The problem will lead to concrete goal-setting.
- The therapist's involvement in the definition was collaborative.
- The therapist refrained from defining the problem for the patient.
- The therapist supported the use of the "reporter's rule."

- Measures of nonspecific therapeutic skill should be included in the tool. Psychotherapy is not just about sticking to a protocol but also relates to how well one engages the patient in the therapy and how flexible the therapist can be with the intervention when necessary. The difference between a good-enough therapist and an exceptional one is in the degree to which the therapist can stick to the therapeutic frame but motivate the patient and adapt the treatment for each patient without violating the therapeutic principle. Below is a list of items that measure these constructs:
  - Communicates without jargon, slang, or unnecessary elaboration.
  - Asks for patient feedback about the session.
  - Asks for the patient's understanding of the material.
  - Is patient.
  - Uses redirection appropriately to minimize distraction.
  - Addresses crises without dropping the therapeutic frame.
  - Conveys warmth and understanding.
  - Adjusts psychoeducation to the patient's understanding of the illness and treatment.
  - Clarifies questions.
  - Maintains the agenda and sticks to the time frame.
  - Covers all the material needed to cover.
- Patient level of difficulty should also be considered in the fidelity measure. Research participants will be a mixed group in terms of how easy they are to work with, how disabled they are by their illness, the degree of affect arousal they experience and how chaotic their lives may be. These factors should always be considered when rating treatment fidelity. In our experience in working with low-income populations, sometimes therapists do not cover all the material they are expected to cover in a session because patients come to treatment in crisis, or they may have a harder time understanding what they are supposed to do in treatment. In our own fidelity measures, we add this one question: "On a scale of 0 to 5, with zero being not at all difficult to five being very difficult, how

would you rate the patient during this session? Does patient difficulty affect how you rate the therapist overall on performance? Please explain."

Most existing evidence-based practices have accompanying fidelity tools. If you are studying an existing intervention, you may not need to create a tool. However, you will still need to ensure that the people who are conducting your ratings are trained in the tool and can maintain good inter-rater reliability when using the tool. This is discussed in greater detail in Chapter 5.

The Test Phase

The next step in manualizing your treatment is to beta-test the whole process on a small sample of clinicians and patients who represent the community your intervention is meant to treat. This test of your procedures allows you to see how the whole treatment process works from beginning to end and allows you to make obvious modifications to the intervention, training, and quality monitoring. The process is as follows:

1. Test the manual on approximately five test cases.
2. Modify the manual and materials based on the test case results.
3. Rerun tests with 10 to 15 more test cases.
4. Finalize the manual and materials.

The process for beta-testing a new intervention manual is simple. Identify representative patients, administer the manual, and based on your experience and feedback from the patients after treatment, adjust the manual. In the first pass, you will want to identify at least five patients. There is no magic number for how many you will need to test the intervention on, but in our experience, you will reach what is called "information saturation," the point at which you no longer identify unique information, after you have tried the intervention with five people. After each person has completed the treatment, you should ask him or her to give you feedback on the intervention. Ask specific questions, such as:

- Did you like the format?
- What did you find most helpful?
- What did you find least helpful?
- What would you change?

This information can be collected via anonymous questionnaires or in focus groups or individual interviews led by someone other than the person providing treatment. After the data are collected, they can be used to further refine the treatment. Once that refined manual is completed, you are ready to test the intervention on another group of participants. The process for further refinement is the same as the first round of edits. Participants provide feedback and therapist observations are used to finalize the manual.

You will also have the opportunity to test your training program and your quality measures. In this case, you would follow the same procedure as outlined for beta-testing the manual.

Ethical Considerations

The process of developing manuals, trainings, and fidelity measures is technically research and should undergo IRB approval. Whenever you are testing a new treatment on a population, particularly those who are at risk for becoming worse if the treatment is not effective, participants should understand that their participation is helping to refine a new treatment, and as such, the treatment may not help them with their problems. Ongoing monitoring of symptoms for populations with mental illnesses will need to occur, with decision rules about when to discontinue treatment. Second, in this stage of treatment development, there is no rule about who should be the therapist providing treatment. Ideally, the developer should have first-hand experience delivering the treatment and is sometimes in a better position to modify the treatment than someone who is not as familiar with the intervention. However, an independent therapist providing the treatment is useful for obtaining objective insights into the intervention's workings. In the second round of modifications, there should be at least one other therapist (i.e., more than two) to provide different perspectives on the treatment and potential modifications.

Equity Issues

As stated previously, there is a considerable push from NIH to be as inclusive as possible in health research, so that results from studies are generalizable to as many communities as possible. Specifically consider the needs of diverse populations when developing your interventions' therapeutic rationale and design. Explore these issues with your participants when conducting the HCD activities during treatment development. The Cultural Adaptation Framework is not limited to post-development modifications but can be used when creating new treatments. As you develop your manuals, you should consider involving test cases and participants who are as close to your target population as possible for the manual to be truly useful in your larger trial.

Budgetary Issues

Creating manuals, training methods, and fidelity measures will involve costs, and for this reason many psychotherapy researchers add this development process to their pilot studies, which can be funded with the pilot R01, R34 and R21 mechanisms from NIH. Some universities have intramural funds that can help support the development of these tools. Other researchers have also relied on graduate students and postdocs as staff to support the development of these tools. In general, when creating these research tools, plan for at least a year for development. The budget will include about 10–20% of your time, about 15–20% therapist time for training and fidelity measure pilots, and 15–20% research assistant time for the fidelity pilot. For expert panel focus groups and patient feedback, you should also budget for compensation for participation. For expert compensation, most researchers will budget for $1000 a day (depending on the expert). For participant compensation, generally researchers pay $20–40 per hour-long interview.

Chapter Summary

Manuals, training, and fidelity measures are critical to the successful execution of a psychotherapy trial. Psychotherapy researchers need to keep these components in mind:

> If using an existing treatment, you will need to demonstrate that you are an expert in the intervention. If adapting an existing treatment, consider whether the adaptation will be simple (e.g., translating materials) or complex (e.g., changing key components of the intervention).

When adapting, creating, or manualizing an intervention, follow these steps:

- Obtain expert feedback on the manual.
- Pilot test the manual on five patients.

- Modify the intervention based on your pilot.
- Test the intervention again on ten patients and use more than one therapist in this test phase.
- Finalize the manual.

When creating training methods, consider one of these three approaches: taped review, expert model training, or patient actor training.

- Always consider the feasibility of replicating your training method if you plan to disseminate your intervention.

When creating your fidelity measure, be sure to include:

- Well-defined anchors that raters can easily follow.
- Detailed descriptions of the intervention.
- Ratings of overall therapy skill/nonspecific therapeutics.
- Rating of patient difficulty for the session.

4

Defining Your Sample, Creating Recruitment Materials, Selecting Measures, and Developing Assessment Procedures

Critical Research Questions This Chapter Will Address

- How do you define your selected population?
- What are the best methods for recruiting your sample?
- What does a good assessment battery look like?
- What are the different assessment methods to consider?

In clinical trials, it is very important to clearly define who your sample is when selecting, creating, or adapting a psychosocial intervention. In this chapter, we discuss the importance of defining your target population, how to thoughtfully select baseline and outcome measures for your study, and different methods for collecting your data. Although pilot studies (discussed in Chapter 7) may be used to finalize your choice of measures, you will still need to select these methods before piloting. We note here that we discuss the inclusion/exclusion criteria for sampling and recruitment of participants in this chapter, but *sample size* determination is discussed in detail in subsequent chapters. Sample sizes for pilot studies are discussed in Chapter 7; sample sizes for large trials are discussed in Chapters 8 and 9. Furthermore, training of research assistants and ongoing monitoring techniques during a clinical trial are discussed in Chapters 5 and 6.

Throughout this chapter, we use the example of Dr. G's study on the treatment of major depression to illustrate our points. In their study, Dr. G is comparing Problem-Solving Treatment (PST) for depression in older adults who are living in poverty and are receiving social services for physical disabilities. They want to determine if adding this treatment to regular clinical case management will improve depression and functional outcomes.

High-Quality Psychosocial Interventions Research. Second Edition. Patricia A. Areán and Michael D. Pullmann, Oxford University Press.
DOI: 10.1093/oso/9780197681923.003.0004

Defining the Target Population

Common sense dictates that if you have a well-defined hypothesis in mind, chances are you have also defined the selected population—that is, the population to which you intend to apply your results. Historically, studies from the psychosocial interventions field have overlooked the importance of clearly defining the intended target population. For instance, far too many "depression" studies have defined their sample as anyone who exceeded a certain score on a depression scale, without extracting any kind of diagnosis to confirm that the participants truly are depressed. The problem with this method is that many patients who score high on depression scales have several disorders, not limited to generalized anxiety, social phobia, eating disorders, psychosis, or personality disorders; or there may be some other, nonpsychiatric explanation for the high score. Thus, it is unclear for whom the intervention is efficacious, since it is unclear who constitutes the population sampled. Even well-designed effectiveness and hybrid trials, which intend to include people with a target condition whether or not they have other psychiatric or medical comorbidities, should also clearly define the target population. Although the selection criteria may be more lenient, how the sample is selected in a well-designed effectiveness study must be made crystal clear. Therefore, it is very important to define whom you intend to recruit and exclude and develop clear criteria—and rationale—for determining participant selection and exclusion.

Selecting Participants for Research Participation (and Exclusion)

The sample in Dr. G's study will be older adults with major depression and functional disability who are living in poverty. They have defined "older adults" to be anyone over the age of 65, a common age cutoff for defining geriatric research. They could have lowered the age to 60, because people aged 60 and older can qualify for the kinds of service settings Dr. G would like to recruit the sample from. Their decision to keep the age at 65 is based on what the scientific field considers late life. Dr. G has also defined "depression" to be limited to Major Depressive Disorder (MDD) as defined in the Diagnostic and Statistical Manual (DSM; American Psychiatric Association, 2022). Dr. G could have also included people with persistent depressive disorder and minor depression, as those two disorders are prevalent in low-income populations. However, Dr. G elected to limit the sample to MDD exclusively, because this is a far more severe illness and the treatments for this illness are better developed.

The definition of low income is complex, and Dr. G considered many different methods for defining it. They elected to use the US Department of Housing and Urban Development (HUD) definition, which uses Area Median Income (AMI) to determine poverty levels. Dr. G could have used the US Census Bureau's definition of poverty, but the HUD metric was expected to lead to a more generalizable sample, as social services agencies in the United States use the HUD metric to determine a person's eligibility for their services. Additionally, the HUD definition incorporates area cost of living, whereas the Census bureau uses on blanket cutoff to define poverty in the United States. Since the research project is to take place in two states where the cost of living is considerably higher than the rest of the United States (California and New York), Dr. G felt the HUD definition was more reflective of poverty in those states than the CDC definition. Defining the population of interest is important because, should another researcher in another location decide to replicate Dr. G's study, that researcher must know exactly whom to include and whom to exclude. Moreover, if a clinician wants to apply the results of this study to a patient, whether that patient is or is not represented in the population sampled must be clear.

Defining the Target Population for Remote Trials

As will be discussed in Chapter 10, remote clinical trials are those that test the efficacy and effectiveness of technology-based interventions, which include internet-based interventions, mobile applications, video games, text messaging, and wearable devices. Defining the target population for these studies is not that different than for any study, but the following sections, recruitment and screening, will be very much impacted by whether the study is done remotely, whether the remote study has a real-time human contact, or if the selection is done in-person. One consideration, however, is that people who have access to technology are often different from the general population (see Chapter 10 for more discussion) and as a result, the study findings are only interpretable to a population with access to technology. Not everyone has access to technology. Many people who live in poverty either share their devices with other family members, which limits confidentiality, or they have limited access to data minutes, making participation in such studies costly. Finally, in the United States and in many low- and middle-income countries, people who live in rural areas tend not to have ready access to broadband.

In one Global Mental Health project Dr. Areán was involved in, one of the countries involved was South Africa, and participation in remote research was complicated by challenges with rolling blackouts as well as well as a large divide in population access to cellular data.

Recruitment Procedures

The method you select to recruit participants will depend on your target population. Common forms of recruitment are *media recruitment*, *telephone/mail recruitment*, *recruitment from research platforms/communities*, and *gatekeeper recruitment*.

Media recruitment is often the most successful form of research participant recruitment. Newspaper ads, radio ads, fliers, web-based advertisements (such as Craigslist and Google Ads) and social-media recruitment (Facebook, Reddit forums) can help you identify a sizable pool of potential participants. However, this recruitment is not without its challenges. Unless your organization can encourage these sources to publish a story about your study, newspaper, TV, radio, and web-based ads are costly. If your study is on a budget, this may not be an entirely sustainable recruitment method. For newspaper, TV, and radio ads, studies have shown that the samples resulting from this method of recruitment tend to be more highly educated and less ethnically diverse than with other modes of recruitment (Iflaifel et al., 2023). When using media-based recruitment, it is very important to word your advertisement carefully. Avoid emphasizing that participants will make money from participation, as this will be considered coercive by most Institutional Review Boards (IRBs). In the social-media and web-based recruitment process, advertising incentives are a good way to attract what are called "gamers" or "fraudulent actors," people who sign up for a study for the financial gain and employ computerized methods to complete as many assessments as possible. In a recent study recruiting participants in the United States for a study to determine if sensors in smartphones can detect COVID, Flu, and common cold outbreaks, initial recruitment efforts included news stories in national newspapers and TV stations as well as recruitment from Google Ads and Facebook. At one point, 3000 people had signed up for the study in a matter of one week, but it was clear from the volume of participants, the way surveys were completed, and IP addresses that not only where these participant gamers, they we were not from the United States (although they claimed to be), and in many cases, one person was managing several smart phones to game the study for money (Li et al., 2022). In another recent study, the inclusion of a video-based interview did not deter the fraudulent actors. Time stamps from video conferencing, and inconsistencies in how questions were answered, identified that many people consenting to participate were not from the selected population (Comtois et al., 2022). In Chapter 10, we discuss methods to prevent such gaming in more detail.

Telephone and mail recruitment can be very helpful in identifying participants for clinical trials, if the rules relate to the privacy laws in your country. The method allows the investigator to select a representative group of participants from a large existing database. Once potential participants are identified, contact is made by mail or telephone with people most likely to be representative of the population of interest. Since privacy laws around the world have been enacted (for instance, the Health Insurance Portability and Accountability Act in the United States), this process is far more complicated; additionally, recent data breaches in social media, financial, and health institutions have led the public to be highly suspicious of how anyone gains access to their information. The investigator usually should not contact participants directly unless the investigator is a member of the organization from which the sample is being recruited; investigators who work for large healthcare organizations can often rely on this method of recruitment. Other investigators will generally be able to use this method only after an internal contact person gains permission from the potential participant pool to share information. We note here that research finds there tends to be greater trust across populations when the research solicitation is from an academic or university setting than from other sources, such as health plans (Pratap et al., 2019).

If you can rely on this recruitment method, we suggest you keep your recruitment materials simple. Letters explaining the study should not be longer than one page, the language should be very simple, and all contact information should be easy to access. Reading grade level is also important to consider. Most modern word processing programs have this feature built in as a tool and can help with suggestions to bring the reading level to an accessible level.

Research Platform/Communities Recruitment

Since the writing of the last edition, a new source of recruitment has emerged, the research community or research platform. Research communities were initially developed for marketing and advertising purposes. People representative of certain populations are hired to complete surveys to test the marketability of a new product. In the last decade, these platforms have been very useful in recruiting participants for mental health surveys, testing new intervention manuals or technologies and even for identifying participants for randomized clinical trials. The earlier version of this is Amazon's Mechanical Turk (mTurk), which early on was useful in identifying representative samples for health research (Forkus et al., 2023) but has lately been subject to gaming (Qureshi et al., 2024). Other platforms are specifically for academic research purposes, such as Prolific (Li et al., 2022), CloudResearch, and Positly (there are many others). Each has a cost associated with its platform but has its own methods for minimizing gaming. These platforms also allow for recruiting specific populations and allow you to oversample populations who have historically not been well represented in psychosocial interventions research. However, like recruitment from web-based or social media sources, samples from these sources will be more comfortable with technology than the general population.

Gatekeeper/referral recruitment is best for identifying potential participants in selected populations that are generally difficult to recruit, which in the United States includes Black, Latine, Asian, Indigenous, and Pacific Islander communities, primary care patients, older adults, and school children. This method is also highly appropriate when studying specific service settings or interventions to be delivered within specific settings. The initial point of recruitment is through a community gatekeeper, someone who is either a respected community leader (e.g., clergy) or a service provider (e.g., a primary care physician). The gatekeeper is then responsible for identifying potential participants and referring them to the research study. This type of recruitment is more labor-intensive for all parties on the gatekeeper, who will need to keep in mind that there is a study while managing all their other responsibilities and the investigative team who will remain in continuous contact with the gatekeeper to keep recruitment active. Often, the investigator will also have to provide community presentations to help the gatekeeper with recruitment.

In recruiting participants who are difficult to reach, we advise investigators to convene a Participant Advisory Board (PAB) to help create recruitment materials and strategies. PABs can be helpful in identifying the best recruitment sources and messages and the common concerns the community will have about participating in research.

A final point about recruitment is that it is essential to maintain your reputation as responsive to the community you are recruiting from. Whether participants self-identify for a study or are referred, it is important that you respond quickly to any requests for information about a study. Most people are generally reluctant to participate in research, and the longer the interval between the time they are referred or called to the study and the time the research team contacts the referral source or returns a potential participant's call, the more likely it is that the potential research participant will decide not to engage in the study. Professional reputation in hard-to-reach communities is particularly sensitive to late follow-up. We have seen investigators damage their reputation with a community because they were late to respond to a call, and it is very hard to gain back a positive reputation once it is tarnished.

Dr. G was primarily interested in recruiting people who qualify for senior services and thus elected to recruit from several agencies in their two catchment areas. They met with the CEO of each organization to discuss the study and to identify the person within each organization who would operate as the gatekeeper. After agencies agreed to serve as a recruitment source, Dr. G met with each gatekeeper and social service staff who would be referring cases to the study. In this meeting, they again described the study, answered any questions and addressed concerns, and then asked the group to identify people who could serve on the Participant Advisory Board (PAB). After the gatekeepers were satisfied with the study and operations, the project coordinator for the study then met with each gatekeeper to develop a recruitment method that would be feasible to implement. The plan they came up with was to have the gatekeeper and selected staff review their cases and to recruit for the study for the investigative team. Recruitment consisted of a flier created by the PAB that the case managers could distribute, and an opportunity for potential participants to meet with the project coordinator to answer any questions or address concerns about the study. This method meant that the coordinator and eventually the research assistants were based at the clinics at least one day a week to be available for questions and to participate in team meetings to keep gatekeepers apprised about recruitment progress.

Selection Process

Once you have your recruitment in place, the next step is to screen, identify, and consent participants. Most studies begin the process with a telephone or in-person screening, and remote trials sometimes use a fully online screen. The purpose of this screen is to identify likely candidates for a full intake interview and to screen out those participants who are obviously not members of your intended population. Those who pass the screen are then seen for a clinical intake assessment or interview, which consists of a longer interview to finalize eligibility and to explain the study to the patient in hopes of gaining informed consent. The intake interview should be kept to under an hour to reduce respondent burden, and for remote trials it should be under 45 minutes, and it should be focused only on the information necessary to determine eligibility and informed consent. Randomization should follow as soon as possible after the determination of eligibility and after informed consent is received. Treatment should begin very shortly after that.

The baseline information necessary for measurement of initial severity, or of possible moderators of interest, should be obtained immediately before randomization and onset of treatment. If "baseline" measures are obtained concurrently with the determination of eligibility, and there is a delay to randomization and onset of treatment, this "baseline" may not characterize the patient at the onset of treatment. The patient's condition may improve or worsen over the time delay. Similarly, it is crucial that the baseline is measured at the time of randomization just before treatment onset. If there is a time gap between eligibility and baseline measurement, some participants whose conditions improve may no longer be eligible for the study at the start of treatment. However, if baseline measures are obtained just before randomization, such a patient can be excluded from the study (although this creates a public relations problem). Any delay between the time of randomization and the onset of treatment may also result in the patient dropping out after randomization but before treatment starts.

Once randomized, every patient must remain in the study sample. You cannot change your mind about eligibility after randomization, and certainly not after the treatment assignment is known, or treatment has begun! Since the analysis of results requires analysis "by intention to treat" (i.e., using everyone randomized), such dropouts will complicate both the analysis and the interpretation of results. If patients are removed from the treatment groups after being randomized, such removal may affect the protection that randomization offers—that the two treatment groups are randomly sampled from the *same* population. This is a particular problem for remote trials where there is no human contact (and in some circumstances, even when there is human contact). Therefore, it is critical that participant eligibility be determined first, then the baseline evaluation, then randomization, followed very quickly by the onset of treatment. For this reason, it is important to work out your post-randomization retention strategy before embarking on a clinical trial. This is discussed in Chapter 7.

Often, due to the complexity of the eligibility criteria or the needs of the patient sample, screening can be a multi-stage process that for practical purposes might not adhere to the recommended quick turnaround in screening and assignment just described. Let us turn to Dr. G and their selection process as an example of real-world screening methodology. Because participants in Dr. G's research sample had less than a high school education and were physically disabled, Dr. G aimed to reduce respondent burden while determining eligibility by using a three-meeting intake approach. When participants were referred to the study, potential participants were told on the phone that there would be three meetings with a research assistant to determine whether potential participants would be eligible. The first interview was a telephone screener, which consisted of questions about income level, a brief disability assessment scale, and a brief depression scale. To qualify for the second interview, those referred had to earn less than $30,000 a year, have a depression score associated with moderate depression or worse, and have at least one functional disability. This telephone interview generally took 15 minutes. The second interview was an intake interview done in person, which consisted of a semi-structured clinical interview to determine the diagnosis of MDD and to rule out other diagnoses, such as psychosis, substance abuse/dependence, and Bipolar Disorder. Additionally, the intake included a memory test to exclude those with moderate memory impairment, a complete demographic interview, a more extensive disability assessment, and a more thorough, reliable, and valid depression scale than the one used for the telephone intake. Dr. G elected to use a different depression measure for the intake and baseline interviews because the intake measure is more accurate than the telephone screener in identifying depression and must be done face-to-face rather than over the phone. Therefore, this second interview varied in length but averaged an hour. Participants who qualified for the study were seen within a week of the intake interview for the baseline assessment and randomization. Baseline assessment included re-administration of the depression severity scale and the assessment of other outcomes, potential moderators such as hopefulness, case management needs, self-efficacy, educational attainment, and number of chronic illnesses. This interview took two hours. Treatment began within a week of this visit.

Participant Selection Tools

Mental health diagnosis

If your target population consists of people with a mental illness, you will need to use a well-validated tool to determine if your sample has that illness. The ideal tool for clinical trials is a semi-structured interview tied to the DSM or International Classification for Disease (ICD; World Health Organization, 2019) criteria. These include the Structured Clinical Interview for DSM (SCID; First, 2015), the World Health Organization Composite

International Diagnostic Interview (CIDI; Kessler & Üstün, 2004), and the Mini International Neuropsychiatric Interview (MINI; Pettersson et al., 2018). Except for the CIDI, which can be administered by lay interviewers, both the MINI and the SCID require that interviewers who administer the tools have some experience in diagnosing mental illnesses and allow the interviewer to amend the diagnosis derived from the instrument. All three have extensive training protocols to ensure that interviewers are administering the interview reliably, and all require ongoing reliability checks to ensure interviewers are not "drifting" from the protocol. The interviews vary in length depending on the severity of mental health issues; the maximum time an interview like the SCID can take is around two hours. All three instruments have a screening section that will allow interviewers to select the diagnostic sections to be administered. On the SCID, if a participant does not appear to be using drugs or alcohol to excess or does not appear to have any psychotic thinking, the interviewer can skip those interview sections.

Some studies will also rely on diagnoses available in clinical charts to identify a potential pool of participants. While this method is useful in identifying potential participants in a study, we advise against relying on those diagnoses for determining eligibility, unless the study is a pragmatic trial, field trial, or implementation trial. In those instances, the intervention to be tested should be on people who have undergone the standard clinical assessment practice. The intervention should already have demonstrated its efficacy in the selected population, thus, the purpose of these trial types is to determine real-world effectiveness. We caution here that many chart diagnoses are not accurate and do not specify how the diagnosis was reached. In many cases, the choice of diagnosis on the record may reflect what diagnoses are covered by the patient's insurance rather than being fully reflective of their presenting problems.

Severity measures

In addition to a well-validated diagnostic tool, you will also need a good symptom or problem severity measure to determine problem severity. Often this same measure will be used to assess the intervention outcome, either at the end of treatment and/or periodically during the treatment. As a result, you will need to make sure that the severity measure you chose is a functional measure. In selecting a problem severity measure, it is important to consider a few factors, specifically the measure's reliability (how consistently a tool measures a construct), validity (how accurately a tool measures a construct), and, if this will be your outcome measure, its sensitivity to change over time (how accurately a tool measures a construct over time). It is important to note that here and throughout this book, we adopt the common approach and refer to a measure being reliable and/or valid, but it is the measurement itself—the data—and not the measure that is reliable and valid. Data produced by a measure may be reliable and/or valid within one context or population, but not another. The simple use of a "reliable and valid" measure does not guarantee quality data. You should consider not only the overall psychometric properties, but also how well it functions in your selected population and how it is being applied. If you are using a translated version of a scale, make sure you know how the scale was translated and how well it functions in your population, compared to how it functions in the populations in which it was originally developed. Many journals that publish data from remote trials require you to also report on the scale's psychometric properties as an online measure. Many scales do have this information, many do not (given the relatively nascent state of the field). As of this writing, it is perfectly fine to say in a report that a scale has not been tested as a remote scale and justify why you selected that scale over others that may have been tested as a remote measure.

It is common to see in psychology journals investigators reporting on the reliability of the measures they chose using the sample they studied. In many cases, what is reported is the scale's internal consistency (i.e., Cronbach's alpha)—that is, how well the items relate to one another. It is possible that Cronbach's alpha is low where the measure has very high test–retest reliability. For example, a general intelligence test featuring items for math, language, music, logic, and social skills may be highly replicable over time but have relatively low internal reliability. Cronbach's alpha may also be high where the measure has low test–retest reliability. For example, a measure of states such as mood or alertness might have several items that are highly correlated but have a low test–retest reliability when administered on different days. Of course, states should be measured with test–retest reliability over minutes rather than days or weeks. While internal consistency is important in measure development, it is test–retest reliability that is important in clinical trials reporting Cronbach's alpha, while common, it is not necessary, and does not replace consideration of test–retest reliability.

Reliability is essentially a signal-to-noise indicator. It is zero either when there is no signal, or if the noise overwhelms the signal. It is perfect (1.0) when there is no noise. "Noise" in this case is measurement error, which is the difference between an individual's true value on a scale and their measured value. Measurement error includes random error, which happens in most measures, and systematic error, which is the result of a measure that is consistently miscalibrated. Participants taking a depression scale who respond differently at different times of day would result in random error; a depression scale that does not include specific symptoms such as anhedonia or lethargy would result in systematic measurement error.

Special consideration must be given to data collected from trained observers or coders. The two major sources of measurement error in this situation are inconsistency in patient response and inconsistency in observer assessments. Intraobserver or intra-rater reliability, where the same observer rates the same patient data multiple times (e.g., multiple readings of the same x-ray), excludes both major sources of random measurement error, but may lead to biased data from systematic measurement error. For example, certain observers may consistently rate patients' behaviors as more severe than other observers. Intra-observer reliability is seldom measured or reported in clinical trials. Interobserver (or interrater) reliability, where two or more different observers independently rate the same participant data (e.g., two observers of the same patient interview), excludes participant inconsistency but acknowledges observer inconsistency. This is probably the most common type of reliability in clinical trials and is essential to validate fidelity ratings and ensure that the intervention was delivered as intended. Test–retest reliability of observational data, where two or more different independent observers rate the same patient at two different times within a time span short enough that the true status of the patient has not changed (e.g., two interviews on two successive days), permits both major sources of measurement error. Generally, given the differing degrees of magnitude of measurement error described above, intra-observer reliability has higher scores than interobserver reliability, which, in turn, has higher scores than test–retest reliability.

In longitudinal clinical trials that incorporate multiple waves of measurement into the analyses, test–retest reliability will have a major impact on statistical power. The power to detect treatment effects depends on the size of the test–retest reliability (called the rho statistic). Generally, the sample size necessary for adequate power is inversely related to the test–retest reliability (N/rho). You will achieve the same statistical power when N = 100 and rho = 1 as you would when N = 200 and rho = .5 or N = 500 and rho = .2! By using a measure that produces data with high test–retest reliability, or training observers to code data with high reliability, a researcher reduces measurement error and increases statistical power. In fact, this is one of the easiest and least expensive ways to increase the statistical power of a longitudinal trial.

Exclusionary measures

In defining your sample, you will also want to make sure you consider whom to exclude from your sample. Ethically, you must exclude those not willing to participate in the clinical trial, those who might be harmed by participation, and those who, based on past research, are unlikely to benefit from the new treatment. Moreover, you will need to consider all the potential co-occurring conditions the population of interest will likely have and decide whether you want to exclude people for having a co-occurring condition or include them because it will be a more representative sample. The decision of whom to include and exclude is largely based on your study's intent.

In Dr. G's case, the prevalence of cognitive impairments in older adults with depression is around 30% and may be higher in low-income populations. Although the study results would be more generalizable if Dr. G were to include all older people with depression, Dr. G knew that people with more moderate to severe cognitive impairments would not benefit from a learning-based psychotherapy without assistance from family or other personal supports. They therefore decided to include people with mild impairment, to be more representative, but to exclude those with early dementia or dementia. Because of the ethnic and educational composition of the sample, and the potential for these patient characteristics to cloud the results from standard cognitive screening tests, Dr. G decided not to rely simply on a cut score from a memory test but to review cases that were close to the cut score for moderate impairment and make a clinical determination about the participant's capacity to participate in the study.

One common exclusion criterion is whether the participant speaks English. Even when not expressed as a formal exclusion criterion, the lack of linguistically appropriate materials and staff can result in the de facto exclusion of non-native English speakers. Several studies, including a systematic review that included over 70,000 individuals from a range of health research (Wendler et al., 2006), have found that racial and ethnic minoritized people are as willing as non-Latine Whites to participate in research studies. Despite this, minoritized individuals are not adequately represented in health research. While translation of materials, using interpreters, and hiring and training multilingual research interviewers can be expensive and time-consuming, it is important that researchers engage in efforts to increase the representation of diverse communities in research. Unfortunately, many of the barriers to the inclusion of diverse individuals lie at the researcher level. While researchers endorse the value of diversity in research participation in general, they are less likely to endorse and prioritize its value in their own research (Passmore et al., 2022). Some of the most important strategies to include marginalized groups are to eliminate exclusionary criteria based on language and make efforts to create a warm and welcoming environment by using culturally appropriate and translated measures, diverse and culturally competent research staff, and hiring research staff who are fluent in multiple languages.

Demographic characteristics

Measuring participant characteristics is important not only for reporting to your funder about your sample, but also for describing to the field the population to whom the results from your study apply. The most common characteristics measured are age, gender, race and ethnicity, marital status, income, education, place of birth, language preference, and, for immigrants, how long they have lived in the country. While these characteristics seem straightforward to measure, a few are not as easy to assess. Definitions of income, race and ethnicity, and gender require some discussion.

Although income is a relatively straightforward variable, it can be a sensitive question to ask and is often not reported accurately. Investigators need to think carefully about their reasons for collecting this information, and if it is important to the study, to be clear about what they mean by income (do you mean salary only, salary plus capital gains, gross income before taxes, net after taxes, individual income or household income?) and allow participants to report their income in the way they feel most comfortable. In Dr. G's study, income was defined as total household income, including any capital gains and other benefits, and was collected as a finite number; in past studies, however, Dr. G found that people were generally uncomfortable reporting total income, but were more willing to provide an income range. Dr. G's current study used income as an inclusion criterion, as she was most interested in recruiting those with low incomes. Dr. G had to consider the various ways that this term could be defined before deciding on the inclusion criteria. Another way to ask about income is to ask whether the participant has the means to meet their basic needs. Although not as accurate a measure of income (and would be insufficient for Dr. G's study), this question does characterize whether one's earnings cover basic needs, as there may be variability between people with the exact same income. For instance, someone making $25,000 a year would surely be struggling in Dr. G's study, but if this person had no debts, $25,000 would go further than for someone who has considerable debt. This nuance is the difference between struggling but basically stable, versus not feeling any financial stability.

Race and ethnicity are also defined differently in different studies. For most psychotherapy studies, in measuring this construct, you will need to consider what you are interested in studying in relation to these variables (and please consider that race is not the same as ethnicity, they are two different variables). Often, consciously or not, researchers include race and ethnicity as a proxy for other variables that are better when measured directly. If you are interested in the role that culture plays in treatment effectiveness, it may not be enough to collect just information on race and ethnicity; you may also need to administer an acculturation tool, because people from the same ethnic background may be differentially ensconced in their culture. Other such variables include experiences of racism, income, education, socio-economic status, political viewpoints, buying habits, adverse experiences, and wealth, just to name a few.

Another factor to consider is when people identify with multiple racial and ethnic categories. A growing number of people report being multiracial. This will make describing the makeup of your sample a bit more complicated. To prevent this from being a problem, some researchers add a "multiracial" category or "select all that apply" to the survey. When reporting race, the current best practice is to report all multiracial combinations, though this may not be practical in large studies or if it might reveal a participants' identity. At the time of this writing, NIH uses limited and outdated racial and ethnic classifications (American Indian or Alaska Native, Asian, Black or African American, Hispanic or Latino, Native Hawaiian or Other Pacific Islander, and White), though NIH has sought input on suggested modifications such as adding North African and Middle Eastern (currently categorized as White), and allowing Hispanic or Latino to be endorsed within a combined list of race and ethnicity rather than separately. (Note that Hispanic refers to people who are from or descend from a Spanish-speaking country, Latine refers to people who are from or descend from the Latin American region, and official US documentation uses Latino to represent people of all genders, despite ending in a masculine -o.) We have found that participants frequently do not distinguish ethnicity from race and we often have a sizable portion of participants who endorse Hispanic or Latino for ethnicity, while for race they endorse "Other" and write in "Latino," essentially leaving the race variable unanswered. As of this writing, there have been some efforts to remove the gendered "-o" for Latino by using terms such as Latinx and Latine. Despite the recent popularity of "Latinx" in academic journals, as of this writing, very few people in this population have embraced this term and some feel that the letter x is a symbol of colonization that erases cultural heritage or ignores linguistic norms that are broadly acceptable to people who are of the Latino culture and minimally identify with the United States or Anglo culture. Latinx is not a word in Spanish, however, Latine is, and Latino as a collective term refers to men, women, and nonbinary. The "x" in Spanish is pronounced three ways depending on the region of the person (either "ekis," "heh," or "sh"), making Latinx unpronounceable in some regions of Latin America. We also often include an open-ended option for tribal affiliation for Native Americans, as this can provide additional insight and demonstrate respect for the widely varying cultures within this population. The primary point of this discussion is that language evolves; we are certain that current best practices will feel antiquated in time. Researchers should not look for the perfect terminology but rather create their demographic survey to include the categories and terminology with which their population resonates, while retaining the ability to re-categorize to fit funder-specified category requirements. Aiming for an inclusive system is always a good practice to positively engage participants.

Regarding gender, current best practice is to include options along with male/female, such as nonbinary or genderqueer. Some researchers will ask people to report if they are cisgender (their biological or assigned sex at birth matches their gender identity) or transgender (their biological or assigned sex at birth does not match their gender identity). Although this is a helpful option to offer participants, we have found that many people who are transgender do not wish to elect this category. Many will indicate the gender they feel closest to, rather than their biological sex. For studies involving basic science principles, you will need to ask about one's biological sex at birth. If this is necessary for your study, provide participants with two questions, the first being the generic "What is your gender?" and the second being "what was your assigned sex at birth?" Again, it is up to researchers to stay current with best practices, as we suspect any recommendations made here might shortly be outdated.

Some funding agencies will want to know specific information about your sample. As of this writing, the NIH requires that applicants provide a targeted enrollment table that details the proportion of women and different racial groups (see example in the Appendix). The terminology on this table is dated, as we just discussed, and further complicated to use the first time, because the "Hispanic or Latino" category is separated out from the racial groups. The rationale for the format is that "Hispanic or Latino" is an ethnicity, not a race, reflecting the fact that many Hispanics are also Black, Asian, Native, or White. The process for completing this table is as follows:

- In Section 1, provide the proportion of Hispanic and non-Hispanic men and women you plan to recruit.
- In Section 2, take your entire sample again (*including those identifying as Hispanic or Latino*), and determine the proportion of racial groups you plan to recruit, but *remember*, your Hispanic groups are to be included in this count. Therefore, you will also need to estimate how many of your Hispanic sample will be Black, Asian, Native, or White.

Defining Your Outcomes

Defining your outcomes and selecting the measures of your outcomes is a very important process. In selecting your outcome measures, consider the following questions:

1. What is (are) the primary outcome(s) to be addressed in my study? Is there a gold standard measure of that outcome in the field I am studying? If so, you will want to use that measure so that your results can be compared with other studies of a similar problem.
2. Is the measure (a) reliable and (b) valid in the population I am studying? If the answer to either question is no, you will need to identify another measure that is more useful for your population. If the answer is not known, you may want to do a pilot study in which the gold standard and instruments known to be useful in your target population are evaluated and compared to choose the most appropriate outcome measure for your study. In the section above, we discuss some of the most important aspects to consider in measurement quality, with test–retest reliability being a highly important aspect of your outcome measure for longitudinal trials.
3. If there is no existing measure for the outcome you want to study, you may need to create a measure. It is a very bad idea to try to develop a primary outcome measure in the same study in which that outcome measure is to be used—if your measure ends up being of low quality, you would be stuck with a nearly useless trial. It is preferable to consider developing the outcome measure first (perhaps in a pilot study), and only then propose to use it in the clinical trial. This is not an easy task, for researchers who specialize in measurement development are not usually the same researchers who specialize in clinical trials.
4. How invasive is the outcome measure? If the outcome measure is burdensome, and no alternative measure exists, you will need to evaluate the effect the measure has on recruitment and retention in a pilot study, so you can either develop a protocol to minimize the burden or determine the need for a new instrument.

Predictors, Moderators, and Mediators

One of the biggest points of confusion for clinical investigators is the distinction between a predictor, a moderator, and a mediator. Allow us to clarify the terms for you here.

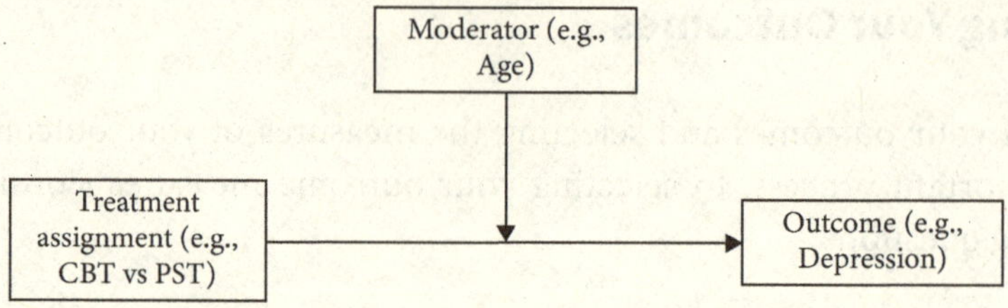

Figure 4.1 Moderation

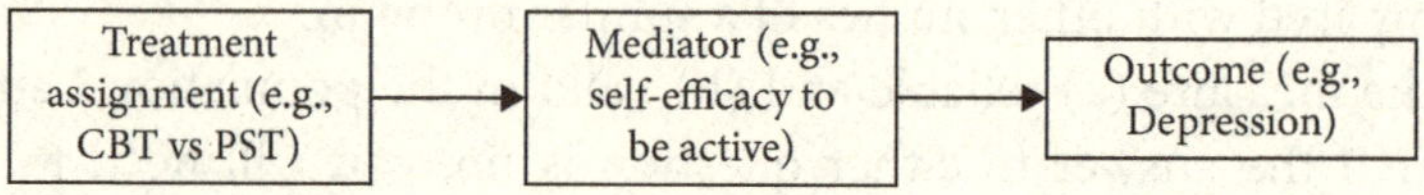

Figure 4.2 Mediation

The first distinction, between a mediator of treatment and a moderator/predictor, is easiest. A moderator/predictor must be a characteristic that exists at the time of randomization (baseline) before treatment is initiated, and thus, with randomization, is uncorrelated with treatment condition (see Figure 4.1). A mediator is an event or change that happens during treatment but before the outcome of treatment is determined, and is correlated with treatment condition—that is, itself is an early outcome of treatment (see Figure 4.2). For instance, treatment A may be better than treatment B at improving the sense of self efficacy to be active (get out of bed, engage with work), which is then related to the outcome (depression).

If the effect of treatment (i.e., the difference between treatment A and B responses) is related to a baseline variable, that baseline variable is a moderator of treatment. Moderators are pre-existing aspects of the individual (e.g., gender, race, openness to treatment), their context (e.g., support of family members, rurality), or the treatment context (e.g., size of clinic, treatment provider years of experience) that differentially impact the effectiveness of the treatment by condition. For instance, treatment A may work better than treatment B for older individuals. A moderator is important because it helps to identify in whom, or under what conditions, A "works differently" than B. It may be that there is a subgroup of patients with a specific characteristic for whom A is strongly preferable to B, another subgroup for whom A and B are clinically equivalent, and the remaining subgroups for whom B is strongly preferable to A. Thus, moderators of treatment provide information about tailoring treatment decisions for individual patients.

If a baseline variable is not a moderator of treatment but predicts outcome in both treatment conditions A and B, that baseline variable is a predictor of treatment outcome. Since it is not a moderator, if treatment A is preferred to treatment B for some patients, it is equally preferred for all. However, whichever treatment is given, one would expect those with high values of the predictor to respond differently from those with low values of the predictor.

An event or change that happens during treatment that is correlated with treatment condition is a mediator of treatment if the treatment effect can be explained partially or entirely by that variable. For example, if depression treatment A leads to a greater change in self-esteem than treatment B and those with the greatest change in self-esteem are those with the largest decrease in depression, the change in self-esteem mediates the treatment on that outcome. Mediators help us understand possible mechanisms of treatment, that is, how or why one treatment "works" and why it may "work better" than another. While mechanisms are mediators, mediators are not always mechanisms. Mechanisms differ in that there is a causal path, both logically/theoretically as well as empirically, where the treatment causes a change in the mechanism, and the mechanism causes the change in the outcome. While mediators and mechanisms can each provide clues as to how we might make the treatment either more effective or more cost-effective, mechanisms are the primary goal of science. It is this principle that drives the experimental therapeutics approach to contemporary clinical trial research.

Let's use again Dr. G's study as an example. Dr. G was interested in the degree to which baseline physical disability affected treatment outcome. They hypothesized that the differential effect of case management plus PST versus case management alone would be greater for participants who had been homebound longer and were frailer. Indeed, it might be possible that the effect of adding PST to case management would be apparent only for such patients. They therefore measured at baseline how long the person had been homebound, how long they had been disabled, and how many disabling conditions the participant had.

Additionally, Dr. G thought that changes in self-efficacy would be found primarily in the participants receiving PST, and that the effect of adding PST to case management might be largely explained by this change in self-efficacy (mediation). They therefore measured self-efficacy at baseline and again a month before the depression outcome measures to determine if a change in self-efficacy led to changes in depression, and if this effect was primarily in the PST group.

It can easily be seen how this approach could lead to changes in the treatment design to make it more efficient or cost-effective. If there was supportive evidence for the moderator, Dr. G. could tailor treatment so only patients with a certain level of disability would receive PST, therefore saving cost and effort on the misapplication of PST for those who didn't need it. If Dr. G. found evidence for self-efficacy as a mediator, they could redesign their training to more efficiently address self-efficacy, or consider other, possibly more effective or less expensive, methods of enhancing self-efficacy.

Assessment Timing and Timelines

One of the biggest problems faced by intervention researchers is balancing the need to adequately assess baseline features, moderators, mediators, and outcomes with the need to ensure that participants are not overburdened by the assessment. Burden can result in two unfortunate outcomes for your study: unreliable results and early participant dropout. Both participants and evaluators simply get fatigued and become less careful in providing thoughtful and accurate responses when an assessment is too burdensome, and this results in decreased reliable reporting. Moreover, participants get annoyed at having to answer many questions, which often seem or are redundant, and may react by withdrawing from the study. With the pilot study (discussed in Chapter 7), you can fine-tune and streamline your assessment, but for the most part for adults without cognitive disabilities you will want to keep your interviews to no more than 90 minutes for an efficacy trial, less than an hour for an effectiveness study and ideally less than 30 minutes for a remote trial. The time difference between trial types has to do with the trial purpose and the burden. In efficacy trials, the study must collect data on mechanisms of change, and often does so using varying levels of analysis, such as self-report, performance data in the form of cognitive tasks, and observational analyses, such as the use of EEG or fMRI devices. In effectiveness trials, the trial intends to be as close to actual practice as possible, meaning assessments should align with typical practice. Assessments should minimize burden to not detract from practice. For remote trials, the rule of thumb for assessment timing has more to do with research pragmatics than study purpose. In remote trials, it is very hard to keep participants engaged. The briefer the assessment, the more likely the participant will remain engaged in the study. In Chapter 10, we discuss methods for managing respondent fatigue in remote trials when it is not possible to keep assessments under 30 minutes. Researchers who have many variables they want to measure will often split their interviews into separate sessions to relieve the burden and address reliability issues. However, requiring too many sessions may even further encourage dropout. The best solution to this problem is to try and keep assessments short, minimize the number of visits needed to complete an assessment, and when this is not possible, create mitigation strategies for response burden.

Here are a few hints on measure selection. First, you should be able to visualize the unique role each variable plays in answering the questions posed in your study. Do not collect measures simply because you think you can. Draw a model of your theory of change, complete with constructs and variables or measures representing each construct, to ensure there is a rationale for including your measure. Second, while you are required to document the reliability and validity of only your primary outcome measure(s), you should assure yourself that all the measures have reasonable reliability and validity. Otherwise, certain measures will be of no use in answering questions and may even mislead. It is important not to collect redundant measures. Having three or four different measures, all measuring the severity of an illness, increases not only the burden but also the probabilities of both false-positive and false-negative results. In such cases, choose the best single measure, or combine the measures into one. The latter strategy, of course, does not decrease burden, but it does increase the reliability of the measurement of the construct they all measure, thus increasing power and precision (Leon, 1995).

While careful selection of measures will reduce the burden, it comes at the risk of not including important constructs. A longstanding but underutilized method for retaining measures in the study but reducing burden is to apply a planned missingness design for your measures. With the near-universal use of computerized administration (via REDCap, Qualtrics, and other applications), researchers have easier and more robust options for planned missingness than ever before. While there are several different approaches to planned missingness designs, they all operate by administering only a partial subset of measure items to each participant. Instead of having to answer a 25-item measure on depression symptoms and functioning, participants might only answer a 10-item measure, but with each participant answering a different 10 items. Because the items are missing at random across the sample, they can be estimated very well by commonly available approaches for addressing missing data. Using a planned missingness design can significantly reduce assessment burden for participants while having a relatively minor impact on the study's statistical power. The benefits that accrue from increased study retention likely outweigh this impact.

Procedure for Collecting Data: In-Person, Telephone/Video, Online, Home-Based, and Mailed Assessments

As an investigator, you will be faced with several decisions related to how your interview will be conducted, and your decision should be based on what makes the most sense for your study and what is the most acceptable and feasible process. You will ultimately arrive at your decision after you do the pilot study, but we felt it important to describe the pros and cons of each method, as well as the importance of using one method consistently over time and for each participant.

The most common form of data collection is the in-person interview. Generally, this will consist of a research assistant working with the participants as they complete the interview. In some studies, apart from observation and clinician-rated measures, participants are handed a packet of instruments to complete while they are at the research setting. The advantage of this method is that the research assistants can schedule more people in a time slot and be more efficient with their time; while one participant is completing measures, an assistant can be collecting data from another participant. Having participants complete measures on their own is also useful in studies of group therapy or classes, where it is not feasible for research assistants to interview several participants at once. The downside of self-administered measures is that participants sometimes skip questions or do not quite understand how to complete the measures, and without a research assistant present to make sure each question is answered and to explain the process, the investigator may end up with missing data. Other investigators administer interviews orally to make sure the participants understand the questions and complete each one. This method is useful for populations where literacy, vision, education, and comprehension issues (e.g., young children, people with severe mental illnesses) may interfere with participants' ability to complete measures on their own. The downside is that this method is expensive, requiring a team of assistants to conduct interviews.

Telephone or video conferenced administered interviews are another common method for assessment that minimizes time and transportation burden on participants. Studies demonstrate that this method of interviewing is a reliable method of data collection and is convenient in that it eliminates travel time for the participant or research assistant to conduct an in-person meeting (Chang, 2009). The main downside of telephone-based or video conference interviews is that these interviews need to be even shorter than in-person interviews, because participants often find such interviews longer than an hour to be very tiring. Imagine yourself talking to someone you do not know well for over an hour, and that conversation consists of questions like "In the last week, would you say you worked none of the time, some of the time, most of the time, or all of the time?" over and over again. After more than 30 minutes of dialogue like this, you would probably become quite tired. We do note here that in the post-pandemic era, and for generations accustomed to video-chat platforms, such burdens may not be as challenging and may be preferred over in-person interviews.

Online or remote assessments consist of participants receiving a link to a computerized survey engine where participants complete their assessments on their own. Like mailed-in assessments, which we see as being used less over time as a data collection approach, unless the survey is programmed to encourage one-sitting completion, participants may complete assessments at their leisure, which could impact the reliability of the assessment. Online assessments are subject to increased respondent fatigue. Respondent fatigue can be mitigated by using progress bars on the assessment screen to show participants how much more time the survey will take, and introducing visual relief, such as rewarding GIFs interspersed through the survey. A hybrid approach can have participants self-administer a survey online while a research assistant is available on the phone or video to answer questions and ensure survey completion. Two of the most common applications for online surveys are Research Electronic Data Capture (REDCap; Harris et al., 2009; Harris et al., 2019) and Qualtrics ((https://www.qualtrics.com); both have similar features such as automated survey invitations and reminders, skip pattern programming, embedded videos, and longitudinal participant tracking. REDCap is available for free through many universities. Both applications feature modes that adjust the presentation of surveys for ease of viewing based on whether the user is on a smartphone or a computer monitor.

Home-based assessments are common for populations where transportation is an issue and access to telecommunication technology is not available. Home-based assessments are not unlike in-person assessments, except that the transportation burden is on the research assistant rather than the research participant. This method of data collection has its own challenges, such as research assistant safety when studies are conducted in high-crime neighborhoods, and the reluctance of some participants to have strangers in their home.

Finally, assessments can be completed by mail. However, this method has fallen out of favor because of the tendency for participants to lose materials, not return them in a timely fashion, and send back incomplete assessments. Although this method is a money-saver in some respects, it is problematic in ways just described and is becoming obsolete when participant pools have ready access to the internet.

Ethical Considerations

In this chapter, the main ethical issues concern recruitment methods, safe data management, and assurance that research assistants keep information confidential and that the consent process is done ethically.

Recruitment Methods

The main issue regarding recruitment is to make sure your advertising is not seen as coercive. As noted earlier, advertisements claiming participants can make hundreds of dollars by participating are often considered coercive, and most IRBs will not approve those methods. In communities with low income, the concept of "therapeutic misconception" is a controversial one that is currently a subject of much study by bioethicists. Therapeutic misconception is the belief that participating in the study will directly benefit the participants in the study. This is not usually the case. The purpose of research is to determine which treatment works better in a population. One of the treatments may well be inferior to the other, and thus may not benefit many patients, or there may be a benefit but not to the degree that the other intervention is beneficial. In low-income communities, where resources are very scarce, some people may believe that participating in a study is better than what they have available to them. To the extent that tender loving care may benefit the patient, this may well be true. However, it is important to explain to all participants the purpose of research and to clarify that there are other therapeutic options available that would not leave the decision of their care to chance. If participants understand the risks of participating in an RCT, and are willing to participate knowing those risks, then the study has met ethical standards.

Data Management and Storage

Now, more than ever, with electronic storage of data, the protection of data must be thoroughly considered. All paper files must be kept in locked cabinets 100% of the time; even if an assistant must leave the room to use the restroom while entering data from a file into a computer, that file must be placed in a secure location before he or she leaves the office. Data stored on a computer or cloud must be kept behind a secure firewall and password-protected at all times. Finally, if data needs to be in transit, perhaps because they are being collected in the field, the data must be kept in a secure briefcase or storage system and immediately brought back to the main storage location. Only certain research personnel should have access to the data files, and very few should be able to enter or change the data.

Data Sharing

The open science movement aims to make research widely accessible to other researchers and the public, not just in the form of dissemination of results but including data, software, and study materials. One aim is to improve the replicability and reproducibility of results, especially in the wake of the "replication crisis," or the growing recognition that many—perhaps even most—published research findings are false (Ioannidis, 2005). Phenomena such as the file drawer effect, p-hacking, and bias (by investigators, reviewers, and editors) result in many published studies not substantiated in future research. By making data and analytic code available, other research teams can attempt to reproduce the original findings, something that appears straightforward but is not. For instance, in a study involving 29 different analytic teams tasked with answering the same research question using the same dataset found odds ratios ranging from 0.89 to 2.93, meaning that some teams came to the exact opposite conclusions and some teams found no effect at all (Silberzahn et al., 2018).

Research teams are now tasked with several activities to increase research transparency. These include publishing protocol papers in scientific journals, government trial registration portals (such as the National of Institutes of Health ClinicalTrials.gov) and making data openly available through secure data sharing portals. In the United States, studies funded by the National Institute of Mental Health must agree to upload data to the National Data Archive (although special exemptions are available, usually when working with Tribal Nations and with data that is highly identifiable). These datasets are nearly always anonymized, which means the removal of any data that can be used to identify the participant. Aside from the obvious, such as names and addresses, removal should also include all dates, such as birthdate and date of services. Sometimes these dates are "jittered" by adding a random day from 0 to 365, or computed to be the number of days since some index date that only the research team has access to. Less obvious is the need to remove or mask variables or categories within variables that can be combined to identify a person. For instance, it may be that in a specific location there are many people who are Black or transgender or who are 52 years old, but only one Black transgender 52-year-old.

Perhaps the easiest—though least open—of these approaches is to include statements that datasets and analytic code will be made available upon request. Researchers draft data sharing agreements to protect the confidentiality of the data with those who request it, which outline the ways in which the data can be used, the research questions to be answered, and dates for data destruction. Researchers can also post their data on publicly available websites. For federally funded research in the United States, as of this writing, the most common repository is the National Data Archive (NDA). NIH-funded clinical trials require certain data to be placed into the NDA. Data that is identifiable, intellectual property from small business grant funding, and data that is tertiary to the study's research question is frequently not required. Other data repositories include the Harvard Dataverse, the Inter-University Consortium for Political and Social Research (ICPSR), the National Center for Educational Statistics, and the Institute for Social Research. Find the archive that best fits your field.

Consenting

As mentioned earlier, consent to participate must be obtained in a noncoercive way, and all elements of the study must be conveyed clearly to the participant. Many universities are beginning to require that any research team member who collects consents must undergo IRB training. Even with this training, audiotaping and regularly reviewing the consent process is a must. We review consent for digital and remote research in Chapter 10.

Equity

The main issues to consider with regard to participant selection and research interviewing are to ensure that (1) your sample is representative of the population you wish to select from; (2) the recruitment, selection, and assessment methods you select will ensure that you will have a representative sample; and (3) the measurements you select function well across genders and in different minority groups, and if you are selecting children, can be completed by or for children. As stated earlier, funders such as NIH require that you ensure representative enrollment of these groups unless there is some valid justification for not doing so. For instance, Dr. G's study is focused on older adults, so they did not need to recruit children.

Budgetary Issues

When you are constructing your budget, make sure you have money to hire good research assistants, money to pay participants for their time in the interview, and money to purchase the right to use the instruments you selected, particularly those that are copyrighted and are not in the public domain. As an investigator, you must do due diligence to ensure that you have permission to use instruments and, for those that require you to purchase their forms, enough money to ensure that you have enough forms for your study. You should also consider budgeting for things that can help reduce the barriers to participation from people who are low-income or do not speak English fluently, such as paying for childcare and transportation, translation and interpreters, and food.

Chapter Summary

How you recruit your sample will very much depend on the population you are sampling from and where they are most likely to learn about research participation; no one method works well across all studies. Once you determine that someone is eligible for a study and has been randomized, you CANNOT change your mind afterward. It is crucial that eligibility be determined first, then baseline assessment, then randomization, followed quickly by the commencement of treatment. In selecting your assessment and outcome tools, be sure to check their reliability, validity, and sensitivity to change over time. When measuring demographics, be careful how you define them. Many people in the United States are multiracial and may not identify fully with any one group. Likewise, it is important to be sensitive to how participants identify themselves in terms of gender. Your methods of data collection are important for ensuring that the data you collect is valid, and with the near ubiquity of smartphones there are more options than ever. Carefully consider how choosing among the options of in-person interviewing, self-administered paper surveys, telephone administration, and online self-administration meets the needs of your study in terms of participants, feasibility, and data quality. Above all else, ensure ethical behavior in your study, especially the full participation of a diverse group of participants who are relevant to your research question.

5

Study Team Composition and Management

Critical Questions This Chapter Will Address

- Who are the members of the research team and what are their roles?
- What are the important tools in managing a research team?
- What are the best approaches to running meetings, so everyone is heard and engaged?
- How do I manage multisite projects?
- How do I manage multidisciplinary projects?

This chapter covers the operations of a study team and introduces the reader to the concept of Team Science. When we are working toward becoming a scientist, we are rarely exposed to the best practices of leading a group, which includes learning how to be a good team member. Most of the skills investigators learn are acquired through an apprentice model, where skills are picked up by working as a member of a team. While the hands-on experience is invaluable, this model runs the risk of learning some bad habits, such as underestimating the amount of work needed to complete a project, micromanaging (doing everyone's job) or seagull managing (a seagull manager swoops in, criticizes the team then swoops out again). Even as seasoned investigators, we are constantly learning new ways to lead and support our team because it's the process of supporting and working with your team members that makes the experience of conducting psychosocial intervention research more pleasant and exciting. Psychosocial interventions research has increasingly needed the infusion of expertise of investigators from other disciplines, collaboration with other research teams and community organizations. Therefore, not only is team building important for the research team, but it is also important for research partnerships.

High-Quality Psychosocial Interventions Research. Second Edition. Patricia A. Areán and Michael D. Pullmann, Oxford University Press.
DOI: 10.1093/oso/9780197681923.003.0005

The Study Team

In this section, we start with the basic study team membership. Under ideal fiscal climates, the basic study team will consist of the following members:

The Principal Investigator

The Principal Investigator (PI) is ultimately responsible for the study's conduct. This means that the quality of the study methods and the data collected reflects on the PI. For this reason, the PI's duties do not end with the research award, but continue throughout the study timeline, from set up to dissemination of the study results (and future management of the study data). The PI sets the tone and culture of the team, although with bigger teams, this is also set by the project or team manager, who is responsible for managing any methodological or clinical issues that arise during the study and is directly responsible for the ethical and equitable management of the study. The PI provides regular reports to the funding organization, provides reports to the scientific community and works closely with the project manager, who oversees the day-to-day conduct of the study. The PI is also the mentor of any junior colleagues who are part of the research team. As such, the PI should be aware of the type of training the study provides to any new investigators and should provide co-authorship of publications or even the opportunity for responsibility for leading some aspect of the study which senior authorship might be appropriate.

In many cases, the senior leadership of a study is done by more than one person. In this instance, the PI is called a multi-PI, or MPI. This is not the same as being a co-investigator, a senior researcher who is on your team to provide some specific support (for instance, therapist supervision). MPIs make distinct and unique contributions to the study hypotheses and methods, overseeing an important aspect of the study and may even have their own team. For example, this book's authors have been MPIs on a study with another investigator, also an MPI. Dr. Areán served as the digital mental health expert and expert in industry partnerships. Her role was to also serve as the contact PI, meaning she conducts all the communication between the team and the funder. Dr. Pullmann was the expert in longitudinal, randomized research and oversaw the methods and data analysis of this very complicated project. His role was more than that of a co-investigator (which most methodologists tend to be on the team) because he was making a significant contribution to the hypotheses, analyses, and methods for activities that Dr. Areán could not provide. Finally, the other MPI, Dr. Tim Althoff, contributed significant methodological and data analytic efforts in Machine Learning and Natural Language Processing. He contributed expertise and insight that neither Dr. Areán nor Dr. Pullmann could provide. Indeed, Dr. Althoff managed his own team which had the expertise to oversee that team's work.

Another MPI scenario is when more than one institution is involved in a multisite trial. Usually, there is one PI for multisite trials, but in some circumstances, the lead investigator at each site will also serve as an MPI for the overall study. For example, Dr. Areán was MPI on a multisite project with Weill-Cornell Medical Center and University of California, San Francisco (UCSF) for a proof-of-concept study of a therapeutic video game. The UW site (Areán) provided the expertise on the randomized trial and psychotherapy aspects of the study, the Weill-Cornell MPI (Dr. Gunning) provided the expertise on the functional Magnetic Resonance (fMRI) data collection and analysis, and the UCSF MPI (Dr. Anguera) provided the expertise in video-game methods. Dr. Areán oversaw the clinical team, Dr. Gunning the fMRI team, and Dr. Anguera the video-game team. Although this is technically a small, proof-of-concept study, the expertise needed to conduct the study was such that no one person could ever effectively lead the project.

For projects funded by the US National Institute of Mental Health, proposed projects that will be led by MPIs must be accompanied by an MPI plan (see Appendix). This plan explains the rationale for why the study is MPI, rather than sole PI, justifies why leadership team members need to be elevated to the role of PI and why their contribution is more than what is expected from a co-investigator, and describes how decisions are made and how disagreements are settled. Having three PIs helps with tie-breaker issues, but when there are only two PIs, the need to spell out the arbitration process is necessary (and can often be very helpful). We note here that it is very rare in the United States to have more than three MPIs in the case of psychosocial interventions research. One of the MPIs is always listed as the "contact" PI. This MPI is essentially the one who put the team together, often had the idea to conduct the study (although to be an MPI, each PI needs to contribute to the creation of the hypotheses), and is willing to take on all the regulatory issues for the project (budgets, conversations with the funder, ethical matters, and final decisions).

The Project Manager

A project manager is responsible for the day-to-day operations of the research study. This person supervises and mentors the research assistants and sometimes the data entry assistants, ensures that the study providers are collecting and submitting appropriate data, such as surveys and session recordings (proof-of-concept, pilot, efficacy, and some effectiveness trials), and co-leads all required meetings with the PI. The project manager helps put together reports to the funders, the DSMB (see Chapter 1), Advisory Boards (see Chapter 1), and the IRB. The project manager often schedules needed meetings, works with the investigator on team management issues (staff attendance, work quality), and ensures that procedures and policies as they are detailed in the research manual and study protocol are being operationalized. In many ways, once the study is underway, the project manager is the key person in ensuring the success of a study, and in our group is a principal team member.

The job qualifications for this position will vary depending on the needs of the study, but in general you will want someone with previous leadership and management experience who has held a supervisory role, dealt successfully with human resource issues and is highly organized. Some investigators will hire upper-level graduate students for this position; others hire people with a master's degree in science, mental health, or administration. Some will assign junior faculty to this role. Assigning postdoctoral fellows or junior faculty to this role has some pros, but also a fair number of cons, mostly for the junior faculty or postdoctoral fellow. This role is not one that can be done part-time. Indeed, most project managers serve at least 50% time on small projects and 100% on larger projects. Some very large projects, like research centers, will have more than one project coordinator. While a junior investigator will learn quite a bit about managing teams when in this position and will often be in line to lead publications from the study, the amount of time and energy needed to lead a research team is such that it may impact the junior investigator's publication and other, independent scientific output. We are not arguing against having junior investigators serve as project managers. Rather, when hiring someone in that position, you must carefully consider the individual's ability to juggle both team management and academics. Further, even when the junior person seems capable of this juggling act, the PI needs to be very clear that the priority is to the research project and that can make for some interesting mentorship challenges. There is much written about the dual role of being one's boss and one's career mentor, and the tendency in the mentoring field is to advise against this dual role, or to acknowledge the dual role and share career mentorship with another, impartial individual (Boswell et al., 2017; Meeuwissen et al., 2019).

Research Assistants

Research assistants are crucial to the operations of the research study. They collect data and interact regularly with the study participants. Depending on your budget, the research assistant can be students or professional interviewers. Research assistants must be kept as blind as possible to the study hypotheses and should be regularly monitored for their ability to conduct research interviews reliably (see below). The qualifications to look for in a research assistant are prior interviewing experience, good organizational skills, and excellent communication skills. In the case of distance or remote research, where data is collected using online or app-based surveys, the research assistant will often have minimal contact with the research participants or may be conducting some aspects of the research interviews (such as eligibility screens or complicated assessment batteries) through secure videoconferencing, an option that became more prevalent during the COVID-19 pandemic. In this instance, the research assistants may also serve as the technology assistance contact to participants who may struggle with remote surveys. In this case, the research assistant will either need to have experience with the technology being used in the study or receive training from the project manager in the study technology.

There is considerable disagreement in the community as to whether each participant should be assigned to one research assistant, or whether the participant can interact with different research assistants. On the one hand, having a participant assigned to one research assistant encourages the establishment of rapport that might help keep the participant engaged in the study. On the other hand, any strong one-to-one relationship might compromise the blindness of assessments and thus undermine the goals of the study. Arguments on this concept will persist, but all in all it would be preferable if a rapport could be established between the project manager and the participants, and research assistants maintain their objectivity with respect to the participants. An offshoot of this argument is whether any repeated measures over time should be done by one research assistant or whether the research assistants should be randomly assigned to the repeated measures. Here, it is far preferable to have random assignment or otherwise research assistant biases may be confounded with participant responses and compromise the recognition of true participant responses.

We advocate having two or more research assistants if the budget allows. This is due to practicality. If you have one research assistant, and that person becomes ill, goes on vacation, or simply leaves, then you have no one to collect your data, and you will need to pause the study. If you have two research assistants, one can fill in for the other when the need arises. Having more than one person responsible for collecting data also allows for opportunities to test interrater reliability. Finally, for some studies, having two or more research assistants may be emotionally helpful to team morale. As an example, a colleague once commented on his mistake of not allowing enough in his budget for two assistants. His study was to assess how patients and families made decisions about invasive procedures in situations where the patient was near the end of life. This investigator had a difficult time keeping his research assistant position filled because the stories the families told were so painful to hear, and the patients were so sick, that the people he hired would leave the project because the job was so upsetting. There are also other options the investigator could have employed to support the one assistant (see below), but nothing beats having a buddy when you are conducting research on emotionally complex problems.

Data Manager

Sometimes the biostatistician covers the data management role, sometimes the project manager has this role, and sometimes an independent person or company manages the integrity of the data. The data manager's responsibilities include creating the database into which the data will be entered, developing the entry methods to ensure the data are entered accurately (even for computerized assessments), and providing the data for milestone and progress reports. The data manager will also oversee and supervise any data entry assistants when those are needed.

Data Entry Assistants

Because most assessments are now conducted using computerized tools, such as REDCap (Harris et al., 2009, 2019), there may not be the need for additional data entry assistants and the data manager can oversee the flow of data. However, there are still instances when data entry is necessary, for instance, in studies of populations where technology is not easily accessible. The data entry assistant's level of expertise varies from undergraduate students to those with a master's degree. Less experienced data entry assistants will require ongoing monitoring by the data manager, and more experienced assistants will still need supervision but will require less supervision and training and student-level assistants. Their job is to ensure that data are entered into the database accurately, in a timely fashion, and kept secure. Experience with database management is a highly desirable skill for this position.

Study Therapists (at Least Two)

The qualifications of the study therapists also vary based on the resources available and the hypotheses to be tested. For efficacy studies, the therapists are expert-level clinicians trained and closely supervised in the intervention and monitored for adherence. In effectiveness and hybrid studies, the degree of training, supervision, and monitoring depends on the study's aims. In most effectiveness, hybrid, and implementation trials, the therapists are selected from the settings in which the intervention is being tested, undergo a typical training and will be monitored for quality, but may not receive feedback on their performance.

Independent Reviewers for Intervention Sessions

Most psychotherapy trials employ some sort of ongoing therapist monitoring to determine if the study therapists are administering the therapy with the quality to which they have been trained, and in some cases to measure skill drift. Even if the study is an effectiveness study, and the goal is to observe how the therapy performs under typical circumstances, it is important for monitoring to be conducted to understand the final outcomes and identify potential challenges with manual adherence. The reviewers should be experts in the interventions they are reviewing and should be trained in the use of the therapist assessment tool, so that they know what is being evaluated when their sessions are reviewed.

The importance of having an independent review cannot be underscored enough. The Treatment Effectiveness Study (Williams, Jr. et al., 2000) is an important example of the importance of independent therapist monitoring. In this multi-site effectiveness trial comparing antidepressant medication to Problem-Solving Treatment (PST) and placebo in the treatment of minor depression in adults and older adults in primary care medicine, the final outcomes indicated that PST resulted in worse outcomes than the placebo condition. However, there were substantial outcome differences between the study sites, with some sites finding PST to be superior to antidepressants and placebo, others finding no differences and still others finding worse outcomes for PST. Upon further investigation, the sites that found PST to be superior to placebo and antidepressant conditions also had therapists who delivered PST of good quality; the sites that found PST to be inferior to placebo had therapists who did a very poor job of PST and of basic psychotherapy skills in general (Hegel et al., 2000). Without these additional data, the public would believe that PST was not only ineffective but a potentially toxic intervention.

Recruitment Team

The PI, research assistants and the project manager usually cover this role, although when conducting community-based research and research in partnership with care organizations and technology companies, recruitment will usually fall to the organization, and they will recruit through their own screening practices, records and registries, websites and other similar sources. For other types of trials, hiring a recruiter can be ideal for research with participants who are hard to reach, as the effort it takes to recruit participants who do not usually participate in research is high and having one person who has the time to develop community partnerships is worth the expense. The recruiter provides community talks and prepares advertisements and recruitment/milestone reports for the investigative team and the funders. As such, the recruiter will need to be a personable and outgoing individual who is comfortable with public speaking and willing to answer questions and concerns about research.

Biostatistician/Methodologist

There is a distinct advantage to having someone who fills the role of a biostatistician or lead methodologist involved in the study. That person may have a PhD in Statistics who has experience in clinical research, or a PhD in a health-related or social-science field with training in advanced statistical and methodological strategies. This is why in this edition, we will use the term "lead methodologist" to refer to the person who will help with methodological decisions that impact data collection, integrity, and quality, analyzes the data and then helps with interpretation. As described in Chapter 2, a lead methodologist or biostatistician often differs from an academic statistician in their knowledge and experience of practical and real-world study design and analytic procedures.

Biostatisticians and lead methodologists may work on some projects as a collaborator, a team member deeply involved in the project, attending research meetings, taking responsibility for design and analysis decisions, and methods implementation. In these cases, they would expect a certain percentage of salary support for the duration of the project, authorship on papers and opportunities to present innovative analytics. More frequently, a biostatistician may serve as a consultant who may consult on one issue or several, with the consultation to be used or not used as the researcher wishes. In those cases, the consultation will be collegial and cost little, or there may be an hourly consulting fee. In most cases, the biostatistician would not expect authorship on any resulting papers. The crucial exception is when the biostatistician recommends an innovative, nonstandard procedure, in which case, authorship both credits them with the innovation and provides protection for the researchers against reviewers who may balk at this type of novel work. If the advice is valuable, acknowledgement is appreciated; if the advice is not followed, then do not credit the biostatistician, as they will be asked to sign forms attesting to their contribution on a paper, and they will be disinclined to attest to analyses they did not support.

You should not expect that the lead methodologist or biostatistician will do the statistical analysis (some may, some may not). For that, you need a data analyst. A data analyst has at least the equivalent of a master's-level training in statistics. Their focus is on data management and analysis and they are often far more expert and experienced than the ordinary lead methodologist or biostatistician in the use of statistical computer packages. However, data analysts typically are not competent or comfortable advising on the design of research studies or the development or adaptation of statistical methods.

Finally, every researcher who proposes to use statistical methods in research should have some basic training and experience in statistics. Indeed, in the early stages of career development, a researcher may serve as their own data analyst. While it is not wise as a later stage of career development to spend the extended time needed to do good data analysis, it is wise early in a career to do enough data analysis to appreciate how demanding this work is, to understand how data analysis "works," and to develop the ability to interpret data output with a sensitivity to possible errors in the data output.

The "data-crunching" aspects of exploratory data analysis are very time-consuming, and errors are likely if great care is not taken. When working with datasets generated in other research studies, it takes a certain degree of expertise to understand the structure and contents of the datasets. Thus, having a data analyst to take charge of the dataset and to run and check all analyses in exploratory data analysis is essential. Involving a consulting or collaborating biostatistician as well is a luxury, and not a necessity, to check all analyses done and perhaps suggest other analyses that might be worthwhile, as well as to serve as a sounding board as to how valid and convincing your conclusions may be.

A good data analyst will always be essential to any research. However, in designing hypothesis testing studies, having good methodological and biostatistical advice early in the process is not a luxury but a necessity. During the study design phase, while writing the grant proposal or before the study begins, this person can provide input on important topics such as methods to ensure adequate statistical power and sample size, limit condition contamination, develop appropriate counterfactual comparisons, select or design measures, and data collection schedules. While the study is collecting data, the lead methodologist provides consultation on the issues that inevitably arise in a study and supervises the data management team. Because it is often difficult to find a lead methodologist who has time to dedicate for the full tenure of the project, as a really good methodologist tends to be in very high demand, a good alternative would be to obtain consultation on the proposal when it is in the last stages of development and then again when the study is almost over and analytic plans are being set up. Depending on the size of your study, consider hiring a data analyst who is supervised by the methodologist, as an analyst can provide cost-effective, regular analytic support. The analyst can also work closely with the research coordinator and research assistants to help design systems and regularly analyze data for progress reporting, data quality assurance, and safety monitoring.

Hiring Your Team

There are excellent books on how to hire and keep great people, but in general, the best way to make sure you hire a great team is to be very clear about what you are looking for, create a clear job description, and create a job interview form that will allow you to assess whether or not the applicant can do the job. Create standard questions to be asked of everyone applying for the job and if possible, include tasks that allow you to test the applicant's skillset. This will allow you to compare skill levels between applicants and allow for an element of objective evaluation. As an example, in hiring research assistants, when candidates say they have experience with a particular assessment tool, we have them administer the instrument to us.

For analysts, in addition to reviewing past materials such as manuscripts written by the candidate, we provide a description of a dataset along with a research question and have the candidate write an analysis plan including the steps they would take to answer the research question. With these types of tasks, we are less interested in the candidate providing a specific "right" answer and instead we look for complexity of thought and robustness of their approach. One colleague who conducts research in the Latine community conducts his interviews entirely in Spanish to assess the degree to which the applicant is truly bilingual. We note here that hiring fully bilingual staff is challenging, so this colleague recommends hiring someone whose language skills are at least passable and then offering that person many opportunities to improve their language skills, such as conducting supervision meetings in the less familiar language. This rule can apply to any skill if you experience challenges in finding the perfect person. In that instance, hire a person who seems able to learn quickly, then support them in their skill development.

After hiring the right people, the next step is to keep them! Very good employees have a habit of getting better jobs and so you will want to keep them as incentivized as possible to stay for the duration of your study (or longer!). Educational opportunities, opportunities for advancement, and other perks are often good ways to keep people on your team. Regular check-ins with team members to discuss how the job is going and whether there is anything the team could do to better support the member are also important—even if members are perfectly happy with their jobs, they often appreciate that you, as a leader are thinking of their well-being.

Training Your Research Assistants

In this chapter, we provide advice about the best methods for training and monitoring research assistants to conduct participant recruitment and data collection. We leave interventionist training to Chapters 6 (proof-of-concept), Chapter 7 (pilot trials), Chapter 8 (efficacy), and Chapter 9 (effectiveness and hybrid trials). If you are to trust the outcomes of your study, your team must collect data reliably. Note that in studies where data is recorded using electronic self-report measures, such training is not always necessary, however, research assistants in these studies will occasionally need to interact with participants, even online, and thus should be trained in best practice communication. The strategies we describe for training in research interviewing apply to these skills too.

The goal of research assistant training is to ensure that the research assistants administer the study consent and research interviews reliably and with compassion, which requires good clinical interviewing skills. The specific goals of training are as follows.

- In structured interviewing and survey administration, training aims to ensure research assistants administer the study questions in an unbiased way and by strict protocol. The assistant must be able to administer the research interviews in such a way that the participants understand the questions, but without deviating from the interview protocol. Some instruments are particularly strict about how questions are to be asked. As an example, cognitive or neuropsychological test items have to be delivered exactly as written, and any deviation from the interview protocol is thought to influence the test results. Further, the research assistants must use the same interview format and cannot differ from one another in how the interview is administered to research assistants.
- For semi-structured and open interviewing, training aims to ensure research assistants understand the primary research questions and the interview protocol. Research assistants will need to become fluent in common and effective probes and prompts to ensure research questions are addressed. Common challenges they should be trained to address include how to draw out shy or terse participants and how to focus on loquacious participants.
- If the interview requires coding, or if research assistants are using a codebook to code or quantify qualitative data, training aims to ensure research assistants code data reliably—that is, with good interrater agreement and adherence to the codebook. Before any coding of data occurs, it is essential to train assistants to a reliability criterion. Periodically during the study, there should be a recheck of reliability to avoid the problem of "drift" in the assessors' skills.
- Research assistants must be trained to accurately record participant responses to interview questions and to agree on how to quantitatively score participant responses. Where possible, computation of scale scores from individual participant response should be done by a computer rather than by hand. In that way, computation errors are avoided, the individual responses are on record, and if later, a different computation is required, that can easily be done.
- Training aims to ensure the interviews are conducted professionally, ethically, and without bias. The goal is to teach interviewers how to talk to research participants in a professional and courteous manner, to ensure

that verbal and nonverbal social behavior does not lead participants to respond in a particular way, and that the interviewers do not overstep their boundaries. We train research assistants to explain and remind participants that they are not clinicians, the goal of the interview is to collect research data, and that any problems or concerns participants raise to the research assistant will be followed up on by the project manager, PI, or clinical supervisor.

- Training aims to ensure participant responses are recorded thoroughly and data forms are complete. This includes ensuring assistants know to include only participant identification codes, not names, on forms, that the date of the interview is included on all pages, and that important observations during the interview are noted in a progress note.

Training method

All research teams develop their own means of training research assistants in the research interview methods, but they all generally follow the same format. In our team, training consists of the following steps:

1. Watching training videos that cover general interviewing skills and methods for specific measures.
2. Reviewing the interview protocol with the project manager. The project manager reviews data recording procedures and progress note documentation.
3. Observing an expert interviewer (generally the project manager) conduct screening, baseline, and follow-up assessments, and consent procedures. The assistants observe the expert until they feel comfortable leading a supervised interview themselves. This generally occurs after observing two or three interviews. An alternative to observing live interviews is to conduct standardized role-play interviews. Role-play has several advantages. First, it is less time-consuming and does not require waiting for participants to be recruited to begin training. It also allows for immediate corrective feedback and can directly calculate interrater agreement. The bulk of the effort in using this method is creating the role-play script and training the standardized patient to engage in the role-play. We have found, though, that the project coordinator and any graduate students or postdoctoral fellows can serve the standardized patient role adequately, with little training.
4. Observing the assistant administering the live interview. The project manager then watches assistants administer interviews until the assistant (1) conducts interviews professionally, (2) administers the

questions without bias, and (3) records the participant's answers reliably and similarly to the expert interviewer.

What if the assistant never learns to administer the interview reliably or professionally? Most institutions have a grace period when hiring staff that allows investigators to let go of staff members without complications. If you hired a research assistant, he or she cannot either meet or maintain your standards, it is best to find a replacement. The research interview is your main method of testing your hypotheses in psychosocial intervention studies, and without reliable data, you will not be able to interpret outcomes with confidence.

Research Assistant Monitoring

Everyone exhibits some drift from a research protocol when they become comfortable with the procedures. For this reason, the research assistant's ability to administer interviews reliably and professionally should be regularly monitored. A supervisor could listen to recordings of research assistant interviews and provide feedback regularly. Similarly, any team members who are engaging in coding qualitative data should be regularly assessed for drift. This process is similar to the original training to achieve interrater reliability. All coders and the project coordinator code a section of qualitative data independently. Each item is then reviewed, and disagreements on how to score the item are discussed to ensure shared understanding and continued interrater agreement. If one rater is consistently not rating reliably, that rater could be temporarily paused in the conducting ratings and retrained until they achieve consistency. We generally have a group of coders simultaneously code about 20% of the material, randomly selected, on an ongoing basis to ensure ongoing interrater reliability and stop rater drift.

Research assistant monitoring also consists of conducting research chart or e-record audits regularly. The data management team can usually help with the process by alerting the project manager to any problems they observe on research forms, such as missing identification numbers and dates on interview packets. Having the research assistant also engage in chart audits can serve as a learning tool to reinforce charting procedures.

What if a research assistant exhibits consistent and troubling drift from the study protocol? This scenario is generally prevented if, during the training phase, people who have trouble staying with an interview protocol are screened out of the study. On occasion, you may encounter a research assistant who needs constant redirection. It is important as a rule of thumb to have ongoing team member appraisals, with recommendations for growth. If over time, research assistants cannot meet those growth goals, despite having access to opportunities to meet those goals, then they should be replaced.

Lines of communication

In putting the team together, it is important to have a clear line of communication among the members and regular oversight. Having an organizational chart for your team will help team members understand the lines of communication. Figure 5.1 shows one of our organizational charts for a study.

Study Management Tools

Once you have your team in place, all you need to do is conduct the study. What could be simpler? Edison is often quoted as saying, "Genius is one percent inspiration and 99% perspiration." For our research, the one percent inspiration lies in the conceptualization, planning, proposal writing, setting up the study, and eventually analyzing and reporting the results (that's a hefty

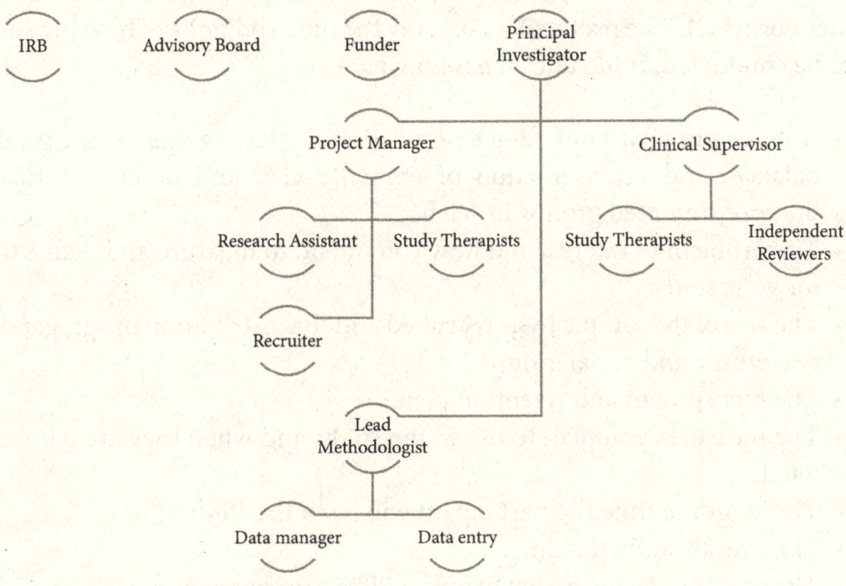

Figure 5.1 Template organizational chart for a research project

1%). The 99% perspiration is in conducting the study, the hardest part of the research process. You need to make sure that to the degree possible, your study is free of bias, that the methods are delivered consistently throughout the study and that any deviations from the original plan are immediately noted and corrected. There are study operations and tools that can help you ensure that your trial maintains high quality throughout its tenure. These tools are the study protocol and manuals, team meetings, study notes, the Consolidated Standards of Reporting Trials (CONSORT) table, and team management platforms.

Study Protocol and Manuals

The study protocol and manuals will be the most important tools in your study toolkit and will ensure smooth operations, provided they are referred to regularly. There are at least three manuals: the study protocol, the treatment manual, and the data management manual and code book. There may be more than one treatment manual based on the study design.

The study protocol

If your work is funded by the National Institutes of Health in the United States, this tool will have already been written for your proposal (its mandatory, under Forms G). The protocol is basically the nuts and bolts of how the study is to be conducted. It includes the following:

- A description of your target population, including age range, gender balance, and representation of ethnic, racial, and other historically underrepresented groups in science.
- The problem of interest and how you intend to measure and define that for your study.
- The size of the sample to be recruited and the distribution of age, gender, and ethnic and racial groups.
- The recruitment and retention plan.
- The measures you plan to use in the study, and when they are administered.
- The length of time the participant will be in the study.
- The overall study timeline.
- The study design and how people will be randomized.
- The statistical analysis plans.

- A plan for identifying, managing, and reporting adverse events and suicide risk.

The protocol can be registered publicly through clinical trials (dot) gov (US) and the World Health Organization's International Clinical Trials Registry Platform. In the United States, trial registration is mandatory before the study can begin, and based on our experience, when a manuscript from a clinical trial is submitted for review in a journal, reviewers go to this website to confirm that the method you describe in your paper follows the registered protocol. Likewise, many people will publish their protocol, and many open-access journals either have a section for protocol papers or their own sub-journal specifically for protocols. The purpose of trial registration (as we discuss in Chapter 2), is to keep you honest.

For the purposes of the team, the protocol may also have information about team culture, work expectations, roles and responsibilities, how to use team technologies, such as the team management platform, and procedures for research assistant and therapist training. These details are not published or registered but are important for making sure team members are on the same page about operations.

Often in the study, unexpected issues arise that must be dealt with. How these issues are dealt with should be added to this protocol (and dated) so that should the same issue arise later, it is handled in the same way.

The treatment manual(s)

The treatment manuals provide instructions about how to do the intervention, with instructions specifically for the study therapists about required documentation, including progress notes, documentation about missed appointments, and so forth. This manual is used for therapist training before the study, for therapist guidance during the study and to document the therapies after the study is done. Depending on the purpose of the study (efficacy, effectiveness, implementation), the manual will likely vary in detail. In efficacy studies, the manual is detailed and is reviewed and referred to throughout the study under supervision. In effectiveness, hybrid and some implementation trials, the manual will be adjusted to fit the needs and experience of the intended clinician. Many clinicians in practice have very little time to read an entire book or a large manual about a particular therapy. The involvement of the intended clinician in the creation of manuals or other therapy support tools is critical for the manuals or tools to be usable and to be disseminated.

The data management manual

This manual provides information about how data is to be managed and includes procedures for proper storage of participant files, data entry procedures, and data security. This manual also includes the data coding book which provides the variable names and how they are coded in the database. It is crucial that the documentation of data be complete enough that at the end of the study, the manual plus the dataset could be analyzed by any other data analyst, and all the data analysis could be reproduced by that analyst.

> *Does anyone ever really check your data?* While it very rarely happens, there is always the possibility that your data will be audited by an outside group. If this should happen to your study, incomplete documentation of the dataset and a resulting inability to reproduce exactly the analytic results reported in any publication would be viewed as something close to scientific misconduct. As such, it is good policy to conduct your study as if your data were going to be audited and that at the end of the study, you will be required to hand over this documentation and the completed dataset to an outside auditor. The current emphasis on data sharing means that it is not unlikely that you will be asked, if not required, to share you your data at the end of the study, and you should be ready to do that.

Meetings

While the importance of meeting with your team would seem to go without saying, there is often variability in how people organize their team meetings. Therefore, it is important to detail the different types of meetings and their content here. This will be the main way an investigator and project manager will ensure the study is being implemented as planned, and it is also an opportunity to troubleshoot any problems that may arise. There are seven types of meetings: the initial launch meeting, the operations meeting, the research assistant meetings, the data management meetings, the study therapist/clinical meeting, the executive meeting, and the data safety and monitoring meeting.

The launch meeting is critical and will set the tone and expectations for the team members. In the typical launch meeting, the study protocol and other procedural manuals are reviewed and training for team members commences. Our launch meetings are generally one to two days long and include a general meeting of all team members, discussion of the study, the study timeline, and team organization. After this general meeting, study therapists begin their intervention training, research assistants begin their interviewer training and calibration, and the data management team members are instructed in their procedures.

Operations meetings, which we call our Get Your Stuff Together (GYST) meetings, happen weekly throughout the study. Depending on where in the study timeline the project is, the focus will shift from initial implementation to data management and analysis. The team members who participate in this meeting regularly are the PI, project manager, research assistants, recruiter, and data manager. It is during this meeting that the research assistants report on their workflow, the recruiter reports on recruitment efforts and recruitment flow, the project coordinator discusses the milestone report, and the data manager reports on data entry efforts and progress. We will sometimes invite the study therapists to this meeting to provide information on participants' availability for interviews, as well as to talk about any participants the therapists think may be at risk for study dropout. The ideal scenario, however, is to keep the study therapist meeting separate from the operations meeting to maintain the research blind as much as possible.

The research assistant meeting is usually led by the project manager. They review any cases screened for the study, discuss issues related to participant eligibility, review follow-up interviews participant retention, and interrater performance. In our research team, this meeting is held weekly. In our meetings, one week is dedicated to inter-rater reliability in those studies where clinical assessments are done with the research assistant, rather than collected electronically, one week is dedicated to career development and one week we hold special topics, for instance an opportunity to discuss the impact of the 2021 George Floyd protests in the United States on each team member and the communities in which we work. The project manager also audits participant charts to ensure data are organized and complete and that identifying information is recorded properly on the research forms (e.g., no names are recorded, participant number, date of assessment, and assessment type are recorded on every page). Any deviation from these procedures is corrected in this meeting.

Data management meetings are often led by the lead methodologist or the project manager, depending on who is directly supervising the data entry team. During these meetings, the data quality is reviewed, including identifying odd values in the dataset, entry procedures, and plans for re-entering data where data entry between assistants disagrees. Descriptive statistics are often generated for crucial variables both to gain experience in the type of data collected and its properties, and to monitor for unexpected changes over time. To give an example, in a study in which cortisol levels were being monitored for one year, the levels reported suddenly increased. When the data manager checked, there was no apparent reason for any sudden increase, and he reported it to the PI. As it happened, the laboratory had changed its assay protocol without realizing the impact of this change on the data being provided in a longitudinal study. Immediate corrective action was taken requiring the repeat assay of many samples. However, had it not been detected, that important aspect of the study would have been completely lost.

As the study end approaches, the emphasis shifts from data entry and processing to data analysis, and ideally, before the last data are in, the programs to analyze the data have been set up and debugged. Then, as soon as the data are finalized, the analysis of the study results can begin without delay. The nitty-gritty of data monitoring and of data accrual, structure of the dataset, analytic approaches and so forth are vital to the success of the study, but the interest and expertise are focused within the data management group.

Therapist/clinical meetings are led by the clinical lead of the study, often the intervention experts (sometimes the PI) and include review of participant safety, participant retention (number of missed appointments, potential study drop-outs), potential co-occurring illnesses that were missed at screening and baseline assessments which could influence the study outcomes, and therapist quality for efficacy, effectiveness and occasionally hybrid trials. In our research team, when we are comparing two interventions, we will hold two separate meetings that alternate weekly, one meeting focused on participants in one intervention and the other focused on participants in the other intervention. When our clinical meetings are done this way, the meeting for intervention A is led by an expert in intervention A and the meeting for intervention B is led by the expert in intervention B. The project coordinator attends these meetings to record any adverse events or safety-related events to be discussed with the PI. In efficacy and effectiveness trials, once a month, information from the external evaluators will be provided and discussed for corrective feedback to the therapists. Often therapists make similar mistakes, and the feedback can be made generically to all the therapists in the meeting. However, any therapist-specific problems that arise in the review should be handled individually, between the expert and the therapist alone.

Executive meetings focus on upcoming reports to funders, data safety and management issues, recruitment and retention problems, funding issues, and staffing issues. The main people attending these meetings are the PI, the project manager, clinical supervisors, and the methodological lead or data manager.

All clinical trials in the United States funded by NIH must have a Data Safety and Monitoring Board (DSMB, see Chapter 1). *DSMB meetings* can occur once a year or up to four times a year, the DSMB usually recommends the frequency of the meetings. DSMBs usually consist of three members, a content expert, a methodologist, and an ethics expert. The DSMB elects the board leader, who will write up the meeting minutes and summary to the PI and funder. Prior to the meeting, the DSMB should have access to the study aims and hypotheses, the recruitment and retention/milestone reports, a report of adverse events (see an example in Appendix), and a progress report on general study activities. The DSMB members, the PI, the lead methodologist, and the project manager attend this meeting to address any questions the board may have and to listen to board recommendations.

Managing the team meeting

Given the number of meetings that happen in a psychosocial intervention trial, meeting management is critical. There is no reason that all meetings need to last more than an hour if the time and topics are well organized and managed. Most business advisors recommend that every meeting include a written agenda that is adhered to in the meeting, that extraneous, non-study related discussion be kept to a minimum, and that all meetings start and end on time. In our meetings, we do allow for some social time in the beginning, usually during our 3-minute buffer to allow people to get to the meeting. This can sometimes be difficult to adhere to, but a trick that has worked well for us in our CREATIV Lab and ALACRITY Center is to promise to end the meeting 10 minutes before the hour so that members have time to travel to other meetings, and in the era of hybrid meetings, have that time to stand up, stretch, and manage Zoom-fatigue. Interestingly, this adherence to this 10-minute rule has led to members showing up right on time to other meetings. Another trick we use is to always start on time (giving people about 3 minutes buffer) and then just start the meeting regardless of who is there (even if the PI is late). Because we keep our notes on our team management platform, late team members know that we will NOT stop everything to catch them up, they can go to the team platform and catch themselves up on the meeting discussion. One team member should be given the task of keeping the time and directing the discussion so that all items are given fair airtime. Everyone in the meeting should be given a task. See the sample team meeting agenda in the Appendix.

Equity and Inclusion in the meeting

We would normally put this discussion in the Equity, Diversity and Inclusion section of the chapter, but we feel a discussion of how to run a meeting so that all points of view are heard is really important to present here. Those of us who are members of historically under-represented in science groups (women, people of color, and cultural groups) can attest to how meetings can lead to feeling valued or feeling devalued. Several books and papers have detailed how common it is for groups who are historically under-represented in science to be interrupted more frequently than usual, have their ideas restated by others who then receive acknowledgement for the idea, or to be educated in the area of expertise they already have, all of which results in historically under-represented team members not participating. A few meeting strategies can help mitigate this problem. The first is role modeling and member support. This is probably the less ideal way to manage the problem but may be the only way teams can overcome the problem if they do not have immediate support from leadership – which as the PI, should be you. For instance, in a government committee during the Obama Administration, women felt that their ideas were only heard if a man repeated them, and often felt they were being interrupted. To mitigate this, the women did the following: they pointed this out to Obama (the team leader) and instructed him to count the number of times women were interrupted in the meeting – the purpose being for him to see how prevalent the problem was first hand; whenever a woman's idea was repeated by another member, the other women immediately said, "Yes, this exactly what X was saying a moment ago." Or "I think X, who raised this idea first, should say more about it." When they were interrupted, the women in the meeting would stop the interrupter and say, "I was not finished speaking." And then start their comment from the beginning. If it happened again, the other women would interrupt the interrupter and say, "I would like to hear the rest of what X was saying." Of course, these methods put the onus on the people directly impacted by the bad behavior. A good leader, you as the PI, should come prepared to advocate for your team members who may have had bad experiences with meetings. You can change the climate of your meetings to be more inclusive by doing the following: (1) encourage diverse points of view upfront and do not allow anyone to interrupt, unless one person is dominating; (2) include everyone as you plan. When everyone has a say in the meeting, it becomes everyone's meeting. We always ask our team members if they have something to add to our agendas and we always get to those items; (3) rotate roles every meeting. Assign roles of facilitator, note taker and time-keeper to different people every week so that the PI isn't always the facilitator, and the junior female member isn't always the note taker; (4) ensure every voice is heard, invite those who are quiet for their impression, even if it's only "Yeah I agree with what was said." (5) Share how decisions are made. When team members see how their input is used, they feel more invested in the team process, which helps them connect more deeply with the work.

Study Notes

We encourage investigators to have study therapists (in efficacy and some effectiveness trials) and research assistants collect as much process information as they can. Progress notes can provide much additional information for hypothesis generation and information to clarify study outcomes. In our experience in publishing study outcomes, we have on most occasions been asked by manuscript reviewers to provide information that is not in the research interview but is in the clinical record. In a publication comparing Problem-Solving Therapy to Supportive Therapy, a journal reviewer asked us to provide information about the types of problems the study participants focused on in therapy. Because we did not collect that information proactively, we had to turn to the study notes. Although the information was available, it required some digging to find it and from that point on, we have included in our clinical notes a section detailing the types of problems discussed in treatment and the treatment plan.

Project managers and investigators should also keep their own study notes to keep track of decisions made in the study and any changes that occurred in the study—there should be NO changes to the fundamental study design, although additional measures may be added to the study, and changes in recruitment sources can be made, although must be documented and reported in any publications, manuals and in trial registries.

The CONSORT table

The CONSORT table is a figure required when one publishes data from a clinical trial. The purpose is to show the reader how the final sample was selected, how many people:

(1) did not screen into the study.
(2) decided not to participate after screening into the study.
(3) were not deemed as eligible to participate after the initial screen, and what the reasons were for being excluded.

(4) were in the final initial sample and the number randomized into each condition.
(5) and completed treatment and follow-up interviews.

We use the CONSORT table to keep track of recruitment and retention. It is a good idea to create this table at the very beginning of the study so that there is an ongoing review of enrollment and retention in the study, as well as any correctable issues related to reasons why participants drop out of the study. The CONSORT table is also a good reminder to be aware of any potential differential dropout at every stage of the study (see Appendix for sample CONSORT). In future chapters, we will review additional reporting requirements, for instance, for remote trials and implementation studies.

Team Management Platforms

Since the last edition of this book, the world of team management software has literally exploded. In the last edition, we talked about how to use Excel spreadsheets and clunky Gantt charts. Today, the tools available make the first edition suggestions very old school. There are so many decent team management programs out there, we will not recommend one over the other. (Although, Prof. Areán (me) prefers Microsoft Teams because is often free to use in most universities and it works well with the other Microsoft such as Outlook, SharePoint, Adobe, OneDrive, Word, PowerPoint and—yes—Excel. It also has plug-ins for Zoom, Calendly, and other non-Microsoft tools.) We will review briefly what you should look for as you select a tool. We provide in the Appendix a non-exhaustive list of management programs we have used and they are all effective.

Why do you need team management software and what to look for in a platform? The reason why you need such a platform is that it will be the place where all your documentation will be stored, where everyone who needs to know can track the study progress, where meeting minutes and decisions made are saved and tracked, and all needed files can be accessed. Having everything in one place so you don't have to ask your project manager "where is the latest recruitment report again?" or "can you send me that manual, I don't think I have the latest version" repeatedly. You go to your platform and, voila! These platforms also allow for as needed tracking and intel gathering, team communications, and secure document curation.

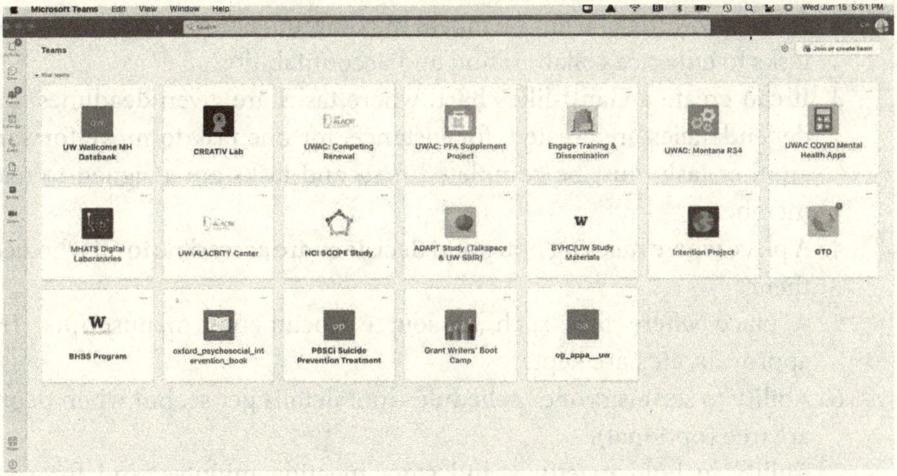

When you get to be as busy as we are (meaning, too many studies we are involved in), most team management platforms allow you to create subfolders where information specific to that study lives. See screenshot of Dr. Areán's Team 3.1. Each icon represents a different study, and each study has its own secure SMS channels, files, agendas, etc. (see screenshot 3.2).

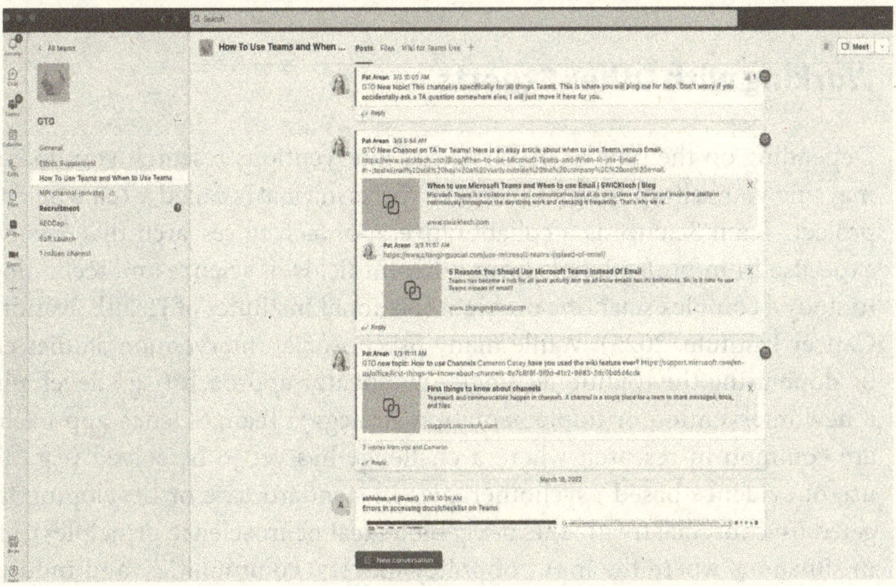

A good team management platform has the following features:

1. It has a place where you can curate internal communication with your team members, minimizing email trails in your inbox.

2. It has a way to tag team members in communications, documents, and tasks to enhance collaboration and accountability.
3. It can create a Gantt-like chart, where tasks are given deadlines, task dependencies are created, for instance, for one task to move forward, another task must be completed first, and tasks are assigned to team members.
4. A place where meeting notes and decisions are accessible to all who need them.
5. A place where files such as source documents, manuscripts, IRB approvals, etc., are kept.
6. Ability to see everyone's schedule—not details per se, but when people are free (optional).
7. Ability to hold meetings and store meeting minutes, and for some programs, record and transcribe the meeting.

For a team management tool to be effective, everyone must use it. This can be hard when you are working with another team on a project, and they have their favorite platform that just happens not to be the one you use. Therefore, you may become an expert in a variety of tools.

Working with Other Experts

Depending on the type of psychosocial interventions research you do, you may find yourself working with other experts in what is called a Team Science project. Team Science is a collaborative approach to research that involves expertise from professionals from different fields of science and technology to study a complex scientific problem (National Institutes of Health, National Cancer Institute, 2025). While many psychosocial intervention studies can be done using the traditional single-investigator approach (e.g., developing a new intervention or implementation strategy), Team Science approaches are common in research where a challenge has yet to be solved (e.g., the use of evidence-based psychotherapies in standard care or developing targeted psychosocial treatments using biological neuroscience principles), and in situations where the input of policy makers, communities, and industry is needed (e.g., targeting psychosocial interventions to address social determinants of mental health). Part of the challenge of Team Science is getting everyone on board and agreeing on a plan. Here are some tips to make that work well:

1. Create a shared vision and mission for the project. The last thing you want to do is to walk in and tell everyone, "OK, this is what we are doing." That is fine if you are the single investigator and everyone else is just a consultant, but in collaborative efforts, you will want to be sure everyone contributes to the project's vision and design.
2. Establish trust. Collaboration rests on trust between investigators. Trust is hard-earned, but can be achieved by being transparent about decisions, coming through on promises, and allowing space for team leaders to express their points of view.
3. Make sure the project benefits everyone's field. This part is tricky, but from our experience it is essential if you want your leadership team—the group of experts on the project—to be engaged. Early in our work in digital mental health, we were told that too often, people in health care approach technology experts to build a tool for a study, and rarely were these outside experts asked to contribute to the study in a way that benefited their own field. This is particularly problematic with the technology expert who is also an academic, because their promotion is based on academic papers, presentations, and other scholarly activities. If you really want to involve an expert from outside your discipline to be engaged in the research agenda you are pursuing, make sure you include them in creating hypotheses, developing the research plan, and you are thoughtful about academic outputs members of your leadership team and lead and own.
4. Be open to other points of view and be prepared to have your ideas challenged. Keep in mind that the reason why you are inviting collaborators to work with you on a project is that they have vital information and perspectives that could result in innovative solutions to a complex psychosocial intervention problem. Everyone will be sharing and challenging perspectives. Remain open-minded, do not be afraid to ask questions, and make sure that the conversation remains respectful. This latter bit of advice is important to heed. Not everyone you invite to collaborate will agree with one another. When this happens, it's important to remind everyone that the purpose is to work together, find the problems in the current thinking about a problem, and that identification of flaws in logic is to be expected and such feedback delivered kindly.
5. Meet regularly and often. Juggling the schedules of busy investigators is definitely a challenge. For people to feel heard and included, they have to be present when critical decisions are being made. It can be tempting to

prioritize (or de-prioritize) a team leader's schedule over other schedules. However, if you want to avoid conflict and the late introduction of ideas to the design of a study, everyone has to be present and that means someone needs to give when it comes to scheduling. During these meetings, make sure everyone reports on the progress they are making on aspects of the project they are the expert in. Clear communication about deliverables and timelines will help, and making sure everyone contributes to the meeting, even if it's only to say, "Nothing yet, but soon."

6. Pick someone to lead, or if you are the person who put the collaboration together, do not be afraid to lead. This means you are accountable for the success of the collaboration, and you will be on the hook to make final decisions and resolve conflicts when they arise. Be clear and transparent about the decision-making process, and truly elicit everyone's input. But do make the decisions.
7. Recognize and share success. Regularly acknowledge the contributions everyone makes, and when it comes to sharing the outputs, make sure credit is shared fairly. This means having a frank discussion up front about products, who should lead the development of manuscripts and so forth. Some Team Science projects give the project a name, and then in acknowledgements in manuscripts, that project name is listed as the author, with a footnote listing all the collaborators.
8. Recognize that teams evolve and with that evolution, so do the team dynamics. In the National Cancer Institute's field guide for Team Science (Bennett et al., 2010). the authors point out that team evolution goes through four stages: *forming*, when the team gets to know each other and agree on a vision and mission; *storming*, which is one of the most critical points in the relationship and is when people are most likely to claim their turf, when different perspectives are shared and disagreements may ensue; *norming* is the stage when the storm has settled and team leaders have established and agreed to their role and the direction of the project; and finally, *performing*, when the team is moving in the agreed upon direction. To ensure the process goes as smoothly as possible, be sure to ensure that the environment is safe and collegial and be sure to build on each other's ideas before narrowing down possibilities to move forward—in other words, allow brainstorming to happen, and collaborative decision making to follow (*What Happens in Each Phase of Forming, Storming, Norming, and Performing, 2020*).

Data Management

Perhaps the most effective method of ensuring the quality of data management is to ask for interim reports, not interim analyses related to the research question (such peeking should be discouraged). But other reports that simultaneously document research progress and the efficiency of database management. Recruitment reports, for example, document that the data being collected are being entered promptly into the dataset. Tracking the number of visits over time ensures that the appropriate corrections can be made for the multiple measures of that same participant over time. Descriptive statistics at baseline as participants are entered into the treatment groups document the success/failure of randomization but also document that the data are entered and cleaned and can be used. As you will see in Chapter 10, Remote Clinical Trials, such data monitoring is critical to ensure a digital study has not been "gamed" for the incentives, or that the study has been hacked by fraudulent actors. To give an example at the other extreme, in a multisite RCT, a request was made to report the number of subjects who had been recruited, and how many had been assigned to the treatment and control groups. This seems a very simple request, but it could not be done apparently because of the way information was coded in the dataset. It was a good thing this problem was discovered very early and repaired.

Ethical Considerations: Reducing Bias in a Psychotherapy Trial

We note that no study is ever bias-free, and as such, investigators should plan their studies to minimize threats to study integrity as much as possible. While randomization covers many problems, it is not a cure-all for reducing bias. Here, we discuss potential sources of bias that team members can introduce in a study, and methods for addressing them.

In a psychosocial interventions trial, one of the most important factors that the research team must stay on top of is the potential for bias. A key principle in clinical trials is the need to keep the research assistants, research clinicians, and research participants naïve about the research hypothesis. It is believed that such knowledge could influence the team's and participants' behavior and, as a result, influence the outcome. Normally, control of this source of bias is managed by keeping the research participants and the research assistants in contact with participants unaware of which condition the participant is assigned to, a methodological feature called research masking. Although complete research masks are common in medication, procedural, and in most implementation studies, or large-scale effectiveness studies, and in most remote trials, where contact between the study team and participants tends to be minimal, this is not hard to do, in efficacy and effectiveness trials, this is almost impossible to do. Regardless of how the therapists are assigned to a condition in any study, they are aware of the treatment they are offering a participant; likewise, participants are also aware of the content of the intervention they are receiving. In these instances, the lack of masking is not a major problem, but a lack of masking for the research assistants conducting interviews is a problem. One way to maintain a mask is to train those who conduct interviews to avoid discussion about the treatment received, and the participants should be warned not to discuss details with the research interviewer. Nevertheless, participants sometimes do let slip the details of their intervention, which can compromise the mask. Another approach is to keep the participants and research assistants unaware of the study hypotheses, or which condition the comparator is, and which is experimental. Although keeping a hypothesis masked for research participants, therapists, and assistants is probably the closest one can get to a research mask, it is still a difficult standard to achieve. Even if the team never figures out the true study hypothesis, they may have some idea of what they think it is and thus may inadvertently behave in a way that will influence the data quality. For this reason, there are no better ways to control bias than to regularly monitor the research therapists and assistants and to maintain a high standard of assessment.

If masking is compromised, researchers should document what happened, notify their Data Safety and Monitoring board, analyze the impact of the breach on the study results, and develop a plan consistent with the type of breach. If the unmasking only impacted data collected from one or a few participants, the simplest approach to mitigation is to remove these data from analyses. If it impacted many participants, the team may need to conduct a sensitivity check to see if any systematic differences in the data resulted. A method of doing that is to use a covariate to indicate affected participants and see if there are differences in outcomes. If the breach occurred in the analytic team, projects may need a separate team to re-mask the data by reassigning condition codes or even to independently conduct the analyses. Depending on the nature of the masking, the team may need to inform participants or even withdraw or end the study. Whatever measures are taken, it is essential that transparent reporting of the unmasking occurs in manuscripts and reports.

Investigator bias

PIs may introduce bias into a study by being closely involved in aspects of the protocol. Sometimes this cannot be avoided, owing to the stage of the study, or the amount of funds available to the project. This is not to say PIs should stay away from all operations, but they should consider when it is critical they be involved and when someone without a else should be responsible for a task. As an example, at times PIs will provide clinical supervision to the study therapists in proof of concept, pilot, efficacy, and some effectiveness trials, particularly when they are the experts in the intervention being studied. Typically, supervision occurs in a team setting and only issues related to confusion over whether a participant can be involved in a study and issues related to participant safety are discussed. However, in situations where the PI, who wrote the hypothesis and is invested in the outcome is also the only expert to provide training and supervision. In this instance, investigator bias is an issue, but can be managed (but not entirely corrected for) in the following ways:

1. Make sure the investigator provides supervision only to cases receiving the treatment that the investigator is an expert in.
2. Regularly monitor the quality of all treatment conditions and ensure that the quality is high in all treatments.
3. Arrange for supervision of therapeutic-specific issues to be conducted by an independent expert who has no investment in the study's outcome.

Chapter Summary

Building your team is an important part of conducting high-quality research. There are many great resources from business management and the Science of Team Science literature. We have provided a few favored resources in the Appendix to this chapter to help you along the way.

6

Proof-of-Concept Studies for Psychosocial Interventions

Critical Questions This Chapter Will Cover

- What is the purpose of a proof-of-concept study, and why are they important?
- What is the difference between a mediator, target, and mechanism?
- What is a go/no-go rule?
- What sample size is needed?
- What is the appropriate way to report on the findings?

What Is the Purpose of a Proof-of-Concept Study and Why Is It Important?

Proof-of-concept research in treatment development is the first line of inquiry when investigating the utility of a new intervention or the use of an existing intervention in a novel context. This research can be thought of as a design tool to understand and provide evidence for the mechanistic therapeutic action of the intervention. This work is very common in the development of pharmaceuticals and is considered a cost saving approach to identifying candidate compounds for the management of a specific illness. The best examples of these studies come from the field of oncology, where after a series of animal trials, a new compound will be tested in a small number of humans with a disease to determine (1) the optimal dose of treatment; (2) the compound's impact on the *mechanism* (the hypothesized cause of the illness; this is determined through a form of mediational analyses); (3) what the potential dosing schedule is for the intervention, and (4) the potential adverse effects of the new intervention (Umscheid et al., 2011). Once you show that your new treatment has an impact on the mechanism, changes in the mechanism appear to be a function of the treatment, and those changes result in improved disease states—in other words, there is mediation—then you are ready to move on to planning a larger trial (see Chapter 7). The cost savings in such studies are that

High-Quality Psychosocial Interventions Research. Second Edition. Patricia A. Areán and Michael D. Pullmann, Oxford University Press. © Patricia A. Areán and Michael D. Pullmann (2026).
DOI: 10.1093/oso/9780197681923.003.0006

if the intervention does not pass a pre-specified *go/no-go criteria*, then investment in the intervention is halted, and no more money is spent on developing it further for the purpose the proof-of-concept study was conducted. The effort is not considered a waste of time, however, because we do learn quite a bit about an illness and its treatment from failed proof-of-concept trials.

Proof-of-concept research is relatively new to the psychosocial interventions field and came into use in the US when the National Institute of Mental Health (NIMH) moved to an experimental therapeutics model (Moran, 2018). For many years, when we studied the impact of a psychosocial intervention, even though these treatments are developed based on theories of behavior, we focused mainly on the question "Does it work?" rather than "Does it work in the way we think it works?" One could argue that the former is more important than the latter. If something works, why do we need to know the mechanics behind its success? Fair enough. However, when you conduct a study on the efficacy of a treatment, all you learn is whether it worked or did not work. And that is all. When you study an intervention's proposed impact on the mechanism as part of the process of determining its impact, you learn much more, even when your study finds the intervention is not effective. These results could serve to improve the theory of the disorder and intervention design.

Let's say you find a new treatment to be effective on depressive disorders, as well as a proposed mechanism, affect regulation. That information becomes very useful to other investigators who may not be interested in the disorder you are trying to treat, but in the mechanism your intervention targets; for instance, investigators who study illnesses with similar underlying causes (anxiety, personality disorder) may find your new intervention quite useful in their work. Now let's say your new intervention is effective for depressive disorders, but not affect-regulation skills. This is still an important finding because, in the end, what matters most to patients, clinicians, and policymakers is that an intervention is effective. From the proof-of-concept perspective, however, what the investigator is trying to do is not treat the disorder per se, but to treat the underlying cause/specific characteristic of the disorder. When we find that the change in clinical conditions is not due to changing the underlying cause, we generally will have to go back to the drawing board to either understand why this novel treatment is effective or to develop a different intervention that will treat the underlying cause of the clinical condition. We do caution here that just because a *mechanistic hypothesis* fails at the proof-of-concept level, this doesn't mean that you would not see an impact in a larger, better-powered study. But, unless you follow our advice, you will have a harder time justifying a proposal for an efficacy study (see Chapter 8).

What Is the Difference Between a Mediator, Target, and Mechanism?

People are often confused by the difference between mediators, targets, and mechanisms. The "target" is the cognitive or environmental problem your intervention will interact with to produce a desired clinical outcome. The mechanism is the causal pathway through which the intervention produces an effect. Mediation is the statistical model that tests whether the intervention affects the outcome through this causal pathway. In the traditional approach developed by Baron and Kenny (1986), statistical mediation is established when an independent variable is correlated with an outcome and a mediator, the mediator is correlated with the outcome, and the correlation between the independent variable and the outcome is statistically reduced or removed when including the mediator in a regression model. Note that these requirements have been criticized and updated by others (Edwards & Lambert, 2007; Rijnhart et al., 2021), but this discussion is still useful for a basic understanding of mediation. A mechanism requires (1) statistical mediation, (2) experimental evidence for causation via longitudinal, experimental manipulation of the independent variable *and* the mediator, even though manipulation of the mediator often proves difficult or impossible to conduct, and (3) strong theory or rationale for why there is an association (Kazdin, 2009; Tryon, 2018). It may also require ruling out alternative explanations or mechanisms that may be a proxy for or correlated with the theoretical mechanism you are testing, which is also difficult or impossible to fully conduct. Therefore, mediation is necessary but not sufficient evidence for a mechanism.

In our example of depression and affect regulation, the novel treatment (cognitive exercises) is hypothesized to improve affect regulation (the target) through repeated training sessions over four weeks. Improvement in affect regulation after four weeks of training results in improvement in depression at six to eight weeks (mediation). It is important to note here that mediation, as a statistical model, is akin to correlation. The most you can say in this research is that changes in affect regulation after four weeks of cognitive exercise are associated with changes in depression six to eight weeks later, and that the statistical association between cognitive exercise and changes in depression is significantly decreased when including the impact of cognitive exercise on affect regulation and the association of affect regulation and changes in depression. However, this is evidence of statistical mediation, not proof that affect regulation is a mechanism. Even though you may find that your intervention is better at improving affect regulation than a comparator, and that changes in depression later are associated with downstream depression improvement, you will never be able to say that your intervention definitively cured depression via the mechanism of affect regulation.

Here is an example. Dr. Areán has studied the psychological treatment of depression in older populations for many years. Her colleagues, Drs. Alexopoulos and Gunning have found that some older adults do not respond well to antidepressant medication. These older adults share a unique cognitive characteristic, *executive dysfunction.* Although the team did not know why those with executive dysfunction would be particularly vulnerable to poor antidepressant response, they did recognize that these are remediable functions that could be addressed through a behavioral intervention focused on improving specific executive functions, such as decision making and goal setting. Dr. Areán had shown that Problem-Solving Treatment is a highly effective treatment for late-life depression. Previous research had shown that this intervention improved executive functions, specifically decision making and goal setting, in older populations and in people with depression. The team decided to test whether Problem-Solving Treatment could treat depression in older adults with executive dysfunction, and if so, whether the improvements were due to changes in executive function. Thus, the experimental, mechanistic model was:

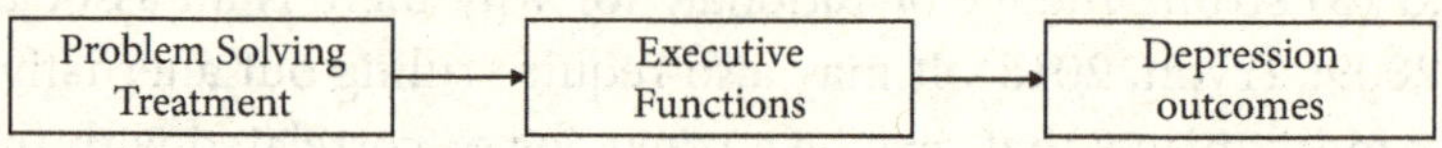

Examples of Targets

In psychosocial intervention research, targets can be anything from biological, neurophysiological systems, cognitive/neuropsychological, behavioral, emotional, interpersonal/social group processes, contextual factors, or social determinants of health. Targets will need to be measured in some way, either through direct measurement of the target through a biological assay to test, imaging technology, or some other form of observation, or through an indirect means, such as self-report measures. Ideally, if you can, it is best at this stage of investigation to pick two to three ways to measure the target. If you only have one method to measure your target, and you do not show that your intervention makes changes to the target (engages or modifies the target), then you will not know if the problem is your intervention or that the measure was not sensitive enough to detect a change in the target. Additionally, these measures can be tested for use as multiple indicators of a latent construct.

What Are the Important Tasks of a Proof-of-Concept Psychosocial Intervention Trial?

According to the NIMH, a proof-of-concept study can engage in the following activities (depending on the nature of the intervention):

1. Defining the target, identifying possible mechanisms to engage or change the target, and identifying objective measures sensitive enough to measure change in the target.
2. Modifying the intervention to maximize change in the target.
3. Demonstrating the intervention engages and changes the target with sufficient dosage, e.g., how intense does treatment need to be, and how long and how often should someone be exposed to the intervention.
4. Demonstrating the intervention as designed is feasible, safe, tolerable, and acceptable.
5. Developing an initial manual with fidelity measures.
6. Demonstrating research feasibility by recruiting and retaining a representative sample.

What you choose to focus on will depend on your intervention, the target, gaps in the literature, and the population. Some of these activities are also often tested in pilot studies (see Chapter 7), such as items 5 and 6. Which activities you choose to focus on will inform your go/no-go rule. If you want to truly test your mechanism, however, focus your proof-of-concept study on items 1–3.

What Is a Go/No-Go Rule?

A go/no-go rule is an a priori benchmark you set to determine if the intervention has preliminary evidence of an effect on the mechanism. In a larger, sufficiently powered trial, this would be achieving a clinically meaningful effect size with statistical significance. However, because proof-of-concept studies are conducted on relatively small samples (for safety and cost purposes), you will need to set a benchmark you can justify being evidence of *preliminary impact*, but not set the bar so high that you will stop investment in a potentially useful intervention. As of this writing, the use of proof-of-concept studies for psychosocial interventions is relatively new, and as such, we have few good examples to share. However, we have some experience with successfully funded proof-of-concept studies we can draw from. Deciding on a reasonable go/no-go rule is based on how you are measuring your mechanism.

Below are examples of go/no-go rules:

Example 1

AIM 1: Test target engagement following four weeks of treatment with GAME:

H1a (Circuitry): Four weeks of GAME use will result in improved Cognitive Control Network activation (CCN; percent signal Δ) and functional connectivity of anterior aspects of the cognitive control network (CCN), Middle Frontal Gyrus (MFG) and dorsal Anterior Cingulate Cortex (dACC) during a Stroop/Flanker task in 66% of study participants.

H1b (Performance): Four weeks of the intervention use will lead to improved performance on the Test of Variables of Attention and a delayed recognition working memory task in 66% of study participants.

H1c (Self-Report): Four weeks of the intervention use will lead to decreased complaints on the Frontal Systems Behavior Scale in 66% of study participants.

To move to the pilot trial phase, H1a and either H1b or H1c must be confirmed.

Example 2

Aim 1: To test whether a digital support tool (DST) improves patient engagement with digital treatment more than would happen if the patient did not have access to the DST

H1a (App Use): Participants who have access to DST will have greater in-app use during the first four weeks of the intervention use than participants who do not have access to DST. We predict that DST participants will use the app daily for the first four weeks, and app-as-usual participants will use the app daily for two weeks, then will discontinue use after week two and week four.

To move to the pilot trial phase, both H1a and H1b must be confirmed.

Example 3

Aim 1: To test the impact of an intelligent tutoring system (ITS) on skill quality in lay providers.

H1a (Time to certification): Participants who have access to ITS will demonstrate skill competency in fewer hours than participants who do not have access to the ITS.

H1b (Self-Efficacy): Participants who have access to ITS will report greater clinical self-efficacy after training than participants who do not have access to the ITS.

To move to the pilot trial phase, either H1a or H1b must be confirmed.

How to Measure the Target and Mechanistic Change in the Target

How you measure your mechanism's effect on the target depends on the nature of the mechanism. As can be seen in example #1 above, some people feel it is important to find changes in multiple measures of the same mechanism using different methods (e.g., objective observation, self-report, other report) and/or different rating scales. If you are interested in testing if your new intervention has an impact on brain function, the first example is a general good rule of thumb, as it requires changes in objective measures, self-report, and a performance measure.

If the mechanism proposed is dosing or the use of a tool or intervention, then you may be fine with just proposing that the intervention improves engagement with the intervention. As illustrated in example 2, the investigators were interested in measuring how engaged people would be with a digital support tool, with the assumption that great engagement would result in great outcomes. This is an objective measure, as digital tools allow you access to "meta-data" (see Chapter 11), which includes when, how often, and how long someone engages with an app. This research team also felt that satisfaction with the digital support tool was an important indicator of engagement, and further hypothesized that greater satisfaction with the digital support tool would result in better clinical outcomes.

If the mechanism changes in behavior, such as in example 3, then you should measure both objective and self-report measures. In example 3, the research team felt that the intelligent tutoring system would help lay professionals learn basic behavioral activation skills faster and increase their perceived ability to use behavioral activation. Here, they collected both objective measures (time to develop competency in behavioral activation) and self-reported efficacy in using the intervention.

When choosing your criteria and measures, note that collecting a variety can be better: estimating a latent variable, which can be very useful when conducting mediation testing, requires three or more measures for each construct. While your small proof-of-concept trial will likely have too limited statistical power to conduct latent factor analysis, you are also identifying candidate measures for a larger trial that will be able to do this. Selecting a mix of measures of the same construct that vary in methods is the best approach, such as including measures that use observation, self-report, performance testing, and reports from others, such as family members.

Who to Sample and What Sample Size Is Needed?

Who should be sampled in proof-of-concept studies is not a difficult decision; it should be representative of the people who are struggling with the problem your intervention intends to solve. However, given the experimental nature of proof-of-concept studies, you may wish to choose participants who are more likely to tolerate participation in a study that may require lengthy assessments, frequent safety checks, and may result in no or worsening response to the intervention. Participants will then be more like samples you recruit for pilot and efficacy trials (Chapters 7 and 8), and less like the typical person suffering from the condition.

The number of people to recruit also depends on the purpose of your proof-of-concept study. In the first example above, to test a therapeutic game on brain changes, this study only recruited 30 people because the go/no-go rule was based on percent improvement, and there was no comparator group proposed. The team felt that it was enough to recruit 30 people to determine with reasonable confidence that if 66% percent of the sample had changes in fMRI, that was good enough to move forward. In fact, they used studies from cancer trials to justify their sample and their go/no-go criteria. In the second and third examples, the samples were even smaller. In both studies, the sample size was 10 (five per group). The main reasons for selecting such small samples are that proof-of-concept studies are meant to provide quick, initial evidence for mediation but are not meant to be powered for mediation. Indeed, many proof-of-concept studies do not measure changes in the clinical outcome. You are uncovering evidence that your intervention might impact a theoretical mechanism. They are not meant to be definitive studies, just the initial step in the intervention testing process.

How to Write Aims and Hypotheses for Proof-of-Concept Studies

In the discussion about go/no-go rules, we provide two examples of how to write hypotheses for the first phase of proof-of-concept studies. First, highlight the purpose of the study (the Aims), and then specify clearly the hypotheses for each Aim. In our experience reviewing and writing grant proposals and applications to foundations and government organizations in the United States, Specific Aims pages are crucial, as they are the very first thing reviewers read in a proposal and create their expectations. Below we dissect each part of the Aims and Hypothesis for a proof-of-concept study.

Aims

In a proof-of-concept study, you will likely have two Aims. The first is to test whether the intervention affects the target, and the second is to test if the mechanism is associated with changes in the clinical condition. The Aim is best stated as an action statement in one to three sentences that reflects one or more of the study's research questions. Aims should include expected outcomes phrased as constructs (e.g., "engagement" instead of "time on task," or "skill quality" instead of "time to certification." Aims might also include time frames or other study-relevant material, but only if this adds important value and does not detract from their clarity.

Hypotheses

Hypotheses tend to be specific questions to be tested and are often detailed. Details include the type of question being asked (outcomes only, mediation, prediction), the measures to be used to determine an outcome (self-reported mood, a biomarker assay), the hypothesized time frame or dose needed to move the target, and what (if any) comparison group will be included. Figure 6.1 shows the anatomy of Aims and hypotheses for a proof-of-concept study.

When is a control condition necessary in a proof-of-concept study?

This question is a subject of much debate. In the pharmaceutical world, these studies are small and usually inexpensive, as a company may simultaneously explore several different compounds for a problem at once, looking for a "winner" for intensive testing. To keep the research budget manageable, these studies are often pre-post designs on a target without a control condition or looking for a safe and optimal dose-effect on a target by varying the intensity of the intervention. In this case, it is expensive and not necessary to have a control group because you just need enough data to see if a change exists at all. There is no reason why this approach would not be useful for psychosocial intervention development.

Once you find an association with a target outcome, the next step is to conduct a new trial to compare that intervention to an inactive or active control, or to another potentially promising intervention. This could be done in a pilot trial (see Chapter 7) where you are testing your methods and finding the best and most robust measures and methods to test a mechanistic hypothesis to scale, or even an efficacy trial (Chapter 8), if sufficient evidence

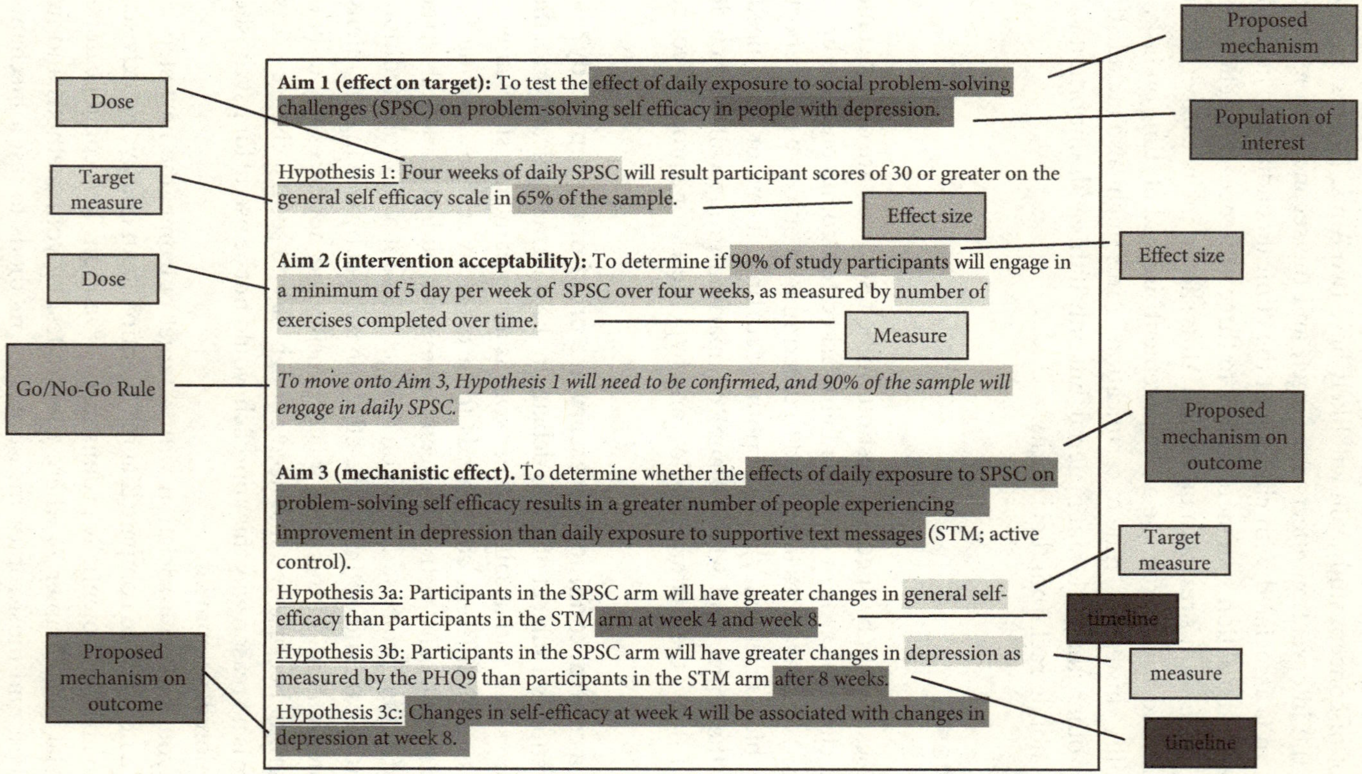

Figure 6.1 The anatomy of aims for a proof-of-concept study

for the feasibility and appropriateness of a larger trial is obtained in the proof-of-concept trial.

How to Analyze Data from a Proof-of-Concept Study

Keep in mind that proof-of-concept studies are quite small, between 10 and 30 participants, and that very early phases of these studies will only have one arm of treatment, the intervention designed to engage/change the target. In this early phase, when testing the go/no-go rule, it is best to rely on visual analysis of graphical depictions of data and simple, parametric statistics when conducting analysis. As in the first go/no-go rule example, the research team set the rule at a percentage of participants demonstrating a sufficient change in the target on at least two different measures of that target. In this case, the analysis was limited to the percentage of people who demonstrated a change in the target on two measures. You can use similar methods to determine if your intervention engages or changes the target enough to continue to the next phase of study.

What Is the Appropriate Use of Proof-of-Concept Findings?

Proof-of-concept studies are very preliminary. Their purpose is to determine if there is enough effect on a proposed target to continue investing in clinical research. While you could publish your findings from these trials, you must be very cautious about making any inferences beyond there being promise in the intervention and must specify that more work is needed to determine its true impact on both the target and clinical outcomes. Always mention that these studies are not powered to test mediation, efficacy, or effectiveness, but are meant to test an intervention's potential impact on theoretical mechanisms. Findings from these studies are never definitive, and to say otherwise is unethical.

Data from proof-of-concept trials is most appropriately used as preliminary data in a proposal to a funder for additional study. The data you report in a proposal or application to support additional research will be your go/no-go outcomes, the preliminary data on associations between changes in the target and eventual changes in the outcomes, and the feasibility of the trial methods. This reporting is important for reviewers for funding agencies to determine if the intervention is worth further exploration and is feasible to conduct.

Ethical Considerations

A proof-of-concept trial usually means you will be studying a novel intervention that has not been studied in the condition you are interested in changing. This means there are several processes your Institutional Review Board, or IRB, will want you to engage in as you manage your trial. Considerations center largely on participant safety as they participate in the trial and the methods you will use to ensure participants understand that the intervention under investigation is novel, with no known effect on outcomes. You will monitor participant safety, address adverse events and the methods by which you will intervene should any one participant experience adverse events. Let's take these in turn.

Informed Consent

In your consent form and consent meeting, you must be clear that the purpose of the study they are participating in is to determine if the intervention under investigation will influence a feature of their illness, not necessarily the illness itself. Some people participate in research in the hopes of getting a new treatment for their condition. This is a concept that research ethicists refer to as "therapeutic misconception" (King, 2014). You will also need to be clear that there is a risk the participant may experience worsening clinical symptoms and uncomfortable side effects, and that the research team will be carefully monitoring for these adverse events. This means that the participant may be removed from the study for their safety, and thus, continued participation is not guaranteed. You will also need to explain what the monitoring methods will be and what the study team can offer participants should there be adverse events.

Safety Monitoring

Likely, you will need to have a data and safety monitoring board (DSMB), as we describe in Chapter 1. The DSMB is responsible for overseeing the safety of your study and has the power to recommend that the study be stopped if too many participants suffer adverse events. To ensure participant safety, you will need to regularly monitor whether participants are experiencing worsening of symptoms, if they are in danger of a bad reaction, such as suicidal thinking or impaired concentration, and any uncomfortable side effects. Appendix provides an example of a suicidal risk assessment that studies might use to monitor patients. If your study is focused on target engagement or change in a clinically ill population, even if you do not intend to measure the impact of your intervention on the clinical condition, you will need to measure the clinical condition periodically to make sure the condition does not worsen.

Not all side effects are initially obvious. In one of our studies of an immersive therapeutic video game, some participants reported motion sickness. While not dangerous, it is uncomfortable; thus, we had to determine how best to address this problem, as well as warn future participants of this side effect. This means the study team must ask explicitly if the participant is experiencing unusual experiences they were not experiencing before participating. These need to be documented for further exploration.

You should report to your IRB and DSMB (and often, your funder) when someone experiences any adverse event, whether you deem it serious or not. It is important that the DSMB and IRB weigh in on the seriousness of the event, and your interpretation may not be consistent with others'. Co-monitoring the safety of research participants is a purpose of the IRB and DSMP. Keep in mind that side effects are not always adverse effects. Your IRB will want to weigh in on the characteristics that distinguish side effects from adverse events, so it is good to discuss a noted side effect with someone who is an ethics expert (Aronson, 2023).

Equity Considerations

Ideally, your sample will need to be representative of the general population, and some funders will require that samples be equitable regarding gender, race, ethnicity, and age. Additional considerations are income, education, and location. These samples are quite small, so disaggregation and testing for differences by groups is not advised. However, you may notice patterns in response and acceptability between groups, and this will be important initial (not definitive) information for your study. You need not be concerned with how diversity impacts your statistical power at this stage because you don't have adequate power to begin with. Therefore, there is no apparent reason to exclude these groups from your research; indeed, you may gather important initial information about the intervention impact in these groups.

Budgetary Considerations

Interestingly, the budgets for proof-of-concept studies can be very small to quite large. It depends on the methods you will need to test the mechanistic proof-of-concept. For instance, if the best measure of a target and target engagement is the use of a functional magnetic resonance imager (fMRI), the time in the MRI can be very expensive, and specialized staff are needed to set up the MRI for the test, prepare the participant, run the scans, upload the data and process, and then analyze it. As an example, one of our proof-of-concept studies at the University of Washington used fMRI, with the task time being 90 min, and each participant having three scans over the course of eight weeks. An hour of scanning time costs about $900. That meant for the scans alone, the budget was $121,500 for 30 participants. This does not include research assistant time, transportation, participant incentives, study management, data analysis, or regulatory reporting. In that study, the budget was about $600,000. However, for other studies that do not use expensive measurement techniques, the proof-of-concept study may be far less expensive. But as we detailed in Chapter 5, even for small studies like these, you will need:

- A project coordinator.
- At least one full-time and one half time research assistant.
- Time for yourself and a methodologist.
- Incentives for your participants.
- Expenses related to measurement.
- Money for your DSMB
- Publication costs (even though you may not want to publish the data, you can still write about your mechanistic hypotheses).
- Safety monitoring costs.
- And for those who receive funds from the National Institutes of Health, time and money to upload data to the National Data Archive (more on that in future chapters).

Chapter Summary

The proof-of-concept trial is the first step in the clinical trials pipeline, the purpose being to determine if a new intervention can have an effect on a specific feature of a clinical condition (the target) and if the impact of the new intervention on that target changes the clinical condition (mechanism). These studies are small and are not at all definitive, but they are useful in determining the next steps in treatment development. Psychosocial intervention development can benefit from this phase of research. Not all targets are biological or neurological; they can be attitudinal, behavioral, environmental, or a social determinant of health. In general, these studies are particularly useful when we learn from much larger studies, when an existing treatment is not effective in a particular patient population, and that population has a unique characteristic that differentiates them from those who do respond to existing treatments. That unique characteristic becomes the target that a new treatment may better address.

7

Conducting a Feasibility Study

Critical Research Questions this Chapter will Address

- What is the purpose of a pilot study, and why is it important?
- Should I use effect sizes from pilot data to justify a proposed sample in a larger trial?
- Can I publish the data from a pilot study?
- What data should be presented in a grant application for a larger trial?
- Even though it is wrong, should I still present the effect size from my pilot study in a future grant application?

In this chapter, we cover the purpose of a pilot feasibility study and the appropriate use of pilot study information to inform a future trial. You will learn what questions can be answered by a pilot study, how many participants you will need to pilot the study, and how to best present your data in a grant application. It is first important to review here the critical design elements of a randomized clinical trial for psychotherapy outcomes. They are:

- Well-defined interventions with clear manuals or protocols.
- Methods for measuring therapist fidelity to all interventions in the study.
- Clearly defined minimal therapist skill and training levels.
- Clear and reasonable inclusion/exclusion criteria.
- A feasible and reliable method to identify and recruit participants.
- A well-defined and feasible participant retention method.
- A reasonable participant incentive.
- A feasible randomization scheme.
- A clear assessment battery using appropriate and established measures.
- A well-trained research team (assistants, data entry experts, project manager, biostatistician, and therapists).
- Pre-specified benchmarks to inform decisions on whether to proceed to a larger trial.

High-Quality Psychosocial Interventions Research. Second Edition. Patricia A. Areán and Michael D. Pullmann, Oxford University Press.
DOI: 10.1093/oso/9780197681923.003.0007

Pilot feasibility studies give you the opportunity to experiment with these design elements and determine the best, most feasible methods for conducting your larger trial.

What Is The Purpose Of Pilot Studies And Why Are They So Important?

Pilot studies, an integral part of the research process, are feasibility studies to ensure that the trial can be successfully done as proposed. Pilot studies are meant to work out the bugs in a study design; to uncover hitherto unforeseen problems with the methods, materials, and any equipment you will be using in your study; and to provide evidence that the design decisions in future proposals can be implemented in the milieu in which the trial is to be done. Pilot studies differ from proof-of-concept trials (Chapter 6) in that pilot studies are focused on establishing the feasibility of study mechanics (e.g., therapeutic protocols, recruitment, retention) while proof-of-concept trials are focused on establishing the feasibility of therapeutic mechanisms. Too often, after investigators begin a large study, they run into problems and are tempted to change the study design mid-study. Generally, this is a very bad decision that could be avoided conducting a pilot trial prior to a definitive trial.

For example, Dr. T was conducting a randomized clinical trial comparing the response of caregivers of patients with dementia to psychotherapy versus an attention-control condition. However, the recruitment protocol was not effective at ensuring adequate numbers of participants. Therefore, the researchers made the difficult decision to loosen the inclusion criteria to allow fewer and less severe symptoms of dementia. This is not rare, as recruitment challenges are the primary reason why clinical trials fail, and loosening inclusion criteria is one of the simplest solutions; indeed, up to 85% of clinical trials fail because of poor recruitment or poor participant retention (Idnay et al., 2023). By changing eligibility criteria to improve recruitment, the trial was split into two: the sub-studies before and after the change in eligibility criteria, with inadequate power to detect treatment effects in either sub-study. This change also likely decreased the effect size for the intervention, as the degree of dementia moderated effectiveness. Any changes during a trial in eligibility criteria, treatment, measurement protocols, and so forth will result, as here, in splitting the study into disparate portions, with inadequate sample size in both portions, and may have other undesirable impacts. What should happen is that if a major change needs to be made, to protect the validity of the conclusions, the study done to date should be closed down and a new study begun. Generally, however, there is neither the funding nor the time to do this. Thus, the best advice is that once a study has begun, it should be completed with the original protocol. No changes should be made during a large efficacy or effectiveness study. This clarifies the importance of a pilot study, as the procedures and protocol should be near perfect for the final trial. We discuss the important dos and don'ts of final trials in subsequent chapters.

To do any pilot study, you will need funding to support your staff. Funding can come from university intramural funds or the National Institutes of Health (NIH; the R34 or R21 mechanisms), and some agencies and foundations will allow a pilot phase as part of a larger study. Of course, continued funding is contingent on the success of the pilot.

How Do I Conduct a Pilot Study?

There are two general types of pilot studies, those focused on portions of the methods, such as technical issues, and those focused on a beta test of the larger trial. When the investigator has previously successful experience with recruitment, delivery of treatments, retention, and so forth, there may be only one or two technical issues about study design that are in doubt. For example, investigators may need to demonstrate that there is a sufficient pool of eligible participants. In this instance, the pilot study may simply be monitoring the flow of eligible participants, using the past year's records in the clinic from which they will be recruited, to document the feasibility of completing the sample in the specified time. Or they may need to determine which of several different outcome measures is most sensitive to individual differences in response to treatment. In this instance, the pilot study might simply be a comparative study of the several measures' psychometric properties for their population, with the best one to be used in the subsequent trial. Frequently, the only issue to work out is to produce a manual or protocol for treatment delivery. The pilot study might involve having different therapists deliver the treatment and together compile and modify the manual that would then be used in the trial. In all such cases, the pilot study is itself not a clinical trial, randomization may not be involved, and so forth.

However, most pilot studies are a dry run or beta test of the larger trial. You would conduct the pilot study the same way as you propose to conduct the larger trial. In the pilot study, though, if you notice that your inclusion/exclusion criteria are too narrow or too wide, you adjust them and determine if this would improve the trial. If you notice that your recruitment strategies do not yield enough participants, you augment those strategies. If you find that your treatment manuals are unclear, incomplete, or flawed, you modify them. If you find that the outcome measure is not as reliable, valid, or sensitive as needed for your target population, you change it. In short, you can adjust the methods you originally planned based on how well the study is progressing.

Methodological adjustments should occur only in pilot studies, never during a definitive trial. If, during a pilot study, there is an indication of problems that involve participant safety that cannot be remedied, the subsequent study will simply not be proposed. If, during a clinical trial, such problems are detected, the study should be halted. For this reason, you should take care in designing the study; you do not want to waste your efforts correcting errors that are obvious from the beginning.

A pilot study will help you answer the following questions:

- Can I randomize and, if so, what is the best way to do it?
- What is the best recruitment method?
- What is a meaningful but minimally coercive incentive?
- Can the therapists deliver the treatment with fidelity using usual supervision, or will they need more oversight? This applies to efficacy and some effectiveness studies.
- Will participants remain in the study? What will be my anticipated dropout rate? Are my inclusion/exclusion criteria too strict?
- Do I have enough staff time and is it correctly allocated?

What Are My Options for Determining the Impact of the Intervention?

Researchers must weigh the feasibility, rigor, and appropriateness of several options for judging the impact of interventions using some method of comparison or determining a counterfactual. A counterfactual literally means "counter to fact," and represents what would have happened to participants had they not received the intervention. A randomized control group provides one type of counterfactual to an intervention. For research procedures, including those used for the counterfactual, to be tested in the pilot, pilot studies usually employ the same approach to the counterfactual as is believed to be needed in the larger study. However, if the primary purpose of the pilot is to test intervention-specific procedures, sometimes a pilot study will use a counterfactual that is less expensive and more feasible, such as a pre-post comparison with the intervention group. Many options for counterfactuals exist, all with benefits and drawbacks, and determining the best counterfactual is a primary job of methodologists. Here we discuss a few of the most common.

Pre-post comparison

In a pre-post comparison, there is no group that is separate from the intervention group. All participants receive the intervention, data is collected at baseline and follow-up, and inference about the effectiveness of the intervention is based on the degree of change between those timepoints (although, as we've discussed, drawing inference about effectiveness is not an appropriate goal of many pilot studies). In this type of comparison, the counterfactual of the intervention effect on functioning is the participants' functioning prior to receiving the intervention. The primary reason to use a pre-post comparison is its high feasibility and reduced cost compared to a control group study, as the complexity of randomization and data collection from a comparison group is unnecessary. Additionally, pre-post comparison studies can be seen by some participants as more appealing and by some scientists and practitioners as ethically preferable to control group studies because everyone receives the intervention. (However, it is important to recognize that this reflects a pro-implementation bias, because many if not most truly new interventions do not work as well as interventionists predict.) The primary weakness of pre-post comparison studies is that they do not control for the passage of time and historical confounds. Just like with the common cold, many people who are experiencing mental distress, especially when related to situational aspects of their lives such as a death of a loved one or marital disruption, will improve over time regardless of whether they receive any services or due to "regression to the mean"—when one observation has an extreme value and the next observation is likely to be closer to the mean. This is extremely common in intervention studies because the clinical criteria to enter intervention studies require an extreme value (such as high scores on depression). Pre-post studies may mistakenly attribute this improvement to the treatment that was provided rather than the passage of time or regression to the mean. Similarly, historical disruptions such as an emotional presidential election may have positive or negative impacts on the entire sample and also be mistakenly attributed to treatment. For these reasons, one may expect the largest effect sizes to emerge from this type of study, though much of the effect may not be appropriately attributed to the intervention. Therefore, pre-post comparison studies are considered to have less inferential strength than other types of comparisons.

Naturalistic control

In a naturalistic control study or a natural experiment, conditions are defined by nature or other reasons that are not directly manipulated by the investigators. For instance, an investigator may compare clients in two mental health provider agencies, one that provides a treatment of interest and the other one that does not. Sometimes investigators will use data to try to statistically balance or adjust for differences between the participants or providers—a common method for this is propensity score modeling or matching (described more in Chapter 11). These types of studies are also highly feasible and cost less to conduct than a similar study using more rigorous methods. Like pre-post comparisons, natural experiments are also more palatable to participants, who may not even know they were part of a study, as these types of studies are often done after the fact and participants' data may be shared with researchers in complete anonymity. The primary weaknesses of natural experiments lie in the high likelihood that the groups differ on important aspects that are correlated with their outcomes but not documented. Because naturalistic experiments use existing data, researchers simply may not have the necessary data to truly balance for differences between the groups, leaving unmeasured confounds that will cloud inference. For instance, a study may compare two groups of people with depression, one group that sought treatment and one group that did not. However, motivation to seek and regularly attend treatment is likely correlated with symptom improvement but this type of motivation is not regularly collected by treatment providers and is difficult to statistically control for. Many studies using statistical adjustment or propensity score modeling still suffer from this limitation, that is, not actually having the correct data needed to statistically adjust for differences between the groups, and therefore, these studies should be viewed with extreme caution. However, naturalistic experiments can be a powerful and inexpensive tool for examining possible trends while addressing the threat to validity from regression to the mean.

No-treatment control

In a no-treatment control study, participants are randomly assigned to receive treatment or no treatment, and the change over time between these two groups is compared. While this approach addresses the problem of regression to the mean (because a group of participants is tracked who are not receiving treatment and therefore the researchers can observe whether and at what rate they improve without the treatment), this type of study is very rare, as it is generally considered unethical to withhold treatment from those in need. Participants may or may not be restricted from seeking treatment elsewhere.

Allowing treatment elsewhere is obviously more ethical but it will confound any inference about the effectiveness of the new treatment. Additionally, participants may be extremely reticent to enroll in a study in which they have a 50/50 chance of not receiving any treatment at all. One might expect large effect sizes from no-treatment control studies, as the control group is not receiving any active care.

Wait-list control

In a wait-list control study, participants are randomly assigned to the treatment group or a control group that eventually will receive the treatment. These types of studies can be more acceptable to participants than other types of comparison studies because they will eventually receive the treatment and are good for situations when it would be unethical to withhold treatment for more than a short duration (usually, the wait time should be equivalent to the length of services). Additionally, if the availability of treatment is limited, this type of study ensures that treatment capacity is filled. Wait-list control studies also address the confounds of the passage of time and regression to the mean because the comparison group will experience these as well, so comparing the groups eliminates any effects of these phenomena from the group differences. However, it can be unethical to withhold treatment for even a short duration, and the need to eventually provide treatment restricts the ability to conduct longer-term data collection. Additionally, in wait-list control and no-treatment control studies, participants are aware of which condition they are in. Their expectations regarding the effectiveness of the treatment can impact the actual effectiveness of the treatment. It may be that those in the wait-list or no-treatment group do not improve because of their awareness of and expectations of not being in the treatment group, rather than what would have happened over the course of time. As with no-treatment control studies, one might expect larger effect sizes with this approach as compared to the next types of comparison we describe.

Placebo control

Placebo control studies attempt to address the weaknesses of no control or waitlist control by providing sham treatment and/or attention to participants. While this is more difficult in psychosocial treatment studies than in studies of medications, it usually means providing brief psychoeducation or commonly available information to patients. The goal is to remove the impact of participants' expectations from the treatment effect that is computed when comparing outcomes between conditions. Similar ethical challenges exist as with wait-list and no-treatment control studies; in addition, researchers sometimes may have to use deception with participants so they believe that they are receiving the treatment. Any time deception is used, participants must be debriefed after the study. Placebo control studies may be combined with wait-list control studies so that participants eventually receive the treatment. One might still expect large effect sizes in this type of study, though not as large as no-treatment or wait-list control studies, because the placebo group may be more likely to show some additional incremental improvement due to the placebo effect.

Usual care control

In a usual care control study, participants are randomly assigned to the new treatment or to treatment as usual. These studies eliminate many of the ethical concerns of the studies above and remove placebo effects from the comparison. However, in usual care comparisons, the usual care is often effective, so the specific treatment effects of the new treatment as compared to no treatment cannot be judged and the effect sizes might be expected to be smaller in this type of study as compared to those described above. Usual care control studies are one of the most common approaches to clinical trials and can be highly feasible and rigorous, as participants are assured they are receiving at least some form of treatment, and the sources of confounds and bias described in other approaches above are eliminated.

Active control

In an active control, participants are randomly assigned to one of at least two conditions: a new treatment and an existing treatment that is shown to be effective. These types of studies are appropriate when there are questions about the effectiveness of the new treatment above and beyond existing approaches, and when researchers are interested in optimizing the treatment approach in areas other than effectiveness, such as cost, efficiency, and patient satisfaction. It may be that the new treatment is equally effective to active treatment but is easier to deliver, less expensive, preferred by patients, or has other elements that might make it more desirable. One might expect the smallest effect sizes on functioning outcomes between conditions in this type of study because it is comparing against an active condition. Often, researchers will propose a non-inferiority or equivalence testing rather than the more typical superiority testing, where the new treatment is designed to have preferable elements while being at least as effective as the existing active treatment. Non-inferiority and equivalence testing require a specialized approach and the involvement of an experienced analyst.

Can I Randomize, and, If So, What Is the Best Way to Do It?

If you have had experience randomizing your selected population in previous studies, you may be able to skip this step. If this is the case, you are fortunate, as you may not need to randomize participants in the pilot study and can focus on other design implementation issues in your pilot study. You should always, however, pilot test the control/comparison condition, at least in some small percentage of the pilot study patients. You need to detect any problems for that condition—for instance, differential dropout rate, premature termination, and so forth.

On the other hand, if you have not had experience randomizing your selected population, and there are concerns that those in the population in question may not accept randomization (e.g., dropping out of the study if they determine they are not in the "new" intervention group), then you should pilot the randomization method and procedure. This will include how you describe the study to potential participants, how you obtain informed consent, and how you randomize. Any flaws in any of these procedures should be dealt with. If you should find that participants will not accept randomization to the control/comparison condition you intended, you may have to change that condition or change the study design to one that does not include randomization or features a more palatable approach to randomization in which all participating groups or individuals eventually receive the intervention, such as a wait-list control or a stepped wedge design. With the "intention to treat" principle for valid clinical trials, those who agreed to be in your study but then dropped out after randomization must be considered as study participants in the analysis of results.

One particularly amusing experience with randomization

Despite the assurances that treatment assignment would be determined by a random process, the participants in a certain pilot study were highly suspicious that some were being selected to get the "preferred" treatment. Despite all the assurances that to do other than random assignment would undermine the validity of the clinical trial, and would not be in the researchers' best interests, the subjects' suspicions remained. To deal with this, we essentially created a bag containing an equal number of red and blue balls, identical except for color. Each patient was allowed to examine the contents of the bag. When they were assured, we allowed them to shake the bag thoroughly, then reach in and draw a red ball (treatment 1) or a blue ball (treatment 2). Never before or since have we encountered participants worried that we were *not* actually randomizing, but it is this kind of unexpected snag that often can be detected and remedied in a pilot study.

Let's turn to Dr. C and their pilot study, where randomization was believed to be a concern for the population under study. Dr. C was interested in the comparison of a computerized asthma support tool for asthma patients suffering from mild depression. They wanted to compare a new computerized intervention to an information-only control condition. Dr. C was understandably concerned that people who would volunteer for the project might be largely attracted to the computer program and would be less interested in participating in the study if they were randomized to an information-only condition that consisted of a one-hour visit with a nurse about depression and given a booklet on how to manage mood. Dr. C worked very hard on the research consent to explain that the computer intervention was experimental and that it may be no more effective than a visit on how to manage mood when suffering from asthma. In an interesting turn of events, Dr. C discovered that some participants were disappointed to be randomized to the computer intervention because it required more of their time! However, Dr. C discovered that, despite this, there was no differential dropout between conditions. Reviewers of the proposal would clearly have the same reservations as Dr. C did initially but reporting the results of the pilot study in the proposal relieved any such reservations.

What Is the Best Recruitment Method?

In all our collective years of conducting randomized behavioral intervention trials, we have learned one important lesson: The best recruitment method for one study will not always be the best method for the next study. You will need to pilot test the best way to recruit your selected population, or at the very least, make sure the method you have used previously is still the best method. Thus, the best recruitment method is the one that you have found works best for your selected population and study type.

In subsequent chapters, we will discuss typical methods for recruitment used in efficacy, effectiveness, hybrid, multisite, remote, and implementation studies. If you are new to recruitment, the best starting point for piloting your recruitment method is to do the following:

- Read the recruitment section from manuscripts reporting on the clinical trial or the selected population you will be working with.
- Search for special issues in journals where methods for ethical and culturally relevant recruitment are discussed.

- Talk to experts and colleagues in your field about what has worked for them in the past.
- Always talk to members of your selected population and the settings you may be recruiting from about what has worked or not worked for recruitment.

These are good starting points, but not always perfect. For instance, we know of one study comparing behavioral interventions for caregiving distress in Hispanic communities in the United States where the junior investigators sought advice from a senior investigator who had been highly successful in recruiting people from Hispanic communities for their behavioral intervention studies. The senior investigator, however, was recruiting from rural counties, and the junior investigators planned to recruit from urban counties. The senior investigator had tremendous success recruiting from local churches, however, when the junior investigators attempted to recruit from local churches, they found that this was a less than ideal approach because (1) there were many churches in the urban county (most rural counties in this context had one or two churches), creating too much recruitment burden for the study team, and (2) many of the caregivers they wanted to recruit simply didn't attend church.

What Is a Meaningful but Minimally Coercive Incentive?

For some studies you will need to make sure that the amount given for participation in a study does not create another unforeseen problem. Most behavioral intervention researchers will offer about \$20 to \$30 per assessment; some may offer more if the assessment is particularly invasive. For instance, it is common to offer \$50 to \$100 for participation in neural assessments like functional MRI, as they are uncomfortable and lengthy procedures. However, in some populations, \$20 is a considerable amount of money (e.g., children, those living in poverty) and may be seen as coercive. The pilot study offers an opportunity to determine the length of time the research procedures demand from participants. It is important to consider the time a participant requires for travel and other expenses, such as childcare. These data can inform appropriate incentives. Low recruitment and retention rates in the pilot study can also indicate that your incentive is insufficient. A simple method to determine if the incentive amount is sufficient but not coercive is to ask your participants survey questions, collecting impressions of the burden of the research and the adequacy of the incentive.

Can the Therapists Deliver the Treatment to Fidelity With Usual Supervision or Will They Need More Oversight?

Your pilot study will give you an idea of how difficult it is to maintain fidelity to the intervention during the trial. As with the larger trial, you should monitor on a regular basis the quality with which your study therapists deliver the treatment and determine what is the best approach to ensure fidelity.

Piloting the fidelity assessments also allows you to determine how much time you will need for the external reviewer to evaluate your therapists' fidelity in efficacy and some effectiveness studies. Never assume that it takes 45 minutes to review a 45-minute session; some more complex interventions require the expert to review the sessions a few times; others may require in-person review for accurate evaluation of therapist fidelity to treatment. The pilot study will allow you to design the best approach to fidelity monitoring as well as the amount of effort needed to do this work.

Finally, if certain aspects of treatment protocols appear to be impossible to deliver with fidelity, during the pilot study is the time to amend those aspects or determine if they are worth attempting to pursue. Recall in Chapter 4, the use of Human Centered Design methods should help you with making the intervention more accessible, and a pilot study is an ideal place to make those amendments.

Will Participants Remain in the Study? What Will Be My Anticipated Dropout Rate? Are My Inclusion/Exclusion Criteria Too Strict?

One of the most important pieces of information the pilot study will provide is the rate at which you can recruit participants, given your inclusion/exclusion criteria and recruitment methods. Additionally, you should have your recruitment methods worked out in advance; it is fine to have different recruitment methods, if you document how each participant is identified. As noted earlier, you should not change the way you recruit partway through a definitive clinical trial. Almost inevitably, the samples you recruit early in a larger clinical trial will be different from the samples you recruit later. Generally, those recruited early are the "low-hanging fruit," those readily accessible and eager to participate. It is not unusual that those later in the study are harder to recruit, either because of availability or enthusiasm issues, factors that can also affect the effect sizes of the treatments. Randomization guarantees that both treatment and control samples are recruited from the same general population, whatever trends occur within that population over time. However, changing the recruitment method midway through a clinical trial introduces a cohort effect in your study, which impacts the power of your study to provide accurate results.

In the pilot study, you will need to keep track of how many people you initially recruit, how many are included and excluded, and finally, how many you can randomize and retain in the trial. During the pilot study, you will begin to identify elements of your inclusion and exclusion criteria that may need to be loosened or tightened to recruit the sample you need to test your hypotheses, as well as the best methods for recruiting the sample in the first place.

Do I Have Enough Staff Time and Is It Correctly Allocated?

There is an adage that a home remodel costs 50% more and requires twice as long as planned. The same is often true for research. One of the most important aspects of the pilot study is to understand whether you have adequate researcher time and if that time is correctly allocated to different procedures. Often, researchers discover that they have not budgeted enough staff time, particularly for research assistants and coordinators, to complete the study. Team science, which involves multiple investigators across diverse domains, may be especially prone to this. When writing grant proposals, it is important to obtain input on the planned budget from experienced research assistants, research coordinators, and project managers, as they often have a much more concrete vision of how much work various activities take. Even when this is done, certain procedures such as interviews, fidelity coding, qualitative analyses, and recruitment may take far longer than initially expected. The pilot study offers an excellent opportunity to examine this and determine if you need to seek more funds, allocate those funds differently, or scale down activities in a larger trial.

How Many Participants Do I Need for a Pilot Study?

If the purpose of the pilot study is only to document patient flow in a clinic source, one might examine the records over the past year in that clinic, with sample sizes of several hundred records. If the purpose of the pilot study is to generate information on the reliability/validity/sensitivity of outcome measures, sample sizes between 50 and 100 would generally be needed.

However, for the typical pilot study that is essentially a dress rehearsal for the clinical trial, generally 20 or 30 participants per condition will suffice, although we have seen smaller samples. Because you would anticipate making modifications to the research design during the pilot study, there is no intent to test hypotheses or to estimate population parameters. Thus, statistical power is not an issue. However, you will need enough subjects to assure yourself (and reviewers) that the methods you propose can be successfully done. If you make major changes during the pilot study, you might have to add more participants to produce the necessary assurances.

Should I Use Effect Sizes from Pilot Data to Estimate the Sample Size for Adequate Power in the Subsequent Trial?

Here is a thorny question. You will still get quite a bit of conflicting information from research experts on this question, even though this is a situation where there really is one correct answer: No, you should not. Historically, researchers have used data from pilot studies to justify proposed sample sizes in a larger trial as well as to justify the pursuit of the final trial. As a result, grant reviewers and writers have gotten into the habit of appealing to such information to make decisions as to whether a trial should be pursued or if the sample proposed is adequate, although we are beginning to see that this is becoming far less common a problem. Although we do see the tide changing in grant reviews, it will still be important for investigators to continue educating reviewers about the ills of relying on data from a pilot trial to make these decisions.

Why should you avoid using data from a pilot study to justify your sample size? Before we address this question, a few terms need to be defined. The first is *statistical power*. Statistical power is computed as 1 minus the probability of a Type II error (a false negative). In plain English, power is the probability that you will reject the null hypothesis of equivalence of treatments (get a "statistically significant result") when the hypothesis is indeed false. Put another way, statistical power represents how likely you will be to detect a *true* difference between treatments. Therefore, 80% power would mean that if there is a true difference between the groups you have an 80% probability of detecting it and a 20% probability of not detecting it. In general, statistical power differs depending on how large the non-zero effect size is comparing treatment versus control. Power isn't one number; it is one number for each possible non-null effect size.

A clinical trial is adequately powered if the power exceeds an arbitrary but pre-specified amount, in the social sciences, usually 80% for all non-null effect sizes greater than a critical value. The critical value is some assessment of how large the effect size must be to be of clinical or practical importance. Technically, a clinically important effect size should be decided in the context of the treatments to be considered using clinical judgment; but in practice, the effect size, standardized mean difference (Cohen's *d*), is often considered "small," "medium," or "large" when it is .2, .5, and .8 (it should be emphasized that Cohen himself expressed reticence and caution over using any sort of effect size interpretation in the absence of clinical judgment). Based on past research, the true effect size would be expected to be greater than the critical value.

Power is driven by your effect size and your *sample* size, the number of people you have enrolled in your study. In fact, "statistical significance" is better interpreted as "my sample was large enough to detect a non-random difference between treatment and control" than as "my treatment is much better than control." This is because two groups are almost always different and with a large enough sample size you are likely to find that difference with statistical significance even if it is of little clinical importance. If the sample is too small, you will have an underpowered study. Not only are you unlikely to get "statistically significant" results, but any estimation of the effect size comparing treatment and control will be inaccurate.

An effect size found in a pilot study is an inaccurate estimate of the true effect size both because the sample size is too small to achieve precision, and because there are often modifications in the protocol that will affect the true effect size. The effect size from a pilot study is very likely to grossly overestimate or grossly underestimate the true effect size. If it is overestimated, the clinical trial based on power calculations using that overestimate will be underpowered. If it is underestimated, the clinical trial will be discouraged or unnecessarily expensive. The point is this: Pilot studies by their nature are too small to produce reliable results; any tests of hypotheses or estimation of parameters based on those results will be either invalid or inaccurate. Therefore, you should never use data from pilot studies to estimate the sample size you will need in a bigger study.

So, what information should you use to justify a sample size? If your aim is to determine whether an intervention results in better outcomes than usual care or an existing intervention, you should always select a sample size based on the detection of a clinically meaningful difference between groups. Often, investigators choose a moderate effect size of .5 or the effect sizes in other studies or related issues that have had an impact on their field of inquiry. However, other considerations apply here. An effect size of this magnitude, though deemed "moderate," is fairly rare in intervention research. Many people in clinical studies improve without any treatment due to natural progression or regression to the mean, and many treatments are not highly effective, meaning that the difference between a control group and an intervention group at the end of treatment is often not very large. Additionally, the approach to comparison strongly impacts the expected effect size. Frequently used comparisons include a single-group pre-post design (comparing the intervention group at the end of treatment to itself at the beginning), wait-list control group, attention placebo group, or active intervention control group. As described above, expected effect sizes will decrease across this range of comparison group options, while the internal validity of the effectiveness aim increases across this range. We will discuss how to conduct sample size estimates for each type of trial in subsequent chapters.

After all of these caveats, there is one situation where you may wish to consider using pilot data to estimate desired effect sizes and resulting sample sizes for a larger trial, and that is when a field of inquiry is completely new and there is absolutely no existing research or clinical guidelines for basing judgment. This situation is exceedingly rare, as practically no field of inquiry is completely new, and it is the exception that proves the rule.

Should I Use Effect Sizes from Pilot Data to Justify the Significance of the Trial?

We have already argued that you should not use the estimated effect size on the primary outcome from a pilot-study randomized controlled trial as a basis of power calculations for the full-scale randomized controlled trial. But what of effect sizes on other outcomes, not for power computations, but for empirical justification for new hypotheses? In small studies (including pilot studies), researchers often examine the results on many possible outcome measures. In such multiple testing, even if there is absolutely no difference between treatment and control conditions, the probability of one or more false positives increases as the number of tests increases.

The biggest mistake we have seen reviewers and grant writers make is using the effect sizes from pilot studies to justify doing the full-scale trial, or more often, as a reason to not conduct the trial. The argument historically has been that if your pilot study shows no difference between treatments, then you would not likely see a difference between treatments in a well-powered study.

This argument is backwards, because the primary explanation for seeing no difference in a pilot study is inadequate power due to the small sample size in the pilot study. Moreover, the argument continues, if we do see an indication of a large effect size in a pilot study, this should encourage doing a well-powered study to confirm that effect. However, not only are these effect sizes (as for the effect size on the primary outcome above) inaccurately estimated, but there is now the additional problem of proliferation of false positives due to multiple testing, and that with a sample this small, even correction methods like Bonferroni tests are ineffective (Kraemer et al., 2006b; Thabane et al., 2010).

Moreover, the pilot trial may detect methodological problems that are then adjusted so as to obviate the problems before the main study starts. The decision as to whether a study is worth pursuing or not should never be based on a pilot study's outcomes, but on the robustness of its theory of change, its public health significance, and potential impact on the field, supported by the research literature, clinical observations, secondary data analysis from previous studies, and so forth.

Can I Publish the Data from a Pilot Study?

If the pilot study were a study of the reliability/validity/sensitivity of various measures important to the field, such a study might well be worth publishing. If the purpose of the pilot study were to finalize the manual for delivering a treatment, that information might well be worth publishing. An interesting case report that may result from a pilot study is worth publishing, as is the literature review that was done to support the study, and a methodological paper on the challenges and solutions for problems encountered in the implementation of a study. One investigator was able to publish the cultural translation method she used for a pilot study of problem-solving treatment for late-life depression in older Chinese immigrants (Chu et al., 2012). Another investigator published the theoretical rationale for the study she piloted on homebound older adults with depression (Areán et al., 2010).

The usual pilot study, a dress rehearsal for the RCT, requires a great deal of time and effort to conduct. However, such pilot studies generally do not yield useful information beyond the feasibility and quality of the study methods. It is difficult to invest years of work into a project and not be able to publish the outcomes from the study. But, as we detail above, data from underpowered pilot studies are simply inaccurate. As a result, it is not ethical to draw any conclusions from a pilot study, because those conclusions are likely to be misleading. This is true even if, in your discussion, you clearly label the study as an underpowered or pilot study.

The purpose of the pilot study is not generally to move the research field forward; rather, it is to avoid expending time, effort, and funding in a full-scale study that will likely fail or produce conclusions that will mislead the field. It is better, we would propose, both for the researchers and for the funders to invest one year and $50,000 in a pilot study to avoid losing the efforts of five years and $5,000,000 in a failed clinical trial.

What Pilot Study Data Should Be Presented in a Grant Application for a Larger Trial?

The data presented in a grant application from a pilot study often includes the following:

- Recruitment rates.
- Retention rates.
- Treatment dropout and data missingness.
- Length of time to complete assessments.
- Ability of therapists to provide all treatments with fidelity.
- Information on how the treatment manual was adapted or created (see Chapter 4).
- Any barriers encountered to implementation, and methods for overcoming them.

We turn to Dr. C again, the investigator who piloted a computer intervention for depression and asthma management. In this application for the larger trial, Dr. C indicated that based on sample size calculations to detect a small critical effect size (the patients were only mildly depressed), the study would need 300 participants. Dr. C first documented in the application that over a 4-year period, they would be able to recruit 300 participants because in the pilot study, they were able to recruit approximately 12 people a month and experienced only a 20% research participation decline rate, equally distributed between the two study conditions. To be conservative, Dr. C indicated that a 30% decline rate was more common in larger trials, and even with that proportion, they would still be able to recruit 300 people in 4 years. Dr. C also reported that no participant required more than 1 hour to complete the assessment battery proposed, that participants were able to tolerate the assessment time well, completing all assessments with few problems and little missing data, that no participant rated the research procedures as overly burdensome, and that 75% of participants felt the incentive was appropriate for the levels of participation. In the grant proposal, Dr. C described how they had originally developed a ten-session computer program but found that a program with only four sessions was better tolerated and seemed to result in outcomes as good as those with the longer intervention. Dr. C documented that for younger participants, the computer program was easy to use, but for older participants, the research assistant would need to walk the participant through the program first. As a result, the intervention included this guidance in the treatment program for anyone with limited experience using computers. By reporting these data, Dr. C was able to show that not only was the proposed study feasible, but it was also well planned and that potential barriers were already determined, and methods created to overcome them.

Even Though It Is Inaccurate, Should I Still Present the Effect Size from My Pilot Study in a Future Grant Application?

Although there has been considerable movement in the field to educate reviewers that nothing can be gained from the review of effect sizes from small pilot, underpowered studies, there are still a few reviewers who want to see effect sizes and equate them with justification to support the study. If you refuse to provide them, suspicion may arise that you are hiding something.

Report the effect sizes if you must. We often preface this by reminding reviewers about the purpose of pilot studies and citing experts about their misuse. Report the effect size for the proposed primary outcome with its confidence intervals, which clarifies how inaccurate it is. If there are multiple outcomes, the confidence intervals should be based on adjustments for multiple testing, which will indicate even more strongly how inaccurate these effect size estimates are. Caution the reviewers about any modifications made during the pilot study, and thus, that the effect sizes are speculative at best. The power of the proposed study would continue to be based on the critical value that determines its public health significance, not on any effect sizes from the pilot study. Beyond that, the justification for the study rests heavily on how innovative it is and its public health impact.

Ethical Considerations

Even though a pilot study is not the final trial, and you will not necessarily be reporting any outcomes of your trial in publications, you will still need to acquire Institutional Review Board (IRB) approval for the study, for the IRB is primarily concerned with the welfare of patients participating in clinical research projects. The IRB for a pilot study is virtually the same as it is for a larger trial, except that you will be indicating to the IRB that this study is to determine the feasibility for a future trial.

Budgetary Considerations

The budget for a pilot study is a scaled-down version of the budget for the final trial. The main difference is that you will not need as much overall staff time to conduct the pilot study, but you need *more* staff time per participant than in a final trial, as procedures will be in development. Some of the decisions around staffing will depend on how much money the funding agencies allow for pilot trials. For instance, most of the institutes at NIH in the United States use the R34 mechanism to support pilot studies. These only allow for $450,000 to be used over three years, total. However, recently, the National Institute of Mental Health began using the modular R01 mechanism, which provides up to $750,000 total to be used over 3 years. The basic pilot budget for a psychosocial intervention trial will need the following items:

Your time. Because you are overseeing a large part of the project and will likely be more involved in the day-in-and-day-out operations, you may need more of your time dedicated to the pilot study than the actual trial. It is not unusual for budgets to include 30% of the investigator's time in oversight and decision-making for a pilot study. Your time may be dedicated to the following tasks:

- IRB acquisition and communication.
- Oversight of the coordinator's duties (should you choose to hire one at this time).
- Supervision of the therapists and research assistants.
- Communication with funders.
- Decisions regarding changes in the protocol.

Your project coordinator. Because you are more involved in the execution of a pilot study than of the larger trial, you may not need as much coordinator time. However, the pilot study is a good time to train your project coordinator and to ensure that the necessary skills are already in place when the clinical trial begins. You will need the coordinator to do the following tasks:

- Oversee recruitment.
- Oversee randomization (if you will be randomizing).
- Oversee research assistant training and fidelity to the assessment protocol.
- Coordinate therapist schedules for patients.
- Coordinate reports from the study team and participants about the acceptability of the study procedures, protocols, and respondent burden.

Research assistant time. Most pilot studies get by with *two part-time* research assistants who perform the assessment battery and data entry of any important process data from the pilot study (patient acceptability of protocols, length of assessments, etc.).

Therapist time. Who the therapist in the study is depends on the purpose of the study. If your pilot study is to prepare for an efficacy trial, the therapists may be advanced graduate students, licensed clinicians, or the investigator (the investigator should see no more than 15% of the participants). When the study is a pilot effectiveness study, then the therapists will be from the setting where the intervention is meant to be delivered, for instance, a school or outpatient clinic. If the intent is to test the effectiveness of introducing a new staff person into a service setting, then the study therapist should be representative of what could be the typical provider in that setting. The percentage of time will depend quite a bit on the number of years you have to do the pilot study and the number of participants you will recruit. Generally, a pilot study can be supported with a 25% time therapist over a 3-year period for study therapists in efficacy trials, and in most cases, you will only need to cover time in research activities that cannot be billed for in effectiveness studies; the National Institute of Mental Health does not pay for clinician time spent in activities that can be billed.

Participant fees. Because you will be asking participants to engage in research interviews and provide you with feedback about the interview, therapy, and research experience, you will need to reimburse them for their time. As we will explain in the next chapter, the amount you give should not exceed a value that can be seen as coercive, and the amount should not be so low that it would not be valuable to the participant. Generally, investigators offer $20 to $30 per hour, per participant, as a standard incentive.

Supplies. You will need some funds for recruitment materials, duplication of measures (in those cases where you can duplicate the assessment), miscellaneous office supplies, audio-recorders for fidelity monitoring, and communication costs.

The National Institutes of Health has three mechanisms that support pilot projects: the R21 (2 years, for no more than $300,000 for all years), the R34 (3 years, $450,000 for all years), and the National Institute of Mental Health now supports pilot studies using the Modular R01 mechanism (3 years, $750,000). Some foundations also have pilot funds; for instance, the National Association for Research in Schizophrenia and Affective Disorders has a junior faculty award, and the Robert Wood Johnson Foundation sometimes offers pilot funding awards.

Chapter Summary

The pilot study serves as (1) a dress rehearsal for a larger trial; (2) an opportunity to test assessment battery accuracy; and (3) an opportunity to test methods and finalize psychotherapy manual development and adaptation. Information you can publish from pilot studies includes the literature review for the proposed study, case reports from the pilot, and descriptions of methods and procedures. What should not be reported are actual outcome data from a pilot study, as you will likely be tweaking your procedures (and hence changing methods midstream) and because effect sizes from these studies are often unstable estimates of outcomes. Although reviewers will often expect to see effect sizes reported from a pilot study, the value of a study proposal should always be based on its public health significance, the impact it may have on the field, and its innovation. In preparing grant applications using pilot data, we recommend that you do provide all information asked but emphasize to reviewers that effect sizes from small studies are unstable and that your study should be considered based on its potential impact. Cite the papers in the Resources section as support for your argument.

8
Efficacy Trials

Critical Questions This Chapter Will Address

- What is the purpose of an efficacy trial?
- When is it appropriate to conduct an efficacy trial?
- Who is appropriate for recruitment into efficacy trials?
- What sample size is needed for an efficacy trial?
- What is the typical timeline of an efficacy trial?
- How do you train and monitor therapists and research assistants?
- Can I change my recruitment strategy or eligibility criteria if I am having trouble identifying participants?
- What are common problems in efficacy trials?
- What do I need to report to my IRB and Data Safety and Monitoring Board?
- What should be reported in progress reports during and after the trial?

What Is the Purpose of an Efficacy Trial?

The purpose of efficacy trials is to determine the relative impact of an experimental intervention versus a control or common standard of care condition under optimal conditions. Efficacy trials give preference to internal validity (controls for confounding) over external validity (generalizability), as the purpose is to determine whether the intervention is safe and efficacious in a large number of participants with the problem. Efficacy trials provide an opportunity to identify the safety and possible risks of the intervention under highly controlled and responsive conditions. You will have already tested the initial hypothesized dose in a proof-of-concept trial and finalized the treatment specifics in a pilot trial. Here, you will be looking to confirm the efficacy of an intervention (Agency for Healthcare Research and Quality, 2006), and in the United States, where federal funders expect the experimental therapeutics approach, you will also be looking to see if the intervention engages the mechanism in your theoretical model. End-point outcomes will include self-reported and objective measures of changes in behavior or symptoms

High-Quality Psychosocial Interventions Research. Second Edition. Patricia A. Areán and Michael D. Pullmann, Oxford University Press. © Patricia A. Areán and Michael D. Pullmann (2026).
DOI: 10.1093/oso/9780197681923.003.0008

that characterize the problem or illness with which you wish to intervene, changes in functioning, and broad safety and tolerability of the intervention. Intermediate assessments will be necessary in testing the impact on putative mechanisms, and those can be, like in the proof-of-concept trial, various levels of assessment: neurological, objective, and subjective, depending on the proposed mechanism.

The design of an efficacy trial is highly controlled, and this is what primarily distinguishes it from an effectiveness trial. Participants are always volunteers and often recruited from and seen in academic research settings, rather than in community settings (although there can be exceptions to this rule). The clinicians will usually be highly trained experts in the interventions you are testing and will be monitored closely to maintain fidelity to treatment. As such, the data from these trials will be useful for determining the therapeutic effect of an intervention, but not how it will function when delivered to scale and in the typical community setting—this latter goal is the purpose of effectiveness and hybrid trials (Chapter 9).

Before we discuss the details of conducting an efficacy trial, it is important to point out the two key issues in conducting a clinical trial that are specific to psychosocial intervention trials. These are:

1) The dose of psychotherapy. People and supporting materials (e.g., participant manuals and worksheets) are the main mode of delivery of the active psychotherapeutic ingredients, and as such, there is inherent variability in the dosing of treatment. For this reason, the psychotherapy sessions and any between-session work participants engage in must be closely monitored. In efficacy trials, any significant deviation in treatment delivery by the therapist must be corrected to ensure that participants are receiving the maximum exposure to treatment.
2) The ability to keep research assistants blind to study conditions and therapists blind to the study hypotheses is another major issue specific to psychosocial interventions. As we will discuss further, study masking is hard to do in psychosocial intervention studies, more so than in device or medication trials. Most of the time, outcomes are assessed through assessor impression or participant self-report, which is subject to respondent bias. However, there are strategies to mitigate the effects of potentially unmasking or accounting for the potential effects of participant, provider, and assessor influence on outcome reporting. You will need to demonstrate in grant proposals, presentations, and manuscripts how you accounted for preserving some degree of masking, or why it was not possible to mask.

These two issues add a layer of complexity to psychosocial intervention trials and mean that the study team is somewhat different than what is seen in other clinical trial teams. It also means that the interpretation of the data needs to be made in the context of how well the study team managed these two factors.

When Is It Appropriate to Conduct an Efficacy Trial?

Traditionally, efficacy trials have been a logical next step for intervention development and testing after a proof-of-concept and/or pilot trial is completed but before an effectiveness trial can begin. The logic has been that it is important to establish that an intervention is safe and efficacious under the best possible circumstances before attempting to discover if it is then effective in real-world circumstances. Highly controlled settings are also a safer way to conduct an initial large-scale test because researchers can be more responsive should problems or adverse reactions arise. However, there are some weaknesses in this approach. First, it may be that an intervention, however efficacious in highly controlled settings, will never work in the real world. In fact, hundreds of evidence-based practices have been developed and tested but very few ever make it into widespread real-world implementation. Implementation factors such as limited resources, lack of access to trained and responsive supervision, high levels of patient comorbidity, lack of leadership support, and clinical social norms that are resistant to implementation act as barriers that make it impractical to ever implement certain interventions. In efficacy trials, researchers attempt to minimize these factors in favor of maximizing clinical impact via experimental control. Researchers often exclude participatory involvement in decision-making by practitioners or community members that might otherwise highlight these factors as essential elements for consideration (Beidas et al., 2023). However, not focusing on implementation factors during the earliest stages of intervention development will lead to the inefficient use of research time and money if the intervention is not feasible in real-world settings or applicable to real-world populations (Chambers et al., 2010). The lack of consideration for implementation challenges and the fact that rarely do consumers seeking care meet the strict eligibility criteria in these studies (having multiple physical and behavioral comorbidities or housing, food and income insecurities) are in large part the reason for the "voltage drop" (the difference in effect sizes in efficacy and effectiveness studies) when a novel, highly efficacious intervention is put into regular practice. This is not to say that efficacy trials are inferior to effectiveness trials. These trials have a very important place in the treatment development pipeline.

In some situations, it might make sense to skip the efficacy trial or to conduct a trial that is less controlled than an efficacy trial but more controlled than an effectiveness trial (Beidas et al., 2023). Many interventions are based on building, adapting, and rearranging well-established treatment components where the efficacy, safety risks, and adequacy of protections have been thoroughly identified in prior studies. For example, many new cognitive behavioral interventions are based on some combination of components such as identifying cognitive distortions, cognitive restructuring, relaxation, and desensitization. These components have been tested in hundreds of prior studies. When clinical safety is established and risks have been identified and are low, researchers may consider moving directly to an effectiveness trial or even a hybrid implementation-effectiveness trial, which would further speed the research-to-practice pipeline. This is particularly true when the "active ingredients" of an intervention are largely based on well-established treatment components.

Who is Appropriate for Recruitment into Efficacy Trials?

Participants in efficacy trials should be members of the population for which the intervention is intended, however, usually participants in such trials tend to be those with minimal co-morbidities and can tolerate participating in demanding assessment schedules. This means the study tends to be higher on internal validity but lower in external validity. Internal validity refers to the degree to which the findings in a study are due to experimental manipulation (the intervention) and not due to other factors in the setting or the population. These other factors are known as confounds. Co-morbidity is a common confounding variable that might weaken the identification of a causal association between the intervention and outcomes. External validity refers to the degree to which the study effects generalize or could be replicated in other settings or with participants who have different characteristics than the participants in the efficacy trial. For example, if you want to test the efficacy of psychotherapy for Major Depression, you will need to ensure the participants have a diagnosis of Major Depression and rule out or at least measure any other potentially confounding conditions, such as anxiety disorder. It is common in efficacy studies of Major Depression to exclude participants who are also drinking heavily, have symptoms associated with psychosis or have an uncontrolled medical condition that could explain the symptoms associated with Major Depression (Thyroid Disease). Other potential co-occurring mental health conditions might not be ruled out but should be measured to control or understand the potential effects of these conditions on treatment outcomes, for instance, symptoms of an anxiety disorder.

A potential participant for an efficacy study will undergo a rigorous series of interviews to confirm they have the problem the intervention addresses, have no other problems or characteristics that may cloud the effects of the intervention, and are willing to accept randomization to a condition that may be a placebo, waiting list condition, standard of care, or experimental intervention that has yet to have any demonstrated efficacy. In recent years in the United States, the need to collect objective measures of mechanisms means these participants may also need to be able to tolerate assessment devices such as functional Magnetic Resonance Imaging (fMRI), electroencephalogram (EEG) recordings, or neuropsychological assessments which are often tedious and frustrating to complete.

Where Can You Recruit a Sample?

There is no hard and fast rule about where to recruit your sample, although for an efficacy trial, most recruitment occurs through radio or podcast advertisements, through fliers, newsletters or, if your institution allows it and you have access to a health center or medical records. In nearly all our in-person trials, we will often give community talks in places where our population is most likely to hear the talk, such as senior centers and senior living facilities for a study in geriatric samples.

What Sample Size Is Needed for an Efficacy Trial?

An a priori estimated sample size should be conducted by your biostatistician based on the effect size you want or expect to detect (Minimum Detectable Effect Size), the psychometrics of your measures, and your study design. Usually, efficacy studies are "superiority trials," to examine whether the new intervention is more efficacious than non-active controls such as a placebo, waiting list, or unproven standard of care, or an active control that has proven to be effective, such as proven standard of care or other evidence-based intervention. However, efficacy studies could also be "non-inferiority trials," testing whether a new intervention has a similar clinical effect to standard of care but is better on another outcome, such as lower costs, fewer side effects, or increased participant engagement. And sometimes efficacy studies might be superiority or non-inferiority trials but are primarily focused on testing mediating mechanisms or moderation. Of these three types of designs, superiority trials with a non-active control condition usually require the smallest sample size because one expects the effects to be large. Superiority trials comparing against an active control condition will require larger sample sizes due to smaller expected differences (effect size). Non-inferiority trials also require larger samples to obtain the precision necessary to determine if the new treatment is within a non-inferiority margin. Trials testing mediation and moderation will likely need to be large to account for the variance used to test these additional hypotheses. Overall, one can expect larger effect sizes from an efficacy trial than from an effectiveness trial because the study design controls for confounds that potentially reduce effect size. Therefore, all else being equal, an efficacy trial will require a smaller sample size than an effectiveness trial.

What is the Typical Timeline of an Efficacy Trial?

There are two things to consider in answering this question: how much time a participant will spend in your study (study timeline) and how long it will take to complete your trial (trial timeline). The study timeline will depend on the hypotheses you are testing, but usually most efficacy trials are pre- and post-trials, with a short follow-up period to test the short-term permanence of treatment effects. If your intervention dose is three months of weekly meetings, the participant will likely be in the study for about six months. Three months for treatment, then a three-month follow-up to test for short-term permanence of intervention effects. There may be an extra week or two to conduct the screening and then the baseline assessment.

The trial timeline for efficacy studies is often four to five years to prepare the study, obtain ethics approval, train the research assessors and study therapists, and recruit the participants and have them complete their study timelines. You will want to reserve time at the end of your trial period to conduct data analysis. In US federally funded studies, most investigators include the data analysis in the trial timeline because they need to fund biostatisticians' time to analyze the data and prepare and upload trial data to the National Data Archive. We have the option in the United States to ask for a no-cost extension, which is an agreement with the funding agency to continue the project without additional funding, but that assumes there is still money left over to conduct analyses and publish the findings.

Here is an example of a trial timeline that includes a pilot year for testing study procedures:

YEAR 1/PHASE 1												
Efficacy Pilot	**M1**	**M2**	**M3**	**M4**	**M5**	**M6**	**M7**	**M8**	**M9**	**M10**	**M11**	**M12**
Finalize protocol, IRB, training, DSMB	XX	XXX	XXX									
Participant recruitment (N = 200)				XX								
Participant follow-up					XXX	XXX	XXX					
Data Analysis/Report to NIMH & DSMB								XXX	XXX	XXX	XXX	XXX

YEAR 2/PHASE 2												
Efficacy Trial	**M1**	**M2**	**M3**	**M4**	**M5**	**M6**	**M7**	**M8**	**M9**	**M10**	**M11**	**M12**
Finalize protocol, IRB, training, DSMB	XX	XX	XX									
Participant recruitment (N = 500)				XX	XX	XX	XX	XX	XX	XX	XX	XX
Participant Follow-up				XX	XX	XX	XX	XX	XX	XX	XX	XX
Progress Report, DSMB												XX

continued

continued

YEAR 3/PHASE 2												
Efficacy Trial	**M1**	**M2**	**M3**	**M4**	**M5**	**M6**	**M7**	**M8**	**M9**	**M10**	**M11**	**M12**
Participant recruitment (N = 500)	XX	XX	XX	XX	XX	XX	XX	XX	XX	XX	XX	XX
Participant follow-up												
Progress Report. DSMB												XX
YEAR 4/PHASE 2												
Efficacy Trial Wrap-up	**M1**	**M2**	**M3**	**M4**	**M5**	**M6**	**M7**	**M8**	**M9**	**M10**	**M11**	**M12**
Participant follow-up	XX	XX	XX									
Data analysis				XX	XX	XX	XX	XX				
DSMB				XX								
Progress/Final report									XX	XX	XX	XX
Final commercialization plan									XX	XX	XXX	XX

Training and Monitoring Therapists

Study Therapist Training

Even if you identify therapists who have expertise in your interventions of interest, or who have worked with you over time and who you know to be talented clinicians, they should still undergo training for the specific study. Best practices in clinician training are an area of considerable interest, and to date, there is no true evidence-based way to ensure therapists will be trained with fidelity. However, we have had considerable experience with study therapists and can share with you our best practices.

Our study therapists undergo a series of training steps. The first step is to participate in a workshop that reviews the intervention theory, strategies, and the manual. In this workshop, we provide videotaped demonstrations of the intervention with actual patients (usually from our pilot study phase) and discuss ways to cope with common challenges that occur in the patient population. For instance, in our research with older adults, we discuss how to manage caregiver demands, illness and disability, mild cognitive complaints, and suicidal ideation. During the last part of the workshop, we studied therapists engage in role-plays with feedback to become familiar with the pace of the therapy.

Next, the therapists administer the intervention to test cases, which are audio-taped for supervision review. These tapes are rated by the intervention supervisor using a therapist adherence/fidelity form, and corrective feedback is provided to the clinician. The study clinicians continue seeing test cases until they reach a specified criterion on the adherence/fidelity scale. If they do not reach this criterion, they should not be part of the study team. One question we get routinely is whether test cases can also be study cases and their data and outcomes are retained in the data analysis. The ideal scenario is to not include them (since these participants may not be getting the true dose of treatment), but limitations in time and the ability to identify participants make this ideal hard to achieve. An argument can be made for inclusion if you've monitored their treatment and can ensure that they received comparable care. If you do decide to keep a test case as a study participant, make sure to indicate in the dataset that the participant was a test case, so that the biostatistician can account for their status in the analysis.

Clearly, this method of observational training can be time-consuming and expensive, and if you need to train a new clinician in the middle of the study, identifying test cases can be problematic. This is why we have now begun to use standardized patient role-plays before study therapists see actual cases for final approval. Using research assistants, students, and other clinicians as standardized patients, study clinicians-in-training conduct therapy sessions and are provided with corrective feedback during the role-plays. The clinicians engage in role-plays until they reach the specified criterion on our adherence/fidelity scale, and then we observe the clinician provide the intervention with one test case. This method is proving to be very cost-effective and time-efficient and allows us to screen out potential study therapists who may not be able to provide the treatment with fidelity.

Study Therapist Monitoring

Ongoing monitoring of therapist adherence and fidelity is important to ensure that research participants are receiving the actual intervention in its true form. The general guideline is to audiotape or videotape every therapy session and review a randomly selected 20% of the taped sessions using the adherence/fidelity form, which also includes items to determine use of other treatments that are not part of the study intervention. In those studies where therapists provide all the treatments, reviewers also listen for instances of intervention contamination (e.g., when the therapist inappropriately starts using components from one treatment when doing the other). In efficacy studies, these ratings are done on an ongoing, monthly basis so that clinician drift can be corrected in supervision and before the drift affects the treatment outcomes.

Randomization

In randomized clinical trials, how one randomizes patient participants to treatment conditions is important. The most common form of randomization is at the patient level (other studies will randomize at the clinician or organizational level, see Chapter 10), and usually involves randomizing participants as they are recruited, and treatment begins almost immediately thereafter. If you decided to assign roughly equal numbers to two groups, you might easily merely flip a fair coin. However, there is always a worry that if the person who flips the coin knows the patient, they might gerrymander it in some way. Consequently, what is often done is to have a statistician flip the coins (typically using a computerized equivalent) for potential future participants and place the assignments in a numbered series of sealed envelopes or into the participant tracking application. REDCap and Qualtrics, two commonly used data collection and participant tracking systems, both allow for predetermined random assignment at the push of a button.

Different randomization schedules, such as assigning one third of the participants to one group and two thirds to another, are also possible using sealed envelopes or computer programming. Randomization means that each patient has an equal probability of being assigned to the treatment group; it does not mean that the probability must be ½. Thus, for example, in a multisite RCT, the costs of recruitment, retention efforts, and measurement were the same in the treatment and control groups, let's say $1000, but the treatment under evaluation was projected to cost, let's say, $6000 per subject per year, while the control (usual care) essentially cost nothing. With 1:1 randomization, the cost per subject was $1000 + $3000, while with 1:2 randomization, it was $1000 + $2000. With a fixed upper cost, the total number of patients who could be recruited into the study was larger with 1:2 randomization than with 1:1 randomization. The reason why 1:1 randomization is frequently preferred is that, with a fixed sample size, the power to detect treatment effects is largest with 1:1 randomization. However, the loss in power is very small in moving to 1:2 randomization, and is easily made up by increasing the total sample size.

For random assignment to ensure baseline equivalence across groups, you must have a large sample. In smaller studies and situations where there is at least one highly critical treatment moderator, you should consider using stratified random assignment. In this approach, groups of potential participants are separated into blocks for each combination of covariates and then use simple randomization within each block. For instance, if it is suspected or known that gender and self-efficacy moderate the efficacy of treatment, you would categorize self-efficacy into high and low and then separate participants into strata of each combination of gender and self-efficacy and randomize within those strata.

Data Management

Data management protocols should be established early and adhered to avoid later errors and inconsistencies. Tracking systems that document participant enrollment, consent, current status, measure completion, and reasons for study exclusion and withdrawal are essential. These can be created in several commonly available applications (Excel, Access, REDCap, Qualtrics). At a bare minimum, a tracking system should ensure that all items on CONSORT diagrams can be addressed (Moher, 2001). A data dictionary that provides variable names, labels, possible values, and value labels, measure administration timepoints and targets, and scale scoring guidelines should be developed early. The National Institutes of Mental Health now requires a Data Management and Sharing Plan to be written with grant applications, though this is a good idea for any trial. These plans describe: the types of data that are being generated or obtained; data standards and formats; methods of collection; security and privacy; data storage, backup, preservation and long-term access; policies for sharing; and compliance and reporting standards.

Perhaps the most effective method of ensuring the quality of data management is to ask for interim reports, not interim analyses related to the research questions (such "peeking" should be discouraged) but other reports that simultaneously document research progress and the efficiency of database management. Recruitment reports, for example, document that the data being collected are being entered promptly into the dataset. Tracking the number of visits over time ensures that the appropriate corrections can be made for the multiple measures of the same subject over time. Descriptive statistics at baseline, as participants are entered into the treatment groups, document the success/failure of randomization and also that the data are entered, cleaned, and can be used. The example given above about the detection of a laboratory error in cortisol assays simultaneously alerted the researchers to a problem and documented excellent data management. To give an example at the other extreme, in a multisite RCT, a request was made to report the number of subjects who had been recruited, and how many had been assigned to the treatment and control groups. This seems a very simple request, but it could not be done apparently because of the way information was coded in the dataset. It was a good thing this problem was discovered very early and repaired.

Reducing Bias in an Efficacy Trial

In an efficacy trial of a psychosocial intervention, one of the most important factors that the research team must stay on top of is the potential for bias. Bias is a systematic deviation or error from the true effect of a study. Bias has many causes, but a common source is intentional or unintentional decision-making in favor of the hypothesis. For instance, an interviewer may subtly and unconsciously influence participants by giving smiles and nods when participants in the intervention condition provide favorable responses. Control of this source of bias is managed by keeping the research participants and any research team members in contact with participants unaware of the treatment condition they are assigned to, a methodological feature often called masking or blinding. In recent years, masking has become a more common term because of the possibility of confusion in ophthalmologic research (Morris et al., 2007) and the two are generally used interchangeably, though some have attempted to draw distinctions (Lang & Stroup, 2020). There are many roles that can be masked, including participants, data collectors, research coordinators, treatment providers, analysts, and manuscript writers. Although attempts for complete masking are common in medication and procedural trials, they are almost impossible to have in psychosocial intervention trials. Regardless of how the therapists are assigned, they are aware of the treatment participants are receiving and can usually guess the study's hypothesis; likewise, participants are also aware of the content of the treatment they are receiving. In this case, this lack of masking is an unavoidable problem. Those evaluating treatment response should be trained to avoid any discussion about the treatment received, and the participants should be warned not to discuss details with the research interviewer. Nevertheless, participants will often let slip details about the treatment they have received.

Keeping research team members blind to the study hypothesis is one way to minimize bias, however this is a difficult standard to achieve. Even if the team never figures out the true study hypothesis, they may have some idea of what they think it is and thus may inadvertently behave in a way that will influence the data quality. For this reason, there are no better ways to control bias than to regularly monitor the research therapists and assistants and to maintain a high standard of treatment delivery and assessment.

Common Problems We See in Efficacy Trials

Conducting an efficacy trial is no small feat. Even with the best-piloted trial, you will run into some challenges along the way, and you will be tempted to make some decisions that may be ill-advised. In this section, we describe the common challenges investigators face and the common errors they make to address them.

Investigator Bias

Often, PIs will provide clinical supervision to the study therapists and research assistants. Typically, this supervision occurs in a team setting, and ideally, only issues related to confusion over whether a participant can be included in a study and issues related to participant safety are discussed. However, it can be difficult not to provide therapy-specific supervision and advice with cases that a study therapist may be struggling with, and we are aware of many studies where clinical supervision on the conduct of therapy is provided by the PI. This is a gray area for psychosocial interventions research because when the investigator, who wrote the hypothesis and is invested in the outcome, begins to give advice on individual cases to the people he or she employs, investigator bias will likely be an issue. Additionally, a major goal of efficacy research is to ensure that the treatment is being delivered with fidelity, which often requires intense observation and supervision with newly developed interventions. Many times, the PI is the sole expert in the interventions under investigation, and even if supervision is the responsibility of another member of the research team, bias can still result. There are three ways to control for potential investigator bias:

- Make sure that the investigator provides supervision only to those cases that are receiving the treatment the investigator is an expert in.
- Regularly monitor the quality of all treatment conditions and ensure that the quality is high in all treatments.
- Arrange for supervision of therapeutic-specific issues to be conducted by an independent expert who has no investment in the outcome of the study.

Data "Peeking"

While it is fine to look at outcomes for safety issues, you should not periodically look at differences between conditions, except for cases where an invasive and potentially dangerous procedure is in use—even in this case, the procedures should have been piloted for safety reasons before there is investment in a larger trial. The reason is simple: if you look too soon at how the data appear to be evolving and find that either your hypothesis is being confirmed or disconfirmed, this knowledge may influence your behavior regarding the conduct of the trial. Most importantly, any test of the hypothesis with too small a sample to accurately test will yield unreliable information, and therefore, there is no reason to peek at the outcomes too early. One exception is in studies with risky interventions, where a researcher may need to examine the data for futility to ensure that no participants beyond those necessary are put at risk. In this situation, one could leave the peeks to be conducted by the Data Safety Monitoring Board (DSMB). Another rare exception is a sequential trial, one in which the study was designed for multiple "peeks," and the tests and computation of significance levels take those "peeks" into account.

To give an example, in an RCT where the outcome was time to an event (like remission), about halfway through the planned study time, the PI asked for the time-to-event curves of the two treatment groups and found that the time to remission for the preferred treatment was statistically significantly better than that of the other treatments. He was convinced by the biostatistician not to publish the result but to wait until the planned study time was completed. Sure enough, by the study's completion, there was no longer a significant difference between the two groups. By sheer chance, the only time there was any appreciable separation in the survival curves was exactly at the time the "peek" was made. This often happens because the results based on too small a sample size are often very unstable. It is best to complete the study as planned and then evaluate the results rather than capitalizing on chance findings during multiple "peeks."

Recruitment Is Slow or Non-existent

Even the best-piloted study will encounter recruitment difficulties, and when this happens it is very tempting to slightly modify the entry criteria. For instance, we have seen investigators who originally excluded participants from the trial taking psychiatric medication, but after recruitment became challenging, they began to allow participants on medications. We have also seen studies change their recruitment methods midway to enhance their recruitment when other methods began to lose their effectiveness.

Unfortunately, changing the study entry criteria and recruitment methods introduces problems for the study. First, both methods may create a cohort effect in your study. Participants recruited earlier in the study will be different than participants recruited later. It is typically much easier to recruit earlier in the study, and those recruited are often those more in need or more enthusiastic: the "lower-hanging fruit." If it becomes necessary to change the recruitment criteria (e.g., if it becomes apparent that one of the treatments was harming a certain kind of patient, who thus ethically will have to be excluded thereafter), the study should be regarded as stratified, and the analysis should include consideration of strata (those before and those after the change), treatment, and treatment × stratum interaction. It may be necessary then to increase the total sample size to achieve adequate power.

To avoid such stratification, a Community Advisory Board (CAB) can be helpful in determining ways to improve recruitment rates without changing methods or entry criteria. As an example, Dr. P had been relying successfully on community talks to recruit participants into their study, but after two years, they began to see a decrease in the number of people self-identifying for the study. Their CAB had determined that the talks were no longer as effective because the community had heard them all before, and the PI needed to develop new topics to discuss that would reengage the community. Dr. P did find that this method increased attendance and interest in participation.

The Issue of Fidelity Measures and When to Look at Them

Investigators must ensure that participants receive a full and untainted dose of the psychosocial intervention through independent fidelity assessments. If you do not pay attention to fidelity until the study's end, you may find that your participants did not receive the treatments they were assigned, and you will have spent several years collecting data that cannot test your hypotheses. In an efficacy study, strong efforts should be made to ensure that each treatment is delivered with fidelity. These efforts go far beyond what would be done in the real world, and this is one of the hallmark differences between efficacy and effectiveness trials.

Random and Assorted Common "Sins"

There are other problems we see in RCTs that investigators are not aware of. The most common are:

- Changing the research question after the RCT is completed or hypothesizing after results are known.
- Interpreting nonsignificant results as proof of equivalence or non-inferiority.
- Multiple testing problems.
- Using outdated and inappropriate data analytic methods.

Changing the question or hypothesizing after the results are known

There are research studies designed and funded to ask one research question, but they change it to another when the original question does not pan out. Sometimes, investigators will find statistically significant results in a large series of analyses, develop new hypotheses after the results are known (HARKing), and then present the data as if the study had been designed with that hypothesis. A major reason why RCTs are required to be registered before they start is that it has been found that this is a very common "sin." It seems such a minor thing to substitute one outcome measure for the one proposed, but the fact is that if the data were random numbers to which interesting-sounding labels were applied, and there were enough of them, one or another would be "statistically significant" or "make for a good story." In an RCT report, a priori primary outcome is reported completely first. Thereafter, a priori secondary hypotheses should be tested, and the results reported. What is reported might be interesting and suggestive but should not be regarded as hypothesis testing or the basis for conclusions. Post hoc and exploratory analyses can then be presented and discussed but with caution and will require confirmation in another study.

Interpreting nonstatistically significant results as proof of the null hypothesis

Two groups are nearly always different on their statistical moments (mean, variance, skewness, kurtosis), even if randomly assigned, and even if the difference is trivial. Nonstatistically significant results are often a result of inadequate power and thus are "hung juries." "Absence of proof is not proof of absence." If you are really interested in determining if studies have equivalent outcomes (non-inferiority trials), you will need larger sample sizes, on the order of 600 to 1000 participants. Even then, the groups will be different but not different enough to surpass a predetermined effect size range. For instance, you may determine that anything smaller than an average one-point difference on the Patient Health Questionnaire is equivalent. Determining what is a small versus a medium effect size is very much driven by clinical context.

Multiple testing problem

In a recent study, 29 analytic teams were provided with the same dataset and the same research question: "Are soccer referees more likely to give red cards (fouls) to dark skin toned players than to light skin toned players" (Silberzahn et al., 2018), but no instructions on how to analyze the data. After each team took its own approach to analyzing the data, over 30 different effect sizes were found, ranging from 0.89 to 2.89 in odds ratios, with 69% of teams finding a positive association and 31% of teams not finding a significant relationship. It is obvious, therefore, that the approach to analysis can make a strong difference to your conclusions. P-hacking is the sin of analyzing data in many different ways until you achieve a statistically significant result. For this reason, it is important to predetermine your analytic strategy, prespecify this in your study protocol, and avoid multiple tests of your data. Otherwise, you may think you have identified an important finding that is really identified only because of chance. If multiple tests are done, you must report the results of every single one of those tests. Some researchers may be resistant to prespecification of the analytic plan because they do not yet know about the form of the data (e.g., data normality, final sample size, degree of intraclass correlation) that might impact their analytic choices and they do not want to tie their hands for future analyses. In these situations, prespecification should be focused on the process and decision-making choices that analysts will make.

Inappropriate data analysis

The next challenge we have seen is in problems with using a statistical analysis inappropriate for the data—for example, univariate repeated measures analysis of variance applied to multiple measures of responses over time. This statistical model is appropriate when the correlation between each pair of observations on the same subject is the same. In a time series, generally, the correlation between two proximal time points is much greater than between two distal time points. The unfortunate fact is that deviation from this assumption inflates the appearance of significance (false-positive results). This fact has now been known for more than 50 years, but many psychotherapy researchers continue to use this approach.

Avoiding these sins

There are many more such "sins," although these tend to be the most common, and most may be avoided by consulting a trained and experienced biostatistician in design and analysis, by peer review (not only those reviewing for funding, but also by colleagues willing to give a critical reading of your proposal/paper), and simply by learning from the mistakes in one study to avoid making the same mistakes in all future studies. Although PhD-level mental health professionals (e.g., Clinical Psychologists) are trained to read, understand, and in some cases conduct data analyses, statistics is an ever-evolving and very specialized field. Unless you are a regular consumer of the statistical literature, you will eventually be using outdated analytic techniques and will be interpreting your data with old assumptions in mind.

Case in point: The first author of this book experienced this issue first-hand when she presented data related to the mediation of treatment outcomes to a group of postdoctoral fellows at another university. A biostatistician of note had recently visited the same group of fellows and presented on the latest issues about testing mediation. The fellows were quick to let the first author know she had conducted her mediation analysis incorrectly—at the time her study was funded (6 years prior), measuring the mediator at the same time as the outcome was deemed appropriate. This is no longer the opinion of the statistical field.

Ethical Considerations

Here, we discuss a few critical issues about the ethical conduct of your study. We mention here that the topics covered here are at best suggestions, and each IRB will have its own interpretation about study risk and methods to ensure risk is minimized. The challenge many investigators face is that IRBs will often have different reactions and recommendations for the ethical management of clinical trials. For instance, Dr. Areán has worked for two state-funded universities. In many ways, those two universities are similar, and you would expect similar IRB experiences. In both instances, Dr. Areán was a professor in a department of psychiatry in a school of medicine that received research funds from federal agencies, such as NIH, DoD as well as from foundations and donations. Both universities were in urban areas and served a diverse population. Both institutions conducted research on psychosocial interventions, service research, epidemiology, and mixed methods studies. Despite these similarities, the IRBs from these two very similar institutions could not be more different from one another. In one, all clinical research was considered high-risk and it would take months (sometimes a year) to get IRB approval. In the other, the IRB would determine risk based on the type of trial conducted—in fact, behavioral intervention research in adults who could consent for themselves would receive minimal risk designations. This is all to say that the advice we provide below is the minimal level of consideration you need, and depending on your IRB, you this may be enough information to receive approval, or you may need more assistance from your IRB.

Obtaining Consent

The only people on your team who can collect consent from participants are the research assistants who interview the potential participants. Although participants can talk with the investigator to answer questions and concerns, the investigator cannot obtain consent, as this runs the risk of participant coercion. Even though the PI may be fair in their consenting process, collecting consent can have the appearance of coercion, and for that reason should be avoided. Just as you train your research assistants to conduct research interviews, you must train your assistants to obtain consents in a way that is not coercive and to explain to the participant what it means to be a research participant. It is required in the United States that anyone obtaining consent must undergo training in research ethics, particularly on the importance of informed consent. In our research group, we train assistants to collect consent the same way we train them to interview participants. We first demonstrate how to explain the study and the participants' role in the study, we then role-play how to provide information to help participants decide if they want to participate, and then we monitor their consent process.

Important Elements to Consider in Obtaining Consents

In the research ethics field, there is much discussion about three important elements of consent forms: understandability, capacity to consent, and therapeutic misconception. Regarding understandability, all consent forms should be written so that the average participant can understand what is being said. Terms like "randomization" should be explained clearly, and some research has found that providing a visual demonstration of research constructs can help participants understand those terms. Consent forms should be written at the sixth-grade reading level. If your target population cannot read either because of vision problems or educational disadvantage, it is important that the consent forms be read to the participant, and that those sessions be audiotaped for quality assurance. Sometimes, family members who can read will be invited in to ensure the participant understands what is read to him or her. Most IRBs include mandatory legal language in their consents that violates the sixth-grade reading rule. In those cases, it is important that the research assistant explain the legal phrases so that the participant understands what is meant.

Regarding capacity to consent, some populations may not be able to consent for themselves. It is a given that children (up until age 18) cannot participate in a study unless they are emancipated minors or their guardians provide consent for them. In these cases, it is important that the parents understand what is expected of the child during the study, and what the risks and benefits are. Older adults with known cognitive impairments and people with mental illnesses or cognitive impairments that will affect their judgment will also need a guardian or conservator to provide consent. In cases where capacity to consent could be an issue (e.g., older adults with mild cognitive impairments, or people with traumatic brain injury), instruments are available to assess whether the participant understands the consent process. One good measure is the MacArthur Capacity Assessment Tool (MacCAT; Hoge et al., 1997), which has been used widely in studies targeting people with psychosis and Alzheimer's disease.

The final issue to be aware of is therapeutic misconception. It arises due to participants not fully understanding the purpose of a research study or not understanding the concept of randomization. Some participants may believe that by participating in a treatment study, the main goal is to treat the problem they have been identified as having, rather than to test the efficacy of the interventions in question. We have had experiences with participants being disappointed that they did not receive a treatment they thought was superior or being annoyed with the research interviews. It is very important that participants understand that the purpose of research is to test a scientific question, and although their safety is very important, assignment to treatment is completely out of everyone's control, only chance decides, and the research interviews are critical to testing the study hypotheses. At the same time, it also behooves researchers to choose control/comparison interventions that are credible. If the patients know that by dropping out of the trials, they can obtain better treatment, they will do that. Also, it is important to repeatedly express to the patients during the trial the value of their contribution, if not to their own improvement, then to that of many other patients like them in the future. If possible, it would be advantageous to offer those patients not benefited by whichever treatment they were assigned to the other treatment, if they wish, when the study is over.

Participant Compensation

Providing compensation to research participants is important; participants are working hard to provide you with useful information, and in their own way, they are also part of your research team. Provision of this incentive, we have found, varies from country to country; it is common in the United States and some low- and middle-income countries. However, there can sometimes be considerable misunderstanding over what is considered adequate compensation. Some investigators feel that participating in treatment is ample compensation. However, these investigators need to remember that the participants receive treatment based on chance, not on need per se, and thus they should be given at least a token reimbursement for participating in the study and providing information about their experiences.

There is also some discussion about what is considered coercive compensation. This has been an interesting discussion among ethicists about research participation in low-income communities. Some believe that compensation should not be financial, or, if financial, it should be a token incentive to avoid the potential of influencing participation solely because of the money being provided. Others who have worked with low-income communities, however, believe that if the participant understands the risks and expectations of participating in a research study, the potential participant is more than capable of deciding whether or not the risks outweigh the financial benefits, and, as such, is capable of making the decision to participate or not.

Although all participants should be given some compensation for participation, how much they are compensated will depend on the population from which you are sampling. Some investigators have been particularly creative regarding the compensation. One investigator studying a weight-loss program for Mexican-Americans in Texas convinced the community to donate important health-related items to the study, such as food scales, running shoes, athletic clothes, and other items. Not only were these highly valued items for participants, but the fact that they were health-based reinforced the new behaviors the participants were learning in the program.

Another interesting dilemma when selecting compensation methods is whether the compensation will create more harm than good. One colleague of ours studied behavioral interventions for people addicted to crack cocaine. During the time she was doing this research, crack was relatively inexpensive to buy, and one rock cost $20. As it happened, our colleague had been reimbursing her participants $20 per interview, which also included a urine screen to assess for cocaine use. One clinic she worked with complained that they were concerned about giving participants $20 as it could result in a relapse, that the participants would use the money to buy a rock of crack. Because our colleague wondered why it would be her $20 that would lead to a relapse, she decided to see if participation in her study (regardless of condition) resulted in any increased risk of relapse. Using the data she collected historically and in the current study, she demonstrated that participation in the study resulted in fewer relapses overall, compared to what the clinic members not in the study experienced. Nevertheless, this concern could have had some teeth to it, and thus it is important to think through the effects that compensation could have on the participant.

It is a courtesy, at the end of a study, to inform participants about the study results. This might be merely a letter with a synopsis of the results and a reference to the journal in which they are published. We have found that most participants are eager to learn about the results and sometimes provide valuable insights as to what they think the next direction in research should be.

Reporting Adverse Events

Although participation in psychotherapy studies is relatively safe, adverse events could occur (e.g., suicide). When adverse events occur, it is important to report the event within a short period of time (which should be specified in your data safety and monitoring plan) to your IRB and DSBM. Both parties will determine if the event is related to participation in the study, and if so, you may need to be prepared to discontinue the study. These situations are extremely rare, however. We provide an example of suicide prevention protocols in Chapter 6 Appendix to demonstrate how to construct a plan to ensure that any participant in research is safe.

Miscellaneous IRB Issues

One issue to consider that we have encountered working in academic medical centers is that some grant reviewers and IRB members are still concerned about the ability of clinical supervisors and PIs who are not psychiatrists to provide clinical supervision for certain patient populations, including patients with depression, psychosis, anxiety, and substance abuse. Although we have taken this battle to the mat several times, explaining that holding a license to practice in a state or having medical staff privileges in a clinic ensures our ability to provide safe treatment to research participants, sometimes this battle is lost and you, the investigator, will have to have some means of assuring reviewers and IRB members how you will ensure the safety of your research participants. The following are options you can use to minimize the need to hire a psychiatrist to be part of a research team when it is not necessary (e.g., when there are no medication-based treatment conditions):

- Create a supervision team that includes outside consultation from a psychiatrist when cases appear to be worsening during the course of the study.
- Establish a relationship with an existing clinic that can provide services to participants who need more intensive services than are provided in the study.
- Include a psychiatrist member on the DSMB.

Equity Considerations

The NIH has historically mandated that investigators ensure research samples include an adequate representation of women, those who experience health disparities, and when appropriate, children and older adults (people 65 years old and older). For federally funded applications, you will be expected to provide a preliminary projection of the likely representation of women and people from different ethnic and racial groups in a projected enrollment table (see Chapter 6 Appendix) and, for any study that recruits more than 100 participants, a quarterly milestone report on recruitment (if under 100, the milestone report accompanies the yearly progress report). You must meet your projected enrollment, so be as realistic as possible. You may also need to recruit from areas outside your region if ethnic and racial minorities are few. For instance, one of our colleagues who works in New Hampshire had to recruit from Boston to ensure his sample included people from different racial and ethnic groups.

Completing the projected enrollment table is not as easy as it looks. There are two sections to the table, enrollment of Hispanic and non-Hispanic members on the top and then recruitment of White, Black, Asian/Pacific Islander, and Native American on the bottom. *These are two separate tables!* Because many Hispanic communities have within them indigenous communities (South America, Central America, and Mexico in particular), African-descent members (Caribbean Hispanics most commonly), some have Asian members (Cuba has a sizable Chinese-origin population, for instance), and there is a large population of Hispanics who are white. When completing the second table, you will need to document all the Hispanics who also identify as Black in the Black category, and those who identify as Native in the Native American category. Sadly, there is no category for those who are mixed races or mixed ethnicities, even though the US population is becoming increasingly mixed. Until there is a category for "mixed," it is important to ask these participants with which they identify most and not make assumptions based on appearances.

Budgetary Issues

In Chapter 6 Appendix, we provide an example of a recent budget justification for an efficacy trial. This will give you a good idea of how to create a reasonable budget for your study. Currently, when research money is tight and money for intervention research is limited, it is important to be as frugal as you can without working on a shoestring. The best way to ensure your budget is reasonable is to use a set of rules that we have used most recently to ensure our budget is approved and remains reasonably funded over time:

- Justify your costs as much as possible. In the United States, the NIMH clinical trials and other foundations, such as PCORI allow for larger budgets, generally because of the costs associated with conducting a high-quality clinical trial. Your budget will be reviewed for its justification, and we have seen budgets that are obviously too large be non-funded and asked to reduce their budget substantially.
- You might have to plan for regular budget cuts. In the United States, the funding budgets for science are at the mercy of congressional budget decisions. Sometimes budgets are cut, sometimes there is no increase (which is basically a small cut to the operating budget) and sometimes there are increases. At some point, you may be asked to reduce your budget to accommodate the lean budget years. It is always prudent to plan for cuts either by identifying other sources of financial matching, or by aggregating effort on your team.
- Rely on students and volunteers when possible. Many of our former volunteers have gone on to graduate school and some to highly successful research careers of their own. Although volunteers often need more supervision in the beginning, they can be a budgetary asset. We use volunteers for recruitment activities, data entry, simple screening tasks, and office duties that research assistants are sometimes used for.

Budgets are based on either percent effort or calendar months for staff, supplies, equipment, and participant fees. Below, we provide a breakdown of percent time and calendar months for each team member and the typical amount of money for other supplies and fees:

- *PI:* 20–30% effort (2.4 to 3.6 months)
- *Project manager:* 50–100% effort (6 to 12 months)
- *Research assistant:* 50–100% effort (6 to 12 months)
- *Data entry assistants:* 25–50% effort (3 to 6 months)
- *Recruitment assistant:* 25–50% effort (3 to 6 months)
- *Study therapist:* 25–50% effort (3 to 6 months)
- *Fidelity rater:* This is usually contracted by the hour. We often pay our raters $125 an hour.
- *Biostatistician:* 25% effort in the first few years, more in the last year (3 months)

- *Data manager:* 25–50% effort (3 to 6 months)
- *Participant fees:* Transportation costs ($3.50 a mile); compensation ($20 to $50 an interview; if more invasive procedures, such as MRI, then more compensation)
- *Equipment:* One or two computers in the first year and any interview material costs.
- *Publication fees.* Since the first version of this book, the number of open-access journals has increased dramatically. The demand for such journals is the result of growing demand from funders to ensure anyone can access publications from a clinical trial (or any study) for free. Further, many journal editors feel it is important to distance themselves from industry advertisers to reduce conflict of interest. This has meant that journals now have a dwindling source of income. Fewer people pay for journal subscriptions and fewer companies advertise. This has put the onus of publication costs on the research team. Hence, you will need to budget for publication costs. In the CREATIV Lab, we try and reserve about $5,000 per study.

Chapter Summary

The purpose of efficacy trials is to determine the relative impact of an experimental intervention versus a control or common standard of care condition under optimal conditions. Typically, this is the next step after the proof of concept or pilot trial, and the intervention is a novel one and has not been tested in larger samples of people with the illness of interest. There are exceptions to the need for an efficacy trial, for instance, when the intervention and its elements have evidence of prior efficacy but the delivery platform is novel (e.g., digital version of an in-person intervention), or when developing an implementation strategy for increased uptake or usability of an intervention. Efficacy trials tend to be more internally valid, and include participants who can tolerate extensive assessments, can come to an academic medical center for care, and do not suffer from other conditions in order to gain a clear signal of the intervention effect on the condition of interest. Clinicians tend to be highly trained and strictly supervised to control the dose of treatment. We do argue here, however, that in the future, some flexibility about participant inclusion (to enhance preliminary generalizability), and study of the potential barriers to intervention uptake should be considered in these trials, if not earlier. The *voltage drop* phenomenon is one where the effect of a new intervention is moderate to large in the efficacy trial but drops considerably in tests of effectiveness. The voltage drops are generally due to several factors, such as the limited representation of the samples in efficacy trials, the inability of representative patients to access the intervention and the ability of clinicians and services to implement the intervention with fidelity. We argue that more consideration of these issues in the design of novel interventions will go a long way toward moving new treatments into common practice.

9

Effectiveness and Effectiveness-Implementation Hybrid Trials

Critical Questions to Be Addressed in This Chapter

- What are the differences between effectiveness trials, implementation trials, and effectiveness-implementation hybrid trials?
- What is the purpose of effectiveness trials?
- What are effectiveness-implementation hybrid trials?
- What are the levels of randomization?
- How are clinicians trained?
- What sample size do I need for an effectiveness trial?
- What is the typical timeline for such trials?
- What are best practices when working with community partners?
- How should clinicians and research assistants be monitored?
- What happens if I need to change partners mid-study?

What Is the Purpose of Effectiveness and Hybrid Trials?

Once an intervention has demonstrated efficacy, the next step is to test the effectiveness of that intervention under less controlled, real-world circumstances. It is often not enough to say that a new intervention works on a specified condition. It is also important to understand in which context the intervention is most effective. *Effectiveness studies* vary in their purpose. Some focus on whether a novel intervention developed for one context maintains its effects when introduced in a different setting. For instance, Interpersonal Psychotherapy (IP) was developed for mental health clinic settings but may not be as effective if delivered in a prison. To know if the context of the prison system would impact the effectiveness of IP, a study needs to be conducted in that setting. Other studies focus on the effectiveness of a novel intervention in populations not involved in the original efficacy study. As an example, the

High-Quality Psychosocial Interventions Research. Second Edition. Patricia A. Areán and Michael D. Pullmann, Oxford University Press.
DOI: 10.1093/oso/9780197681923.003.0009

efficacy of Cognitive Behavioral Therapy (CBT) was determined to be efficacious in a sample that was predominantly White and female. To be sure the intervention was effective in other populations, such as Latine or Black populations, CBT was culturally translated and then tested in several effectiveness trials. Effectiveness studies also study the impact of the novel intervention in people who not only suffer from the condition for which the intervention was designed to treat, but also suffer from other, co-occurring conditions. Thus, the questions that the effectiveness studies answer are:

1. Is the novel intervention as clinically effective in different settings as it was for the context in which it was originally studied?
2. Is the novel intervention clinically effective with different populations with the specified condition?

Another important question that effectiveness trials answer is how a novel intervention compares to an existing standard of care, often termed "Treatment As Usual." These trials are called *Comparative Pragmatic Effectiveness Trials* and these studies tend to focus on whether the novel intervention is as good as to or better than the standard of practice at producing clinical outcomes. These trials may also examine whether there are benefits of the novel intervention over the existing standard of practice, such as a reduction in side effects, costs, or user burden, or on any of the Institute of Medicine's standards of care, including efficiency, safety, equity, patient centeredness, and timeliness (Institute of Medicine, 2001). In this and all types of studies, it is important to track whether the participant also received other treatment outside of the research study, including medication, therapy, and counseling. Some questions comparative effectiveness trials answer are:

1. Is the novel intervention as effective as or more effective than standard practice?
2. Does the novel intervention have fewer side effects compared to standard practice?
3. Is the novel intervention less costly compared to standard practice?
4. Does the novel intervention have less patient burden compared to standard practice?
5. Does the novel intervention have more equitable outcomes compared to standard practice?

Implementation trials evaluate methods and strategies to improve the adoption of evidence-based treatments as standard practice. Rather than testing if an intervention works, the assumption is that the intervention does work but there are challenges that get in the way of the intervention's adoption. An implementation scientist may study methods to train clinicians in best practices or compare incentives for adopting new treatments into practice. They may also study methods for redesigning systems of care so that new or existing interventions can be implemented. While the focus of effectiveness research is on the intervention's impact (whether "the thing" works), the focus of implementation science is on how to help people adopt and use the intervention (the optimal methods to help "do the thing"; Curran, 2020). Implementation science is its own field of study, outside of the scope of this book to address in detail, however, a few important concepts and references may be of interest if you would like to explore more.

The Consolidated Framework for Implementation Science (CFIR) is an ecological framework for studying implementation (Damschroder et al., 2009, 2022). The CFIR views interventions as existing five major domains: (1) characteristics of the innovation/intervention (e.g., complexity, strength of evidence); (2) outer setting (e.g., policies and incentives for implementation); (3) an organizations' inner setting (e.g., implementation climate and culture, communication networks); (4) individual characteristics (e.g., knowledge, attitudes); and (5) implementation process (e.g., planning, engaging, and executing the intervention). These domains provide a structure for researchers and practitioners to examine and address factors associated with the success of implementation strategies for integrating best practices into standard care. At least 73 *implementation strategies* have been identified (Powell et al., 2015), including well-known and often used strategies such as training and coaching, mandating implementation, creating implementation teams, and identifying implementation champions, as well as softer or less used strategies such as promoting adaptability, involving patients in implementation, and modeling and simulating change. The effectiveness of these strategies is determined by several identified *implementation outcomes* (Proctor et al., 2011): adoption (the actual use of the intervention within a setting), fidelity (degree to which people implement the intervention as intended), penetration (extent to which the intervention is adopted), sustainability (long term use of the intervention), acceptability (willingness to adopt the intervention by people in the setting), appropriateness (perceived fit of an intervention with an setting), feasibility (degree to which an intervention can be implemented within a setting), and cost (money, time, and infrastructure required to implement an intervention). Investigators conducting a classic implementation trial will develop an implementation model using the CFIR to identify the possible determinants of implementation success within that setting. Implementation strategies will be selected, adapted, or developed, and groups will be randomly assigned to receive these strategies. Implementation outcomes will be measured and analyzed to determine whether an implementation strategy is superior. In an implementation trial, the intervention selected will usually not vary across groups, as the effectiveness of the intervention should have been well established in other studies and it is not the research goal. Instead, the goal is usually to determine the best implementation strategy for setting characteristics. Some questions an implementation trial might address include:

1. Does a novel implementation strategy result in higher rates of adoption for the same cost as usual implementation?
2. Does adapting or tailoring an implementation strategy for a specific setting result in better implementation outcomes?
3. What combination of implementation strategies results in the best implementation outcomes?

Effectiveness-Implementation Hybrid Trials are a relatively new trial type (Curran et al., 2012, 2022). Hybrid trials are meant to accelerate the time between establishing an intervention's effectiveness and its eventual implementation into practice by simultaneously studying an intervention's effectiveness and the best methods to implement it. Most effectiveness studies funded by the National Institute of Mental Health in the United States are now hybrid trials.

Hybrid trials exist on a continuum but have been categorized into three broad types. Type 1 focuses mainly on the clinical effectiveness of a novel intervention but also explores the potential challenges a system may experience in implementing it. The intervention described in Chapter 3 was tested as a hybrid type 1 trial, where the main hypothesis was one of comparative effectiveness, testing whether the new intervention was as effective as Problem-Solving Treatment (PST). However, the trial also tested questions about how much time it would take to train clinicians in the new intervention as compared to PST and how many hours of corrective feedback clinicians would need to maintain quality.

Type 2 hybrid trials equally focus on intervention effectiveness and implementation strategy effectiveness. Usually, this trial type compares the new intervention to an existing intervention, while conducting a pilot study of an implementation strategy, but it can also include comparisons of two or more implementation strategies. Because a new implementation strategy may adversely impact the effectiveness of the intervention if it is not effective, usually the new implementation strategy is added to or compared to a traditional implementation strategy in each condition. An example of a hybrid type 2 trial is the Beliefs and Attitudes for Successful Implementation (BASIS) study, which evaluates the effectiveness of an implementation strategy to increase providers' likelihood of adopting an intervention. BASIS is a training that occurs before and after providers receive training on the intervention. In one Type II study, the researchers are examining whether BASIS enhances provider adoption of and fidelity to Trauma Focused Cognitive Behavioral Therapy (TF-CBT) in schools, while simultaneously testing the effectiveness of TF-CBT at reducing trauma symptoms and behaviors (Lyon, et al., 2021a).

Type 3 hybrid trials are essentially implementation trials that also collect information on clinical and functional outcomes. The primary goal of a hybrid type 3 is to determine if a strategy improves the implementation outcomes described earlier (e.g., adoption, fit, fidelity, cost, etc.). However, information on whether the strategy impacts improved clinical outcomes is also collected as a secondary outcome. An example of a hybrid type 3 trial is the Adolescent and child Suicide Prevention in Routine Encounters (ASPIRE) study, which primarily compares two implementation strategies to determine the best method to ensure clinicians are using evidence-based firearm safety protocols, with the secondary assessment being youth mental health and suicide safety (Beidas et al., 2021).

An easy mnemonic to remember how the types are distinguished is that type 1 is focused primarily on effectiveness, which is the first word in Effectiveness-Implementation, type 2 equally emphasizes both, and type 3 is focused primarily on Implementation, the last word in Effectiveness-Implementation. Also, the traditional sequence of clinical trials has been to establish effectiveness before exploring implementation issues in a variety of settings.

Rigor in Effectiveness Trials

One major difference between efficacy and effectiveness trials is in the degree of control the investigator has over the clinician delivering the treatment, the setting in which the treatment is delivered, and the selection of cases for the experiment (Enrique & Marta, 2020; Gartlehner et al., 2006; Singal et al., 2014; Stricker, 2000). In efficacy studies, the main point is to determine if the intervention influences a specific illness (see Chapter 8), whereas effectiveness studies, the main point is to determine whether the

Table 9.1 Distinctions between efficacy and effectiveness trials

	Efficacy	Effectiveness
Clinician	Highly trained and supervised, experts	Non-expert, typical for setting, supervision only to measure quality
Training	Expert led	Depends on hypothesis
Monitoring	Regular observation and supervision with feedback	Often just monitoring, but may provide feedback depending on hypothesis
Setting	Usually academic clinics	Community-based organizations
Comorbidity	Co-morbidity is rare; many exclusions	Comorbidity is measured, with a few exclusions
Control Condition	Placebo, Active Control, Wait-list, Mechanistic Control	Standard of Care
Assessment	Often lengthy and frequent	Often low burden and minimal
Outcomes	Emphasis on clinical and mechanisms	Emphasis on clinical and implementation (depending on hybrid type)
Validity	Internal	External

effects of the treatment are maintained under less-than-ideal circumstances (see Table 9.1). Let's take each study component in Table 9.1 and dive into the details.

The Study Clinician

A primary distinction between efficacy and effectiveness studies is that clinicians in efficacy studies are usually highly trained and closely supervised psychologists, often clinical interns or postdocs in an academic research institute. In effectiveness trials, the study clinician is a clinician in a real-world setting, often community mental health centers, who has agreed (or been volunteered) to participate in the study. For example, in the IMPACT study of collaborative care for depression in late life, clinicians were nurses and social workers employed in the primary care clinics (Unützer et al., 2002).

Clinician Training and Monitoring

The degree to which the investigative team interacts with the clinician, from training to monitoring, will vary depending on the study's intent. In pure effectiveness studies where the focus is mainly on the replication of treatment effects in a unique population, the investigative team will be involved in training the clinicians and will engage in monitoring and feedback to the clinicians as they deliver the intervention. In a hybrid type 1 study, the clinician will undergo training by the investigative team, and quality will be closely monitored, but depending on the hypothesis, feedback may or may not be given to the clinician during the study. As an example, in the study from Chapter 4, they hypotheses were to study the comparative effectiveness of the new intervention to PST and to determine the amount of skill drift post training clinician in each condition would experience over time. Thus, clinicians were trained by the developers of the new intervention, were closely monitored for quality, and received corrective feedback from the experts. The number of hours in corrective feedback was one of the study outcomes so that the burden of implementation in the real world could be examined.

In hybrid type 2 and 3 studies, the clinicians will likely be randomized to different types of training and ongoing support, particularly if the intent of the implementation hypothesis is about how to best train and support clinicians in an intervention. If the implementation question is not about training and support, then the training may remain training as usual.

The Setting

In all types of effectiveness studies, the setting for the trial will be representative of the typical setting, clinic, school, hospital, etc. where the intervention will be offered. Even though this improves the generalizability of the study results, you will still need to be clear in describing the setting in which your study is to be conducted. For example, let's say you want to study whether a suicide prevention intervention will work when delivered by nurses in public schools. It will be important to describe where the school is (urban or rural), what resources the school has (access to school foundations), and to describe the children, nurses and teachers. While you may find the suicide prevention intervention to be effective in the school district you conducted your study, it may only be effective in school settings most likely the one you conducted your research.

Comorbidity

An important distinction between efficacy studies and effectiveness studies is that efficacy studies tend to have many participant exclusion criteria. In efficacy studies, the participant must have a verified diagnosis provided by a clinical expert using a standardized instrument and typically do not have any other behavioral conditions unless the purpose of the efficacy trial is to test treatment effects in co-occurring disorders (see Chapter 8 for examples). In an effectiveness study, the participants will be representative of the typical patient in the setting or community of interest. Participants will certainly be evaluated for whether or not they have the diagnosis or behavioral challenge in question, but the assessment will be similar to what is done in practice. While an effectiveness study may elect to conduct a standardized assessment of the participant to verify they have the condition to be studied, most effectiveness studies will rely on the clinical judgment of the clinic evaluation. Effectiveness studies have fewer exclusions, but will still have some, for instance, the patient participants will likely have some other medical or behavioral co-morbidity, but it usually be considered secondary to the primary diagnosis. Some conditions may be excluded if they are deemed to either interfere with the ability to participate in the intervention or the research. Let's take the example of CARED (Areán et al., 2015), a study of case management and Problem-Solving Therapy for late life depression in low-income communities. In this study, the patient participants were older adults with Major Depression who qualified for home-based meal programs. The team was interested in whether Problem-Solving Therapy was effective for treating depression in homebound, low-income older adults, or if clinical case management should be added to address social determinants of health. Additionally, the team wanted to test if social workers in senior service agencies could effectively deliver these treatments. Patient participants in this study only needed to meet criteria for major depression to qualify. They could also have co-morbid anxiety, substance misuse and chronic illnesses. However, potential patient participants who had significant memory impairment were excluded because it was unlikely that they would be able to consent to be randomized to treatment.

The Control Condition

While efficacy studies may use no-treatment, placebo, or active control conditions, the typical control or comparison condition in effectiveness and hybrid type 1 and type 2 research in psychosocial intervention research is standard of care (Areán & Alvidrez, 2002). Standard of care, sometimes called usual care or usual treatment, is an intervention broadly used and adopted by the typical settings and clinicians from whom the typical patient seeks care. Standard of care is not always another evidence-based treatment, although evidence-based treatments are sometimes used in effectiveness and hybrid type 1 studies. Often the standard of care is whatever is already offered, and you as the investigator will need to determine and then define what the standard is in each community. Sometimes the standard of care is nothing. In this instance, you will need to either monitor the people randomized to the control closely for safety reasons, or you may need to consider an enhanced usual care condition. The PROSPECT study (Bruce et al., 2004) was an effectiveness trial to study the integration of mental health services in primary care medicine to prevent suicide events in people over the age of 65. In planning the study, the team determined that the standard of care in primary care medicine was basically nothing; clinicians did not screen for suicide, and if suicidal ideation was expressed by patients, the clinicians tended to attribute the statement to normal aging (Uncapher & Areán, 2000). For ethical reasons, the PROSPECT team elected to create an enhanced usual care intervention that included teaching primary care physicians how to recognize suicide in late life and what to do if they determined risk. While this is more than what was typical in primary care settings at the time, it was still the more ethical decision in choosing a control (Alexopoulos & PROSPECT Group, 2001). Whatever the standard of care is in a community, you will need to describe it for readers of your data to understand the findings (see Chapter 4).

Assessment Times

In an effectiveness and hybrid trial, you will want to keep the assessment times as low a burden as possible. Most investigators try to keep the patient participant assessments under 45 minutes to reduce respondent fatigue and to minimize the tendency for patient participants to drop from the study. Efficacy trials often involve multiple assessments and sometimes multiple assessments of one outcome. In effectiveness trials, assessments are tied to key periods when you expect a change in the outcome (or mediator) to occur, and often, only one measure of each outcome is collected.

Outcomes

The typical outcomes for effectiveness trials are clinical symptoms, psychosocial functioning, intervention acceptability, intervention implementability, clinician quality over time, and burden/side effects. Table 9.2 highlights the primary differences in outcomes between efficacy, effectiveness, and hybrid trials.

Table 9.2 Differences in outcomes among efficacy, effectiveness, and hybrid trials

	Efficacy	Effectiveness	Hybrid type 1	Hybrid type 2	Hybrid type 3
Symptoms	Primary	Primary	Primary	Primary	Exploratory
Functioning	Secondary	Primary	Primary	Primary	Exploratory
Mechanisms	Primary	Primary	Primary	Primary	Exploratory
Burden/side effects	Secondary	Secondary	Secondary	Secondary	Secondary
Acceptability	—	Primary	Secondary	Primary	Primary
Adoption	—	—	Secondary	Primary	Primary
Appropriateness /Fit	—	—	Secondary	Primary	Primary
Costs	—	Secondary	Secondary	Primary	Primary
Feasibility	—	—	Secondary	Primary	Primary
Fidelity	Secondary	Primary	Secondary	Primary	Primary
Penetration/reach	—	—	Secondary	Primary	Primary
Sustainability	—	—	Secondary	Primary	Primary

Symptom measures in effectiveness studies include measures that the typical clinician and setting will use in practice. Because some practices do not use outcome measures, you will need to conduct your own assessment of symptoms but be sure to select measures that are low-burden, most likely to be used in typical practice, and at the same time are valid and reliable. The same is true of *functional outcomes*, but in the case of effectiveness trials, the functional outcome will likely be one that is important in informing policy (absenteeism), or outcomes that patient advisors suggest are as important as symptom change, such as improved concentration, better social engagement, and improved well-being and quality of life. Finding brief measures of these constructs can be challenging, but the National Institute of Health provides a library of outcome measures available for free. You can search on the NIH Toolkit or the PROMIS measures website by outcome of interest, age group, language, and length.

Intervention acceptability is an outcome that is increasingly important for implementation questions. Acceptability of an intervention can happen at the patient level and clinician level. Collecting information about acceptability can help us understand how well or how hard it would be to implement an intervention in a particular community and with clinicians and help point the way toward improving aspects of the intervention to make it more acceptable. An example of an acceptability measure is the Theoretical Framework of

Acceptability Questionnaire (TFAQ), which assesses affective attitude, burden, ethicality, intervention coherence, opportunity costs, perceived effectiveness, and self-efficacy in clinicians using an intervention (Sekhon et al., 2022).

Fidelity is measured for different reasons in these study types. In efficacy studies, you will be monitoring fidelity to be sure that patient participants are receiving the treatment condition as assigned and providing feedback and corrections to clinicians if any drift is detected to improve the delivery of the psychosocial intervention in the study. In effectiveness and hybrid type 1 studies, clinicians may or may not be given feedback (that depends on the purpose of the study), but in hybrid type 2 and 3, quality is measured but feedback is not typically given because the intent of these studies is to determine what degree of skill drift you can anticipate when the intervention is provided in the real-world context. Sometimes, the outcome of interest in a type 3 trial is the degree to which an implementation strategy is effective in reducing skills drift. You will want to use measures of intervention quality to measure that outcome.

Intervention Burden is the degree to which patient and clinician participants find the intervention to be difficult to use or burdensome. In a way, for psychosocial interventions, burden is a primary side effect of the intervention that impacts intervention usability. If the intervention is onerous, time-consuming, and difficult to learn, then it will be less likely to be used in the real world. Hopefully, some of these issues will be addressed when you create or modify the intervention (see Chapter 3), but there are cases where burden may be something that cannot be addressed. Take the example of exposure therapy, an intervention for the treatment of PTSD. Indeed, exposure therapy is the leading evidence-based treatment for PTSD, and there are aspects of exposure therapy critical for treating OCD. Most clinicians' initial reactions to this intervention are that it is overly time-intensive (90-minute–2-hour sessions, a few times a week) and can be uncomfortable for the patient because they are being asked to confront the trauma or anxiety in a non-avoidant way. While the exposure is done ethically and gently, the active ingredient of exposure therapy is facing the feared event until the anxiety extinguishes (hence the long therapy sessions and frequency of sessions). In this case, the intervention may be deemed burdensome, and thus implementation strategies to support clinicians in the delivery of this intervention would need to be developed to reduce (but likely not eliminate) user burden. There are not many good measures of intervention burden or usability, but we do recommend the Intervention Usability Scale (Lyon et al., 2021b) as one potential measure that has good preliminary psychometric validity and reliability, and the User Burden Scale (Suh et al., 2016). An alternative to this is to conduct focused interviews with clinicians to assess burden and usability.

Validity

Effectiveness studies are noted for having high *external validity*, the degree to which the results from a trial can generalize to other settings and populations. When a study has high external validity, the results from the study are likely to inform public health and public policy because the sample is more representative of the general community and the intervention is delivered in settings and by clinicians that the typical patient is mostly to encounter (Steckler & McLeroy, 2008). The more that patient participants share with the typical patient population, the more study clinicians represent the typical clinician seen by the typical patient, and the more settings are real settings where patients seek or receive care, the more generalizable the findings are and the better the external validity. *Internal validity*, the degree to which the findings of the study reflect what would happen under the most ideal conditions without confounds or bias, is important in early phases of research (efficacy research), but the findings are only limited to the highly controlled and selected populations and settings in which the study was conducted.

It's important to note here that effectiveness studies must strive to be rigorous and trustworthy, even though they may have more limited internal validity than an efficacy trial. Effectiveness studies do define the population, setting, and clinicians being studied; measures used do have to be valid and reliable; the control condition also has to be defined; and there is a defined study protocol that the effectiveness trial should follow, with any deviations from that protocol reported.

Randomization

Effectiveness and hybrid effectiveness trials always involve randomization, but random assignment to different study conditions can happen at different levels. The first is participant-level randomization which we discussed in detail in Chapter 8. Another common level of randomization is at the *clinician level*. This is usually done when there are concerns that clinicians may not be able to be trained in two different interventions, when there are concerns that clinicians may behave differently (beyond the treatment being offered) with patient participants assigned to one condition than they do when working with patients assigned to another condition, or when there are concerns that patients within the conditions will interact and influence each other's behavior. This phenomenon is called study contamination. To avoid this contamination, clinicians are randomized to the study conditions instead of patients, and all patients receiving care from that clinician receive that condition. Similarly, *organization-level randomization* tends to be more common in hybrid type 3 studies and pure implementation studies. In this instance, entire organizations (e.g., clinic offices, provider organizations, schools, prisons) are randomized to receive the new intervention or implementation strategy. Imagine, for instance, a study of a new therapy being done in one clinic with randomly assigned clinicians to different conditions. Clinicians will interact with each other and discuss their new techniques. The clients may also interact in the waiting room or their neighborhoods and discuss the therapy they are receiving. This might destroy study masking and result in contamination if a therapist in one condition attempted to implement strategies from a different condition.

However, randomizing at higher levels comes at a statistical price. Clusters of people in nested settings tend to share characteristics that influence treatment including demographics, attitudes toward therapy, exposure to trauma, and socio-economic level. These shared characteristics result in shared variance within the cluster that will confound treatment effects, especially when there are a relatively small number of clinicians or organizations in the study, which is almost always the case. This requires different methods of data analysis and could impact the power of the study. Statistically, we refer to the degree of shared variance among groups as the Intracluster (or Intraclass) Correlation Coefficient (ICC). Computing the ICC is simple: it is the variance between clusters divided by the total within and between variance. Unfortunately, correcting for the ICC can be difficult and choosing among the several options is confusing. An appropriately trained biostatistician can help your team navigate these issues. In recent years, it has been noted that a common family of approaches—known as hierarchical linear modeling, mixed effects modeling, or multilevel modeling—is often overkill if your goal is simply to adjust your statistical estimates due to clustering. While these analytic approaches feature a great deal of analytic flexibility, they also have stringent assumptions that are often not met or analytic choices that can lead to bias if made incorrectly. Other options to consider include generalized estimating equations and cluster-robust standard errors (McNeish et al., 2017).

Because the number of higher-level units for randomization is often small (e.g., therapists, agencies, schools, classrooms), yet simple randomization is a large-sample procedure, it can be helpful to block and/or stratify your randomization unit to help balance conditions on important baseline covariates. We described stratified and blocked randomization at the client level in the chapter on efficacy trials (Chapter 8). The process for higher-level units is the same, except you use variables at the level of randomization. For instance, if you are randomizing therapists you might stratify by therapists' years of experience or attitudes toward implementation. If you are randomizing agencies, you might stratify by the size of the agency and proportion of clients in different races. We have found that blocking by using nearest neighbor matching is a convenient method of balancing conditions across multiple continuous and categorical covariates. Your biostatistician can help with these details.

What Sample Size Do I Need for Effectiveness and Hybrid Trials?

The issues discussed for sample size estimation for efficacy trials (Chapter 8) are pertinent here, especially to determining your minimum detectable effect size (superiority versus non-inferiority, active control versus placebo or no-treatment). An additional consideration here is clustering. As described above, clustering results in shared variance within clusters, which will lower your statistical power, all else being equal. Clustering will weaken your statistical power even if you are not randomizing at that level. You may even have a study with multiple levels of clustering. For instance, in our studies in school mental health, it is common for us to have four levels of clustering—timepoint within student, within clinician, and within school. It is important for you to include a range of ICC estimates in your power analyses at each level of clustering and, to be conservative, to estimate these ICCs at the high end of the range. These estimates can be obtained from your pilot data and other studies. An important and useful resource is a paper that defines estimates of therapist ICCs across a meta-analysis of 20 different psychotherapy trials and found a range from 0.001 to 0.05 at the clinician level.

What Is the Typical Timeline for These Trials?

Effectiveness and hybrid effectiveness trials take a while to conduct, the usual timeline for such trials is five years. You may have noticed that psychosocial interventions study timelines vary from long-term studies (1- to 2-year follow-up) to shorter timelines (a few weeks after treatment ends). There is no one correct answer for the best timeline in psychosocial interventions research in general, thus, the length of time you will follow your participants depends on what you have learned from previous studies of related issues and on the purpose of your study. If your study's purpose is to determine acute response to treatment (Do people recover from depression after receiving treatment?), then you will not need to follow your participants past a month after treatment. If you wish to determine response to treatment and stability of treatment gains once the participants are no longer receiving care, you may want to follow your participants for a year after treatment ends. If you are interested in determining the number of people who relapse after they recover from treatment, or you are interested in long-term costs of care, you may want to follow participants for one to two years (depending on the disorder you are treating).

It often makes sense to address such questions sequentially. First, question the acute effect of treatment. Very seldom does a treatment that shows no clinically significant effect in the short term become effective in the long term ("sleeper effects"). Once the acute effect of treatment is shown, one might ask the next question in a separate study by delivering the effective treatment to all in the sample, then randomizing to a "usual follow-up" group and to a maintenance treatment group (e.g., amplifying the preferred treatment for those who initially did not respond, and giving "booster" treatment for those who did).

Determining the length of follow-up is not the only issue to consider in specifying your study timeline. You will also want to define how often during the follow-up period you will want to track the outcomes of interest. In depression studies, most researchers will assess every one to three months. However, if the follow-up period is up to two years, that timeline may change to every six months to minimize respondent burden. How many times you assess participants will depend on what makes the most sense for your study.

The trajectory of response during and after treatment is generally nonlinear. Change often happens immediately after the start of treatment (much of this may be due to statistical regression to the mean, expectation effects, and other such artifacts). Thus, if your interest lies in acute response to treatment, it is wise to obtain observations more frequently in the early stage of treatment—perhaps a baseline measurement, followed by measurements at monthly intervals for half the duration of treatment, and then every three months thereafter. By the end of treatment, there is likely to be an approach to stabilization, and less frequent measurement is necessary. For very long-term follow-up after treatment, there is often a trend back toward baseline values, but this is generally a slow enough change that once every six months might suffice. In some studies, it may suffice to take a pretreatment and posttreatment measurement—a wise choice if the assessment of outcome is costly (e.g., brain scans) or painful (e.g., spinal taps). In other studies, even daily observations might be best—particularly if the response can be obtained from a quick self-report from the participant. What is crucial is that you use the information gained from other studies to make the most cost-effective choice of timing to answer the questions of greatest interest to you.

A final word here about "measurement exhaustion." If you require too much follow-up (both very long measurement sessions at each follow-up, or many follow-ups closely spaced), the participants, the evaluators, and the measures themselves can become "exhausted." In this case, participants and evaluators may become less careful and focused, with a consequent loss of reliability of the measures. Moreover, some measurement procedures lose their value with too frequent use. The extreme example is a learning task. Once the subject has accomplished the task, asking him or her to do it again at another time will not elicit a valid independent result. In making decisions about the duration and frequency of follow-up, such factors should also be considered.

What Are the Best Practices with Community Partners?

Effectiveness, Hybrid Effectiveness-Implementation, and Implementation studies all involve creating partnerships with community-based organizations. Finding community partners can sometimes be challenging, and it may take time to identify a partner who would be willing to participate in research. If you follow the key principles embodied in Community-Based Participatory Research (CBPR), you should be successful in finding and working with a partner. Briefly, CBPR is a research partnership approach where the scientific group and the community group share the same concerns about a public health problem and are equal partners in developing methods to study and solve the problem (Holkup et al., 2004). CBPR has been a partnership method that has been around since the 1940s, when Kurt Lewin, a social psychologist, developed the method to promote social change. A recent study (2020) conducted a synthesis of principles, strategies, and approaches to CBPR and created six subcategories of successful community research partnerships (SCI Guiding Principles Consensus Panel et al., 2020). They are:

1. *A collaborative and equitable relationship between the researchers and community partners in all phases of research.* The main thing you will need to keep in mind as a scientist is that scientists have not always been ethical or fair in their community-based work, so trust will be hard earned. You should approach work with your partners with the expectation that they know more about their community than you do,

and they will bring to the partnership an invaluable source of information. The community partner should be involved in the study design from the project's start and should have a say in the hypotheses to be tested and the methods used to conduct the study. For instance, Dr. R, a geropsychologist, was interested in documenting the extent of mental health problems in older homeless communities and the treatment options currently available to them. Dr. R sought a partnership with a Federally Qualified Health Center that served older adults who are homeless. The clinic's chief medical officer was interested in this question, too, but also asked Dr. R to include assessments for cognitive impairment and adherence to treatment recommendations so he could use this data for fundraising purposes. Dr. R also worked closely with the clinic team to develop methods for identifying participants, conducting interviews and incentivizing participation that did not interrupt the clinic workflow, nor was seen as coercive in any way. Thus, not only did the study Dr. R wanted to pursue benefit her work, but it also benefited the clinic.

2. *Co-production of knowledge.* CBPR approaches emphasize that researchers and community partners co-own the products and data that come from the research. As we discussed in Dr. R's example, not only did she collect the data for her own needs (to identify pertinent research needs she could pursue), but also for the chief medical officer's needs. In addition to shared data, she also helped to validate a mental health screener that this clinic could use. She also shared all publications with the clinic leadership so that they could review the language to be sure it was not derogatory toward older homeless communities nor the clinics that served this community. In some CBPR projects, researchers and community partners will co-write publications and co-conduct presentations.
3. *Meaningful stakeholder engagement.* At times, funding agencies will make the CBPR approach mandatory and will insist on the creation of a community advisory board. While these are very important aspects of research, they can be used superficially. Authentic engagement means that the researchers and community partners engage in a shared decision-making process for all scientific decisions from the creation of the hypotheses, the selection of methods and measures, how to engage with the community and how data and findings will be shared with the community. As illustrated in Dr. R's example, she agreed to add screening for dementia to her research, investigate the use of health services, and collaborate closely with the clinic personnel to ensure the methods would not be burdensome.

4. *Capacity-building, support, and resources.* The benefit of the research should be bi-directional. Many CBPR-based projects provide additional training to community members in research skills, shared data, and as was done in Dr. R's project, she created a screening measure that would fit into the normal workflow of the clinic. The community also provides resources in the form of access to participants, education about cultural nuances about health and mental health that may not be obvious. In a different study with Indigenous populations in the United States, Dr. R learned a considerable amount of history about the treatment of this community she did not have, which helped her to understand why it would be difficult to have neighboring tribes collaborate on research projects unless it was clear that the project would serve everyone's needs fairly.
5. *Communication processes.* For a successful partnership, both the researchers and community partners will need to have frequent, open, and clear communication. Regular check-ins, discussions about how decisions are made, and openness to hearing different opinions are important for CBPR to succeed.
6. *Ethical collaboration.* Collaboration between partners needs to consider respect for community autonomy and the fair allocation of limited public resources. The community should be able to partner in research without negative impacts from participation. As we described above, Dr. R shared her results with the clinic leadership before publishing her data to ensure the community was fairly described and to ensure her interpretation of the data made sense in the community she was studying. Regarding resources, particularly with treatment studies, there is a perception that once a research team has collected its data, it tends to disappear and with it take the resources that were available to the community as part of the partnership. This is why point 4 above is important to attend to.

What Should I Do If I Need to Change Partners or Methods Mid-Study? The Example of COVID-19

Usually, when you have conducted your pilot study in the community or with an organization, the methods and partnerships will be stable and unintended changes in procedures are likely to be small. However, there are situations where you will need to change research partners and research procedures, owing to unanticipated environmental challenges and practices. We have had to face this challenge working with health companies which often have frequent turnover in leadership, resulting in a diminished interest in participating in research. Sometimes, these issues can be worked around with a renewed commitment to finish a project, other times you may be in the position of needing to find a new partner, or stopping the study. If you are in a position to change partners and if your new partner has access to a similar population and can deliver a similar intervention, then the only concern you may have is in a cohort effect: you may not be able to analyze combined samples from two different organizations without some statistical adjustment.

Another challenge is when there is an environmental event that impacts everyone. The global pandemic of COVD-19 introduced enormous challenges for public health and had a significant impact on research projects that were actively collecting data before the pandemic. Most investigators had to stop their studies early in the pandemic, and almost all investigators had to change the way they delivered study interventions and collected data. In some cases, particularly in studies conducted in medical settings, if the study was not specifically focused on the pandemic, study sites elected to stop participation in research. In the former case, where study procedures had to change, like changing study partners, data collection could continue, but adjustments to the data analysis plan needed to be made to account for any differences remote treatment and assessment may have had on treatment outcome and assessment accuracy. In the latter case, many investigators could not find replacements for their organizational partners and had to postpone their studies until the challenges of working in health settings during a pandemic were resolved. For some people, this took a year or two. In all situations where a planned partnership is fraying, it is important to communicate with your funder early and often so they can help you determine alternatives, whether those involve delaying the study, changing partners, changing the study, or some combination of these alternatives. Thankfully, most funders are understanding of these challenges and in the United States, NIH may have supplemental money to help investigators with supporting staff for a period until the study can resume.

Ethical Considerations

Here, we discuss a few critical issues regarding the ethical conduct of your study. The ethical considerations for effectiveness and hybrid effectiveness trials are like those in efficacy trials. However, there are additional considerations that need to be addressed for effective trials regarding informed consent, participant compensation, and working with vulnerable populations and communities who have historically been abused by research.

Informed Consent

The discussion in Chapter 9 details how to obtain an informed consent from research participants in clinical trials. All of what is discussed there applies to effectiveness and hybrid trials. Additional considerations for effectiveness trials are the need to ensure that there are accommodations for populations where English is not the first language, for people with low literacy (even below 6th grade), or in populations that cannot read due to visual impairments and other sensory disabilities. Effectiveness and hybrid effectiveness trials are more likely to have diverse populations in terms of education and sensory disabilities, thus, always consider these issues when planning your consent procedures.

For people living in poverty or in regions where access to health services is scarce, Therapeutic Misconception could be a very real problem. Therapeutic Misconception is the belief that participation in research will resolve the problem under study. For people who have no or limited access to health care, they may be particularly motivated to participate because they have no other option. This is not to say you should not include people who have poor access to health care in your research. However, participants must understand that there may be no benefit to them for participating in research.

A final thought on informed consent is to be clear about who your research participants are. Particularly in hybrid effectiveness trials, participants are not limited to the people with the condition under study, but also the clinicians and organizations who are providing the treatment. You will likely have an implementation outcome focused on the impact of an implementation strategy on clinician behavior or accessibility of treatment. You will also need to obtain consent from those clinician and organizational participants and ensure that their participation in research will not impact their employment in their work settings. Indeed, organizational leaders will need to know that your study cannot share information on participants, the exception being when someone is dangerous or in danger. Not all organizations understand this requirement, thus, they will need to be informed about the need for participant confidentiality.

When should you use "usual care" in an effectiveness or hybrid effectiveness trial?

As you may recall in our discussion of control conditions, in some situations usual care may be no care. For some study questions, it will be important to demonstrate that a new intervention or implementation strategy is better than the existing level of care, even if it is no care or limited access to care.

Studies that include usual care conditions are highly informative for policy makers and insurers who want to be sure the new intervention or implementation strategy is truly better than what already exists. However, you will need to consider the risks of participating in a protocol where you will study a condition that may have a high risk of mortality if not treated. Indeed, most IRBs will want some assurance that you are at a minimum monitoring outcome and removing participants in the case that they are becoming worse over time. As in the PROSPECT study, it may be best to at least provide some minimal level of care in communities that have no or limited access to health care (Areán & Alvidrez, 2002).

If usual care is not ideal but a necessary comparator, there may be trial designs that may be more appropriate such as a wait-list control, so all participants will eventually receive treatment. Your team may also consider a Cluster Randomized Stepped Wedge Design, wherein clusters of participants such as entire clinics all begin the study in usual care and then move from usual care to the treatment condition over time (Harvin et al., 2020). This has the advantage of all participating clinics eventually being trained on the intervention (this could also be done in a traditional RCT at the end of the study). However, clients in the study may exit treatment before their clinic transitions to the intervention condition, so this will not benefit all participants. You will still need to closely monitor people who are still in the usual care condition, and analysis of these designs is highly complicated; you will need a biostatistician or methodologist with expertise in this trial methodology. Another design approach is to use unequal or unbalanced randomization, wherein the number of people exposed to usual care is smaller than the intervention (Sverdlov & Ryeznik, 2019). This method, too, has its own analytic challenges and for conditions where the incidence of the outcome you are preventing is low (for instance, death by suicide), comparing samples with different numbers may lead to misleading results. For all of these design considerations, it should be reinforced that there is no guarantee the new intervention is more effective than usual care. In fact, probabilistically, the study team should always remember that most new interventions do not work better than usual care.

Participant Compensation

Participant compensation in hybrid effectiveness trials is usually at a smaller scale than efficacy trials, largely because participant burden is not as high. The research assessments in these trials tend to be scaled down to a manageable level and are scaled to minimize the perception of coercion in populations where a financial incentive for participating in research may be a highly motivating variable in willingness to participate. The ethical writings on the impact that financial incentives have on the willingness to participate in people with financial insecurity is mixed. With some ethicists reasoning that if the risks of participating are clear and understood, and the monetary incentive is reasonable for the effort, then there should be no concerns about using them (Resnik, 2015). Others reason that monetary incentives could be the variable that makes a person agree to participate in a study they normally would not participate in because of the risks involved (Klitzman, 2013). So far, there is no data-driven research to verify which position is correct. Likely, the decision to use monetary incentives will be up to your community partners and your IRB. Keep in mind that incentives to participate do not have to be monetary. Access to services and goods, providing feedback about the study, and gift cards can also be used as an incentive, if you are unable to provide a monetary incentive.

Journal Reporting Considerations

Several guidelines exist for reporting your study. It is important that you preregister your study's protocol including hypotheses, variables, data collection plan, and analyses. The Standard Protocol Items: Recommendations for Intervention Trials (SPIRIT; https://www.spirit-statement.org/) provides guidance for researchers when reporting protocols, including a checklist with sections detailing instructions for administrative information, introduction, methods, ethics, and appendices. For instance, item 10 addresses the need to include inclusion and exclusion criteria for all participants including agencies and clinicians. Though developed for study protocols, this document is a useful resource for reporting any clinical trial. Similarly, the Consolidated Standards of Reporting Trials (CONSORT) provides detailed descriptions of the elements to report in clinical trials across 25 areas (Schulz et al., 2010). A helpful checklist that can be used to draft and proof your report is located at http://www.consort-statement.org/. For example, under title and abstract, the checklist includes "1a. Identification as a randomized trial in the title; 1b. Structured summary of trial design, methods, results, and conclusions." Additionally, professional organizations and journals often provide reporting recommendations and requirements. For example, the American Psychological Association has developed the Journal Article Reporting Standards (JARS) for quantitative, qualitative, and mixed methods research (https://apastyle.apa.org/jars), and the JARS for Race, Ethnicity, and Culture (JARS-REC; https://apastyle.apa.org/jars/race-ethnicity-culture). The JARS are designed to be used for all psychology reporting and includes guidance for authors, reviewers, and editors. For instance, one standard in the JARS-REC is "When applying a theoretical framework to a group that is not consistent with the group that the framework was developed in/for, explicitly state this and detail the strengths and limitations of applying the framework to this group." Finally, some funding agencies require you to complete a PRECIS-2 diagram if you are conducting a pragmatic effectiveness trial. PRECIS-2 (PRagmatic Explanatory Continuum Indicator Summary, Loudon et al., 2015) is a chart that show how pragmatic a study is on nine indicators: participant eligibility (how strict the entry criteria are), recruitment source, setting (academic medicine versus community), organization (who the clinicians are), intervention delivery flexibility, treatment monitoring, follow-up methods, relevance of the outcome to the patient population, and intent to treat versus as-treated.

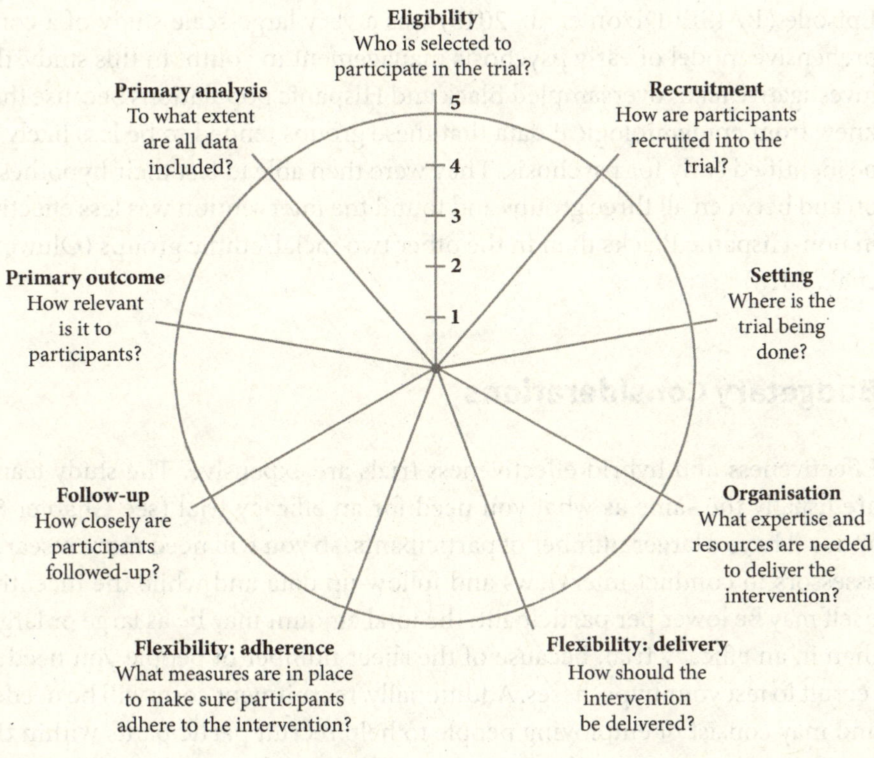

Equity Considerations

The purpose of effectiveness and hybrid effectiveness trials is to ensure a new intervention works in the typical person with the condition in question, what the impact of co-occurring illness has on intervention effects, and what conditions are needed to ensure the intervention can be used by the typical clinician working in a particular setting. In effectiveness and hybrid effectiveness trials, sample diversity is key, and you will want to do more than sample the proportion of people in your area but oversample a representative group of people to ensure the results are generalizable to more than the majority community. You do not have to necessary recruit every potential age, racial, ethnic, gender group in your study, in fact, some studies on representation in research finds that those studies that do recruit historically under-represented samples, tend to conduct White versus Non-White analyses, which leads very little information on the differential response to treatment by group (Alvidrez & Areán, 2002). Instead, it may be wiser to hypothesize in advance which groups you believe may have a differential response to treatment and over-recruit those groups. As an example, the Recovery After Initial Schizophrenia Episode (RAISE; Dixon et al., 2015) was a very large-scale study of a comprehensive model of early psychosis management in youth. In this study, the investigative team oversampled Black and Hispanic populations because they knew from epidemiological data that these groups tended to be less likely to be identified early for psychosis. They were then able to test their hypotheses on and between all three groups and found the intervention was less effective in non-Hispanic Blacks than in the other two racial/ethnic groups (Oluwoye et al., 2018).

Budgetary Considerations

Effectiveness and hybrid effectiveness trials are expensive. The study teams are usually the same as what you need for an efficacy trial (see Chapter 8). You will have a larger number of participants, so you will need more research assessors to conduct interviews and follow-up data and while the incentive itself may be lower per participant, the total amount may be as large or larger than in an efficacy trial, because of the sheer number of people you need to recruit to test your hypotheses. Additionally, recruitment costs will be needed and may consist of employing people to help recruit participants within the organization you are conducting your study. In studies conducted in service settings (most of these trials are conducted in settings outside academia), you will need to include money for subcontracts to those organizations. In effectiveness and hybrid effectiveness trials, you will be using clinicians who work in the organizations you are studying. Although you will not pay for the service being provided (unless there is no way for the organization to bill for that service), you will need to pay for clinician time spent in research activities, such as training, supervision, and completing research assessments. You may also want to have access to data the organization collects for billing or service purposes, such as electronic health record data from medical organizations to look at service use over time, and this will require help from the people who manage that data. Most trials of this nature hire a community or organizational champion who will help to implement your study. Below is a list of staff and items you will need for your budget:

- *PI:* 30% effort (3.6 months): Effectiveness and hybrid effectiveness trials are time-intensive, and the investigator will be maintaining the partnership with the organization where the research is occurring. Thus, you should put aside as much of your time as you can to lead the study. Often, these trials will be Multiple PI (or MPI), because you may need an expert in the intervention to be the study and an expert in implementation research. MPI teams tend to have the same or similar percentage of time effort on awards.
- *Project manager:* 100% effort (12 months). Because of the regulatory burden and the need to maintain communication between the research team and the organizational partner, most managers on these trials are full-time.
- Two *Research assistants:* 100% effort (months). As we noted above, you will be recruiting a larger sample of participants than you would for an efficacy trial. You will need about two research assistants to manage that effort.
- *Data entry assistant:* 25–50% effort (3 to 6 months)
- *Site champion:* 25% effort (3 months). Site champions are much like recruiters for the study, and often have other duties in the organization, for instance, they may be a clinician, supervisor, or unit chief. They are unlikely to ask for more than 25% of their time to work on research, but the decision about effort on a project should really be left up to the organization and champion.
- *Study clinicians:* You will likely have many study clinicians because you will have implementation outcomes that in all likelihood would be based on clinician use and implementation of the intervention. Normally, you would not pay for their time providing the intervention, unless that

intervention has no way to be paid for, so most of the costs will be in study activities completed. The amount you set aside for these activities will need to be based on the number of hours required of the clinician and the clinicians' hourly rates. The organization will want to calculate what they think should be included as part of their subcontract to you, so make sure you start this discussion early.

- *Fidelity rater:* This is usually contracted by the hour. We often pay our raters $125 USD an hour. However, hybrid type 2 and type 3 may not collect information on clinician fidelity unless that is an important part of their hypothesis.
- *Biostatistician:* 25% effort in the first few years, more in the last year (3 months)
- *Data manager:* 25–50% effort (3 to 6 months)
- *Participant fees:* Transportation costs ($3.50 a mile); compensation ($20 to $50 an interview.
- *Equipment:* One or two computers in the first year, any interview material costs.
- *Publication fees.* Since the first version of this book, the number of open-access journals has increased dramatically. The demand for such journals is the result of growing demand from funders to ensure anyone can access publications from a clinical trial (or any study) for free. Further, many journal editors feel it is important to distance themselves from industry advertisers to reduce conflict of interest. This has meant that journals now have a dwindling source of income. Fewer people pay for journal subscriptions and fewer companies advertise. This has put the onus of publication costs on the research team. Hence, you will need to budget for publication costs. In the CREATIV Lab, we try to reserve about $5000 per study.

Chapter Summary

Effectiveness and hybrid effectiveness-implementation trials' purpose are to test the effects of a novel intervention when delivered in the typical service setting (school, medical, community, and other settings), with the typical clinician. Hybrid type 1 trials emphasize the effectiveness of an intervention while also looking for the challenges and barriers in successful implementation. Hybrid type 2 trials simultaneously test the effectiveness of an intervention and implementation strategies. Hybrid type 3 trials compare different implementation strategies, while also ensuring implementation methods preserve the intervention effects. While most studies of this nature employ 1:1 randomization, quite a few employ cluster randomization and other methods to test hypotheses at the system or community level when 1:1 randomization is not possible. Clinicians in these studies are the typical clinician you would find in the organization in which you are conducting the study, and while you may monitor the quality of intervention delivery, that data is typically outcome data, and rarely are clinicians given feedback to adjust quality unless clinician feedback is an implementation strategy you are testing. Sample sizes in these trials are usually large to very large and can last 4–5 years. You will also be working with community partners in research, so familiarity with community-based participatory methods of engagement is important to maintain the partnership.

10

Remote Clinical Trials and Working with Industry

Critical Questions This Chapter Will Address

- What is a remote clinical trial?
- What do I need to do to create my own digital tool?
- How do I work with an industry partner?
- What recruitment and retention challenges will I face?
- What is data collection like in a remote clinical trial?
- How should I manage the transfer of data from people's mobile devices?
- What ethical issues should I be aware of?

What Is a Remote Clinical Trial (and How Are They Different from Traditional Trials)?

A remote clinical trial is a study that uses distance technology to conduct research. Distance technology includes everything from telephone-based recruitment, assessment, and treatment to the use of digital tools such as mobile phone applications, computer-assisted assessment and treatment, and sensor-based systems such as smart watches and other wearable health devices. Usually, these studies are collecting data on mobile mental health offerings, such as digital mental health smart phone applications, online interventions via the internet, secured messaging interventions, and more recently generative artificial intelligence chatbot for delivering psychotherapy. In many ways, remote clinical trials are not different from the traditional clinical trials we discussed in previous chapters. In fact, the main differences between these trial types are:

- The intervention is often either all digital (like an app) or a traditional treatment supported by technology (psychotherapy using text messaging).

High-Quality Psychosocial Interventions Research. Second Edition. Patricia A. Areán and Michael D. Pullmann, Oxford University Press.
DOI: 10.1093/oso/9780197681923.003.0010

- Assessment is often conducted through an online or digital assessment tool. Because the tools are available through smartphones or other devices, you can collect data more frequently through brief notification-based surveys or continuously through wearable sensors like smartwatches.
- Recruitment is not limited by geography: you can recruit people from anywhere you are ethically and legally allowed.

The main difference between a traditionally run clinical trial and a remote clinical trial is that participants do not come into a lab, they do all their research activities through technology. Some remote clinical trials are *fully remote*, meaning that there is limited involvement of research staff beyond checking data quality, technical assistance, bug-fixes, and monitoring for adverse events. Most are "human-in-the-loop" remote trials, where a research team member is involved in some aspects of the study, either delivering treatment, or conducting initial screenings to verify participant-study fit. We discuss the pros and cons of each type of remote clinical trial later in the chapter. Because remote clinical trials are so similar in design to traditional clinical trials, we will only discuss in this chapter the unique aspects of remote trials. Previous chapters on intervention development, proof of concept, pilot, efficacy, and effectiveness studies already cover what you need to know about randomized psychosocial intervention trials in general.

Remote clinical trials are not novel approaches to testing the effects of an intervention. In fact, clinical trials of internet-based psychosocial interventions for mild forms of mental health conditions and behavioral health interventions such as smoking cessation have been around since the late 1990s (Taylor et al., 2017), and telephone-based treatments have been around since the late 1980s (Corry et al., 2019). However, many of those early studies were limited to prevention studies or studies with low-risk populations and many were more hybrid remote studies, where the treatment may have been delivered over the phone or the internet, but recruitment and assessment were local and often in-person. Fully remote clinical trials were first launched around the time that personal, Wi-Fi-enabled smartphones came to being in the mid to late 2000s. The first fully remote clinical trial of behavioral interventions was launched in 2013 (Areán et al., 2016, where recruitment was conducted over the internet, assessments were self-guided, and three mobile applications based on evidence-based treatments for depression were tested using only smartphones.

There are several advantages and disadvantages to these types of trials. We will go over how to manage the disadvantages of such trials later in this chapter. The main advantage of remote clinical trials is the participant reach and opportunities for better participant inclusion/diversity. By not requiring participants to come to a university or health center to participate, research teams can include participants from around the globe. The sample may be more representative of the typical patient who would use technology for mental or behavioral health concerns. People often use such tools because of time constraints and other barriers to accessing health and mental health services. A participant who can make the time to attend in-person assessments at a clinic or university may not be typical of the person who would use these tools. The ability to recruit large samples into remote clinical trials allows research teams to answer questions that require larger samples, such as the impact of clinical or participant characteristics on treatment effects (moderation, see Chapter 4) and mechanistic hypotheses (mediation, see Chapter 4). Often, remote clinical trials using smartphones or wearable health devices can gather information about behavior on a moment-to-moment basis that can provide clarity and nuance about mental health and behavioral states which in turn could help the field better understand the progression of illness and the course of treatment.

Like all scientific methods, there are challenges associated with this type of research. While recruitment is typically easier, it can also be fraught with the potential for manipulation by bad actors and fraudulent respondents who participate for money and do not provide valid data (Rogers et al., 2022; Salinas, 2023). Retention in such studies is much more challenging than it is in traditional trials, particularly as there is limited or no human contact with research participants. While the potential for better population representation is greater than in local clinical trials, the samples will not be representative of people who do not use or cannot access mobile technology. Additionally, devices are always updating faster than science can keep up with, which results in considerable expense and data collection challenges every time the software being tested needs to be updated. Finally, the use of digital data and research conducted over devices and Wi-Fi is being highly scrutinized at the government level for concerns about privacy and ethics, concerns shared by the general population (Carlo et al., 2020; Pratap et al., 2019; Renn et al., 2019). Indeed, there are significant differences in the type of data that can be collected in the United States and in the United Kingdom, with the United Kingdom and European Union having adopted stronger privacy restrictions about the type of digital data that can be accessed (Regulation 2016/679 of the European Parliament and of the Council, 2016). It is therefore important for researchers interested in using these technologies to be familiar with the challenges of remote clinical trials and how to address them proactively. There is very little in the literature as of this writing to guide research teams.

What Is the Participant Journey Like in a Remote Trial?

Participant experience in remote trials will mostly depend on the trial type (fully remote or hybrid/human-in-the-loop), the length of the study, the frequency of assessment and assessment type, and the intervention to be studied. A remote trial is a study that uses distance technology only and does not require in-person interaction. Even those remote trials that involve a human-in-the-loop still use distance technology (video conferencing or text messaging). As soon as a participant meets someone in person for treatment or assessment, it is no longer a remote trial.

Fully Remote Trials

Fully remote trials are those where the only human contact is for technical assistance. Everything is conducted online, from the recruitment and consent process to follow-up assessment. These trials are fast and efficient but do have their challenges (see section on Fraudulent Acting under Recruitment section in this chapter). These trials are best used for initial proof of concept or to answer a question about the effectiveness of digital health tools when you need answers quickly. As an example, our research group conducted a fully remote trial of free commercial apps for mood that could be downloaded from the App and Play stores to study the utility of these commercial apps for coping with COVID-19 during the lockdown phase of the pandemic. Because we did not know when the lockdown would end, and because access to mental health care was limited, there were grave concerns about potentially increased rates of suicide and the availability and potential effectiveness of support provided to them. We were interested in learning what apps people were most likely to use, how satisfied people were with free offerings, and which seemed to have the greatest impact on mood over time.

Our method was to conduct two studies. The first was a fully remote survey of people's preferences for apps to cope with distress during COVID-19 and to ask participants to design the ideal app for themselves. This first study was to determine which were the most popular apps people were turning to, so that we could select apps we wanted to compare in a subsequent remote clinical trial (Mata-Greve et al., 2021). Using a research community called

Prolific (see details in the Recruitment section of this chapter), we identified approximately 2000 US-dwelling adults who were 19 years old and older and had varying degrees of risk for suicide. From this pool of participants, participants could consent to be contacted for the second part of the study. Those who consented were contacted via email and given a code to access a website for the second study.

In the second study, the participants completed an eligibility screen, including an online informed consent and a consent quiz to ensure the participants read the consent and understood the risks and benefits of participating (see Ethics section in this chapter). Once they consented, participants completed an online assessment using a data collection application called REDCap (Harris et al., 2009, 2019) and then were randomly assigned to one of four free-of-charge commercial apps. As our team did not work directly with these app companies, the process of downloading the app and using it was entirely done by the research participant. One limitation of this study (and a limitation of not partnering with a company) is that we were not able to access use or meta data, such as whether the participant downloaded the app and used it as recommended other than through a self-report four weeks later. In this trial, all assessments were self-report via REDCap, for which people received text reminders to complete, and were only pre-post between week one and week four of the study. Other remote trials go for longer, sometimes up to six months, with daily surveys, and the collection of "passive" data such as information from smartwatches about physical activity, heart rate, and ambient sound and light. The only contact our study team had with participants was to send participants links to our study website and survey, and to troubleshoot any problems with completing surveys and receiving incentives. Thus, to a participant, the journey in a fully remote clinical trial will look completely automated.

Retention in a fully remote clinical trial is very challenging, and while we do not know for sure why retention is a problem, we suspect it may have to do with the level of commitment the participant may have and the degree to which they have had a personal connection with the study. One meta-analysis of remote longitudinal studies found that while fully remote studies had the best recruitment and population representation, these studies at best kept participants engaged for no longer than four weeks. However, when there was a personal connection to the study, for instance, recruitment from a health center, or some contact with the research team, recruitment was slower, but retention was better and there were far fewer problems with fraudulent participation (Li et al., 2022; Pratap et al., 2020). For these reasons, we highly recommend using remote trials with some human-in-the-loop.

Hybrid Remote/Human-in-the-Loop Clinical Trials

There are several ways that a human-in-the-loop clinical trial can operate. For instance, study participants may interact initially with a research assistant to complete eligibility screening and consent but then all remaining procedures are conducted remotely. In other studies, a research assistant will meet via video conferencing with participants periodically in the trial, to collect more extensive assessments and analysis. Sometimes the treatment you are studying will involve engagement with a clinician or coach who will either guide the participant in using a digital mental health tool or will provide real-time treatment through a remote platform. While the treatment and assessment are done over distance technology, a study team member is always involved in some aspect of the study procedures.

Our research team completed a remote, human-in-the-loop clinical trial comparing psychotherapy delivered over video conferencing to psychotherapy delivered through text messaging (Areán et al., 2021). The purpose of this study was to determine the effectiveness of text-based psychotherapy in treating depression, the rationale being that many such companies were beginning to offer psychotherapy in this manner, but there had been no study to determine if it was effective. The process of conducting psychotherapy by text messaging is very different than the traditional process: in videoconference psychotherapy, people meet their therapists about once a week for close to an hour, just like in face-to-face therapy. Text-based psychotherapy, on the other hand, was semi-on demand; a person could contact their therapist as often as they liked during the day, with therapists replying either immediately or at some point within 24 hours of receiving the text. Participants in this study were recruited through radio ads and through contact with the company that provided these therapy options. Screening, consent, and assessment were conducted in a fully remote manner, but treatment involved contact with a licensed clinician employed by the company. In this case, the human-in-the-loop was part of the treatments being studied, but the research tasks were all done remotely.

Are There Remote Research Platforms I Can Use to Conduct a Remote Clinical Trial or Do I Have to Build My Own?

In this section, we discuss remote research platforms to help you recruit, consent, and collect data remotely, and to provide technical assistance. We discuss building a digital behavioral health intervention in the following section.

Several online data collection and participant tracking systems exist, with two of the most common being REDCap and Qualtrics. REDCap is free to use by thousands of universities and research institutions that are part of its consortium. It requires some training and expertise to develop complex surveys and tracking, but it also features extensive documentation, and many institutions provide robust support. Qualtrics is a for-profit company, and the app is more user-friendly for programming than REDCap, but both offer highly similar features. There are also companies that will help you conduct a remote research platform from the point of recruitment to study completion (end-to-end platforms). These companies will help you design a website, post ads (sometimes even have curated research participant communities) and collect all your data (and can even help you develop your digital intervention). For instance, Google Health has a research platform called Open Health Stack (https://developers.google.com/open-health-stack) where Google can help you use their tools to build a remote research platform. Apple ResearchKit provides a similar service to research teams (https://www.apple.com/lae/researchkit/). These tools are open source, so teams with software engineering expertise can create a research platform and provide some technical assistance at no cost or at a small cost. A quick internet search will show you that some universities have created end-to-end remote research platforms, and that there are independent companies that also offer these services. However, we have never used any of these end-to-end platforms and so cannot really evaluate the pros and cons of them. These companies may be most useful to a research team that needs software engineering help or that does not want to or know how to create a customized experience.

For our remote research, we have used a combination of existing research tools (Qualtrics or REDCap) and home-spun tools (websites, consent videos). The main advantage of creating your own is direct control over the process of data collection and data warehousing, as well as some economy.

Recruitment and Enrollment Tools

As with in-person trials, remote trials require a process by which participants will receive information about the study, informed consent, and begin the assessment and study procedures. Whether you intend to provide a study website for providing material or solely communicate via email or text messaging, here are some possible features to consider:

- *Study overview*: An overview of the study, including a lengthier explanation of the purpose of the study, study procedures, and contact information, can be provided using a PDF or a link to a study website. Webpages should be created such that they are visible on both a laptop and a smartphone. There are many free website builders you can use to create your own website, or you can hire someone at a minimal cost to create one for you. Whether you use a website or a PDF flier, it's a good idea to brand your study with a consistent color scheme, font, and appealing study logo to professionalize the experience, so participants can easily identify the study, and so participants begin to build a relationship with the study.
- If you're using a study website, it should have a simple homepage with basic information as to the study purpose and who you are looking for. The landing page (the first webpage seen) may contain the consent screener, which will let the participant know whether they initially qualify, or may contain a button that asks if the participant wants to learn more (see Figure 10.1)
- *An informed consent page or link (optional)*. This will often come before a full eligibility screen because in the eligibility screen, you will collect and record personal information, which you cannot do without a person's consent. The consent, which can consist of text or a video, introduces the study and explains what the participant can expect once they enroll. Some research teams will put an entire consent form on the website for people to read. Othersprovide both a video and a guided tour of a study along with a printable consent form. If the consent is taken online without a human in the loop, you can verify participant engagement and comprehension using a consent quiz that the participant must

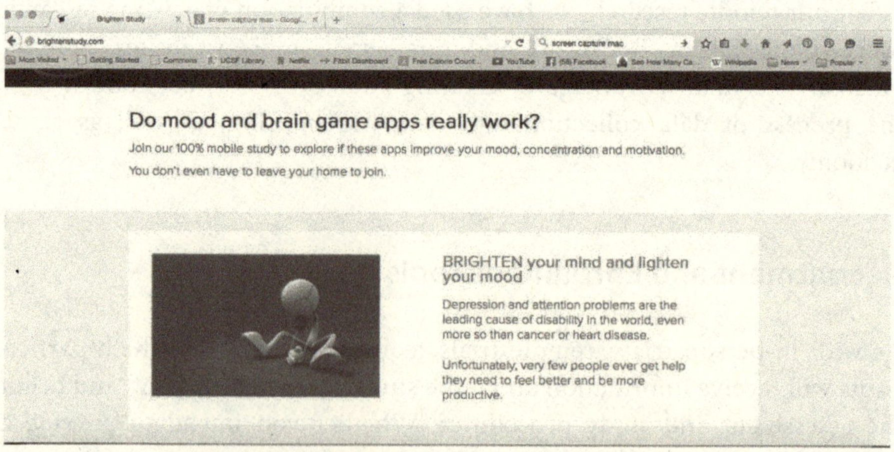

Figure 10.1 Example homepage for study website

pass to proceed. The quiz covers various aspects of the study, with a True/False format. If the participant selects the incorrect answer, they are given a written explanation of the correct answer and may be re-asked another comprehension question. If the consent is to be collected by a research team member, that will occur in the first eligibility meeting (and you likely will not need this page). See Appendix for a quiz example.

- *An eligibility survey.* You can design your survey collection software to automatically email, or your website will include a link to the eligibility survey after the participant completes the consent quiz. This link is to a survey package (see below) where data will be collected and stored on your university or health system's secure server.
- *A link to the study calendar for a video conference appointment (human-in-the-loop only).* Depending on the study design (fully remote versus human-in-the-loop), you may or may not need to include a calendar link. If you intend to collect the consent remotely but conduct the eligibility screen through videoconference, the calendar link can appear after the informed consent is taken. If you plan to collect consent and eligibility over videoconferencing, then the link will appear after the initial eligibility screen. There are many companies that provide online appointment scheduling services, and many universities already have access to these tools. The convenience of these tools is that people can schedule the initial step at their convenience. The challenge is that you may find yourself with many missed appointments, particularly if the appointments are too far out into the future. You will need to plan for the fact that a sizable proportion of people will not show (about 75% in our experience), so plan for this. You can also try double appointments and have research assistants back each other up if more than one person shows up for a time slot. This is no small feat, however, it is one of the reasons research teams prefer fully remote trials. However, it is an illusion that there is a time or monetary cost savings to fully remote assessment; the time and money saved by having people conduct assessments on their own is usually spent on cleaning up data from the number of fraudulent participants you will get without the video-conference screener (see Fraudulent Actors under Recruitment below).

Assessment Tools

Which tools you need will depend on the frequency and type of data you intend to collect. There are three types of remote data collection you may consider for your trial: Fixed schedule assessments, momentary data collection collected randomly throughout the day or triggered by a wearable sensor, and passive data from wearable sensors. Let's address fixed schedule surveys and assessments first, as these are the easiest and least expensive to collect. Commonly used commercial or academic survey tools include REDCap, SurveyGizmo, Qualtrics, and SurveyMonkey (there are many others, but we have had the most experience with these tools). These will carry a cost for you, although REDCap is free to most academic institutions. Each of these tools can conduct surveys on a website interface or by text messaging. REDCap, SurveyGizmo, and Qualtrics have the added advantage of being able to randomize participants to conditions, should you choose not to verify your participants first (something we do not recommend you do). You can even build in non-monetary incentives, such as information, progress in a study, and funny gifs or inspirational images (see Retention section in this chapter). These surveys can also set up schedules for fixed survey times, sending reminders and surveys at a prespecified time. Some can even conduct random daily surveys.

Sensor-triggered surveys and passive data collection are more complicated, and you may need to work with a platform like Open Health Stack or ResearchKit to collect this data. Sensor-triggered surveys are generally used to collect data to validate information from a wearable sensor. For instance, a participant may get a survey when there is no movement detected on their sensor, along the lines of "You haven't moved in a while. Did you forget to put your watch on? Are you working? Are you sick?" Passive data collection is currently a popular mode of data collection to understand the nuances of participant behavior and how environmental factors contribute to treatment response. Location data on these devices can help with understanding how phenomena like noise or air pollution may impact physical activity or sleep; data on when a phone screen is on or off can provide valuable information about sleep quality. The potential for this data is very appealing, but we warn that it is not perfect. See below under the data collection section and the ethics section for more on the challenges of passive sensing data.

Randomization and Intervention Link

Once participants are deemed eligible to participate, you will want to randomize them and sign them into their study condition. If you are conducting eligibility over videoconferencing, it may be best to conduct the random assignment then and help the participant sign into their study condition. If you are not conducting a videoconference screening, you can randomize participants immediately using a software program. As we mentioned above under Assessment, some survey tools have intervention randomizers included, and that feature may drive your decision as to which survey tool you use.

Final Note on Platforms

Regardless of whether you build your own platform or invest in an end-to-end platform, you will need time to test the participant journey. The steps are:

- *Cognitive Interviews* (or alpha test). Select about 10 people to test your platform and complete the surveys. This will identify bugs in the process, survey questions that may be confusing and any broken links.
- *Beta test.* Sometimes you only need one beta test, sometimes you need several. It very much depends on how complex the platform is. Prepare for about three of them. Each beta test will need about 50 or more people, the more people who use your platform, the more likely you are to catch a bug. Once you get feedback and fix the problem, you will then move to conducting a soft launch.
- *A soft launch.* A soft launch is a form of a pilot, where you test your study methods on about 25–100 participants. They will go through the entire study process, and you should warn them that they may encounter bugs because they are the first to participate. In fact, having an easy-to-find portal where people can report bugs would be ideal in this phase of testing. Soft launches are characterized by many stops and starts, so do not recruit 100 people all at once, stage your recruitment so you can solve problems without too much burden on participants. Once you have found all the bugs, you can now go to your full launch, but continued quality assurance and improvement is needed.
- *Continued quality improvement.* You will need to continuously be on alert for new bugs as they pop up. Some bugs are due to a change in the software you are using, changes to phone or web operating systems that trigger new bugs in your programming (or shut your study down), and device generation problems (see Representation in this chapter).

Creating Your Own Digital Intervention

A question we get all the time is, should one create their own clinical tool and if so, how should they go about doing that? The answer to this question depends on whether there is a similar intervention on the market, and if so, whether the owner will work with you. Descriptions and reviews of existing mental health and wellness apps are available at some websites, such as https://mindapps.org/. If an intervention does not exist, do you have the money for development? In our experience, it is often less expensive and time-consuming to work with an existing intervention, although that option is never problem-free. We discuss partnering with technology companies in the next section.

Building your own intervention has certain advantages, for instance, you control the content, and you can be sure the intervention has all the active components you feel need to be included. If you do decide to build your own intervention, you should consider becoming familiar with Human (also called User) Centered Design methods (HCD, described earlier in this book). This approach is one that is commonly used by software and device developers, the aim being to make sure the intervention's *usability* is good, and that it does not require someone needing to read a manual to use it. Usability is the extent to which an intervention can be used to achieve specific goals with effectiveness, efficiency, and satisfaction (Lyon et al., 2021b). Interventions with too many buttons, writing, and decision points all confer a burden on the person using the intervention, which may increase the probability that the person using the intervention will stop using it before they have had a full dose of treatment. In fact, most digital interventions are often abandoned within the month of downloading the intervention (Borghouts et al., 2021; Lipschitz et al., 2022). There are many reasons why people abandon these interventions, from poor usability to having reached maximum benefit from using them (Gan et al., 2023). Understanding how your intervention may be used by the typical participant in your study is an important step in its design.

The HCD process is iterative and collaborative. The design expert will begin with an initial, usually paper version of the digital intervention to be developed. Through a series of interviews and observations, the designer will watch the participant engage with the digital intervention and will ask the participant questions about the layout of the intervention, how hard it looks like to use, and will solicit ideas for how to make it better. The designer uses this information to create new versions that they will continue to iterate on until the designer and participants are satisfied with the digital intervention. The designer will then create a workable (but often not final) version of the intervention and will then ask participants to use it as they normally would in their daily life. The participants may be asked to keep a diary of use or may simply be interviewed at the end of a week of use, with the aim of identifying new usability challenges that need to be addressed. Once this data is collected, the new version is tested with a larger sample of participants in a proof-of-concept manner.

Who Should You Have on Your Intervention Design Team?

You will need to add new teammates to your research team to build your own tool. Depending on what you are building, you will need a design expert with user experience research skills, a software developer for mobile applications, an engineer for devices, and a web developer for any websites you are creating. Depending on the resources available to you, you may be able to identify people in your university who would be willing to partner with you to design your new tool. There are also small businesses that will work with you to build your tool as work-for-hire.

If you do have colleagues in your system who could work with you (for instance, other faculty in engineering or design departments and schools), please keep in mind that their interest in your project will need to be high. These are not "work-for-hire" staff but rather people who have their own academic and research careers. If the project is not interesting to them, they will not partner with you, and even if they did agree to partner, you will not be at the top of their priority list if the project is not interesting or beneficial to their career. If you cannot find a colleague with the skills you need and an interest in your project, you may be better served working with a small business. If you do find such a person, make sure that the colleague is engaged at every step of the planning and data collection and has an outcome or product that will benefit their career. In our experience, colleagues whom we have worked with will want to present the engineering or human-centered design findings to professional conferences in their field or may ask to support a graduate student who can use similar data for a publication. The more your colleague has invested in the project, the faster the development process will be and the higher the quality of the tool.

If you do decide to work with a company, get quotes and references from at least three companies. Read about their process for development and meet the team. Ask them these questions:

- What design approach do you use? Can I see samples?
- Who are your customers usually? Can I speak with some of them?

- How many projects do you have going on currently? How many projects do you usually handle at a time? What is your process for prioritizing tasks and projects?
- How long do you think it will take to build my tool? (add about 3–6 months to that estimate).
- How much will this cost?
- Who is on your team?

Be very wary of anyone who says they will design your tool for free, for minimal cost, or will get you a final product in three months. That is not realistic.

Word of Warning Regarding App-Based Interventions or Assessment

Whether you are building your own software app or partnering with someone else (see below), you will need to keep a software engineer on board throughout the study to address bug fixes as well as operating system updates and changes in digital technology policy. Your software engineer will need to stay up to date on any potential operating system updates, as these updates can result in app crashes. Trust us, we have had this happen in our work several times. If you are prepared and know of an update coming, you will need to pause your study and warn your participants of that pause, to make sure the app or digital tool will function smoothly with the update. This can happen with web-based digital tools, too.

How Do I Partner with a Company?

Our preference is to work with companies with existing interventions who are interested in verifying that their tool is effective for the conditions for which it was designed. In the United States, there is a growing interest by companies to have credible evidence that their intervention can effectively treat the condition it is designed to manage. Some devices will require FDA approval, while others will want data to convince insurers to reimburse their members for using these digital interventions. While some companies will have their own internal research team, most will want to partner with academics. Sometimes companies will reach out to you to work with them, other times, you will have to be the one to reach out.

What to Know When a Company Reaches Out to You for a Research Partnership

If a company reaches out to you, be sure to review our discussion about agreements below, as you will want to be sure your interests are protected first. Assuming you have all your paperwork lined up and can speak freely with a company, you will want to ask several questions to determine what to expect in your partnership.

Question 1: What led you to think of me? Most company representatives will volunteer this information, but if they don't, be sure to ask. For instance, did someone recommend you to them? If so, who, why, and what was the context? Did they read a paper or see you present on a topic of interest to them? What was it about the presentation or publication that led them to consider you as a partner? It is important to know why they thought of you as a partner and what they expect you can do for them, as you may have to clear up some expectations.

Question 2: Why do they want to do a clinical trial? This is an important question because you will want to manage your expectations for what they want from a study and what you will be getting into. Do they want to have objectively collected data and a fair evaluation of their tool? Do they want to get regulatory clearance for their product, for instance, FDA approval in the United States? Do they want to test and refine their product for a different use than the tool was originally intended? How they answer those questions may inform your interest in partnering with them.

Question 3: What will be my role on the study team? Some companies will reach out to you just for the sake of having a researcher/scientist on their masthead. In this instance, your involvement may be limited to providing advice and guidance, but you will not be involved in designing the study, collecting the data, or interpreting the findings. The company may even put your name on papers that you had no direct involvement in the design and interpretation. Be very careful about agreeing to this sort of arrangement. Adding your name to a study that you did not design or inform can be hazardous to your reputation.

Some companies will want you to be part of their research team. In this instance, you may be involved as a content expert, providing your expertise on the tool's design and content, the study design, and even some aspects of data interpretation and collection. For instance, we have been involved in remote trials where our sole role was as experts in recruitment, data collection, and ethics. In others, our role was in advising the best assessment tools or content expertise. When engaged in this way, it is important that you are clear at the beginning about your ability to publish from the data and clarity about data sharing when publishing from such data.

Some companies will want you to be an independent investigator. In this case, the company's role is to provide access to the product to be studied and engineering support. Your role is to test hypotheses, collect research data, and evaluate the tool's impact on the condition it is designed to manage. In this instance, you will need to have a conversation about who owns the data and publication rules. In our experience, most companies will want to own any proprietary data, but the research data belongs to the research team. There may be some instances where research data is shared with the company and the company shares its proprietary data. In almost all our partnerships, we have had to have our presentations and manuscripts reviewed by the company. But in our agreements with the company, we make it clear that while they can review and comment, they cannot prevent us from publishing the findings, regardless of the outcome.

Question 4: What is your timeline? Companies and academics work on different timescales, with companies usually living by the "move fast and break things" motto, whereas academics live by the "slow and steady wins the race" motto. Also, most academic institutions are stable institutions, whereas most tech companies tend to have short lifespans. Therefore, you need to be sure that the company's timeline fits with yours. We have had experiences where companies will meet with us in say, late January, wanting to submit a research application to a funder by the end of March. That is usually too fast and too short a timeline to submit a competitive application. While you will have to get used to moving faster than usual, the company will also need to be realistic about your timeline.

Question 5: What is your business plan? Learning about a company's business plan will help you understand what stage of development they are in. Some companies are still dependent on venture capital, and do not have a sustainable income model yet; these companies are usually more cutting edge, but also at greatest risk of either failing or changing their entire model out of necessity. Sudden change in business models and financing is one of the most difficult aspects of working with companies. You can literally be in the middle of data collection, only to learn that the company has a new CEO who is not as friendly to research as the last one was, or that the company is about to declare bankruptcy. One of the biggest challenges in working with technology companies is their failure rate. About 90% of all tech startup companies fail, with 60% failing in the first five years of business (Chakraborty et al., 2023; Rigg, 2022).

Question 6: Can I access your intervention and make suggestions for improvement? You will probably not be able to gain full access to the intervention until you have at least a Nondisclosure Agreement (NDA) in place (see below under Agreements section of this chapter). Most companies will show you images of the intervention initially to get your input, but you should always have a chance to use the intervention yourself to make sure it has all the active ingredients you are interested in studying. Having some ability to make improvements will be important, even for minor changes. For example, we partnered with a company who had developed a therapeutic videogame we thought may have benefits for older adults with depression. In our pilot studies, many older participants claimed that they had trouble seeing important images because in one level, the digital environment was too dark. The company agreed to "brighten" that level for us, which resulted in better usability for the older participant. In another example, we partnered with a company who delivered therapy largely using text-messaging, sometimes in combination with video-conferencing, but did not offer video-conferencing alone. We explained that to study the effects of text-messaging therapy alone, we would need to compare it to an accepted delivery mode of psychotherapy, which in this instance was video-conferencing without access to text messaging. For the purpose of the study, they agreed to provide a video-conferencing only condition.

Finding a Partner

If no one is knocking on your door to partner with you, you can knock on theirs. Finding a company to partner with is not unlike finding a community or clinic partner. You will have to do some research to see who has a tool that you are interested in researching and is willing to partner. Here are some ways to initiate a research partnership with a company:

- Look for an existing history of doing research with outsiders. Look into publication databases and see whether the tool you are interested in has been published before and if they have an existing partnership. You may be able to make inroads by contacting the outside researcher first about a potential partnership with the company.

- Some companies have on their websites the names of people on their scientific advisory boards whom you can reach out to. Some even have research request portals where you can describe (in very general terms) your interest in their product and the type of research partnership you are looking for.
- See if the company attends any of the health technology conferences. If so, sign up and meet the people presenting.

As with building a partnership with communities and clinics, building a partnership with a company can take time and be a slow process of building trust. Your research project may be one aspect of your overall job, whereas their product may be their entire focus. When you first initiate contact, it is important to be honest about your limitations on time as well as your dedication to scientific integrity and openness.

Agreements

When working with a company or developer, expect some initial paperwork. While the paperwork is a bit of a nuisance, it is important to protect your (and the company's) intellectual property. Never sign anything a company gives you without looking it over first. You would be surprised at what is in these existing boiler-plate agreements, including that the details of any conversation you have belong to the company and they can sue you for using those ideas. Most of our readers will be working in an academic or healthcare setting, and most of these settings have teams of lawyers and contracts people who can help you with these agreements. The type of agreements you will likely need to put into place are:

1. *Nondisclosure Agreement (NDA).* The very first document you will need to create, in fact, most companies will not talk to you before you have an NDA in place. An NDA is the initial agreement that allows you to just have a conversation without making any other commitments. You will need to agree not to share anything the company shares with you outside of the partnership and they will need to do the same.
2. *Data Use Agreement (DUA).* This agreement usually happens after you have decided to work together and have an initial plan. It is necessary if you are to use any data that the company owns for pilot data, publications, and future research. For instance, your research team may be

collecting research data that the university owns but may need to combine that data with data the company owns. As an example, you may be collecting periodic outcome data on your own assessment app but may not have data that an app or device collects, such as number of times the app is opened, or number of steps on a device. You will need the DUA (and participant consent) to access that data.

3. *Master Service Agreement (MSA).* An MSA is a contract that is usually created at the beginning of a business arrangement and lays out the basic terms and conditions between you and the company. This usually precedes a full contract and allows you to work together to plan and allows you to make amendments and future contracts. You will be creating a scope of work for each party, how you will work together, what data you will have access to, who owns what data, protects each party's intellectual property. This will be your initial agreement on how you will work together.
4. *Contract.* A contract is like a service agreement only in tremendous detail and will involve lawyers talking to lawyers. This will be your final working document where your scope of work is finalized, a detailed budget is created, and milestones are laid out, with language concerning data ownership and use, publication rights, and how to terminate the contract.

Recruitment and Retention in Remote Trials

One of the main advantages of remote clinical trials is the speed at which one can recruit participants, as well as the reach your study will have. You will be able to access communities that you may not reach in traditional studies. There are challenges with recruitment that should not be ignored and that we will discuss in detail, namely the potential challenge with "gaming," that is, accidental recruitment of participants who are not who they say they are and are only participating for the incentive or just to mess with a study. We will cover that in detail soon. While recruitment can be easier with remote trials, retention is much more difficult but not impossible.

Recruitment

The use of distance technology allows research teams to extend their reach into communities beyond those around an academic or research center. If you use a fully remote clinical trial, you may be able to recruit large numbers of participants in a very short period. For instance, in one of the very first remote clinical trials for depression, the research team screened 2923 people and enrolled 1098 participants in as little as five months, and the final sample was representative of the population of the United States (Anguera et al., 2016). However, this recruitment, and recruitment in other studies, was met with challenges that are not as common in traditional studies. Before we get into the details about the best recruitment methods, it is important to first explain what the challenges are with remote recruitment, namely, fraudulent participation (sometimes referred to as gaming a study) and sample representativeness.

Fraudulent participants/gaming

Fraudulent participants (also known as gamers or bad actors) are people who misrepresent who they are with the intent of financial gain or to disrupt a study. Fraudulent actors can be individuals who enroll in your study and do the bare minimum they need to obtain a financial incentive. They can be one individual posing as several different people, signing up with different accounts and IP addresses. They can also be bots run by one person or a team of people who try to sign up as many as possible for financial gain or malicious motives. While gaming has always been a problem in online research, the problem has increased considerably over the last few years (Pozzar et al., 2020) and you should be prepared upfront for this problem. Just one bad actor can send thousands of fraudulent entries.

Several studies have reported problems with fraudulent participation, but most publications addressing this issue have mainly focused on gaming of surveys and not clinical trials. While many strategies to reduce gaming are available and should be used, there is no research yet to determine the relative cost and benefits these strategies have on recruitment and which are the most successful methods for preventing fraudulent data. However, this is a real and problematic phenomenon in clinical trials, and practices to make sure anyone randomized to a condition is an actual participant are critical to the validity of the study. While survey research can remove participants from the survey data for being fraudulent after the study is completed, this cannot be done in clinical trials. Once someone is randomized, they must be included in the final data set. Another challenge with fraudulent participants is how insistent they can be that they are in fact, who they say they are, no matter how clear it is that they are fraudulent participants. This sets up an ethical challenge (see discussion of this under Ethical Considerations) because it can sometimes be hard to prove they are not who they say they are. The effort required to address this challenge should not be underestimated.

We have had experiences where one person has claimed to be three different people to the same research assistant over video conferencing, literally wearing a different wig as a disguise.

Best places to recruit

The first method for preventing fraudulent participation is to be careful about where you recruit. Social media recruitment is highly risky, though some social media platforms and processes are less risky than others. Ads placed on platforms like Craigslist in the United States, X (formerly Twitter), search engine (like Google Search) ads, and open ads on Meta products like Facebook and Instagram result in the largest amount of fraudulent activity (Wang et al., 2023). This is likely because anyone can see your ad and then share the ad with other people. If you recruit from these sources, you will need to have a team of research assistants monitoring incoming data for signs of fraud, which can get expensive and tedious. There are also services that have a pool of potential participants they can recruit for you, for a price, but these can also run the risk of fraudulence. As of this writing, MTurk is a customer survey platform created by Amazon to help companies with marketing strategies. In the early days of MTurk, this platform was useful for recruiting participants in health surveys (Cunningham et al., 2017). MTurk and other research communities like it consist of tens of thousands of people who sign up to complete studies and are paid small amounts of money for participating. While other companies do as thorough a job of vetting their community members as possible, many have found that MTurk has historically not screened their community as well, and many will game studies (Dennis et al., 2020). Still some researchers use this platform, but most recommend using it only with specific safeguards and never alone (Ipsen et al., 2021. (see Remedies below). We do hope one day, these venues for recruitment will improve their screening, but as of this writing, they confer a considerable risk to clinical trials.

We have found that the best places to recruit potential participants are secured research communities, in partnership with online advocacy communities or through clinical networks. This results in a smaller volume of people seeing your ads but can also result in more targeted recruitment. You will still need to incorporate the remedies outlined below, but the number of people you screen out for fraud will be smaller and more manageable. These companies conduct several layers of screening to ensure their members are who they say they are and recruitment in this manner can prevent the instance where one person tries to sign up as several different people. As of this writing, Prolific is one such example. You will have to pay a fee and you cannot use the platform to conduct clinical trials, however, we have used this platform to identify potential participants from a survey study, asking them to provide us with contact information if they are interested in participating in a future study (https://www.prolific.com/).

Recruitment from an advocacy group that has an online presence or a clinical network is another way to ensure you will not be swamped with fraudulent participants. You will need to build a relationship with these organizations first and be ready to provide them with financial support to help with recruitment. It is no small thing to ask these organizations to post an ad or send out announcements, as someone in their company will need to do that (and do not expect them to provide you with a list of names).

Advertising methods

One of the biggest reasons for fraudulent participation is to gain a financial incentive. Some research groups have been successful in recruiting participants without providing a financial incentive, but participants are less likely to engage long-term in a study without some form of compensation (Bickman et al., 2021). We discuss compensation under the Retention Section of this chapter. One way to avoid gaming is to not advertise that there is a financial incentive for participating. While this may work early in the study, at some point, the word will get around that your study does provide a financial incentive, and the chance of gaming will increase.

Remedies for proactive fraud screening

There are several prevention tactics that can be used to prevent gaming and you have likely encountered them when trying to gain access to secure websites. This includes the use of Authentication apps which generate a code that is used to open a survey, Computer Automated Public Turing Test to tell Computers and Humans Apart (CAPTCHA) which employs the use of images or words to authenticate that the user is indeed a human and not a bot, and the use of random questions, called attention checks, to make sure the responses are not random or careless (Teitcher et al., 2015). Over the years, however, fraudulent participants have become more sophisticated, and these methods have become less reliable (Wang et al., 2023). This is not to say they should be abandoned; in fact, you will need to use as many tactics as you can to ensure people are who they say they are and are serious participants. However, you will need to employ additional methods which include the following:

1. *Recruit from trusted sites.* As we mentioned above, try to avoid the use of social media platforms and search engine ads to recruit.

Your recruitment will be slower, but more accurate. It will not be immune to gaming, however, so always continue to employ other prevention and intervention tactics.

2. *Screener question checks.* Like the use of attention checks, this remedy is rather labor-intensive. Our team checks certain answers to screening questions first before a participant moves on to randomization. This includes comparing age to stated year born, we ask where the participant grew up and what high school they went to and compare the location of both. If recruitment increases suddenly and drastically, we look for patterns in responses, for instance, in one study, we found in our data a consecutive run of 50 people who shared very unique characteristics (51-year-old Black men living in New Mexico, all interested in yoga). Before participants make it to the randomization phase, double-check their answers to survey questions.
3. *Use of browser cookies to prevent one person from acting as more people.* Most survey programs will be able to immediately screen out someone who is attempting to participate more than once based on their browsing history. REDCap and other programs all have this feature that can be enabled. This is also not foolproof. We have had experiences where a group of people will work together to game a study. While they are indeed different people, they are still fraudulent participants, and this method alone will not screen them out.
4. *Sophisticated, multiple-step CAPTCHA.* It is possible to create more sophisticated CAPTCHA that includes more complex responses or puzzles and "speed bumps," questions that require participants to slow down their responses.
5. *Use of unique study links.* This is also a time-consuming practice, but you can assign unique survey links that can only be used once by a participant. These can be generated before study launch and given to participants as they pass other screeners. It is ideal to have a personalized, one-time use link for each step in the research process. This will prevent participants from sharing their link with someone else. Qualtrics and REDCap can generate unique links for your study participants.
6. *Internet Protocol Address Logging.* Some survey programs (REDCap) can detect whether someone is posing as two people but using the same device or computer through the device/computer's IP address. IP addresses are sensitive and private information that may not be collected in some institutions or countries. However, REDCap is one program that can anonymize the IP address to the research team but still detect if more than one person is using the same IP address

(Pozzar et al., 2020). This still does not prevent the instance where a group of people will work together to game a study.

7. *Run-in periods.* This method is specifically useful for clinical trials. The process involves providing people with a task for a week after they are deemed eligible but before they are randomized. While we have not seen this method used in practice as of this writing, the concept is that those who are expecting compensation will be less likely to complete tasks that will not provide them with financial gain. The assumption is, those who are serious will complete the tasks, those who are not will complete some or none of the tasks. Those people can be excluded from the study before randomization, thus preserving the randomization of your trial.
8. *Graduate or save incentives until the end.* Most fraudulent participants will try to do as little as they can to participate, so making incentives complex to earn, based on engagement or saving the incentives until the end of the study may deter many fraudulent participants from your study. For instance, you can state early in the study description that incentives will be earned based on the number of assessment surveys completed and that compensation will be made at the study's end.
9. *If possible, perform your eligibility screen and at least one other assessment over video conferencing.* Video conferencing software has the advantage of detecting time and region the participant is dialing in from. Region can be game using a VPN from your country, but it is much harder to game time zone information. Seeing someone in person allows you to have them provide proof of identity to you without having to store that personal information, and fraudulent participants will be less likely to volunteer for a videoconference. Some still will try to game a study and claim they are someone they are not, but that is likely to be far less frequent and easier to identify.
10. *Require individualized information, such as a photo ID or work email address to participate.* Sites like Prolific reduce fraud by requiring participants to submit a photo ID. In our studies that are work-focused (such as the impact of an online training designed to increase therapists' attitudes toward implementing new treatments), we require therapists to provide the name of their employer and use their work email address which can be verified. Both strategies are laborious and may disincentivize authentic participants who may be reluctant to provide this type of information.

Recommendations for recruitment

1. Recruitment using a company or advocacy partner.
   - If you can afford it, use a recruitment company which already has several safeguards in place to identify and prevent fraudulent actors.
   - If you partner with an advocacy group that has an online presence, do not underestimate the effort it takes them to help you recruit. Be upfront about your needs and timeline and work on a payment that would help offset the time and effort it would take for them to help you recruit.
2. If you decide not to use a partner (and even if you do partner), put up as many safeguards as possible to avoid fraudulent activity. These safeguards include:
   - Unique or frequently updated URLs to access your study.
   - Include quality check questions in your survey.
   - If possible, ask for a picture of a driver's license or passport.
   - If possible, schedule in-person meetings via video conferencing.
   - Include sophisticated Captcha or other keys to screen out bots.
3. Check your recruitment activity frequently. If you notice extreme upticks in recruitment, be sure to check the quality questions to be sure you have not been gamed.
4. Be aware that your sample may be large and enriched with historically underrepresented research participants, but it is also only representative of people who would use technology to manage the condition you are studying. For example, in many preference studies across demographic groups, on average, only 60% would use technology to manage a mental health condition (Pratap et al., 2019; Renn et al., 2019; Topooco et al., 2022; Woerner et al., 2022).

Retention

One of the biggest challenges of remote clinical trials is keeping participants engaged in the study over time. Roughly speaking, retention rates that fall below about 80% of the sample introduces bias in the data (Bell et al., 2013), so you will want to do all you can to keep at least 80% of your sample into the study. Newer data analytic methods, such as multiple imputation, weighted approaches, and Bayesian models will allow you to go as low as 70% (Abshire et al., 2017). In the early days of this research, scientists believed that because the samples in these studies were so large, and thus technically powered to detect an accurate effect of treatment, that participant drop off was not a problem. However, the sample, no matter how large, can still be biased due to participant dropout, it just happens to be a large, biased sample.

Retention rates in remote clinical trials tend to be low (10–40%), and discontinuation from a study by participants tends to happen very early in the trial (Anguera et al., 2016; Areán et al., 2016; Pratap et al., 2020). This is a problem that all clinical trials face, particularly when participants are randomized to treatment without choice (Fogel, 2018; Inan et al., 2020) but usually it is mitigated by having a human connection to a study. The worst rates of retention tend to occur in remote clinical trials where the only contact with a study team member is for technical assistance and regular human-in-the-loop strategies result in better retention (Anguera et al., 2016; Areán et al., 2016; Pratap et al., 2020), but still not high enough to mitigate bias (Torous et al., 2020).

Given the risk of poor retention in these trials, you may be wondering why you would use this method at all. The key here is that there are advantages to these trials in that they can test hypotheses rather quickly, allow research teams to recruit from all around the world, not just their back yard (external validity), many people are truly using digital health interventions to manage their problems, and it permits data collection on not just outcomes but acceptability and use of these interventions, which is very important to the field. There is a lot to be learned about why people may or may not continue to use a digital intervention and what the use-to-response (does-response) ratio is for these types of interventions. The trick is to keep people engaged in completing assessments, even if they stop using the digital intervention, and there are methods you can use to increase the chances of adequate retention. The limitation to this discussion, however, is that remote clinical trials are so novel and so few have been conducted in behavioral health that many of the methods for improving study retention are relatively untested or based on what we know about incentives from either longitudinal survey studies or traditional clinical trials. We suspect that over time, the methods we discuss below will evolve, and we encourage readers who wish to conduct these trials not to rely solely on this chapter, but to look at contemporary publications. However, these methods are in use as of this writing and serve as an initial resource.

Prevent fraudulent participants from gaming your study

Although we cannot prove this statement, we suspect that much of the early discontinuation in clinical trials is from people who are fraudulent participants and don't realize how much time and effort it takes to participate in a remote clinical trial. This is not to say a remote clinical trial will eventually screen out fraudulent participants, we have had instances where people will complete an assessment but never engage in the intervention (this behavior is probably gaming behavior). But the effort to incentive ratio, given up front, may deter people from participating who may not be who they say they are. See Remedies for Proactive Fraud Screening above for preventing fraudulent participation.

Provide financial incentives

While providing financial incentives increases the risk of fraudulent participation, it will also likely increase the retention rates in your remote trial. There are few studies that have directly investigated the impact of financial incentives and incentive size on retention, however, a meta-analysis of longitudinal, remote clinical trials has found that financial incentives do result in better longitudinal retention than providing no financial incentive (Pratap et al., 2020). Additionally, other studies have found similar effects for long-term retention in remote studies (Kolovson et al., 2020; Pratap et al., 2019). Although not a randomized clinical trial, the Verily Mood Baseline Study compared varying levels of financial incentives on long-term retention in a twelve-week, daily assessment study about depressed mood. In this study, the research team found that large monetary incentives of about $250.00 for full participation resulted in 83% of the sample completing the entire twelve-week study, answering at least 75% of the surveys (Nickels et al., 2021).

A challenge with providing financial incentives in remote clinical trials is the cost to reimburse large samples of participants and, as we discussed above, the risk of fraudulent participation. There does seem to be a monetary sweet spot that encourages participation but is not so high that the study becomes too costly. For example, the Verily Baseline Mood Study described above found that an incentive of $250.00 USD retained a larger proportion of participants than when participants were paid $75 USD. However, a much larger amount ($600) did not improve retention. But paying participants $250.00 for twelve weeks of participation may be too expensive for most funders and may also be seen as coercive by IRBs. Most ethicists and IRBs will argue that while a small monetary incentive of $25.00 USD may be nominal for some participants, for those who are unemployed or living in poverty, that same incentive may be seen as seductive. Also, keep in mind that incentives as large as $90.00 USD for twelve weeks of participation will trigger fraudulent activity, so be prepared and have fraud prevention strategies in place.

Gamification

Study gamification (not to be confused with study gaming described above under fraudulent participation) is a method of study design meant to encourage participation using competition for points or digital "jewels" that can be used to unlock study benefits, leaderboards, return of information about health or study participation, motivational images (or GIFS), or "easter eggs," which are intentional inside jokes or messages about the study. These approaches to incentivize participation are seen as enjoyable by participants, but some methods are more appealing to certain participants than others, and thus they require you to use Human Centered Design approaches to pick the best incentives. Some gamification methods are easier to program than others. In our own experience, most participants we have interviewed over the years have said they would be more likely to stay in a study if they could be given information about how they are doing compared to other people like them (Anguera et al., 2016; Kolovson et al., 2020). However, whenever we have tried to program that feature into a study, software engineers have told us that this is very hard to program. Leaderboards and easter-egg type incentives are not as hard to create, but the easiest and as effective method is to use text-based health tips, and humorous and inspirational gifs at the end of each survey. The data on gamification has been mixed. One meta-analysis of gamification methods found that this can be a good way to increase intrinsic motivation to participate (Teague et al., 2018; Xu et al., 2021). As of this writing, there has been no study of gamification for remote clinical trials, but one meta-analysis of traditional clinical trials found that these incentives did nothing to impact study retention (Teague et al., 2018; Xu et al., 2021).

Incentives based on behavioral economics

Behavioral economics is a branch of behavioral science that seeks to understand how people make financial, time, or opportunity cost decisions, particularly those decisions that seem irrational, borrowing from the fields of sociology, economics, and psychology (Rice, 2013). In the context of research participation, incentives based on behavioral economic strategies include using social norms, where participants incentive can be donated to a charity of their choice, giving participants a variety of incentive options to choose from, using an incentive lottery, whereby each participant has an equal chance of getting an expensive, tangible incentive such as a fitness tracker, or using fixed variable reinforcement methods, where participants are given varying levels of incentives after completion of a study task, in a seemingly random manner such as receiving $10 for completing a survey one week, and $1 the next (Stevens, 2015; VanEpps et al., 2016). Like gamification, these approaches have been variably successful in survey-based and clinical trial research across age groups and populations.

Combined incentives

Another option you can try would be to provide a combination of each approach to enhance retention. As of this writing, there has only been one study of a remote clinical trial comparing combined incentives to financial incentives, one of our own (Griffith Fillipo et al., 2022). To prepare for a large-scale remote clinical trial using a Sequential Multiple Assessment Randomized Trial (SMART see Chapter 11), we studied what incentive types would enhance retention in the trial. We were particularly concerned about retention because by design, all participants were evaluated six weeks after treatment initiation for response to treatment, and those who did not respond were re-randomized to a treatment enhancement. We were also concerned that our budget would be too high for this study if we used a large financial incentive. We randomized participants in the pilot study to receive either $125.00 USD for twelve weeks of participation or $75.00 USD coupled with gamification strategies that included encouraging messages for completing daily assessments ("you're doing great, keep at it!"), facts about depression, humorous GIFs after completing surveys, and reflection exercises. We found there was no real difference in retention and data quality between the two conditions, with approximately 75% of the sample completing the essential assessments (baseline, mid-study, and final). We also found that participants who felt the incentive was fair and the assessments were not burdensome were more likely to stay in the study than those who either felt the incentive was not fair (very few participants) or was too burdensome.

Pilot test your methods with soft launches

As we discussed above under testing research platforms, a soft launch of the full study design will be necessary to find bugs and areas of user burden. Even when you have conducted proof-of-concept and pilot research of your intervention and your study design, a final test never hurts. In a soft launch, participants are made aware that part of their participation in the study is to help the research team improve the methods and fix any bugs. For the purposes of retention, this is an opportunity to test the assessment burden and evaluate the impact of the incentive you have chosen to use. We usually begin with a sample of fifty people who provide us with secure messaging feedback throughout the study. If you receive consistent reports of the study being too burdensome, you would do well to consider how to reduce the burden to enhance retention.

Data Collection and Analysis

One of the biggest advantages of remote clinical trials is the ability to collect data easily and when needed, rather than relying on participants to schedule appointments to come to a research center or clinic or requiring staff to conduct field or home visits. As we mentioned in methods to reduce fraudulent activity, having some human-in-the-loop assessment is helpful, but these can be conducted over secure video internet services. Remote clinical trials also allow for different types of data sources, which we discuss below. Some assessment types have been around for a long time (ecological momentary assessment) and thus are valid methods for data collection, facilitated by technology. Other methods (passive sensing from smart devices) are reliable for some measures (heart rate monitoring, step counting), but not yet technically reliable for other measures at the time of this writing (emotion-based voice capture). We explain each with examples of how these methods are used.

Assessment and Data Collection

Online video assessment

This form of assessment is a valid and reliable way to conduct in-person interviews, particularly since the advent of the COVID-19 epidemic. The COVID-19 pandemic resulted in valuable technological solutions that make video conference assessment easier and greater population familiarity with this form of communication. However, not all video conference products are equal, with some being better suited for confidential assessment and survey than others, and some products having different price points, depending on the features you need. You will want to look for these features that are common in many products:

- Privacy and security features that make it difficult for anyone to accidentally or intentionally break into your meeting (Zoom-bombing).
- Transcription software, so you can keep transcripts of your assessments. This is extremely valuable for qualitative analyses.
- Recording features, which allow research teams to conduct reliability checks on assessments.
- Closed captioning for people who may have difficulty hearing.
- Chat features, which allow you to share questions, response formats, or other images with the participant. While this feature is not essential, it can also be valuable for qualitative analyses and permits participation from people who may be more introverted.
- Screen-sharing, to share information with the participant.

Some companies also have a calendar feature which allows participants to sign up for a meeting with a member of your research team on their own.

If your video conference software does not have this feature, there are many free or low-cost programs you can find to help with online scheduling.

Video assessments function much like in-person assessments. You will be using the same tools and asking the same questions you would ask if the interview were in person. However, some features of in-person assessment may be missed with video assessment. For instance, body language is harder to assess.

Remote, SMS or app-based survey assessments

Conducting periodic assessments of important behavioral outcomes, such as mood or functioning, can be reliably collected by web-based, secure messaging/texting (SMS), or through an assessment app. Online and SMS based assessment is less costly than purchasing a license to use a mobile application but may not be quite as convenient or engaging as a commercial mobile application. Data collection in this manner is like in-person data collection. Regardless of the platform the data is collected in, the participant completes a survey at a specified time and enters responses into an electronic form. SMS and online surveys tend to look like most other online forms, where a question is presented to the participant, and using either radio buttons, scroll bars, or open text fields, the participant provides their answer. In mobile apps, the assessment interface may look more engaging, with the use of chatbots and other imagery to reduce participant burden. Main concerns research teams will need to consider in using any of these data collection methods are how the data will be securely transferred from the app and securely stored in your database. Methods for secure transfer of participant assessments use a secure file transfer protocol (SFTP) with cloud file sharing services. SFTP is one of the oldest ways to send information across networks. Coupled with cloud file sharing services, the data are automatically transferred to the cloud using end-to-end data encryption software. Encryption software is a program that scrambles the data so that anyone looking at it without the encryption software and the passcode cannot make sense of what they see.

Ecological Momentary Assessment (EMA)

EMA is a survey method that collects repeated sampling of participant behaviors in their natural environment and throughout the day. Before the availability of wearable sensors and smartphones, EMA was conducted using telephone reminders, beepers (these were small devices people used to carry, usually on their belt, to alert them that someone was trying to reach them), and a set of forms people completed when reminded to do so and were later collected in person or mailed to the research team. Now, these data are typically collected using an electronic diary or smartphone application, which will remind the participant that it is time to complete an assessment, then transfer the data securely to the research server. EMA is usually a brief assessment, along the lines of yes/no questions, collected daily or multiple times a day. A recent meta-analysis found that as long as there is financial compensation for assessments, six assessments a day is tolerable and the number of assessments per day does not influence participant drop-out (Wrzus & Neubauer, 2023). EMA studies vary on when the data collection occurs. There are fixed EMAs, where participants are asked to complete the EMA in the morning, afternoon, and evening, or during a ritualized event, such as "first thing in the morning" or "before and after you eat." There are also variable/random EMAs, where participants are warned they will complete surveys during the day, but the surveys are generated at random points in the day. The advantage of random EMA is that you may capture a more accurate picture of one's behavior or mood than if the assessments are scheduled. However, you also risk having missing data, as someone may be too busy to complete the survey when alerted to complete a survey or may not have their device nearby. There is also triggered EMA, a relatively new approach where EMA is triggered when another, passive assessment identifies an activity you may want to capture. For instance, if you are interested in measuring one's activity on a continuous basis, you may want to have an EMA triggered by a phone or wearable sensor detecting heart rate. In this instance, an EMA would be triggered when one's heart rate is above a certain number, say 90, and may ask the participant, "are you exercising now?" The answer to that EMA may trigger another EMA once the heart rate lowers, such as "how are you feeling now?"

Timing out a survey

With EMA, it is important to make sure you have a process whereby the survey is considered past its time, and no data collection can proceed. For instance, if an EMA is timed for 8 a.m., but there is no response by 11 a.m., you may want to close that survey, particularly if the next EMA is at noon. This means you may run into issues with missing data, indeed missing data is common in this type of data collection. You will need to work with your methodologist or biostatistician about how to best monitor missingness that has a pattern, for instance, most assessments across participants happen in the evening, but rarely in the morning, so that data analysis plans can account for that missing data.

When is it important to use EMA?

Not every study needs an EMA. As is always true in research, the need for a particular method depends on the question you are asking. EMA is useful when there is behavior you need to capture at specific times of day but it is subject to inaccuracies if you need to rely on one's memory. For instance, if you are conducting a study of an intervention on food choices, the data you collect will be more accurate if the food choices are recorded immediately after the food is eaten, than if you ask the participant at the end of the week (or even end of the day). Another case where EMA is useful is transitory experiences or states such as daily mood fluctuations. Depression is a mental health condition where many people report feeling better or worse over the course of a day. Weekly assessments of mood, while reliable over time, can be subject to "mood induction," a phenomenon where a negative or positive event can influence how someone responds to a survey asking about their mood over the past week.

Passive sensing

Passive sensing is the use of electronics in wearable health monitors, like a fitness watch, or in smartphones to measure behavior. For behavioral interventions, this type of assessment can be invaluable to understanding how an intervention you are studying impacts a potential mediator on the outcome. For instance, if you are studying a method to increase physical activity in children with obesity, with the goal being improving health outcomes, you will benefit from having a continuous monitor of heart rate or step count to accurately assess that moderator. If you are studying an intervention for anxiety and want to know what the pre- and post-intervention heart rate and blood pressure are in participants, wearable sensors can collect that information remotely and continuously. As of this writing, some sensors are more accurate and reliable than others, and there can be variability between devices (Dudarev et al., 2023). There is even international variability as to what sensors one can collect from smart devices (see ethics section below). Sensors that are deemed to be reliable are:

- **Accelerometers** are sensors in phones and devices that detect changes in speed or direction, bumps and vibrations, sharp increases or decreases in velocity and are often used to determine physical activity. It can also be used to determine if someone is exercising and the quality of one's sleep (based on tossing and turning). Accelerometers are available on wearable sensors and smartphones.

- **Geospatial Positioning System** (GPS), found in both wearable devices and smartphones, is often used to determine where people have been and can be used to measure "activity spaces," which is a measure of social activity. GPS is considered a highly sensitive data source, as it can be used to find out one's address, place of work, and common place of business, and raw GPS data is not permitted to be collected in many countries. There is software, however, that can measure activity space without using exact location, but rather the number of different locations and the distance between locations.
- **Heart rate** is usually collected from wearable devices, such as smart watches, and can accurately measure heart rate from moment to moment. This is useful if you wish to study the impact of an intervention on heart condition, anxiety, or exercise intensity. There will be variation from device to device. As of this writing, it is best not to conduct a study collecting heart rate with different devices, as is commonly done in studies where participants use their own devices, rather than being sent a study device (Nelson et al., 2020). In this instance, it may be best to either recruit participants who have access to the same type of device or to distribute devices to participants.
- **Skin conductance** is generally collected from wearables and can be used to measure stress response in participants and is highly correlated in some studies with cortisol levels (a marker of prolonged stress. Studies are mixed as to whether skin conductance is reliable across devices, however, a 2023 study did find that among commercial products, there was enough correlation between their sensors to reliably use different sensors across participants (Ronca et al., 2023).
- **Microphones** on smartphones and some wearables can collect information about noise pollution, exposure to loud sounds, social exposures (how many distinct voices are in close proximity to the participant and the participants level of engagement in conversation), vocal features that allow for natural language processing, such as words spoken, emotional content of words, and vocal inflection (voice volume, tone, pace, pitch, and modulation or intonation and cadence). These devices can also record what time of day the participant is speaking. Although this data collection has the potential for many areas of social and behavioral sciences, the *ethical* use of microphones is challenging. Recording conversations with other people, collecting ambient noise information when there are other people in the participant's environment raises an informed consent issue; people in your participants' environment did not agree to have their voices or sounds collected. Some of the data you

may be interested in, such as social connections, may not be possible to collect unless there is a way to either mask the other people's identity or by having the participant ask for consent to have the conversations recorded.

- **Keyboard data** from smartphones can collect information about the number of typing errors one makes, corrections made, and the length of messages or emails. This information has been deemed useful for measuring cognitive functions, with some data showing errors in typing being associated with cognitive decline in older people (Hossain et al., 2021). Access to the resident keyboard on a phone is challenging. Many smartphone companies have put restrictions on outside party access to this data. However, there are keyboard apps that can be used for this data collection. The challenge is that participants will need to use the keyboard app to collect the data, and not the resident app.
- **Screen time** is the time spent using a smartphone. This data is useful in determining how much one spends on one's phone as well as the time of day one is using a phone. This data can be helpful in sleep research and research into social connections.

Data Analysis

Analyses of remote data come with several common challenges, the most common of which is missing data. Remote studies tend to experience higher rates of missing data due to missed data collection points, which is particularly prevalent in EMA data as described above, and low retention or dropout, which results in monotonically missing data from the dropout point forward. This is sometimes referred to as "right censored" data when you are studying the length of time until an event occurs. Each of these situations requires a different approach to analyses which is outside the scope of this book. Addressing missing data begins with understanding the nature of the missing data, which begins by plotting data points to understand which time points, variables, and participants are associated with the data. You may also look at associations between variables, such as demographics or baseline functioning and the amount of missing data to understand whether the missing data is biased. For instance, older people who are not as comfortable with technology may be more likely to leave the study or skip assessment points. This process will help you understand whether the data may be missing not at random (MNAR), missing at random (MAR), or missing completely at random (MCAR). MNAR is the most common and should be assumed—it means that the missing data are systematically associated with data that were not collected. For instance, it is likely that much missing data is the result of a lack of motivation to participate. This is also likely related to clinical outcomes and is difficult to measure and rarely captured by studies. MAR means that missing data can be completely explained by existing variables and that, by including these variables in your analyses, you can control for the missing data. For instance, if all missing data were the result of motivation and your study used a high-quality measure of motivation, you could with accuracy control for this missing data in your analyses. MCAR means that there is no systematic reason for the missing data. This is almost never the case unless the missingness was intended by the researchers (in a planned missingness design, for instance). MCAR cannot be proven, unfortunately, because you don't know what you don't know—there always may be some external variable that is associated with missingness but that you did not collect. Therefore, in practice, we find these distinctions to be academic and not particularly useful, because real-world data are almost always MNAR to some extent and because MCAR cannot be proven. The best course of action is usually (1) avoid missing data by using study design strategies, (2) explore data for the type of missingness and reasons for missingness, and (3) address the inevitable missing data by treating your data as if it were MAR, and (4) conduct sensitivity checks post-analyses (analyses with and without statistical adjustments for the missing data).

The easiest methods of addressing missing data are to ignore it by pairwise or listwise deletion or to replace the data with the individual's mean from prior timepoints or the group mean for the target timepoint. All of these approaches might be borderline acceptable when you have very small amounts of missing data (say, less than 1%). Other, more complex but very common approaches include predicting and replacing scores using regression, using inverse probability weighting, and multiple imputations. Researchers will sometimes combine the last two (Seaman et al., 2012), or even use a variety of approaches to address different types of missing data. Inverse probability weighting assigns weights to each participant based on the inverse probability of their participation, and then uses these weights in a regression adjustment. Multiple imputation creates many datasets with the missing data replaced by estimates generated through regression-based predictions based on other variables in the dataset. Addressing missing data can be a complex topic best handled by an experienced biostatistician, especially for the type of intensely collected data often found in remote research trials.

Journal Reporting Requirements

In addition to needing a CONSORT table (required of all clinical trials), some journals may require you to complete a CHERRIES checklist, particularly if you are collecting your data fully remotely. CHERRIES is a quality reporting tool reserved for online survey studies, but in our experience, we have sometimes been asked to use this checklist to describe the quality of the remote data collection we conducted. The CHERRIES checklist has sections reporting on the research method, recruitment method, survey types, documented reliability, and validity of the remote data collection methods. As noted above, some remote data collection is still lacking in validity and reliability. Nevertheless, you will still need to report that information in your manuscript (Eysenbach, 2004).

Ethical Considerations

Data Security

Data security, in particular, the secure transfer and protection of information from remote research studies is an area of considerable interest that is continuously evolving, owing to data breaches and the misuse of information collected from digital platforms. In the section on remote data collection, we discussed the importance of using secure file transfer protocols, data encryption software, and secure cloud data storage, or local data storage. Be sure these issues are addressed in any consent form and be sure to check that participants are aware of the potential problems that can arise from data sharing.

Another important consideration regarding data collection is making sure you have a way to turn off remote data collection, particularly if you are collecting passive sensor data. Many people do not remember to turn off sharing in the settings of their phones and many forget to remove apps from their phones. You will need to have a proactive way of removing apps and turning off permissions to collect data.

Participant Safety

If you are conducting a remote trial of a condition that has a clinical risk associated with it, for instance, cardiac disease, depression, or psychosis, you will need to ensure you have several safety features associated with your study. While our research team has conducted fully remote trials with people at risk for suicide (Comtois et al., 2022) and with major depression (Areán et al., 2016), we do not recommend you conduct these studies without having some human-in-the-loop. Although neither of these studies resulted in adverse events, the potential for unanticipated adverse events is certainly there, as we experienced in a recent trial that did include human-in-the-loop (therapists providing text-based therapy). Fully remote trials should be reserved for mild conditions with low risk for adversity.

Online Consent Procedures

When conducting a fully remote study where even the consent is done without a human-in-the-loop, the collection of consent can be challenging. Most people do not read online terms and conditions thoroughly and may apply this behavior to a consent form. In our research group, we have used the following practices to ensure participants understand what they are signing up for.

- Video description of the study. It is not very difficult to record a research assistant explaining the important facets of a study, or to create a PowerPoint presentation. These videos can be created such that the participant has to watch them before moving on to the next section. Potential participants could multitask or leave the room while the video is playing, so you will need the next recommendation to make sure the video was watched.
- Consent quizzes. The use of consent quizzes came from research with participants who may have trouble comprehending consent forms, for instance, in studies where someone may be experiencing some mild cognitive impairment. In remote research, we use these quizzes not only to test if the participant paid attention to the consent form or video, but also as an opportunity to highlight the important aspects of participation. Since our research teams conduct research on mental health conditions, some aspects of fully remote trials are very important to highlight in a quiz. For instance, if someone is experiencing increased mental health symptoms, the participant will need to know how to access a team member or other service. Examples of quiz questions for the trials we have conducted are:
    - I will not have a choice in the treatment I am given, but will be randomized, like a coin flip, to a treatment. True or False?

- The purpose of this study is to understand the usefulness of commercial phone apps to cope with mood. We make no claims that any of the apps will help you with your mood. True or False?
- I am a volunteer and can discontinue from the study without penalty to me. True or False?
- My information will be encrypted and kept in a secure location at the university. True or False?
- There is no clinician monitoring my mood over time. If I am in distress, please reach out to your doctor or call 988 (crisis line) for assistance. True or False?

Is someone really a fraudulent actor?

Our research team has debated this problem for a few years and our IRB has at times challenged us to reconsider if the behavior we see in a remote trial really is fraudulent. There are certain patterns of behavior that are correlated with the probability that someone is not who they say they are (see above under fraudulent acting), but there is always the risk that you may exclude someone who is an actual participant. We offer no real solution to this quandary other than to be thoughtful as to whom you exclude from your study.

Understanding phone sharing issues

If you are asking people to use their own phone for a remote trial, keep in mind that for some populations, they are not the sole users of the phone. There are many situations where families living in poverty share their phones with spouses and children, thus confidentiality could be compromised and could compromise data accuracy of passive sensing. Some researchers manage this problem by providing the participant with a private device. If you do decide to provide devices for your research, be sure the device is locked so that other software cannot be downloaded. Regardless of whether participants use their own phone or your research phone, be sure participants know not to complete surveys in public places where others may be able to see their screen.

Age Considerations

Older Adults Are Likely to Be Underrepresented

In conducting a remote trial, be aware that you may be limited in your age representation. Although more people over the age of 60 are using smartphones and have computers, many do not and prefer not to use these devices.

Even tech-savvy older adults complain that screens are too small to read and experience data entry errors owing to age-related changes in dexterity. Sadly, tech companies have not addressed the issue of device accessibility in older populations, so be prepared that your samples may be younger than the average sample.

Representation and Equity

Poverty

As we mentioned above under ethics, the digital divide by income is a real challenge. The COVID-19 pandemic highlighted the challenges families who have lower incomes face when using distance technology, including limited availability of computers and multiple users of a single phone. Not only is smartphone use limited, but many people who also struggle financially use older generation phones that may not be capable of running the current software or even current operating systems. In addition to these challenges, there are regional differences in access to the internet, for instance, many rural areas in the United States have no or slow broadband, and people in low- and middle-income countries have unstable electricity (if any). Technology is not the access panacea many think it is, so be aware that your samples may not be representative of all people with the condition you are using.

Disability Issues

Be aware that people with vision challenges may not be able to use or make sense of your app. While nearly all devices have reader software and magnifiers, this software does not work as well with some mobile apps because of the app layout. If there is poor contrast between the background and the text on the screen, the reader software may not function. If there are too many images on a screen, magnifiers and readers will also not function well.

Chapter Summary

Remote clinical trials are a relatively new way of conducting research. These trials have the advantage of collecting data and testing interventions from anywhere in the world, without the need for participants to come to a research center to access their intervention or complete assessments. This can result in better representation than local study representation. Fully remote trials rely heavily on distance technology to recruit, randomize, and assess participants, which can result in rapid and large recruitment. However, these trials have challenges, including low retention rates and the potential for fraudulent participation. Human-in-the-loop remote trials can address issues with retention and fraudulent participation, but because of the cost of research staff, they are subject to recruitment rates like in-person trials. Software used for these trials will need frequent updates and team members who can ensure functionality. There are several ethical considerations for these trials, including participant safety, data security, and privacy. However, these issues are addressable. The value of these trials is high, in that they can answer important research questions quickly and can result in a highly representative sample in ways that local trials cannot.

11

Additional Designs and Other Considerations for Psychosocial Intervention Trials

Questions This Chapter Will Address

- What purpose does MOST serve in clinical research?
- What is a pragmatic clinical trial?
- What is a SMART?
- What is a micro-randomized trial and how does it differ from a Just In Time Adaptive Intervention Trial (JITAI)?
- What is a Stepped Wedge Design and when is it needed?
- What is a Random Cluster Design and when is that needed?
- What is the main role of Services and Systems research in psychosocial intervention research?

In the previous chapters, we described the basic methods for testing the efficacy and effectiveness of psychosocial interventions and presented to you how one studies the different phases of intervention development and testing using a person-level randomized design. There are different approaches to testing psychosocial interventions that are important for you to be aware of, but we will not explore these models in depth. In the resource section of this book, we will provide you with important readings and texts that describe in more detail the ins and outs of these methods. Here, we provide an overview of other methods you are likely to encounter, with the aim of explaining their purpose and role in generating evidence for psychosocial interventions.

Multi-phase Optimization Strategies (MOST)

Studies based on the MOST framework are used to refine existing psychosocial interventions to maximize the efficiency, scalability, and/or economy of

High-Quality Psychosocial Interventions Research. Second Edition. Patricia A. Areán and Michael D. Pullmann, Oxford University Press.
DOI: 10.1093/oso/9780197681923.003.0011

an intervention without a significant decrease in effectiveness (Collins et al., 2007). Counter to traditional studies, which prioritize effectiveness, optimization acknowledges the constraints of real-world practice, such as economic and resource costs. This framework is very similar to the proof-of-concept to effectiveness pipeline we describe in previous chapters but is meant to streamline complex interventions for better efficiency, generally once they are created and an evidence base exists. These studies are conducted in the following sequence:

1. A screening phase to identify which components of an intervention are most effective, where those that are most effective are retained in the intervention and those that are not removed from the intervention. In this phase, the therapeutic elements of an intervention are identified, and the treatment is dismantled into its effective components. A *factorial design* is often used to test which elements are effective, the best combination of elements, and the structure of the intervention. A factorial design trial compares each element as well as its combination. Figure 11.1 displays how participants were randomized in a factorial trial of Trauma-Focused Cognitive Behavioral Therapy (Deblinger et al., 2011), which simultaneously examined a research question about whether effectiveness and important mechanisms of treatment were impacted by the length of treatment impacted and the inclusion of the trauma narrative as a treatment component (a type of exposure, conducted by recounting a traumatic event). Factorial studies are elegant and efficient because they permit testing the main effects of multiple questions without loss of statistical power.

   While factorial designs are often discussed as almost synonymous with MOST, other designs may be appropriate during this phase, some of which we describe in this chapter, including Sequential Multiple Assessment Randomized Trial (SMART) and Micro-randomized trials.

		Type of treatment	
		TF-CBT without Trauma Narrative	**TF-CBT with trauma narrative**
Length of treatment	**8 sessions**	Group 1	Group 2
	16 sessions	Group 3	Group 4

Figure 11.1 Randomization of a factorial trial

2. A refining phase to narrow down the selected therapeutic elements and test hypotheses about optimal dosage. Like step 1 above, the candidate elements are again tested in a second study, often a factorial design, to finalize the optimal dose of treatment. A SMART may also be used, if the purpose is to determine the best process or sequence for introducing different components, for instance, which component should be given first and if there is no response, which components should be added.
3. A confirming phase to compare the newly optimized intervention to the original intervention standard, typically conducted through a randomized effectiveness trial.

The importance of these types of studies arises from the need to simplify and optimize psychosocial interventions. Most psychosocial interventions are *complex interventions*. A complex intervention is largely defined by having several interacting therapeutic elements which often require skilled providers to deliver and typically require the consumer or patient to learn as well. Complex interventions often have different forms for different situations based on a specific theoretical principle (Petticrew, 2011). An example of a complex intervention is Cognitive Behavioral Therapy (CBT). While CBT tends to look uniform across disorders, CBT has a minimum of four different yet interacting therapeutic components (i.e., psychoeducation, cognitive restructuring, behavioral activation, and skill rehearsal), with additional components needed for anxiety disorders (e.g., exposure therapy), and personality disorders (emotion regulation strategies). Additionally, the elements emphasized vary by age group, for example, CBT for older adults relies more heavily on behavioral activation and less on cognitive restructuring (Bilbrey et al., 2022). The challenge with complex interventions is that they are very hard to implement in settings outside of academic medicine or specialized health centers, and clinicians are required to undergo rigorous training to be certified in this intervention. Methods to streamline complex psychosocial interventions, such as MOST studies fit the bill nicely for this work.

One example of a MOST for a psychosocial intervention is the Healthy Campus Trial (Uwatoko et al., 2018), where the investigators plan to optimize the delivery of an evidence-based, smartphone CBT intervention. In this study, which is underway as of this writing, the project will optimize the smartphone-based CBT intervention by randomizing college students exhibiting emotional distress to various combinations of assertiveness training, cognitive restructuring, behavioral activation, symptom monitoring, and problem solving. Rather than compare the individual components to each other, the study will compare different sequences of each component.

For instance, some will start with assertiveness training, the move to cognitive restructuring, followed by problem solving, behavioral activation or symptom monitoring (in this order), others will start with cognitive restructuring, followed by the other components in different orders. This study will compare 64 combinations of these strategies to identify which sequences are the most optimal.

Generally, MOST is often used to streamline existing treatments with an evidence base but deemed too complex to deliver into practice. One may be able to use this approach in developing a novel intervention; in fact, this model's principles may encourage early implementation if the efficiency of practices is considered in the treatment's design. Criticism of the MOST framework for existing treatment centers around the delay in making evidence-based treatments available to the public, that to study a complex intervention first and then dismantling it results in delays in delivery (Collins et al., 2007). However, there are examples of multicomponent interventions being made available to the larger public, where larger-scale optimization occurred after broad-scale deployment (for instance, collaborative care).

In sum, MOST studies:

- Are used to streamline and optimize existing, complex interventions.
- Consists of at least two rounds of optimization before the new intervention is compared to the standard.
- Usually involves factorial designs in the early phases.

Sequential Multiple Assignment Randomized Trials (SMART)

The SMART determines the best sequence of treatment based on a set of decision rules for when to adjust treatment for a given population. These studies are often used to create *adaptive interventions* (also known as stepped care), which are interventions that feature clinical decision-making rules to help providers understand when to adjust treatment and predict which treatments or levels of care are likely to be matched to patient characteristics. The way these designs work is that everyone with a condition is initially randomized to one of two (sometimes more) types of treatment. After a clinically meaningful period, or a point in treatment where one expects to see improvement in the condition, participants complete an assessment to determine if participants are improving as expected. Important to this design is the need for a *tailoring variable*, an assessment that determines when participants should be randomized to another type of intervention or receive an augmentation to care, and is often a measure of patient symptoms or functioning. The tailoring variable should be used in normal practice or can be easily adopted in the typical practice setting. Using a tool already commonly used in practice as the tailoring variable will increase generalizability and streamline real-world implementation. If a group of participants shows improvement, they continue in the treatment condition they were originally assigned. If a group of participants is not improving, they are then randomized to receive either a new treatment (a switch), the other treatment condition (also a switch), or a new treatment is added to the one they were originally assigned (an augmentation). This reassessment and randomization can happen more than once, depending on the study question. Everyone is followed until the end of the study timeline.

We recently completed a SMART of digital mental health care to determine who responds to different types and levels of intervention intensity. In this study, called ADAPT (Areán et al., 2021), we compared the effectiveness of psychotherapy delivered over on-demand secured messaging, once-a-week psychotherapy delivered over video conferencing and two combinations of these interventions, either on-demand messaging plus weekly video conferencing or on-demand messaging plus monthly video conferencing. Participants with depression were first randomized to receive either weekly video-conferenced psychotherapy or on-demand, message-based psychotherapy. After five weeks of treatment, participants were reassessed for depression using the nine-item Patient Health Questionnaire (Kroenke et al., 2001), which is a measure that the company providing care already used as standard practice. Participants who were showing improvement stayed in their assigned condition. Participants who do not show improvement were re-randomized to receive either on-demand message-based psychotherapy plus weekly video conferencing sessions or on-demand message-based psychotherapy plus monthly video conferencing sessions. Participants were in the study for 12 weeks total.

In sum, SMART designs:

- Are used to determine optimal treatment sequences of established treatments.
- Involve the use of a tailoring variable to determine when participants should be re-randomized.
- Can have multiple levels of assessments.

Micro-Randomized Trials (MRTs)

Like SMART trials, MRTs randomly assign participants at key decision points, when an intervention is deemed to be needed and likely efficacious. Unlike SMART trials, MRTs may randomize participants over dozens or even hundreds of decision points and may feature many different conditions. MRTs are generally used in developing Just-In-Time-Adaptive-Interventions (cite), where treatment is rapidly tailored in real time to the participant's needs. MRTs can be used to determine how to deliver the best intervention when participants need it to support behavior change. MRTs are rather complicated studies to conduct and most likely to be used in remote clinical trials of digital health interventions, when computers can be programmed to construct conditions and manage randomization and data collection. Because of their repeated and intensively longitudinal nature, MRTs are often used to study the impact of small prompts or nudges digitally delivered, such as using cell phone push notifications. They are useful for answering research questions about the effectiveness of these prompts to increase patient engagement, identifying the context (e.g., time of day, needs of patient) when it is most beneficial to intervene, and identifying what type of prompt is most beneficial for different types of outcomes.

As an example of a micro-randomized trial, researchers sent push notifications to 1255 users to increase engagement in a commercial well-being intervention application over 89 days (Bidargaddi et al., 2018). The outcome was whether participants used the app to self-monitor behaviors and feelings within a day after receiving the notification. The timing of the message was randomly chosen each day, and all messages were tailored to the user's data from self-monitoring and the time of day. Results found a 3.9% increase in the likelihood of using the app after a push notification and this varied by time of day and day of the week, with weekend afternoons being the most effective.

In sum, MRT designs:

- Are used in the development of Just-In-Time Adaptive Interventions.
- Randomize participants at dozens or even hundreds of timepoints.
- Are most feasible using digital health interventions.

Stepped-Wedge Randomized Trials

Stepped wedge randomized trial designs are used when traditional randomization is either not feasible (as is often the case in implementation trials or in services/systems research) or is not ethical, for instance, when there is no known treatment for a disabling disorder and the intervention in question is better than offering no treatment. In these studies, after a period of usual care, an intervention is delivered to groups of people or settings in phases via rolling implementation over time. Stepped wedge designs are mixed within-group and between-group designs such that each unit has a pre-intervention data collection period while also receiving rolling within-group randomization over phases. As an example, a study may want to test the impact of an intervention in schools, and rather than randomizing some schools to receive the intervention and others to be control all at one point in time, as would be typical in a randomized controlled trial, schools are randomly assigned a position in the study timeline when they will receive the intervention. Typically, data would be collected from students in all participating schools during service delivery for three months. After this, then school A would be randomized to deliver the intervention in the second three months of the study, while schools B-Z provide outcome data but do not deliver the intervention, then schools A and B would deliver the intervention during the second three months, while schools C-Z provide outcome, and the process continues until all schools are delivering the intervention (Brown & Lilford, 2006).

Stepped wedge designs can also be useful when a traditional RCT is not feasible due to resource constraints associated with simultaneous intervention initiation. They are also useful when an intervention is highly desirable and community decision-makers who need to agree to the study (e.g., school district superintendents) do not want the risk of being randomized to a control condition. Stepped wedge designs increase equity because all groups eventually are randomized to the intervention. The primary criticism of stepped wedge designs is that this design is susceptible to historical confounds. However, because all participants receive the intervention, yet between-group comparisons are retained, certain statistical approaches can help address this critique, and in some situations, stepped wedge designs can even be more statistically powerful than traditional RCTs given the same sample size and length of data collection.

An example study using a stepped wedge design is one where investigators aim to study the outcomes of a telephone-based intervention for mental health management in primary care medicine (Owen et al., 2019). The study used a stepped-wedge design by having groups of clinics randomized to when they would begin their implementation of this intervention. The intervention was conducted in three steps of six-month intervals each, with new clinics assigned to receive the first step every six months.

In sum, stepped wedge designs:

- Are most useful when randomization is either not feasible or unethical.
- Typically used in implementation studies, however, could also be used in effectiveness studies.
- Are susceptible to confounding via temporal trends, as compared to a traditional RCT.

Pragmatic Trials

Pragmatic Clinical Trials are basically clinical or comparative effectiveness trials whose main purpose is to test the effects of one or several interventions in real-world practices, with as little interference from the research team as possible (Patsopoulos, 2011). It is also assumed that the interventions themselves have already demonstrated efficacy, and that the mechanisms of treatment are well understood. These tend to be rather large studies because while the design may be simplified, the questions being answered are complex. Pragmatic trials answer the following types of questions:

1. What is the effect of treatment when delivered by the typical provider in the usual practice setting?
2. Which consumers do and do not respond to treatment A?
3. Does population X respond better to intervention B than population Y?
4. How acceptable is the treatment compared to other treatments?
5. Can providers deliver the treatment effectively in their routine practice?
6. What is the cost-effectiveness (the return on investment) of an intervention compared to existing interventions?

There can be variability in the degree to which a trial is pragmatic. This can be determined by using the Pragmatic-Explanatory Continuum Indicator Summary (PRECIS-2). This tool helps investigators determine where on the spectrum between explanatory (efficacy) and pragmatic their study lies. Each indicator is measured on a scale of 1 to 5, with five being highly pragmatic and 1 being highly controlled (see Figure 11.2). This figure is often used in grant applications to help reviewers and the funders understand where compromises are made to pragmatism, which sometimes happens when a novel, evidence-based treatment is one of the comparators, and requires provider training to deliver that would not normally be available to the typical provider in a setting. Figure 11.2 below shows an uncompleted version of PRECIS-2

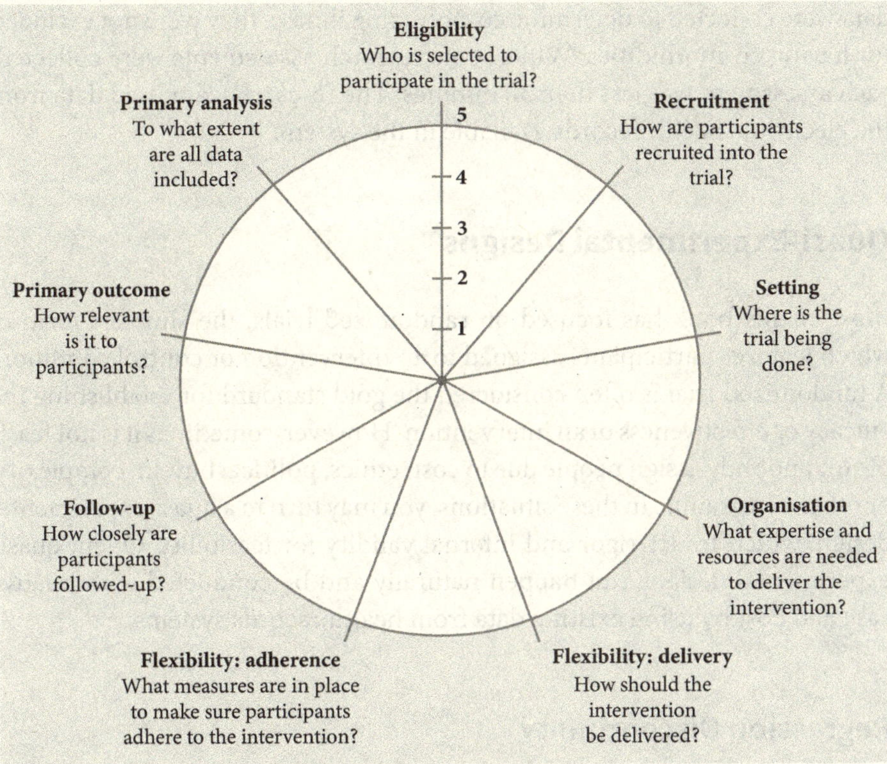

Figure 11.2 Uncompleted PRECIS-2 diagram template

diagram. We provide one we created for an application, with the written justification for it in the appendix.

The need for pragmatic trials is driven largely by the types of questions policymakers find are most relevant to deciding to support or invest in an intervention. As a result, policy and decision-makers, and consumers are involved in the pragmatic trials' design. They are not mere advisors, rather, these parties contribute to the scientific question, how it is measured, and the means by which the study will be implemented.

An example of a pragmatic trial for psychosocial interventions is the comparison of telemedicine-delivered treatments for Post Traumatic Stress Disorder (PTSD) and Bipolar disorder in rural primary care clinics in the United States (Fortney et al., 2021). The pragmatic aspects of this study were in the measurement of cost-effectiveness of training local clinicians to deliver evidence-based practices by phone to consumers and using expert clinicians housed in tier 1 academic institutions to deliver care. This study included all people who were referred for treatment for these two disorders, and while data were collected to determine co-occurring illness, they were not excluded for having co-morbidities. While some research assessments were collected, each assessment was less than 30 minutes. The research team used data from the electronic health records available in the system.

Quasi-Experimental Designs

Most of this book has focused on randomized trials, the simplest form of which features participants assigned to an intervention or control condition. A randomized trial is often considered the gold standard for establishing the efficacy or effectiveness of an intervention. However, sometimes it is not feasible to randomly assign people due to cost, ethics, political buy-in, complexity, or other constraints. In these situations, you may turn to a quasi-experimental design, which trades rigor and internal validity for feasibility. Often, quasi-experimental designs can happen naturally and be conducted with relative ease and cost by using existing data from health records systems.

Regression Discontinuity

A regression discontinuity design can be useful in situations where the decision to apply treatment or not is based on a strict screening cutoff score on an assignment variable. By examining the difference in outcomes for people who scored near the cutoff, both above and below, and capitalizing on data from the full distribution of scores to plot a linear relationship between assignment and outcome scores for these two groups, researchers can make assumptions about the causal effects of the treatment. A regression discontinuity design can be useful to control for natural change over time that is likely to occur even in the absence of treatment. This commonly occurs in treatment studies due to regression to the mean. People seek mental health treatment when they are feeling badly, and these feelings are likely to improve—to regress to the mean or to their "usual" state—even if no treatment is provided.

Here is how a regression discontinuity design works. Let's say a certain treatment for depression was only made available to people who score above a 10 on a pretest screener, the Patient Health Questionnaire-9, which is a common screen for depression. If the treatment is effective, those who receive it will have greater improvement than those who do not receive it. By comparing outcomes for those who scored a 9 and did not receive treatment to those who scored a 10 and did receive treatment (and are essentially the same), one can separate out the causal effect. In reality, researchers will take a bandwidth of pre-test scores—say, 5 to 15 on the PHQ—and compute separate regression lines predicting the post-test scores from the pre-test scores for the groups below and above the cutoff. These can be plotted and the gap between the lines is the assumed causal effect (in fact, this gap is the "discontinuity" in the discontinuity design).

A strength of the regression discontinuity design is that it can sometimes be used on historical or naturally collected data that exists in medical records. Or it can be used in a regular RCT as an additional arm of participants who would not otherwise qualify for the study, allowing an additional point of comparison and strengthening the study's conclusions. This can especially be true when a study is struggling to recruit participants, as those below the cutoff would otherwise be ignored as data points.

The regression discontinuity design, though it can provide unbiased treatment effects when assumptions are met, has weaknesses. It has less statistical power for the equivalent sample size of a randomized trial. This is especially true when there is multicollinearity between the treatment and the assignment variable and when the average pre-test screening score is highly different from the cutoff value. It also relies heavily on correctly specifying the relationship between the assignment variable and the outcome variable. This is usually shown as a linear relationship in examples but if the true underlying functional form is more complex yet not identified and appropriately specified, your conclusions will not be valid.

Interrupted Time Series

An interrupted time series design can be thought of as an intensive AB or pre-post test design. Instead of collecting one round of data before and after an intervention, the interrupted time series will collect several time points to establish a rate or slope of change over time (the "time series") before and after a new intervention or policy change (the "interruption"). Inference on the intervention's impact will be made by observing changes to the level and rate of change of scores on the observed variable. The researchers will examine whether the time series pattern of data changes after the interruption. While these designs are more commonly used in broad, contextual social science like examining the impact of policy change on behavior, economic decisions (e.g., interest rates) on spending, and the impact of historical events, these designs can also be useful when examining interventions, especially in naturalistic settings. For instance, one could examine patient outcomes before and after clinicians are trained and begin to implement a new treatment, or the impact of implementation strategies such as state mandates to use evidence-based practices.

A challenge of an interrupted time series design is knowing exactly when an intervention occurs. For instance, in the example just provided, a state mandate may roll out slowly or not have a direct impact on services for years, so the "interruption" is not clearly defined. This opens the possibility for historical confounds, which are always a problem for interrupted time series designs, as other events may be responsible for any change in the pattern of data. Seasonality and cyclical patterns can also pose a threat to validity unless enough data is collected and examined in the proper manner to identify and model those patterns.

Propensity Score Modeling and Matching

Propensity score modeling and matching (PSM) is a method of identifying a control group without random assignment. Researchers will statistically identify a group of people who did not receive the intervention but who are very similar to those who did receive the intervention. The difference between matching and modeling is that matching will identify a 1:1 match for each person in the intervention and exclude individuals for whom a match is unable to be made. In modeling, a statistical prediction value will be placed on every person for the likelihood that they would be in the intervention group based on their characteristics. This is a "propensity score," for their propensity to be in the intervention. This propensity score, or statistical prediction value, is included as a covariate in all statistical tests to control for this probability. This is similar to how one might include gender or race as a covariate in a regression model to "control for" those variables. As with other quasi-experimental designs, PSM can be highly useful with existing data or when random assignment is unethical or unfeasible.

We used PSM to examine the impact of a family treatment court, a specialized court working with parents in the child welfare system who are impacted by addiction and substance use (Bruns et al., 2012). We collected historical records collected by the court and by the child welfare agency to match 76 participants with 76 similar parents who did not participate in the treatment court, and found positive outcomes including higher treatment completion, faster time to end out-of-home care, and higher reunification rates. However, this study likely suffers from an important limitation that, in our experience, many if not most PSM studies also have, which is that it may not accurately specify the model. The PSM depends upon identifying the probability of treatment assignment. The true probability for this often depends on variables not collected or observed (e.g., motivation, timing, relationships) or is completely unknown. This is a missing data problem. Due to this issue, many PSM studies are little more than an efficient method of controlling for baseline covariates (age, race) that might have little to do with the actual propensity to be in the intervention group. While tests exist to examine and diagnose balance among the groups, the problem of missing data due to unknown determinants of treatment assignment will always remain. We encourage researchers to acknowledge this in their analyses, as PSM offers a halo of robustness and validity that it may not always deserve. Despite this and other limitations, PSM can be an extremely powerful method of using existing data or collecting data in a quasi-experimental study to draw conclusions that could not otherwise be found.

Services Research: Why Is It Important for a Psychosocial Interventionist to Know About This Area of Science?

Services and systems research focuses on methods for increasing access, reach, and quality of evidence-based treatments, such as the use of digital platforms, the governance of evidence-based treatments, health policy, health system quality, best methods for delivering care (implementation), access to care, health care disparities, healthcare financing, health care reform, and health care workforce design. Many times, these studies look at the impact of a bundled set of implementation strategies on access, reach, and quality of already established and effective evidence-based treatments. This stage of the clinical trials pipeline is the stage after which we have determined that an intervention is safe and effective and understand the challenges systems of care may encounter in delivering the intervention. Rather than randomizing consumers to treatments, consumers, or more commonly practitioners, practices, systems, and regions, are randomized to an implementation model that includes some form of clinical support and system redesign, and collects information on access to care, quality of care, gaps in care, and cost-effectiveness compared to practice as usual. These studies will also include implementation strategies that have been developed in implementation studies targeting a particular barrier to care, such as overcoming stigma for using health care, or making health services more accessible to people with housing insecurity.

An example of a services intervention to improve access to psychosocial interventions would be to compare the Increasing Access to Talk Therapies Program (IAPT) that was developed in England to how talk therapies are supported and delivered in the United States. IAPT is a system design program that tackles poor access to evidence-based psychotherapies and includes (Clark, 2018):

- Area analysis of clinical needs to inform the number of clinicians needed and what types of interventions they should be delivering.
- Close communication between health policy leaders in a region and clinical services.
- Developing a workforce to provide stepped care, that is, varying levels of clinical intensity from well checks to inpatient services.
- Preparing and supporting the workforce in delivering evidence-based, guideline-level care.
- IAPT-compliant supervision system that allows for periodic quality checks.
- Negotiated prices for service between systems and providers that reflect the realistic cost of providing effective, evidence-based treatment for consumers with varying service needs (value-based care).
- Inviting consumer voice in the choice of how services should be received (digitally, telephonically, in person).
- Ongoing clinical assessment for decision-making, quality monitoring, and program evaluation (measurement-based care).

A study that would test such a model in the United States could involve studying the entire package, modified for the US health care system, compared to how psychotherapy is delivered and supported currently and likely would need to utilize a cluster randomized design, time series, or a stepped wedge design to test the impact at scale. However, there are examples of system and service redesign studies that have randomized people at the individual level, for instance, the Collaborative Care Study for depression management in primary care medicine (Unützer et al., 2002), where older adults from 18 healthcare systems where randomized to receive stepped care for depression or to care as usual.

Even if you never participate or lead a services research study to implement psychosocial interventions, you should be aware of this body of science, as the questions it addresses should inform decisions you make about intervention design, and can also inform additional information you should collect to assist in the creation of system-level interventions to support the delivery of your new treatment. Be aware that these studies directly address questions that policymakers consider when deciding to support a program. If you want your new treatment to be used outside of your lab or local setting, questions about who should deliver the treatment, who the treatment is for, how flexible it is in being used in different settings and contexts, the upfront and downstream costs of using the intervention, and the potential barriers the current system of care may experience in implementing will help you design interventions with a greater chance of uptake. More information can be found in texts such as *Mental Health Services: A Public Health Perspective* (Lubotsky et al., 2010).

Chapter Summary

There are many other methods beyond the randomized clinical trial to test the effect of a new intervention. When a new intervention is ready to be used in practice, larger-scale pragmatic and systems research is needed to identify if there are populations or settings where the new intervention is less effective, there are contexts in which the intervention cannot be delivered to quality or with equity, and what is the best place in a sequence of services for the intervention. These questions usually require different research models other than the randomized trial. MOST designs are used to streamline complex interventions. SMART designs are used to study intervention sequences. MRTs are used to study the rapid delivery of intervention components. Stepped Wedge Designs are used when randomization is not possible or ethical. Finally, service research designs are the last step in supporting the use of new, evidence-based treatments.

Appendix

Chapter 2 Appendix

Data Use Agreement Example

[DATA USE AGREEMENT]

This **DATA USE AGREEMENT** ("**Agreement**") is entered into effective as of the date last set forth on the signature page hereto by and between (the "**Effective Date**") [COMPANY] on behalf of its Investigator [NAME] ("**Data Provider Investigator**") and ________________________, a ________________________ corporation located at ____ ("**Data Recipient**"), on behalf of its Investigator ________________ ("**Data Recipient Investigator**"), and (each to be referred to herein as a "**Party**" and collectively, as the "**Parties**").

RECITALS

WHEREAS, the US Department of Health and Human Services ("**HHS**") has issued regulations, pursuant to the Health Insurance Portability and Accountability Act of 1996 ("**HIPAA**") and the Health Information Technology for Economic and Clinical Health Act of 2009 (the "**HITECH Act**"), governing the privacy of individually identifiable health information obtained, created, or maintained by certain entities, including health care providers (the "**HIPAA Privacy Rule**"); and

WHEREAS, the HIPAA Privacy Rule requires that Data Provider enter into this Agreement with Data Recipient in order to protect the privacy of certain individually identifiable health information created, obtained, or maintained by Data Provider or by Data Recipient on Data Provider's behalf ("**Protected Health Information**," or "**PHI**"); and

[IF CONDITION: ONLY USE WHERE LIMITED DATA SET IS PROVIDED] WHEREAS, Data Provider holds data, as further detailed in Exhibit A ("Data"), which is a Limited Data set as defined by HIPAA and its accompanying regulations, including but not limited to the Standards for Privacy of Individually Identifiable Health Information ("Privacy Rule"), at 45 CFR 160 and 45 CFR 164; and

WHEREAS, Data Provider desires to enter into this Agreement with Data Recipient pursuant to which Data Recipient will use the data identified on Exhibit A for research, as detailed within Exhibit A and, in accordance with the terms and conditions set forth hereinafter and in accordance with the HIPAA Regulations (such data hereinafter referred to as the "**Data**"); and

WHEREAS, Data Recipient requests access to the Data from Data Provider in the United States for the conduct of its IRB-approved Protocol No. ______________ for the project entitled, ____ described in Exhibit B (the "**Project**");

NOW, THEREFORE, in consideration of the foregoing premises and mutual promises, covenants, and conditions contained in this Agreement, the Parties hereby agree as follows:

1. **Definitions.** Unless otherwise specified in this Agreement, all capitalized terms used in this Agreement not otherwise defined have the meaning established for purposes of the "HIPAA Regulations" codified at Title 45 parts 160 through 164 of the United States Code of Federal Regulations, as amended from time to time.

2. **Obligations and Activities of Data Recipient.**

   2.1. **Non-disclosure**: Data Recipient may only disclose the Data to its faculty, employees, fellows, students, and agents that have a need to use the Data in connection with performing the Project ("**Recipient Personnel**"). Data Recipient is not permitted to share the Data with any third parties, agents, or subcontractors. Data Recipient will not use or disclose the Data other than as permitted or required by this Agreement or as required by law or as otherwise authorized by Data Provider.

   2.2. **Safeguards**: Data Recipient will use appropriate safeguards to prevent use or disclosure of the Data other than as provided for by this Agreement. Data Recipient will develop, implement, maintain, and use appropriate administrative, technical, and physical safeguards to preserve the integrity and confidentiality of and to prevent non-permitted or violating use or disclosure of the Data which is transmitted electronically. Data Recipient will document and keep these safeguards current.

   2.3. **Mitigation**: Data Recipient will mitigate, to the extent practicable, any harmful effect that is known to Data Recipient of a use or disclosure of the Data Set by Data Recipient in violation of the requirements of this Agreement.

   2.4. **Reporting**: Data Recipient will report to the Privacy Officer of Data Provider, in writing, any use and/or disclosure of the Data that is not permitted or required by this Agreement of which Recipient becomes aware. Such report shall be made as soon as reasonably possible but in no event more than five (5) business days after discovery by Data Recipient of such unauthorized use or disclosure. This reporting obligation shall include breaches by Data Recipient, its employees, subcontractors and/or agents. Each such report of a breach will, to the extent possible: (i) identify the nature of the non-permitted or violating use or disclosure; (ii) identify the Data used or disclosed; (iii) identify who received the non-permitted or violating use or disclosure; (iv) identify what corrective action Data Recipient took or will take to prevent further non-permitted or violating uses or disclosures; (v) identify what Data Recipient did or will do to mitigate any deleterious effect of the non-permitted or violating use or disclosure; and (vi) provide such other information as Data Provider may reasonably request.

   2.5. **Identification and Contact of Individuals**: Data Recipient will not identify or attempt to identify the individuals whose Protected Health Information appears in the Data. Data Recipient will not contact or attempt to contact the individuals whose Protected Health Information appears in the Data.

   2.6. **Publication**:

      2.6.1. Data Recipient Investigator is encouraged to publish any results derived from this Agreement and agrees to recognize the contribution of the Data Provider as the source of the Data in all written, visual, or oral public disclosures concerning Data Recipient's research using the Data, as appropriate in accordance with scholarly standards. [COMPANY] asks that Data Recipient send publications or presentations thirty (30) days before submission of publication or presentation to enable [COMPANY] to identify and request removal of its confidential information, as applicable.

2.6.2. In the event that Data Recipient obtains Summary Aggregate Data for use and would like to publish results or analysis, authorship and attribution of the publication shall adhere to academic standards. Data Recipient shall acknowledge the support of Data Provider whenever publicizing the work based on, or developed under this Agreement, in any media, whether copyrighted or not, by including an acknowledgement.

2.7. **Data Transfer and Use:**

2.7.1. To the extent the Data includes PHI, Data Provider will disclose, and Data Recipient will request, only the minimum amount of PHI reasonably necessary to achieve the purpose of the Project. If the Data being provided is coded, the Data Provider will not release, and the Recipient will not request, the key to the coded data.

2.7.2. Data Provider represents that it has complied with all relevant institutional requirements, including the completion of any IRB or applicable ethics review or approval that may be required, prior to transferring the Data to Data Recipient. To the extent the Data includes Protected Health Information ("PHI") under HIPAA, Data Provider represents that the use of PHI for the Project is consistent with such consents or authorizations, if any, as Data Provider has obtained from individuals who are the subjects of the Data.

2.7.3. By signing this Agreement, Data Recipient provides assurance that its relevant institutional policies and applicable federal, state, or local laws and regulations (if any) have been followed, including the completion of any IRB or ethics review or approval that may be required. Data Recipient must provide a copy of the approved protocol and IRB letter to [COMPANY], if applicable.

2.7.4. In accessing the Data, Data Recipient will:

2.7.4.1. use and disclose the Data only for purposes of conducting the Project;

2.7.4.2. not use or disclose the Data other than as permitted by this Agreement or as otherwise required by law, and shall not use or further disclose the Data in any manner that would violate the Privacy Rule if done by Data Provider;

2.7.4.3. use and/or implement appropriate safeguards to prevent the use or disclosure of the Data except as provided for by this Agreement;

2.7.4.4. ensure that any third-party collaborator, subcontractor, and/or agent to whom it provides the Data agrees to the same standards, restrictions, and conditions that apply to the Recipient with respect to the Data; [COMPANY] must approve of any third-party collaborator prior to any sharing of the Data;

2.7.4.5. refrain from using the Data either alone or in concert with any other information to identify or to contact individuals who are or may be the sources of Data without specific written approval from Data Provider and appropriate IRB approval, if required pursuant to 45 CFR 46; and

2.7.4.6. report to Data Provider any use or disclosure of the Data not provided for by this Agreement of which it becomes aware, including and without limitation, any disclosure of Data to an unauthorized third party, within five (5) days. Data Recipient acknowledges that Data Provider may have an obligation to make further notifications as set forth in Subpart D of 45 CFR § 164 or under applicable state law and shall cooperate with the Data Provider to the extent necessary to enable Data Provider to meet all such obligations.

This Article will survive the termination or expiration of this Agreement.

2.8. **Summary Aggregate Data:**

2.8.1. "Summary Aggregate Data" shall be defined as a collected data set from multiple sources compiled into data summaries, summary reports, or summary analyses such that the individual human subjects/patients in the data set are no longer discernible according to HIPAA.

2.8.2. Data Provider may request in writing that Recipient share a copy of the Summary Aggregate Data for use.

3. **Term and Termination.**

3.1 **Term.** The term of this Agreement shall commence as of the Effective Date, and shall terminate when all of the Data provided by Data Provider to Data Recipient, or created or received by Data Recipient on behalf of Data Provider, is destroyed or returned to Data Provider, or, if it is infeasible to return or destroy the Data, protections are extended to such Data in accordance with the provisions of this Section 3.

3.2 **Termination without Cause.** Either party may terminate this Agreement upon thirty (30) days' written notice to the other party.

3.3 **Termination for Cause.** Either party shall have the right to immediately terminate this Agreement upon written notice of such termination to the other party in the event that: (1) either party is in material breach of any provision of this Agreement; (2) the business of either party is terminated or suspended; (3) a petition for bankruptcy is filed by or against either party; (4) a receiver is appointed on account of either party's insolvency; or (5) if any assignment is made of either party's business for the benefit of its creditors.

3.4 **Effect of Termination.** At termination of this Agreement, return or destroy all PHI received from, or created or received by Data Recipient on behalf of, Data Provider, which Recipient still maintains in any form and retain no copies of such information; or if the return or destruction of the PHI is not feasible, extend the protections of this Section to the PHI received from Data Provider and limit any further uses. This provision shall survive the termination of this Agreement.

4. **Notices.** Any notices to be given under or relating to this Agreement shall be in writing and shall be given to the respective Party (i) by overnight courier service (and shall be deemed to have been duly given upon receipt), or (ii) by prepaid registered or certified mail, return receipt requested (and shall be deemed to have been duly given or made on the earlier of receipt or three (3) business days after being deposited in the US mail). Notices may be sent to:

If to [DATA RECIPIENT]:	**If to [COMPANY]:**
[insert address]	[insert address]
[insert Attn:]	[insert Attn:]
With an electronic copy sent to:	With an electronic copy sent to:
________________	________________

Either party may update its notice address by notice to the other party in accordance with this Section 4 (Notices).

5. **Independent Contractor Relationship**. None of the provisions of this Agreement is intended to create any relationship between the parties other than that of independent entities contracting with each other solely for the purpose of effecting the provisions of this Agreement. Neither of the parties, nor any of their respective officers, directors, employees, or agents, shall have the authority to bind the other or shall be deemed or construed to be the agent, employee, or representative of the other except as may be specifically provided herein. Neither party, nor any of their employees or agents, shall have any claim under this Agreement or otherwise against the other party for Social Security benefits, workers' compensation, disability benefits, unemployment insurance, vacation, sick pay, or any other employee benefits of any kind.
6. **Confidentiality**. As noted above, the parties shall maintain the confidentiality of patient medical records and treatment in accordance with state and federal laws. In addition, Data Recipient acknowledges that information regarding Data Provider's business operations, including, but not limited to, procedures, programs, and reimbursement schedules is proprietary and confidential, and agrees to hold such information in strict confidence and not to disclose or make available such information to any third party, except as required by law. This provision shall survive termination of this Agreement.
7. **Liability.** Except to the extent prohibited by law, the Data Recipient assumes all liability for damages that may arise from its use, storage, disclosure, or disposal of the Data. The Data Provider will not be liable to the Data Recipient for any loss, claim, or demand made by the Data Recipient, or made against the Data Recipient by any other party, due to or arising from the use of the Data by the Data Recipient.
8. **Third-Party Beneficiaries.** Nothing in this Agreement shall confer upon any person other than the parties and their respective successors or assigns, any rights, remedies, obligations, or liabilities whatsoever. Data Recipient and Data Provider agree that individuals whose Protected Health Information appears in a Limited Data Set are not third-party beneficiaries of this Agreement.
9. **Waiver**. No provision of this Agreement may be waived except by an agreement in writing signed by the waiving party. A waiver of any term or provision shall not be construed as a waiver of any other term or provision. Nothing in Section 2 of this Agreement shall be deemed a waiver of any legally recognized claim of privilege available to Data Recipient.
10. **Representations and Warranties.** Each Party represents, warrants, and covenants to the other Party that (a) it has the right to enter into this Agreement, and the right and the ability to perform its obligations hereunder; (b) it will comply in all respects with applicable laws, regulations, and rules in the operation of its business and in fulfilling its obligations under this Agreement.

11. **Assignments**. Neither party may assign this Agreement or delegate its performance without the other Party's prior written consent, and any attempt to do so is void; except either party may assign this Agreement to an affiliate or in connection with a merger, acquisition, corporate reorganization, or sale of all or substantially all of its assets to which this Agreement relates. This Agreement and everything herein contained shall inure to the benefit of and be binding upon each of the Parties hereto and upon their respective successors and assigns.
12. **Use of Name**. Neither Party may use the name of the other Party, nor any adaptation of its name, nor the name of any staff member, employee, agent, or student of the other Party, trademarks, or other logos in any publicity, advertising, promotional materials, sales literature, or publicity without obtaining prior written approval of the Party whose name is to be used. For the Data Recipient, approval must be obtained from [COMPANY] Legal Counsel.

    The Parties agree that each Party may disclose factual information regarding the existence and purpose of the relationship that is the subject of this Agreement or other purposes without written permission from the other Party, provided that any such statement shall accurately and appropriately describe the relationship of the parties and shall not in any manner imply endorsement by the other party whose name is being used.
13. **Severability**. Each clause of this Agreement is distinct and severable. If any clause is deemed illegal, void, or unenforceable by any court of competent jurisdiction or is otherwise deemed unenforceable under the current applicable law, the remainder of this Agreement will not be affected. For each provision deemed unenforceable, a provision as similar as possible in its economic and business objectives will be intended.
14. **Force Majeure.** In the event either Party is unable to perform its obligations under the terms of this Agreement because of acts of God, strikes, equipment or transmission failure or damage reasonably beyond its control, or other causes reasonably beyond its control, such party shall not be liable to the other for any damages to the extent resulting from such failure to perform as a result of such causes.
15. **Entire Agreement**. The Parties agree that this Agreement supersedes any prior agreements or understandings between them, written or oral, that pertain to the subject matter hereof. This Agreement supersedes any and all existing contracts and agreements by the Parties with respect to the subject matter covered herein.
16. **Governing Law.** This Agreement is governed in all respects by the laws of the State of [STATE], without giving effect to principles of conflicts of law thereunder.
17. **Survival.** All terms and conditions that by their nature are intended to extend beyond the expiration or termination of this Agreement shall survive the expiration or termination of this Agreement.
18. **Amendments.** This Agreement shall not be changed, modified, altered or amended in any respect without the mutual consent of the Parties, which consent shall be evidenced by a written amendment to this Agreement executed by the Parties, with the exception to amend this Agreement as necessary to comply with HIPAA, the HIPAA Privacy Rule, and the HITECH Act, as amended from time to time. The parties further agree to execute such other agreements as may be required by law.
19. **Counterparts.** This Agreement may be executed in one or more counterparts and by facsimile, each of which when executed shall be deemed to be an original but all of which taken together shall constitute one and the same document.

IN WITNESS WHEREOF, the parties have executed this Agreement as of the date and year first above written.

[RESEARCHER]	**[COMPANY]**
By:	By:
Name:	Name:
Title:	Title:
Date:	Date:

Exhibit A: Data

[DESCRIBE EACH DATA ELEMENT TO BE PROVIDED]

Chapter 4 Appendix and Resources

Resources for measurement development

1. Ball, H. L. (August, 2019). Conducting online surveys. *J Hum Lact.*, *35*(3), 413–417. doi:10.1177/0890334419848734. Epub: May 14, 2019. PMID: 31084575.
2. Jones, T. L., Baxter, M. A., Khanduja, V. (January, 2013). A quick guide to survey research. Ann R Coll Surg Engl., *95*(1), 5–7. doi: 10.1308/003588413X13511609956372. PMID: 23317709; PMCID: PMC3964639.
3. Zimba, O., Gasparyan, A. Y. (December 11, 2023). Designing, Conducting, and Reporting Survey Studies: A Primer for Researchers. *J Korean Med Sci.*, *38*(48), e403. doi: 10.3346/jkms.2023.38.e403. PMID: 38084027; PMCID: PMC10713437.
4. Tabernero, P., Parker, M., Ravinetto, R., Phanouvong, S., Yeung, S., Kitutu, F. E., Cheah, P. Y., Mayxay, M., Guerin, P. J., Newton, P. N. (June, 2016). Ethical challenges in designing and conducting medicine quality surveys. *Trop Med Int Health.*, *21*(6), 799–806. doi: 10.1111/tmi.12707. Epub: May 20, 2016. PMID: 27102573; PMCID: PMC4913736.
5. Goodfellow, L. T. (September, 2023). An overview of survey research. *Respir Care.*, *68*(9), 1309–1313. doi: 10.4187/respcare.11041. Epub: April 18, 2023. PMID: 37072162; PMCID: PMC10468179.

Chapter 5 Appendix and Resources

Sample agenda for GYST
Study XYZ
1st and 3rd Thursday of each month at Noon
(Meeting Link)

Date: September 15, 2022 **Location:** Remote
Objective: Planning for development and distribution of survey on using search data and other technology for NEW intervention
Invitees: All team members
Recording: (link to Zoom recording)

Attendance:

Upcoming Absences:	

Name	Attend	Name	Attend
PI	y	CRA	y
PM	Y	CRA	y

Agenda for this meeting

Discussed	Topic	Leading Discussion	S/D/G	Desired Outcome
	Minutes review	PIs		
	Tasks	See below		

Meeting Minutes
Notes taken by Brittany

Decisions/Discussion

Topic	Decision/ Discussion
Task 1	**Next steps**
Task 2	Next Steps

Tasks

What	Lead	Others Involved	Due Date	Done	Comments
Task 1					
Task 2					
Task 3					

RESOURCE: PROGRAM MANAGMENT SOFTWARE TOOLS WE HAVE USED

Product Name	licensing	Collaborative software	Issue tracking	Document management	Workflow management
Asana	Yes	Yes	No	No	Yes
Basecamp	Yes	Yes	No	No	No
Jira	Yes	Yes	Yes	No	Yes
Microsoft SharePoint	Yes	Yes	Yes	Yes	Yes
Microsoft Teams	Yes	Yes	Yes	Yes	Yes
Smartsheet	Yes	Yes	Yes	Yes	No
Trello	Yes	Yes	Yes	No	No

Chapter 6 Appendix

Suicidal Risk Assessment

Complete on all patients who report thoughts about suicide or killing themselves (active suicidal ideation) or thoughts that life is not worth living or that they would be better off dead (passive suicidal ideation). Otherwise, skip the suicide risk assessment. Unless otherwise noted, questions pertain to the past month. If patients are seen weekly, then questions pertain to the past week.

[SRA]

1. Can you tell me more about that?
   [1]
   - What specifically have you been thinking about?
     ____
   - How frequently do you have these thoughts?
     ____
   - How long do they stay on your mind?
     ____
   - *If thoughts about suicide or killing self*: What makes you want to commit suicide/kill yourself?
     ____
     ____

2. Have you attempted suicide in the past month?

   No (*go to 3*)........... 0 [2]
   Yes...................... 1 **(Criterion A = YES)**

2a. [*If yes, inquire for details and for other suicide attempts.*]:
   [2a]
   - What did you actually do?
     ____
   - How were you found?
     ____
   - Did you really want to die?
     ____
   - How many times have you attempted suicide?
     ____

   (If completing 2a, Skip to 4)

3. Have you **ever** attempted suicide?

No (*go to 4*)............	0	[3]
Yes	1 **(Criterion A = YES if any attempt required medical attention)**	

3a. [*If yes, inquire for details and for other suicide attempts*]:

[3a]

- What did you actually do?

___

- How were you found?

___

- Did you really want to die?

___

- How many times have you attempted suicide?

___

3b. How long ago was your last attempt?

[3b]

Number of months .... ___ ___ ___

4. How strong has your wish to die been in the past month?

None......................	0		[4]
Weak......................	1		
Strong....................	2	**(Criterion A = YES)**	

For patients who report thoughts about suicide or killing themselves (*active suicidal ideation*), continue with the remainder of the assessment. Otherwise, go to the Algorithm.

5. In the past month, have you made any plans or considered a method that you might use to commit suicide? [*If suicide attempt in past month, ask*: Have you made any plans or considered a method that you might use to commit suicide again?]

No (*go to 6*)	0 (i.e., has thoughts of killing self but has *not* considered a method)	[5]
Yes (*go to 5a*)...........	1	

Criterion A = YES if answer is Yes or No

5a. What method would you use to commit suicide? [*Use probes to determine how well-formulated the plan is.*]

___

[5a]

___

Considered, but details not worked out.............1

Details worked out; well-formulated plan...........2

6. If you decided to commit suicide at this point in your life, would the means for carrying out such an act be available to you?

No	0	[6]
Yes, possibly.............	1	
Yes, definitely............	2	

7. How much do you really intend to make a suicide attempt right now?

Not at all	0	[7]
Uncertain, not sure....	1 **(Criterion A = YES)**	
Certain	2 **(Criterion B = YES)**	

8. Do you feel hopeless about the future? 8a. How hopeless?

No *(skip to 9)*	0	[8]	A little	1	[8a]
Yes (go to 8a)..........	1		Somewhat	2	
			Very	3	

9. Is anything preventing you from committing suicide?

If Yes – record reasons for living:____
[9]

____

____

____

____

Answer 9a based upon the patient's response from above. Inquire about any remaining items in 9a if the subject has not already identified them.

9a. *Circle all that apply, and record evidence*:

(1) Has a desire to live
[9a]
(2) Has purpose in life/reason to live
(3) Has hope for the future
(4) Strongly fears the consequences of a failed attempt
(5) Considers suicide morally wrong or against religious beliefs
(6) Wouldn't want to cause family and friends pain
(7) Believes in the ability to resist suicidal impulses
(8) Other (specify:_______________________________________)

If nothing is preventing the patient from committing suicide: What has kept you from acting on your thoughts so far? (example of possible response: "I don't know, I just don't have the energy"):

____

____

____

____

Also inquire about alcohol and/or drug use, particularly the extent to which it affects the patient's impulse control:

____

9b. Convincing evidence that s/he will not make a suicide attempt, and good impulse control.........0

[9b]

Nothing preventing patient from attempting suicide, or questionable impulse control..................1

(If "1" then Criterion B = YES)

Algorithm for Determining Course of Action for Suicidal Patients

<u>**Criterion A.**</u> Thoughts about suicide, strong wish to die, or past history of suicide attempt.
(Check box, if YES)

[10]

Yes if **any** of the following are endorsed:
2 (attempted suicide in the past month) is "yes"
3 (any previous attempt requiring medical attention) is "yes"
4 (wish to die) is "strong"
5 (considered a method in the past month) is "yes" or
"no" (i.e., thoughts of committing suicide but has not considered a method)
or 7 (intent) is "uncertain/not sure"

If Yes, proceed to Criterion B

If No, stop..**1 MILD RISK**

<u>**Criterion B.**</u> Suicide intent, nothing preventing patient from attempting suicide, or questionable impulse control.

- If Yes on Criterion A, and if 7 (intent) is "certain" **or** 9 (nothing preventing) is "1"........

  ....**3 HIGH RISK**

- If No on Criterion B, consider patient Intermediate Risk, make contract, and report (*see below*)...........................**2 INTERMEDIATE RISK**

1, 2, or 3:__________________

Risk level [11]

Suicide Risk Action Plan

LEVEL OF SUICIDE RISK	*RA ACTION PLAN*
None	Nothing
Mild Risk	Recommend patient speak to their clinician.
Intermediate Risk: Reportable	*In-person*: Review with supervisor immediately. The supervisor will determine appropriate clinical action, e.g., may recommend encouraging patient to make an appointment with a clinician; establishing a safety plan with the patient (i.e., call 911 if needed); and may call patient's clinician or family member with patient's knowledge. *Via telephone*: Keep patient on phone and review with supervisor immediately. The Supervisor will determine appropriate clinical action, e.g., may recommend encouraging patient to make an appointment with a clinician; or establishing a safety plan with the patient (i.e., call 911 if needed); and may call patient's clinician or family member with patient's knowledge.
High Risk: Urgent	*In-person at Cornell*: Review with supervisor immediately. The supervisor will determine appropriate clinical action, e.g., may take patient to the NYPH Evaluation Center. *In-person in community*: Review with supervisor immediately via phone. The supervisor will determine appropriate clinical action, e.g., may call 911 or have a family member bring patient to a local ER. *Via telephone*: Keep patient on the phone and review with supervisor immediately. The supervisor will determine appropriate clinical action, e.g., may call 911 or have a family member bring patient to a local ER.

Procedures for Intermediate Risk Patients

(please document steps below):

The supervisor will determine appropriate clinical action, which may include:

- Encourage patients to make an appointment with their doctor or clinician and reveal their suicidal thoughts immediately.
- Instruct patients that if they do not feel in control of their thoughts in the future, they are to call a family member, their doctor or clinician, or 911 themselves.
- Supervisor may call patient's doctor, clinician, or family member with patient's knowledge, depending on setting of research study.

Patient Name: ______________________________

Patient ID: ________________________________

Interviewer: _______________________________

Date: ____________________________________

Describe actions taken, including who contacted and their response. Supervisor to review and sign.

Chapter 10 Appendix and Resources

1. Online consent quiz example

The study this quiz was designed for was a fully remote randomized trial of three different mobile applications for depression. All assessments were in-app and there was no CRA or clinician in the loop.

1. I am a volunteer in this study and can stop at any time without penalty to me. (**T**/F)
    a. Post selection pop-up: True, I can discontinue anytime.
2. There is no clinician I can contact while I am in the study. (**T**/F)
    a. Post selection pop-up: True, while we will be checking to see how you are doing, we are not providing any in-person care. If you are feeling worse or no better, please reach out to your doctor for help, or dial 988.
3. I will be assigned the treatment I am to use, and I do not have a choice. (**T**/F)
    a. Post selection pop-up: True, you will be randomized to a treatment app.
4. I will be dropped from the study if it appears that I am falsifying my answers. (**T**/F)
    a. Post selection pop-up: True, if your behavior in the study appears you are not who you say you are, we have the right to discontinue your participation.
5. There will be a direct benefit to me by participating in this study. (T/**F**)
    a. Post selection pop-up: False, this is a research study. Research participants do not necessarily benefit from participation.
6. I will be paid $200.00 no matter how many surveys I answer (T/**F**)
    a. Post selection pop-up: False. We will reimburse you for the time you spend in completing surveys. Each survey is worth $10.00.

Chapter 11 Appendix

Pragmatic design considerations. In Figure A1.1, we use the PRECIS-2 Tool to provide a visual display of the study design. Our study has design features that are more pragmatic than explanatory (the shaded area nearly fills the outer circle). Pragmatic features include:

- Eligibility criteria mirror exactly of clinical practice in determining treatment with psychotherapy for mild to moderate depression.
- Recruitment from primary care practices where psychotherapy—in particular Problem Solving Therapy—is offered to patients with mild to moderate depression.
- Organization: Clinicians are practicing clinicians (IP-PST and SIB-PST) and peer specialists (SIB-PST), in concert with recommendations that services be delivered by providers from a diverse range of clinical settings.
- Flexibility—Delivery: We will assess fidelity, but will not provide feedback to clinicians; primary care practices that provide psychotherapy do not offer ongoing supervision to practicing clinicians.
- Flexibility—Adherence: We will monitor consumer engagement with both treatment arms. We will not encourage engagement beyond what is already part of normal outreach practice by clinicians and coaches in these interventions (see Section 3d for comparator description).
- Follow-up intensity: We only survey consumers when it makes the most clinical sense to do so: we conduct a baseline assessment to determine consumer characteristics, capture data on illness severity, comorbidities, functioning, quality of life, primary language, and geographic location. We reassess consumers at 10 weeks to measure the immediate response to treatment, and again at 6 months to measure the stability of outcomes. Outcomes at six months are a HEDIS requirement for healthcare organizations and are based on NCQA and CMS criteria.
- Outcome surveys will use online study portals to minimize participant burden and attrition and focus on consumer-centered outcomes.
- Analysis of all data will use intention-to-treat as the primary evaluation.

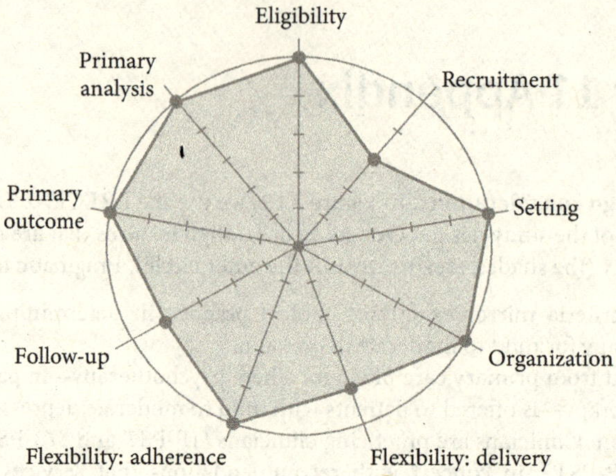

Figure A1.1 PRECIS-2 criteria for our study

References

The National Institute of Mental Health Strategic Plan—National Institute of Mental Health (NIMH). (May 24, 2024). https://www.nimh.nih.gov/about/strategic-planning-reports

Abshire, M., Dinglas, V. D., Cajita, M. I. A., Eakin, M. N., Needham, D. M., & Himmelfarb, C. D. (2017). Participant retention practices in longitudinal clinical research studies with high retention rates. *BMC Medical Research Methodology*, *17*(1), 30. https://doi.org/10.1186/s12874-017-0310-z

Agency for Healthcare Research and Quality. (2006). *Criteria for distinguishing effectiveness from efficacy trials in systematic reviews* (No. 12; Technical Reviews). https://www.ncbi.nlm.nih.gov/books/NBK44028/

Alegria, M., Atkins, M., Farmer, E., Slaton, E., & Stelk, W. (2010). One size does not fit all: Taking diversity, culture and context seriously. *Administration and Policy in Mental Health and Mental Health Services Research*, *37*(1–2), 48–60. https://doi.org/10.1007/s10488-010-0283-2

Alexopoulos, G. S., & PROSPECT Group. (2001). Interventions for depressed elderly primary care patients. *International Journal of Geriatric Psychiatry*, *16*(6), 553–559. https://doi.org/10.1002/gps.464

Alexopoulos, G. S., & Areán, P. A. (2014). A model for streamlining psychotherapy in the RDoC era: The example of "Engage." *Molecular Psychiatry*, *19*(1), 14–19. https://doi.org/10.1038/mp.2013.150

Alvidrez, J., & Areán, P. A. (2002). Psychosocial treatment research with ethnic minority populations: Ethical considerations in conducting clinical trials. *Ethics & Behavior*, *12*(1), 103–116. https://doi.org/10.1207/S15327019EB1201_7

American Psychiatric Association. (2013). *Diagnostic and statistical manual of mental disorders* (5th ed.). https://doi.org/10.1176/appi.books.9780890425596

Andrade, C. (2021). HARKing, cherry-picking, p-hacking, fishing expeditions, and data dredging and mining as questionable research practices. *The Journal of Clinical Psychiatry*, *82*(1). https://doi.org/10.4088/JCP.20f13804

Anguera, J. A., Jordan, J. T., Castaneda, D., Gazzaley, A., & Areán, P. A. (2016). Conducting a fully mobile and randomised clinical trial for depression: Access, engagement and expense. *BMJ Innovations*, *2*(1), 14–21. https://doi.org/10.1136/bmjinnov-2015-000098

Areán, P. A., & Alvidrez, J. (2002). Ethical considerations in psychotherapy effectiveness research: Choosing the comparison group. *Ethics & Behavior*, *12*(1), 63–73. https://doi.org/10.1207/S15327019EB1201_4

Areán, P. A., Ayalon, L., Jin, C., McCulloch, C. E., Linkins, K., Chen, H., McDonnell-Herr, B., Levkoff, S., & Estes, C. (2008). Integrated specialty mental health care among older minorities improves access but not outcomes: Results of the PRISMe study. *International Journal of Geriatric Psychiatry*, *23*(10), 2047. https://doi.org/10.1002/gps.2047

Areán, P. A., Gum, A., McCulloch, C. E., Bostrom, A., Gallagher-Thompson, D., & Thompson, L. (2005). Treatment of depression in low-income older adults. *Psychology and Aging*, *20*(4), 601–609. https://doi.org/10.1037/0882-7974.20.4.601

Areán, P. A., Hallgren, K. A., Jordan, J. T., Gazzaley, A., Atkins, D. C., Heagerty, P. J., & Anguera, J. A. (2016). The use and effectiveness of mobile apps for depression: Results from a fully remote clinical trial. *Journal of Medical Internet Research*, *18*(12), e330. https://doi.org/10.2196/jmir.6482

Areán, P. A., Hull, D., Pullmann, M. D., & Heagerty, P. J. (2021). Protocol for a sequential, multiple assignment, randomised trial to test the effectiveness of message-based psychotherapy for depression compared with telepsychotherapy. *BMJ Open*, *11*(11), e046958. https://doi.org/10.1136/bmjopen-2020-046958

Areán, P. A., Pullmann, M. D., Griffith Fillipo, I. R., Wu, J., Mosser, B. A., Chen, S., Heagerty, P. J., & Hull, T. D. (2024). Randomized trial of the effectiveness of videoconferencing-based versus message-based psychotherapy on depression. *Psychiatric Services*, *75*(12), 1184–1191. https://doi.org/10.1176/appi.ps.20230176

Areán, P. A., Raue, P., Mackin, R. S., Kanellopoulos, D., McCulloch, C., & Alexopoulos, G. S. (2010). Problem-solving therapy and supportive therapy in older adults with major depression and executive dysfunction. *American Journal of Psychiatry*, *167*(11), 1391–1398. https://doi.org/10.1176/appi.ajp.2010.09091327

Baron, R. M., & Kenny, D. A. (1986). The moderator–mediator variable distinction in social psychological research: Conceptual, strategic, and statistical considerations. *Journal of Personality and Social Psychology*, *51*(6), 1173–1182. https://doi.org/10.1037/0022-3514.51.6.1173

Becker, K. D., Boustani, M., Gellatly, R., & Chorpita, B. F. (2018). Forty years of engagement research in children's mental health services: Multidimensional measurement and practice elements. *Journal of Clinical Child & Adolescent Psychology*, *47*(1), 1–23. https://doi.org/10.1080/15374416.2017.1326121

Beidas, R. S., Ahmedani, B. K., Linn, K. A., Marcus, S. C., Johnson, C., Maye, M., Westphal, J., Wright, L., Beck, A. L., Buttenheim, A. M., Daley, M. F., Davis, M., Elias, M. E., Jager-Hyman, S., Hoskins, K., Lieberman, A., McArdle, B., Ritzwoller, D. P., Small, D. S., ... Boggs, J. M. (2021). Study protocol for a type III hybrid effectiveness-implementation trial of strategies to implement firearm safety promotion as a universal suicide prevention strategy in pediatric primary care. *Implementation Science*, *16*(1), 89. https://doi.org/10.1186/s13012-021-01154-8

Beidas, R. S., & Kendall, P. C. (2010). Training therapists in evidence-based practice: A critical review of studies from a systems-contextual perspective. *Clinical Psychology: Science and Practice*, *17*(1), 1–30. https://doi.org/10.1111/j.1468-2850.2009.01187.x

Beidas, R. S., Saldana, L., & Shelton, R. C. (2023). Testing psychosocial interventions in the contexts they are meant to be delivered. *Journal of Consulting and Clinical Psychology*, *91*(4), 189–191. https://doi.org/10.1037/ccp0000797

Bell, M. L., Kenward, M. G., Fairclough, D. L., & Horton, N. J. (2013). Differential dropout and bias in randomised controlled trials: When it matters and when it may not. *BMJ*, *346*, e8668–e8668. https://doi.org/10.1136/bmj.e8668

Bennett, L. M., Gadlin, H., & Marchand, C. (2010). *Collaboration and team science field guide* (p. 138). National Cancer Institute. https://www.cancer.gov/about-nci/organization/crs/research-initiatives/team-science-field-guide/collaboration-team-science-guide.pdf

Bickman, L., Domenico, H. J., Byrne, D. W., Jerome, R. N., Edwards, T. L., Stroud, M., Lebo, L., Mcguffin, K., Wilkins, C. H., & Harris, P. A. (2021). Effects of financial incentives on volunteering for clinical trials: A randomized vignette experiment. *Contemporary Clinical Trials*, *110*, 106584. https://doi.org/10.1016/j.cct.2021.106584

Bidargaddi, N., Almirall, D., Murphy, S., Nahum-Shani, I., Kovalcik, M., Pituch, T., Maaieh, H., & Strecher, V. (2018). To prompt or not to prompt? A microrandomized trial of time-varying push notifications to increase proximal engagement with a mobile health app. *JMIR mHealth and uHealth*, *6*(11), e10123. https://doi.org/10.2196/10123

Bilbrey, A. C., Laidlaw, K., Cassidy-Eagle, E., Thompson, L. W., & Gallagher-Thompson, D. (2022). Cognitive behavioral therapy for late-life depression: Evidence, issues, and recommendations. *Cognitive and Behavioral Practice*, *29*(1), 128–145. https://doi.org/10.1016/j.cbpra.2020.02.003

Borghouts, J., Eikey, E., Mark, G., De Leon, C., Schueller, S. M., Schneider, M., Stadnick, N., Zheng, K., Mukamel, D., & Sorkin, D. H. (2021). Barriers to and facilitators of user engagement with digital mental health interventions: Systematic review. *Journal of Medical Internet Research*, *23*(3), e24387. https://doi.org/10.2196/24387

Boswell, J., Stark, M. D., Wilson, A. D., & Onwuegbuzie, A. J. (2017). The impact of dual roles in mentoring relationships: A mixed research study. *The Journal of Counselor Preparation and Supervision*, *9*(2), 1–18. https://doi.org/10.7729/92.1175

Brown, C. A., & Lilford, R. J. (2006). The stepped wedge trial design: A systematic review. *BMC Medical Research Methodology*, *6*(1), 54. https://doi.org/10.1186/1471-2288-6-54

Bruce, M. L., Ten Have, T. R., Reynolds Iii, C. F., Katz, I. I., Schulberg, H. C., Mulsant, B. H., Brown, G. K., McAvay, G. J., Pearson, J. L., & Alexopoulos, G. S. (2004). Reducing suicidal ideation and depressive symptoms in depressed older primary care patients: A randomized controlled trial. *JAMA*, *291*(9), 1081. https://doi.org/10.1001/jama.291.9.1081

Bruns, E. J., Pullmann, M. D., Weathers, E. S., Wirschem, M. L., & Murphy, J. K. (2012). Effects of a multidisciplinary family treatment drug court on child and family outcomes: Results of a quasi-experimental study. *Child Maltreatment*, *17*(3), 218–230. https://doi.org/10.1177/1077559512454216

Butler, A. S., England, M. J., Gonzalez, M. L., & Institute of Medicine (U.S.) (Eds.). (2015). *Psychosocial interventions for mental and substance use disorders: A framework for establishing evidence-based standards.* National Academy Press.

Carlo, A. D., Hosseini Ghomi, R., Renn, B. N., Strong, M. A., & Areán, P. A. (2020). Assessment of real-world use of behavioral health mobile applications by a novel stickiness metric. *JAMA Network Open*, *3*(8), e2011978. https://doi.org/10.1001/jamanetworkopen.2020.11978

Chakraborty, I., Edirippulige, S., & Ilavarasan, P. V. (2023). What is coming next in health technology startups? Some insights and practice guidelines. *Digital Health*, *9*, 20552076231178435. https://doi.org/10.1177/20552076231178435

Chambers, D. A., Wang, P. S., & Insel, T. R. (2010). Maximizing efficiency and impact in effectiveness and services research. *General Hospital Psychiatry*, *32*(5), 453–455. https://doi.org/10.1016/j.genhosppsych.2010.07.011

Chang, L., & Krosnick, J. A. (2009). National Surveys Via Rdd Telephone Interviewing Versus the Internet. *Public Opinion Quarterly*, *73*(4), 641–678. https://doi.org/10.1093/poq/nfp075

Chu, J. P., Huynh, L., & Areán, P. (2012). Cultural adaptation of evidence-based practice utilizing an iterative stakeholder process and theoretical framework: Problem solving therapy for Chinese older adults. *International Journal of Geriatric Psychiatry*, *27*(1), 97–106. https://doi.org/10.1002/gps.2698

Clark, D. M. (2018). Realizing the mass public benefit of evidence-based psychological therapies: The IAPT program. *Annual Review of Clinical Psychology*, *14*, 159–183. https://doi.org/10.1146/annurev-clinpsy-050817-084833

Cochrane Methods Equity. (2025). PROGRESS-Plus. https://methods.cochrane.org/equity/projects/evidence-equity/progress-plus

Cohen, J. (1988). *Statistical power analysis for the behavioral sciences* (2nd ed.). Academic Press.

Cohen, J. (1990). Things I have learned (so far). *American Psychologist*, *45*(12), 1304–1312. https://doi.org/10.1037/0003-066X.45.12.1304

Collins, L. M., Murphy, S. A., & Strecher, V. (2007). The Multiphase Optimization Strategy (MOST) and the Sequential Multiple Assignment Randomized Trial (SMART). *American Journal of Preventive Medicine*, *32*(5), S112–S118. https://doi.org/10.1016/j.amepre.2007.01.022

Comtois, K. A., Mata-Greve, F., Johnson, M., Pullmann, M. D., Mosser, B., & Areán, P. A. (2022). Effectiveness of mental health apps for distress during COVID-19 in US unemployed and essential workers: Remote pragmatic randomized clinical trial. *JMIR mHealth and uHealth*, *10*(11), e41689. https://doi.org/10.2196/41689

Conway, M., & O'Connor, D. (2016). Social media, big data, and mental health: Current advances and ethical implications. *Current Opinion in Psychology*, *9*, 77–82. https://doi.org/10.1016/j.copsyc.2016.01.004

Corry, M., Neenan, K., Brabyn, S., Sheaf, G., & Smith, V. (2019). Telephone interventions, delivered by healthcare professionals, for providing education and psychosocial support for informal caregivers of adults with diagnosed illnesses. *Cochrane Database of Systematic Reviews*, *2019*(5). https://doi.org/10.1002/14651858.CD012533.pub2

Crabb, R. M., Areán, P. A., & Hegel, M. T. (2012). Sustained adoption of an evidence-based treatment: A survey of clinicians certified in problem-solving therapy. *Depression Research and Treatment*, *2012*, 986547. https://doi.org/10.1155/2012/986547

Cunningham, J. A., Godinho, A., & Kushnir, V. (2017). Using Mechanical Turk to recruit participants for internet intervention research: Experience from recruitment for four trials targeting hazardous alcohol consumption. *BMC Medical Research Methodology*, *17*(1), 156. https://doi.org/10.1186/s12874-017-0440-3

Curran, G. M. (2020). Implementation science made too simple: A teaching tool. *Implementation Science Communications*, *1*(1), 27. https://doi.org/10.1186/s43058-020-00001-z

Curran, G. M., Bauer, M., Mittman, B., Pyne, J. M., & Stetler, C. (2012). Effectiveness-implementation hybrid designs: Combining elements of clinical effectiveness and implementation research to enhance public health impact. *Medical Care*, *50*(3), 217–226. https://doi.org/10.1097/MLR.0b013e3182408812

Curran, G. M., Landes, S. J., McBain, S. A., Pyne, J. M., Smith, J. D., Fernandez, M. E., Chambers, D. A., & Mittman, B. S. (2022). Reflections on 10 years of effectiveness-implementation hybrid studies. *Frontiers in Health Services*, *2*, 1053496. https://doi.org/10.3389/frhs.2022.1053496

Damschroder, L. J., Aron, D. C., Keith, R. E., Kirsh, S. R., Alexander, J. A., & Lowery, J. C. (2009). Fostering implementation of health services research findings into practice: A consolidated framework for advancing implementation science. *Implementation Science*, *4*(1), 50. https://doi.org/10.1186/1748-5908-4-50

Damschroder, L. J., & Lowery, J. C. (2013). Evaluation of a large-scale weight management program using the consolidated framework for implementation research (CFIR). *Implementation Science*, *8*(1), 51. https://doi.org/10.1186/1748-5908-8-51

Damschroder, L. J., Reardon, C. M., Widerquist, M. A. O., & Lowery, J. (2022). The updated Consolidated Framework for Implementation Research based on user feedback. *Implementation Science*, *17*(1), 75. https://doi.org/10.1186/s13012-022-01245-0

Deblinger, E., Mannarino, A. P., Cohen, J. A., Runyon, M. K., & Steer, R. A. (2011). Trauma-focused cognitive behavioral therapy for children: Impact of the trauma narrative and treatment length. *Depression and Anxiety*, *28*(1), 67–75. https://doi.org/10.1002/da.20744

De-identification of protected health information: How to anonymize PHI. (2025). *The HIPPA Journal.* https://www.hipaajournal.com/de-identification-protected-health-information/

Dennis, S. A., Goodson, B. M., & Pearson, C. (2020). Online Worker Fraud and Evolving Threats to the Integrity of MTurk Data: A Discussion of Virtual Private Servers and the Limitations of IP-Based Screening Procedures. *Behavioral Research in Accounting*, *32*(1), 119–134. https://doi.org/10.2308/bria-18-044

Dixon, L. B., Goldman, H. H., Bennett, M. E., Wang, Y., McNamara, K. A., Mendon, S. J., Goldstein, A. B., Choi, C.-W. J., Lee, R. J., Lieberman, J. A., & Essock, S. M. (2015). Implementing coordinated specialty care for early psychosis: The RAISE connection program. *Psychiatric Services (Washington, D.C.)*, *66*(7), 691–698. https://doi.org/10.1176/appi.ps.201400281

Dudarev, V., Barral, O., Zhang, C., Davis, G., & Enns, J. T. (2023). On the reliability of wearable technology: A tutorial on measuring heart rate and heart rate variability in the wild. *Sensors*, *23*(13), 5863. https://doi.org/10.3390/s23135863

Eysenbach, G. (2004). Improving the quality of web surveys: The checklist for reporting results of internet e-surveys (CHERRIES). *Journal of Medical Internet Research*, *6*(3), e34. https://doi.org/10.2196/jmir.6.3.e34

Fancourt, D., & Tymoszuk, U. (2019). Cultural engagement and incident depression in older adults: Evidence from the English Longitudinal Study of Ageing. *British Journal of Psychiatry*, *214*(4), 225–229. https://doi.org/10.1192/bjp.2018.267

Farber, G., Wolport, M., & Kemmer, D. (2020). *Common measures for mental health science: Laying the foundations* (p. 3). Wellcome Trust.

Farrand, P., Raue, P. J., Ward, E., Repper, D., & Areán, P. A. (2024). Use and engagement with low-intensity cognitive behavioral therapy techniques used within an app to support worry management: Content analysis of log data. *JMIR mHealth and uHealth*, *12*, e47321. https://doi.org/10.2196/47321

Fendt-Newlin, M., Jagannathan, A., & Webber, M. (2020). Cultural adaptation framework of social interventions in mental health: Evidence-based case studies from low- and middle-income countries. *International Journal of Social Psychiatry*, *66*(1), 41–48. https://doi.org/10.1177/0020764019879943

First, M. B. (2015). Structured clinical interview for the DSM. In R. L. Cautin & S. O. Lilienfeld (Eds.), *The encyclopedia of clinical psychology* (1st ed., pp. 1–6). Wiley. https://doi.org/10.1002/9781118625392.wbecp351

Fogel, D. B. (2018). Factors associated with clinical trials that fail and opportunities for improving the likelihood of success: A review. *Contemporary Clinical Trials Communications*, *11*, 156–164. https://doi.org/10.1016/j.conctc.2018.08.001

Forkus, S. R., Contractor, A. A., Goncharenko, S., Goldstein, S. C., Weiss, N. H. (2023). Online crowdsourcing to study trauma and mental health symptoms in military populations: A case for Amazon's Mechanical Turk (MTurk) platform. *Psychol Trauma*, *15*(8), 1238–1247. doi: 10.1037/tra0001235

Fortney, J. C., Bauer, A. M., Cerimele, J. M., Pyne, J. M., Pfeiffer, P., Heagerty, P. J., Hawrilenko, M., Zielinski, M. J., Kaysen, D., Bowen, D. J., Moore, D. L., Ferro, L., Metzger, K., Shushan, S., Hafer, E., Nolan, J. P., Dalack, G. W., & Unützer, J. (2021). Comparison of teleintegrated care and telereferral care for treating complex psychiatric disorders in primary care: A pragmatic randomized comparative effectiveness trial. *JAMA Psychiatry*, *78*(11), 1189. https://doi.org/10.1001/jamapsychiatry.2021.2318

US Federal Government. *Freedom of Information Act FOIA 5 U.S.C. 552*. (2025). https://www.foia.gov/

Gaias, L. M., Arnold, K. T., Liu, F. F., Pullmann, M. D., Duong, M. T., & Lyon, A. R. (2022). Adapting strategies to promote implementation reach and equity (ASPIRE) in school mental health services. *Psychology in the Schools*, *59*(12), 2471–2485. https://doi.org/10.1002/pits.22515

Gallo, J. J., Hwang, S., Joo, J. H., Bogner, H. R., Morales, K. H., Bruce, M. L., & Reynolds, C. F. (2016). Multimorbidity, depression, and mortality in primary care: Randomized clinical trial of an evidence-based depression care management program on mortality risk. *Journal of General Internal Medicine*, *31*(4), 380–386. https://doi.org/10.1007/s11606-015-3524-y

Gan, D. Z. Q., McGillivray, L., Larsen, M. E., & Torok, M. (2023). Promoting engagement with self-guided digital therapeutics for mental health: Insights from a cross-sectional survey of end-users. *Journal of Clinical Psychology*, *79*(5), 1386–1397. https://doi.org/10.1002/jclp.23486

Griffith Fillipo, I. R., Pullmann, M. D., Hull, T. D., Zech, J., Wu, J., Litvin, B., Chen, S., & Areán, P. A. (2022). Participant retention in a fully remote trial of digital psychotherapy: Comparison of incentive types. *Frontiers in Digital Health*, *4*, 1–14. https://doi.org/10.3389/fdgth.2022.963741

Harris, P. A., Taylor, R., Minor, B. L., Elliott, V., Fernandez, M., O'Neal, L., McLeod, L., Delacqua, G., Delacqua, F., Kirby, J., & Duda, S. N. (2019). The REDCap consortium: Building an international community of software platform partners. *Journal of Biomedical Informatics*, *95*, 103208. https://doi.org/10.1016/j.jbi.2019.103208

Harris, P. A., Taylor, R., Thielke, R., Payne, J., Gonzalez, N., & Conde, J. G. (2009). Research electronic data capture (REDCap)—A metadata-driven methodology and workflow process for providing translational research informatics support. *Journal of Biomedical Informatics*, *42*(2), 377–381. https://doi.org/10.1016/j.jbi.2008.08.010

Harris, P. A., Taylor, R., Minor, B. L., Elliott, V., Fernandez, M., O'Neal, L., McLeod, L., Delacqua, G., Delacqua, F., Kirby, J., Duda, S. N. (2019). The REDCap consortium: Building an international community of software partners. *J Biomed Inform*, doi: 10.1016/j.jbi.2019.103208

Harvin, J. A., Zarzaur, B. L., Nirula, R., King, B. T., & Malhotra, A. K. (2020). Alternative clinical trial designs. *Trauma Surgery & Acute Care Open*, *5*(1), e000420. https://doi.org/10.1136/tsaco-2019-000420

Hegel, M. T., Barrett, J. E., & Oxman, T. E. (2000). Training therapists in problem-solving treatment of depressive disorders in primary care: Lessons learned from the "Treatment Effectiveness Project." *Families, Systems, & Health*, *18*(4), 423–435. https://doi.org/10.1037/h0091866

SCI Guiding Principles Consensus Panel, Hoekstra, F., Mrklas, K. J., Khan, M., McKay, R. C., Vis-Dunbar, M., Sibley, K. M., Nguyen, T., Graham, I. D., & Gainforth, H. L. (2020). A review of reviews on principles, strategies, outcomes and impacts of research partnerships approaches: A first step in synthesising the research partnership literature. *Health Research Policy and Systems*, *18*(1), 51. https://doi.org/10.1186/s12961-020-0544-9

Hoge, S. K., Bonnie, R. J., Poythress, N., Monahan, J., Eisenberg, M., Feucht-Haviar T. (1997). The MacArthur adjudicative competence study: development and validation of a research instrument. *Law and Human Behavior*, *21*(2), 141–179. https://doi.org/10.1023/a:1024826312495

Holkup, P. A., Tripp-Reimer, T., Salois, E. M., & Weinert, C. (2004). Community-based participatory research: An approach to intervention research with a Native American community. *ANS. Advances in Nursing Science*, *27*(3), 162–175. https://doi.org/10.1097/00012272-200407000-00002

Hossain, M. N., Uddin, M. H., Thapa, K., Al Zubaer, M. A., Islam, M. S., Lee, J., Park, J., & Yang, S.-H. (2021). Detecting cognitive impairment status using keystroke patterns and physical activity data among the older adults: A machine learning approach. *Journal of Healthcare Engineering*, *2021*, 1302989. https://doi.org/10.1155/2021/1302989

Idnay, B., Fang, Y., Butler, A., Moran, J., Li, Z., Lee, J., Ta, C., Liu, C., Yuan, C., Chen, H., Stanley, E., Hripcsak, G., Larson, E., Marder, K., Chung, W., Ruotolo, B., & Weng, C. (2023). Uncovering key clinical trial features influencing recruitment. *Journal of Clinical and Translational Science, 7*(1), e199. https://doi.org/10.1017/cts.2023.623

Iflaifel, M., Hall, C. L., Green, H. R., Willis, A., Rennick-Egglestone, S., Juszczak, E., Townsend, M., Martin, J., & Sprange, K. (2023). Widening participation – recruitment methods in mental health randomised controlled trials: A qualitative study. *BMC Medical Research Methodology, 23*(1), 211. https://doi.org/10.1186/s12874-023-02032-1

Inan, O. T., Tenaerts, P., Prindiville, S. A., Reynolds, H. R., Dizon, D. S., Cooper-Arnold, K., Turakhia, M., Pletcher, M. J., Preston, K. L., Krumholz, H. M., Marlin, B. M., Mandl, K. D., Klasnja, P., Spring, B., Iturriaga, E., Campo, R., Desvigne-Nickens, P., Rosenberg, Y., Steinhubl, S. R., & Califf, R. M. (2020). Digitizing clinical trials. *Npj Digital Medicine, 3*(1), 101. https://doi.org/10.1038/s41746-020-0302-y

Institute of Medicine (US) (1994). Committee on Ethical and Legal Issues Relating to the Inclusion of Women in Clinical Studies. In Mastroianni A. C., Faden R., Federman D. (eds.), *Women and Health Research: Ethical and Legal Issues of Including Women in Clinical Studies: Volume I.* Washington (DC): National Academies Press (US). B, NIH Revitalization Act of 1993 Public Law 103–143. https://www.ncbi.nlm.nih.gov/books/NBK236531/

Institute of Medicine. (2001). *Crossing the quality chasm: A new health system for the 21st century.* National Academy Press.

Ioannidis, J. P. A. (2005). Why most published research findings are false. *PLoS Medicine, 2*(8), e124. https://doi.org/10.1371/journal.pmed.0020124

Ipsen, C., Kurth, N., Hall, J. (2021). Evaluating MTurk as a recruitment tool for rural people with disabilities. *Disabil Health J, 14*(1), 100991. doi: 10.1016/j.dhjo.2020.100991

Jacobson, N. S. (1999). The role of the allegiance effect in psychotherapy research: Controlling and accounting for it. *Clinical Psychology: Science and Practice, 6*(1), 116–119. https://doi.org/10.1093/clipsy.6.1.116

Kane, J. C., Murray, L. K., Cohen, J., Dorsey, S., Skavenski Van Wyk, S., Galloway Henderson, J., Imasiku, M., Mayeya, J., & Bolton, P. (2016). Moderators of treatment response to trauma-focused cognitive behavioral therapy among youth in Zambia. *Journal of Child Psychology and Psychiatry, 57*(10), 1194–1202. https://doi.org/10.1111/jcpp.12623

Keepers, B. C., Easterly, C. W., Nora Dennis, Domino, M. E., & Bhalla, I. P. (2023). A survey of behavioral health care providers on use and barriers to use of measurement-based care. *Psychiatric Services, 74*(4), 349–357. https://doi.org/10.1176/appi.ps.202100735

Kessler, R. C., & Üstün, T. B. (2004). The World Mental Health survey initiative version of the World Health Organization Composite International Diagnostic Interview. *International Journal of Methods in Psychiatric Research, 13*(2), 93–121. https://doi.org/10.1002/mpr.168

King, N. M. P. (2014). Ethics in regenerative medicine and transplantation. In Giuseppe Orlando, Jan Lerut, Shay Soker, Robert J. Stratta (eds.), *Regenerative medicine applications in organ transplantation* (pp. 977–986). Elsevier. https://doi.org/10.1016/B978-0-12-398523-1.00071-9

Klitzman, R. (2013). How IRBs view and make decisions about coercion and undue influence. *Journal of Medical Ethics, 39*(4), 224–229. https://doi.org/10.1136/medethics-2011-100439

Kolovson, S., Pratap, A., Duffy, J., Allred, R., Munson, S. A., & Areán, P. A. (2020). Understanding participant needs for engagement and attitudes towards passive sensing in remote digital health studies. In *Proceedings of the 14th EAI international conference on pervasive computing technologies for healthcare* (pp. 347–362). Association for Computing Machinery. https://doi.org/10.1145/3421937.3422025

Komaromy, M., Duhigg, D., Metcalf, A., Carlson, C., Kalishman, S., Hayes, L., Burke, T., Thornton, K., & Arora, S. (2016). Project ECHO (Extension for Community Healthcare Outcomes): A new model for educating primary care providers about treatment of substance use disorders. *Substance Abuse, 37*(1), 20–24. https://doi.org/10.1080/08897077.2015.1129388

Kraemer, H. C., Frank, E., & Kupfer, D. J. (2006a). Moderators of treatment outcomes: Clinical, research, and policy importance. *Journal of the American Medical Association, 296*(10), 1286. https://doi.org/10.1001/jama.296.10.1286

Kraemer, H. C., Mintz, J., Noda, A., Tinklenberg, J., & Yesavage, J. A. (2006b). Caution regarding the use of pilot studies to guide power calculations for study proposals. *Archives of General Psychiatry, 63*(5), 484–489. https://doi.org/10.1001/archpsyc.63.5.484

Kraemer, H. C., Wilson, G. T., Fairburn, C. G., & Agras, W. S. (2002). Mediators and moderators of treatment effects in randomized clinical trials. *Archives of General Psychiatry, 59*(10), 877. https://doi.org/10.1001/archpsyc.59.10.877

Kroenke, K., Spitzer, R. L., & Williams, J. B. W. (2001). The PHQ-9: Validity of a brief depression severity measure. *Journal of General Internal Medicine, 16*(9), 606–613. https://doi.org/10.1046/j.1525-1497.2001.016009606.x

Lang, T. A., & Stroup, D. F. (2020). Who knew? The misleading specificity of "double-blind" and what to do about it. *Trials, 21*(1), 697. https://doi.org/10.1186/s13063-020-04607-5

Leon, A. C. (1995). More reliable outcome measures can reduce sample size requirements. *Archives of General Psychiatry, 52*(10), 867. https://doi.org/10.1001/archpsyc.1995.03950220077014

Leon, A. C., Davis, L. L., & Kraemer, H. C. (2011). The role and interpretation of pilot studies in clinical research. *Journal of Psychiatric Research, 45*(5), 626–629. https://doi.org/10.1016/j.jpsychires.2010.10.008

Li, S. X., Halabi, R., Selvarajan, R., Woerner, M., Fillipo, I. G., Banerjee, S., Mosser, B., Jain, F., Areán, P. A., & Pratap, A. (2022). Recruitment and retention in remote research: Learnings from a large, decentralized real-world study. *JMIR Formative Research, 6*(11), e40765. https://doi.org/10.2196/40765

Lilienfeld, S. O., Ritschel, L. A., Lynn, S. J., Cautin, R. L., & Latzman, R. D. (2013). Why many clinical psychologists are resistant to evidence-based practice: Root causes and constructive remedies. *Clinical Psychology Review, 33*(7), 883–900. https://doi.org/10.1016/j.cpr.2012.09.008

Lipschitz, J. M., Van Boxtel, R., Torous, J., Firth, J., Lebovitz, J. G., Burdick, K. E., & Hogan, T. P. (2022). Digital mental health interventions for depression: Scoping review of user engagement. *Journal of Medical Internet Research, 24*(10), e39204. https://doi.org/10.2196/39204

Loudon, K., Treweek, S., Sullivan, F., Donnan, P., Thorpe, K. E., & Zwarenstein, M. (2015). The PRECIS-2 tool: Designing trials that are fit for purpose. *BMJ, 350*, h2147–h2147. https://doi.org/10.1136/bmj.h2147

Lubotsky L., B., Hennessy, K. D., & Petrila, J. (2010). *Mental health services: A public health perspective.* Oxford University Press.

Lyon, A. R., Brewer, S. K., & Areán, P. A. (2020). Leveraging human-centered design to implement modern psychological science: Return on an early investment. *American Psychologist, 75*(8), 1067–1079. https://doi.org/10.1037/amp0000652

Lyon, A. R., Munson, S. A., Renn, B. N., Atkins, D. C., Pullmann, M. D., Friedman, E., & Areán, P. A. (2019). Use of human-centered design to improve implementation of evidence-based psychotherapies in low-resource communities: Protocol for studies applying a framework to assess usability. *JMIR Research Protocols, 8*(10), e14990. https://doi.org/10.2196/14990

Lyon, A. R., Pullmann, M. D., Dorsey, S., Levin, C., Gaias, L. M., Brewer, S. K., Larson, M., Corbin, C. M., Davis, C., Muse, I., Joshi, M., Reyes, R., Jungbluth, N. J., Barrett, R., Hong, D., Gomez, M. D., & Cook, C. R. (2021a). Protocol for a hybrid type 2 cluster randomized trial of trauma-focused cognitive behavioral therapy and a pragmatic individual-level implementation strategy. *Implementation Science, 16*(1), 3. https://doi.org/10.1186/s13012-020-01064-1

Lyon, A. R., Pullmann, M. D., Jacobson, J., Osterhage, K., Achkar, M. A., Renn, B. N., Munson, S. A., & Areán, P. A. (2021b). Assessing the usability of complex psychosocial interventions: The Intervention Usability Scale. *Implementation Research and Practice, 2*, 2633489520987828. https://doi.org/10.1177/2633489520987828

Mata-Greve, F., Johnson, M., Pullmann, M. D., Friedman, E. C., Griffith Fillipo, I., Comtois, K. A., & Areán, P. A. (2021). Mental health and the perceived usability of digital mental health tools among essential workers and people unemployed due to COVID-19: Cross-sectional survey study. *JMIR Mental Health, 8*(8), e28360. https://doi.org/10.2196/28360

McNeish, D., Stapleton, L. M., & Silverman, R. D. (2017). On the unnecessary ubiquity of hierarchical linear modeling. *Psychological Methods, 22*(1), 114–140. https://doi.org/10.1037/met0000078

Meeuwissen, S. N. E., Stalmeijer, R. E., & Govaerts, M. (2019). Multiple-role mentoring: Mentors' conceptualisations, enactments and role conflicts. *Medical Education, 53*(6), 605–615. https://doi.org/10.1111/medu.13811

Merlin-Knoblich, C., Harris, P. N., & Mason, E. C. M. (2019). Examining student classroom engagement in flipped and non-flipped counselor education courses. *The Professional Counselor, 9*(2), 109–125. https://doi.org/10.15241/cmk.9.2.109

Merton, R. K. (1936). The unanticipated consequences of purposive social action. *American Sociological Review, 1*(6), 894. https://doi.org/10.2307/2084615

Moher, D. (2001). The CONSORT statement: Revised recommendations for improving the quality of reports of parallel-group randomized trials. *JAMA, 285*(15), 1987. https://doi.org/10.1001/jama.285.15.1987

Moreno, M. A., Goniu, N., Moreno, P. S., & Diekema, D. (2013). Ethics of social media research: Common concerns and practical considerations. *Cyberpsychology, Behavior and Social Networking, 16*(9), 708–713. https://doi.org/10.1089/cyber.2012.0334

Morris, D., Fraser, S., & Wormald, R. (2007). Masking is better than blinding. *BMJ, 334*(7597), 799–799. https://doi.org/10.1136/bmj.39175.503299.94

Munson, S. A., Friedman, E. C., Osterhage, K., Allred, R., Pullmann, M. D., Areán, P. A., Lyon, A. R., & UW ALACRITY Center Researchers. (2022). Usability issues in evidence-based psychosocial interventions and implementation strategies: Cross-project analysis. *Journal of Medical Internet Research, 24*(6), e37585. https://doi.org/10.2196/37585

Murman, D. L. (2015). The impact of age on cognition. *Seminars in Hearing, 36*(3), 111–121. https://doi.org/10.1055/s-0035-1555115

National Institutes of Health, National Cancer Institute. (2025). *What is team science?* https://cancercontrol.cancer.gov/brp/research/team-science-toolkit/what-is-team-science

National Institutes of Mental Health. (2025). *About RDoC.* https://www.nimh.nih.gov/research/research-funded-by-nimh/rdoc/about-rdoc

Nebeker, C., Torous, J., & Bartlett Ellis, R. J. (2019). Building the case for actionable ethics in digital health research supported by artificial intelligence. *BMC Medicine, 17*(1), 137. https://doi.org/10.1186/s12916-019-1377-7

Nelson, B. W., Low, C. A., Jacobson, N., Areán, P. A., Torous, J., & Allen, N. B. (2020). Guidelines for wrist-worn consumer wearable assessment of heart rate in biobehavioral research. *NPJ Digital Medicine, 3*, 90. https://doi.org/10.1038/s41746-020-0297-4

National Institutes of Health (NIH). (2024). *NIH's Definition of a Clinical Trial*. https://grants.nih.gov/policy-and-compliance/policy-topics/clinical-trials/definition

National Institutes of Mental Health. (2025). *Research Domain Criteria (RDoC)—National Institute of Mental Health (NIMH)*. https://www.nimh.nih.gov/research/research-funded-by-nimh/rdoc

NHS talking therapies for anxiety and depression. (2025). https://www.england.nhs.uk/mental-health/adults/nhs-talking-therapies/

Nickels, S., Edwards, M. D., Poole, S. F., Winter, D., Gronsbell, J., Rozenkrants, B., Miller, D. P., Fleck, M., McLean, A., Peterson, B., Chen, Y., Hwang, A., Rust-Smith, D., Brant, A., Campbell, A., Chen, C., Walter, C., Areán, P. A., Hsin, H., ... Fromer, M. (2021). Toward a mobile platform for real-world digital measurement of depression: User-centered design, data quality, and behavioral and clinical modeling. *JMIR Mental Health, 8*(8), e27589. https://doi.org/10.2196/27589

Nuendorf, K. A. (n.d.). *The content analysis guidebook* (2nd ed.). SAGE Publications.

Oliver, S., Kavanagh, J., Caird, J., Lorenc, T., Oliver, K., Harden, A., Thomas, J., Greaves, A., & Oakley, A. (2008). *Health promotion, inequalities and young people's health. A systematic review of research* (No. 1611). EPPI Center, University of London.

Oluwoye, O., Stiles, B., Monroe-devita, M., Chwastiak, L., McClellan, J. M., Dyck, D., Cabassa, L. J., & McDonell, M. G. (2018). Racial-ethnic disparities in first-episode psychosis treatment outcomes from the RAISE-ETP study. *Psychiatric Services (Washington, D.C.), 69*(11), 1138–1145. https://doi.org/10.1176/appi.ps.201800067

Owen, R. R., Woodward, E. N., Drummond, K. L., Deen, T. L., Oliver, K. A., Petersen, N. J., Meit, S. S., Fortney, J. C., & Kirchner, J. E. (2019). Using implementation facilitation to implement primary care mental health integration via clinical video telehealth in rural clinics: Protocol for a hybrid type 2 cluster randomized stepped-wedge design. *Implementation Science: IS, 14*(1), 33. https://doi.org/10.1186/s13012-019-0875-5

PAR-21-131: Pilot Effectiveness Trials for Treatment, Preventive and Services Interventions (R34 Clinical Trial Required). (2025). https://grants.nih.gov/grants/guide/pa-files/par-21-131.html

Passmore, S. R., Kisicki, A., Gilmore-Bykovskyi, A., Green-Harris, G., & Edwards, D. F. (2022). "There's not much we can do..." Researcher-level barriers to the inclusion of underrepresented participants in translational research. *Journal of Clinical and Translational Science, 6*(1), e4. https://doi.org/10.1017/cts.2021.876

Patsopoulos, N. A. (2011). A pragmatic view on pragmatic trials. *Dialogues in Clinical Neuroscience, 13*(2), 217–224. https://doi.org/10.31887/DCNS.2011.13.2/npatsopoulos

Pettersson, A., Modin, S., Wahlström, R., Af Winklerfelt Hammarberg, S., & Krakau, I. (2018). The Mini-International Neuropsychiatric Interview is useful and well accepted as part of the clinical assessment for depression and anxiety in primary care: A mixed-methods study. *BMC Family Practice, 19*(1), 19. https://doi.org/10.1186/s12875-017-0674-5

Petticrew, M. (2011). When are complex interventions "complex"? When are simple interventions "simple"? *The European Journal of Public Health, 21*(4), 397–398. https://doi.org/10.1093/eurpub/ckr084

Pilot studies: Common uses and misuses. (n.d.). NCCIH. (Retrieved March 5, 2025). https://www.nccih.nih.gov/grants/pilot-studies-common-uses-and-misuses

Powell, B. J., Beidas, R. S., Lewis, C. C., Aarons, G. A., McMillen, J. C., Proctor, E. K., & Mandell, D. S. (2017). Methods to improve the selection and tailoring of implementation strategies.

The Journal of Behavioral Health Services & Research, 44(2), 177–194. https://doi.org/10.1007/s11414-015-9475-6

Powell, B. J., Waltz, T. J., Chinman, M. J., Damschroder, L. J., Smith, J. L., Matthieu, M. M., Proctor, E. K., & Kirchner, J. E. (2015). A refined compilation of implementation strategies: Results from the Expert Recommendations for Implementing Change (ERIC) project. *Implementation Science, 10*(1), 21. https://doi.org/10.1186/s13012-015-0209-1

Pozzar, R., Hammer, M. J., Underhill-Blazey, M., Wright, A. A., Tulsky, J. A., Hong, F., Gundersen, D. A., & Berry, D. L. (2020). Threats of bots and other bad actors to data quality following research participant recruitment through social media: Cross-sectional questionnaire. *Journal of Medical Internet Research, 22*(10), e23021. https://doi.org/10.2196/23021

Pratap, A., Allred, R., Duffy, J., Rivera, D., Lee, H. S., Renn, B. N., & Areán, P. A. (2019). Contemporary views of research participant willingness to participate and share digital data in biomedical research. *JAMA Network Open, 2*(11), e1915717. https://doi.org/10.1001/jamanetworkopen.2019.15717

Pratap, A., Neto, E. C., Snyder, P., Stepnowsky, C., Elhadad, N., Grant, D., Mohebbi, M. H., Mooney, S., Suver, C., Wilbanks, J., Mangravite, L., Heagerty, P. J., Areán, P. A., & Omberg, L. (2020). Indicators of retention in remote digital health studies: A cross-study evaluation of 100,000 participants. *NPJ Digital Medicine, 3*, 21. https://doi.org/10.1038/s41746-020-0224-8

Pritchard, I. A. (2011). How do IRB members make decisions? A review and research agenda. *Journal of Empirical Research on Human Research Ethics, 6*(2), 31–46. https://doi.org/10.1525/jer.2011.6.2.31

Proctor, E., Silmere, H., Raghavan, R., Hovmand, P., Aarons, G., Bunger, A., Griffey, R., & Hensley, M. (2011). Outcomes for implementation research: Conceptual distinctions, measurement challenges, and research agenda. *Administration and Policy in Mental Health, 38*(2), 65–76. https://doi.org/10.1007/s10488-010-0319-7

Qureshi, N., Hays, R., Herman, P. (2024). Dropout in a Longitudinal Survey of Amazon Mechanical Turk Workers with Low Back Pain: Observational Study. *Interact J Med Res, 13*, e58771. https://www.i-jmr.org/2024/1/e58771

Regulation 2016/679 of the European parliament and of the council. (2016). *Official Journal of the European Union, 119.* https://gdpr-info.eu/

Renn, B. N., Hoeft, T. J., Lee, H. S., Bauer, A. M., & Areán, P. A. (2019). Preference for in-person psychotherapy versus digital psychotherapy options for depression: Survey of adults in the U.S. *NPJ Digital Medicine, 2*, 6. https://doi.org/10.1038/s41746-019-0077-1

Resnik, D. B. (2015). Bioethical issues in providing financial incentives to research participants. *Medicolegal and Bioethics, 5*, 35–41. https://doi.org/10.2147/MB.S70416

Rice, T. (2013). The behavioral economics of health and health care. *Annual Review of Public Health, 34*, 431–447. https://doi.org/10.1146/annurev-publhealth-031912-114353

Rigg, K. (July 29, 2022). *The top 3 reasons health tech startups fail.* Health Tech World.

Rogers, K. M., Trubey, E., & Oard, D. W. (2022). A user study in a pandemic: Some lessons learned. *Proceedings of the Association for Information Science and Technology, 59*(1), 785–787. https://doi.org/10.1002/pra2.726

Ronca, V., Martinez-Levy, A. C., Vozzi, A., Giorgi, A., Aricò, P., Capotorto, R., Borghini, G., Babiloni, F., & Di Flumeri, G. (2023). Wearable technologies for electrodermal and cardiac activity measurements: A comparison between fitbit Sense, Empatica E4 and Shimmer GSR3+. *Sensors, 23*(13), 5847. https://doi.org/10.3390/s23135847

Salinas, M. R. (2023). Are your participants real? Dealing with fraud in recruiting older adults online. *Western Journal of Nursing Research, 45*(1), 93–99. https://doi.org/10.1177/01939459221098468

Schulz, K. F., Altman, D. G., Moher, D., & CONSORT Group. (2010). CONSORT 2010 statement: Updated guidelines for reporting parallel group randomised trials. *BMJ (Clinical Research Ed.)*, *340*, c332. https://doi.org/10.1136/bmj.c332

Seaman, S. R., White, I. R., Copas, A. J., & Li, L. (2012). Combining multiple imputation and inverse-probability weighting. *Biometrics*, *68*(1), 129–137. https://doi.org/10.1111/j.1541-0420.2011.01666.x

Sekhon, M., Cartwright, M., & Francis, J. J. (2022). Development of a theory-informed questionnaire to assess the acceptability of healthcare interventions. *BMC Health Services Research*, *22*(1), 279. https://doi.org/10.1186/s12913-022-07577-3

Silberzahn, R., Uhlmann, E. L., Martin, D. P., Anselmi, P., Aust, F., Awtrey, E., Bahník, Š., Bai, F., Bannard, C., Bonnier, E., Carlsson, R., Cheung, F., Christensen, G., Clay, R., Craig, M. A., Dalla Rosa, A., Dam, L., Evans, M. H., Flores Cervantes, I., ... Nosek, B. A. (2018). Many analysts, one data set: Making transparent how variations in analytic choices affect results. *Advances in Methods and Practices in Psychological Science*, *1*(3), 337–356. https://doi.org/10.1177/2515245917747646

Simon, G. E., Shortreed, S. M., Rossom, R. C., Beck, A., Clarke, G. N., Whiteside, U., Richards, J. E., Penfold, R. B., Boggs, J. M., & Smith, J. (2022). Effect of offering care management or online Dialectical Behavior Therapy skills training vs usual care on self-harm among adult outpatients with suicidal ideation: A randomized clinical trial. *JAMA*, *327*(7), 630. https://doi.org/10.1001/jama.2022.0423

Steckler, A., & McLeroy, K. R. (2008). The importance of external validity. *American Journal of Public Health*, *98*(1), 9–10. https://doi.org/10.2105/AJPH.2007.126847

Stevens, J. (2015). Behavioral economics strategies for promoting adherence to sleep interventions. *Sleep Medicine Reviews*, *23*, 20–27. https://doi.org/10.1016/j.smrv.2014.11.002

Suh, H., Shahriaree, N., Hekler, E. B., & Kientz, J. A. (2016). Developing and validating the User Burden Scale: A tool for assessing user burden in computing systems. *Proceedings of the 2016 CHI Conference on Human Factors in Computing Systems*, (pp. 3988–3999). https://doi.org/10.1145/2858036.2858448

Sverdlov, O., & Ryeznik, Y. (2019). Implementing unequal randomization in clinical trials with heterogeneous treatment costs. *Statistics in Medicine*, *38*(16), 2905–2927. https://doi.org/10.1002/sim.8160

Taylor, G. M. J., Dalili, M. N., Semwal, M., Civljak, M., Sheikh, A., & Car, J. (2017). Internet-based interventions for smoking cessation. *The Cochrane Database of Systematic Reviews*, *9*(9), CD007078. https://doi.org/10.1002/14651858.CD007078.pub5

Teague, S., Youssef, G. J., Macdonald, J. A., Sciberras, E., Shatte, A., Fuller-Tyszkiewicz, M., Greenwood, C., McIntosh, J., Olsson, C. A., & Hutchinson, D. (2018). Retention strategies in longitudinal cohort studies: A systematic review and meta-analysis. *BMC Medical Research Methodology*, *18*(1), 151. https://doi.org/10.1186/s12874-018-0586-7

Teitcher, J. E. F., Bockting, W. O., Bauermeister, J. A., Hoefer, C. J., Miner, M. H., & Klitzman, R. L. (2015). Detecting, preventing, and responding to "fraudsters" in internet research: Ethics and tradeoffs. *Journal of Law, Medicine & Ethics*, *43*(1), 116–133. https://doi.org/10.1111/jlme.12200

Thabane, L., Ma, J., Chu, R., Cheng, J., Ismaila, A., Rios, L. P., Robson, R., Thabane, M., Giangregorio, L., & Goldsmith, C. H. (2010). A tutorial on pilot studies: The what, why and how. *BMC Medical Research Methodology*, *10*(1), 1. https://doi.org/10.1186/1471-2288-10-1

Topooco, N., Fowler, L. A., Fitzsimmons-Craft, E. E., DePietro, B., Vázquez, M. M., Firebaugh, M.-L., Ceglarek, P., Monterubio, G., Newman, M. G., Eisenberg, D., Wilfley, D. E., & Taylor, C. B. (2022). Digital interventions to address mental health needs in colleges: Perspectives of student stakeholders. *Internet Interventions*, *28*, 100528. https://doi.org/10.1016/j.invent.2022.100528

Torous, J., Lipschitz, J., Ng, M., & Firth, J. (2020). Dropout rates in clinical trials of smartphone apps for depressive symptoms: A systematic review and meta-analysis. *Journal of Affective Disorders*, *263*, 413–419. https://doi.org/10.1016/j.jad.2019.11.167

Tryon, W. W. (2018). Mediators and mechanisms. *Clinical Psychological Science*, *6*(5), 619–628. https://doi.org/10.1177/2167702618765791

Tukey, J. W. (1977). *Exploratory data analysis*. Addison-Wesley.

Uncapher, H., & Areán, P. A. (2000). Physicians are less willing to treat suicidal ideation in older patients. *Journal of the American Geriatrics Society*, *48*(2), 188–192. https://doi.org/10.1111/j.1532-5415.2000.tb03910.x

Unützer, J., Katon, W., Callahan, C. M., Williams, Jr., J. W., Hunkeler, E., Harpole, L., Hoffing, M., Della Penna, R. D., Noël, P. H., Lin, E. H. B., Areán, P. A., Hegel, M. T., Tang, L., Belin, T. R., Oishi, S., Langston, C., & For The Impact Investigators. (2002). Collaborative care management of late-life depression in the primary care setting: A randomized controlled trial. *JAMA*, *288*(22), 2836. https://doi.org/10.1001/jama.288.22.2836

Uwatoko, T., Luo, Y., Sakata, M., Kobayashi, D., Sakagami, Y., Takemoto, K., Collins, L. M., Watkins, E., Hollon, S. D., Wason, J., Noma, H., Horikoshi, M., Kawamura, T., Iwami, T., & Furukawa, T. A. (2018). Healthy Campus Trial: A multiphase optimization strategy (MOST) fully factorial trial to optimize the smartphone cognitive behavioral therapy (CBT) app for mental health promotion among university students: study protocol for a randomized controlled trial. *Trials*, *19*(1), 353. https://doi.org/10.1186/s13063-018-2719-z

VanEpps, E. M., Volpp, K. G., & Halpern, S. D. (2016). A nudge toward participation: Improving clinical trial enrollment with behavioral economics. *Science Translational Medicine*, *8*(348), 348fs13. https://doi.org/10.1126/scitranslmed.aaf0946

Wager, E., & Elia, N. (2014). Why should clinical trials be registered? *European Journal of Anaesthesiology*, *31*(8), 397–400. https://doi.org/10.1097/EJA.0000000000000084

Waldman, S. A., Kraft, W. K., Nelson, T. J., & Terzic, A. (2009). Experimental therapeutics: A paradigm for personalized medicine. *Clinical and Translational Science*, *2*(6), 436–438. https://doi.org/10.1111/j.1752-8062.2009.00146.x

Wang, J., Calderon, G., Hager, E. R., Edwards, L. V., Berry, A. A., Liu, Y., Dinh, J., Summers, A. C., Connor, K. A., Collins, M. E., Prichett, L., Marshall, B. R., & Johnson, S. B. (2023). Identifying and preventing fraudulent responses in online public health surveys: Lessons learned during the COVID-19 pandemic. *PLOS Global Public Health*, *3*(8), e0001452. https://doi.org/10.1371/journal.pgph.0001452

Wendler, D., Kington, R., Madans, J., Van Wye, G., Christ-Schmidt, H., Pratt, L. A., Brawley, O. W., Gross, C. P., & Emanuel, E. (2006). Are racial and ethnic minorities less willing to participate in health research? *PLoS Medicine*, *3*(2), e19. https://doi.org/10.1371/journal.pmed.0030019

What happens in each phase of forming, storming, norming, and performing. (2020). *Six Sigma Daily*. https://www.sixsigmadaily.com/what-is-forming-storming-norming-performing/#:~:text=The%20concept%20of%20Forming%2C%20Storming,on%20accomplishing%20a%20shared%20goal

Williams, Jr., J. W., Barrett, J., Oxman, T., Frank, E., Katon, W., Sullivan, M., Cornell, J., & Sengupta, A. (2000). Treatment of dysthymia and minor depression in primary care: A randomized controlled trial in older adults. *JAMA*, *284*(12), 1519. https://doi.org/10.1001/jama.284.12.1519

Wittes, J. (1993). Behind closed doors: The data monitoring board in randomized clinical trials. *Statistics in Medicine*, *12*(5–6), 419–424. https://doi.org/10.1002/sim.4780120504

Woerner, M., Sams, N., Rivera Nales, C., Gorstein, T., Johnson, M., Mosser, B. A., & Areán, P. A. (2022). Generational perspectives on technology's role in mental health care: A survey of adults with lived mental health experience. *Frontiers in Digital Health*, *4*, 840169. https://doi.org/10.3389/fdgth.2022.840169

World Health Organization. (2019). International Statistical Classification of Diseases and related health problems (11th ed.). https://icd.who.int/

World population aging 2019: Highlights. (2019). United Nations Department of Economic and Social Affairs. www.un.org

Wright, J. H. (2010). *High-yield cognitive-behavior therapy for brief sessions: An illustrated guide* (1st ed.). American Psychiatric Pub.

Wrzus, C., & Neubauer, A. B. (2023). Ecological momentary assessment: A meta-Analysis on designs, samples, and compliance across research fields. *Assessment*, *30*(3), 825–846. https://doi.org/10.1177/10731911211067538

Xu, J., Lio, A., Dhaliwal, H., Andrei, S., Balakrishnan, S., Nagani, U., & Samadder, S. (2021). Psychological interventions of virtual gamification within academic intrinsic motivation: A systematic review. *Journal of Affective Disorders*, *293*, 444–465. https://doi.org/10.1016/j.jad.2021.06.070

Index

For the benefit of digital users, indexed terms that span two pages (e.g., 52–53) may, on occasion, appear on only one of those pages.

Note: page numbers followed by *f* and *t* refer to figures and tables respectively.